Ironic victory

Ironic victory

LIBERALISM IN
POST-LIBERATION
SOUTH AFRICA

EDITED BY   R W JOHNSON

AND DAVID WELSH

with the assistance of   LIBBY HUSEMEYER

OXFORD UNIVERSITY PRESS
Cape Town / 1998

Oxford University Press

Great Clarendon Street, Oxford OX2 6DP, United Kingdom

offices in
Oxford, New York
Athens, Auckland, Bangkok, Bogotá, Buenos Aires, Calcutta
Cape Town, Chennai, Dar es Salaam, Delhi, Florence, Hong Kong
Istanbul, Karachi, Kuala Lumpur, Madrid, Melbourne, Mexico City
Mumbai, Nairobi, Paris, São Paulo, Singapore, Taipei, Tokyo
Toronto, Warsaw

and associated companies in
Berlin, Ibadan

Oxford is a trade mark of Oxford University Press

Ironic victory: Liberalism in
post-liberation South Africa

ISBN 0 19 571684 1

© R.W. Johnson and David Welsh 1998

First published 1998

DESIGNER: Mark Standley
INDEXER: Jeanne Cope

Published by Oxford University Press Southern Africa
PO Box 12119, N1 City, 7463, Cape Town, South Africa

Set in Minion
Cover reproduction by RJH Graphic Reproduction, Cape Town
Printed and bound by Creda Communications, Cape Town

Contents

Contributors

DENIS BECKETT has a BA LL B from the University of the Witwatersrand. Editor of *Frontline* magazine from 1979 to 1990, he is currently editor of *Sidelines* quarterly journal, a columnist for *Rapport*, presenter of *Beckett's Trek* on SABC television, and author of, most recently, *Madibaland* (Penguin 1998).

MONICA BOT has a Masters degree in Orthopedagogics from the Rijksuniversiteit Leiden in the Netherlands. She has researched and written widely on education during the past fifteen years. She is presently research and publications manager at Edusource.

JOHN DUGARD is professor of law at the University of the Witwatersrand. He specializes in international law and is presently a member of the United Nations' International Law Commission. He was a member of the technical committee responsible for advising the Constitutional Assembly on the drafting of the bill of rights in the 1996 constitution. He was president of the South African Institute of Race Relations 1979–1980.

RACHEL JAFTA is a lecturer in economics at the University of Stellenbosch. Her research interests include the economics of technology, black economic empowerment, and affirmative action, as well as economic development issues. She maintains close ties with academic institutions in Africa and Europe.

ANTHEA J. JEFFERY holds the degrees of BA LL B (Wits), LL M (Cantab), and PH D (Lond). She has been admitted as a solicitor in England and as an advocate in South Africa. Since 1990 she has been special research consultant to the South African Institute of Race Relations. She is the author of five books. She has also written some thirty articles on different aspects of law, political violence, and the 1993 and 1996 constitutions.

R. W. (BILL) JOHNSON is an Emeritus Fellow of Magdalen College, Oxford, and the author of seven books and several hundred articles. Currently he is director of the Helen Suzman Foundation.

PATRICK LAURENCE is an assistant editor of the *Financial Mail*. He is the author of two books, one on South Africa's politics of partition with a special focus on Transkei, and the second on death squads in South Africa during white minority rule. The holder of an MA in history and politics, he was political editor of the *Rand Daily Mail* when it was closed in April 1985. He has met and interviewed many of South Africa's leaders, from Robert Sobukwe and Steve Biko to Nelson Mandela and Thabo Mbeki. He contributes articles on South Africa to the *Irish Times*.

M. W. MAKGOBA is currently professor of molecular immunology at the University of the Witwatersrand. A graduate of Natal and Wolfson College, Oxford, he is the current chairperson of the South African Medical Research Council Board, the National Science and Technology Forum, and the National Accelerator Centre. He is general secretary of the Academy of Science of South Africa, a Fellow of the Royal College of Physicians of London and the Royal Society of South Africa, and was Reader at the University of London's Royal Postgraduate Medical School. He is an author and commentator on the transformation process in South Africa.

KEN OWEN was for many years the editor of the *Sunday Times* and now writes a regular column for *Leadership*.

LAWRENCE SCHLEMMER is probably the most experienced social scientist working in South Africa. A vice-president of the South African Institute of Race Relations, he is also chair-person of the Centre for Policy Studies and was until 1995 vice-president of the Human Sciences Research Council. Formerly dean of the faculty of Social Science at the University of Natal (Durban), he is currently a private consultant and director of a market research firm.

CHARLES SIMKINS is Helen Suzman professor of political economy and head of the department of economics at the University of the Witwatersrand. He has written *Reconstructing South African liberalism* (1986) and *The prisoners of tradition and the politics of nation building* (1988), and has edited *State and market in postapartheid South Africa* (1993) with Merle Lipton. A study of dominant party democracies in upper middle-income countries edited by Hermann Giliomee and Prof. Simkins is in press. He is vice-chairperson of the executive committee of the South African Institute of Race Relations and a board member of the Centre for Development and Enterprise.

THEMBA SONO is Professor Extraordinaire at the Graduate School of Management at the University of Pretoria. He is president of the South African Institute of Race Relations and of the Free Market Foundation. He is executive councillor of the Human Sciences Research Council of South Africa, exec-utive chairperson of Africa Lebone Information Technologies, and director of several companies. Author of numerous pub-lications, he has taught at universities in the US and South Africa for more than two decades.

RACHEL TINGLE is an economist and journalist who has worked in economic consultancy, newspaper and television journalism, and for a number of senior British politicians. Her articles on economics, politics, and church affairs have appeared in a wide range of publications. She is the founder director of the Christian Studies Centre through which she has published *Another Gospel? An account of the growing involvement of the Anglican Church in secular politics* (1988) and *Revolution or reconciliation? The struggle in the Church in South Africa* (1992).

CHARLES VAN ONSELEN is director of the Institute for Advanced Social Research, University of the Witwatersrand, and *ad hominem* professor of southern African social history. He is the author of the acclaimed *The seed is mine: The life of Kas Maine. A South African sharecropper, 1894–1985.*

DAVID WELSH was professor of southern African studies at the University of Cape Town. He retired from UCT at the end of 1997. He has written extensively on South Africa and on the politics of divided societies. In retirement he is a writer and an independent political analyst.

MARTIN WILLIAMS is the acting editor of the *Citizen* and a former managing editor of the *Natal Witness*. He is a political science honours graduate of Natal University.

Preface by Helen Suzman
Patron of the Helen Suzman Foundation

In my long years as an opposition M P, the day when South Africa would acquire a constitution that entrenched core liberal principles such as civil rights and the rule of law seemed impossibly distant. I personally doubted that it would occur in my lifetime. However, it did occur, and I am delighted that South Africa is rid of apartheid at last.

Liberals have always been vigilant in the defence and pursuit of freedom, and it is clear from many of the contributions to this book that they must continue to play their historic role as society's watchdogs. South Africa's new democracy is still fragile, and it faces many threats from both Left and Right. In the long run, consolidating democracy may prove to be more difficult than opposing apartheid; we always knew that we were fighting a deeply unpopular minority regime, but liberals today and in the future may be required to stand up against abuses of power that have the weight of a popular majoritarian movement behind them.

The current tendency to carp against liberals as covert racists is not only an insult to those of us who spent a lifetime fighting racism, it is also bad history. The commitment of liberals of all races to non-racialism and to democracy is clearly shown in this book.

Unlike many other ideologies, liberalism not only tolerates but indeed welcomes vigorous internal debate. Liberals can – and often do – disagree with one another while still belonging to the liberal family. This is as it should be. If this book succeeds in encouraging creative debate among liberals as well as introducing non-liberals to liberalism, it will have achieved its objective.

Acknowledgements

THE EDITORS would like to acknowledge their gratitude to all the contributors who first delivered earlier versions of their papers to a two-day workshop held in Johannesburg in March 1997, and for their assistance throughout. Our thanks also go to Mrs Helen Suzman, who attended the workshop and passed on her typically acute observations on the contemporary scene to a younger generation who are attempting to follow in her footsteps. We would also like to thank a number of others who gave papers at the workshop who are not represented in this book, as well as those who attended the workshop and played a vigorous role in its debates.

Beyond that, our thanks go to Rolf Freier of the Friedrich-Naumann-Stiftung who first suggested the idea of such a project and gave his enthusiastic support throughout. We are also grateful to the Friedrich-Naumann-Stiftung, the Anglo American and De Beers Chairman's Fund , Standard Bank of South Africa, South African Breweries, and The Liberty Life Foundation, whose generosity to the Helen Suzman Foundation enabled us to mount the project in the first place.

Finally, and by no means least, our thanks go to Conny van Hout and Priscilla Gololo, who typed up endless versions of the papers and dealt with scores of inquiries and deadlines for us: without them we would never have managed.

Introduction DAVID WELSH

The liberal inheritance

HISTORICALLY, the liberal tradition in South Africa has been a diffuse one, lacking organizational focus for much of its existence. It has never been a dominant political force in that no party espousing specifically liberal principles has ever governed South Africa.

Yet, as I will try to show, liberal values have long possessed the capacity not only to survive but also to nag at governments and other official and unofficial bodies whose commitment to illiberal values is often profound. In this sense, liberalism has acted with catalytic force. Exactly how much influence or leverage this force has actually exerted will be a matter for debate. Enthusiastic liberals will exaggerate the extent of its influence; anti-liberals of both right and left will dismiss it as irrelevant. The truth probably lies in some grey middle area that has varied over time and place.

The core values of liberalism are:

- a commitment to fundamental human rights and those procedural safeguards known as the rule of law;
- a commitment to constitutionalism, meaning that state and government are to operate under law and that certain fundamental principles must remain beyond the reach of any (temporary) government;

- a belief in equality (whose exact parameters remain a matter of on-going debate, but implying at least equality before the law and (for most liberals) the dismantling of entrenched political, economic, and social inequalities;
- an emphasis on the primacy of the individual as the possessor of inalienable rights, though by no means, as critics allege, unmindful of the need for, and claims of, community;
- tolerance of conflicting viewpoints (spelled out with force in John Stuart Mill's great essay *On liberty*). Tolerance is perhaps the logical consequence of the right to freedom of expression, but its centrality in liberal thinking requires that it be regarded as a separate principle;
- an optimistic belief in the possibilities of individual and social 'improvement' (to use a word favoured by late Victorian liberals), with the implication that no individual, community, or society is irretrievably damned as hopeless; and
- compassion.

It will be noticed that democracy has not been included among these core values, although the cumulative consequence of the seven listed values would be a democratic system. Liberalism predates democracy by at least 150 years; but liberals, by pushing their values to their logical conclusion, were often in the forefront of processes of democratization. Nowadays, notwithstanding the analytical distinction, liberalism is virtually coterminous with democracy, as the category 'liberal-democratic' connotes. Indeed, liberals may legitimately inquire, given the appalling failures of 'people's democracies' and 'one-party democracies', whether there is any actually existing credible alternative to 'liberal democracy'.

Several of the core values generate conceptual problems. For example, what should human rights cover? Should they include 'second-generation' rights? Should 'groups' have rights? Does 'individualism' imply that unrestrained or maximal priority be accorded to market forces and the principle of 'possessive individualism'? Should tolerance extend to pornography? How should compassion cope with the habitual criminal, the chronically poor, those reliant on welfare, and other hard-luck cases? How should equality be understood – according to Rawls or to Nozick? And, perhaps most difficult of all, if freedom and equality, both cherished liberal values, stand in a certain antithetical relationship (famously noted by De Tocqueville), how shall they be traded off against each other? This, it might be noted, is a vexing issue in the new South Africa.

It is one of liberalism's most attractive features that it not only tolerates but welcomes internal debate. Mercifully, no liberal has ever produced a canon of 'scientific liberalism' in terms of which ideological purity or reliability must be measured. Liberalism's very flexibility and its open-endedness within the broad parameters of its core values have enabled it to be dynamic, adaptable, and pragmatic.

In view of liberalism's inherent internal diversity, it is hardly surprising that South African liberals have been a pretty mixed bag. It is worth noting that the term 'liberal' has different implications in different parts of the world. In the United States, 'liberal' is a word for 'tax-and-spend' politicians, often those who in European terms would be described as social democrats; in much of Europe, on the other hand, 'liberal' tends to be associated with conservatism.

In South Africa, the term liberal has been loosely applied to all those who opposed racial discrimination and favoured the retention of, or the extension of, rights to people of colour. Liberals in this sense were 'inclusivists'. William Porter, the liberal attorney-general of the Cape Colony, trenchantly expressed this perspective in defending a low franchise qualification for the Cape Colony's representative government in 1852:

> Now, for myself, I do not hesitate to say that I would rather
> meet the Hottentot at the hustings, voting for his represen-
> tative, than meet the Hottentot in the wilds with his gun
> upon his shoulder. (McCracken 1967, 68–9)

His comment went to the heart of what politics is all about: the
regulation of conflict by non-violent institutional means. For
most liberals this has been an important argument for the progressive extension of political rights. Continued exclusion, coupled
with pervasive exploitation and discrimination, was the recipe for
a dangerous backlash among the excluded. From William Porter
to Albert Luthuli, Alan Paton, and Helen Suzman, the role of
Cassandra has come naturally to liberals – and for good reason.

Perhaps the most magisterial of warnings came from the pen
of Olive Schreiner (whose self-description was that of a 'progressive liberal'), who pleaded in 1908 for the just and humane treatment of 'our dark races' as a means of binding them in a social
accord:

> ... if, blinded by the gain of the moment, we see nothing in
> our dark man but a vast engine of labour; if to us he is not a
> man, but only a tool; if dispossessed entirely of the land for
> which he now shows that large aptitude for peasant propri-
> etorship for the lack of which among their masses many
> great nations are decaying; if we force him permanently in
> his millions into the locations and compounds and slums
> of our cities, obtaining his labour cheaper, but to lose what
> the wealth of five Rands could not return to us; if, unin-
> structed in the higher forms of labour, without the rights
> of citizenship, his own social organization broken up,
> without our having aided him to participate in our own; if,
> unbound to us by gratitude and sympathy, and alien to us
> in blood and colour, we reduce this vast mass to the condi-
> tion of a great seething, ignorant proletariat – then I would

rather draw a veil over the future of this land. (Schreiner 1960, 29)

(Many white liberals did, in fact, 'draw a veil over the future of this land' and emigrated. This weakened the liberal cause in obvious ways, but the interesting question, to this writer, at any rate, is the extent to which this emigration not only weakened the liberal opposition but also delayed the break-up of apartheid. Probably the question is unanswerable, at least with any precision.)

Cape liberalism, of which Olive Schreiner and her brother William were two of the finest exponents, has a very spotty record, especially after the progressive incorporation of African territories that began in 1865. However attenuated the Cape's non-racial franchise became after restrictive changes in 1887 and 1892, it survived into Union. No person of colour, however, ever managed to be elected to the old Cape Parliament. On the one occasion in 1893 when a Muslim candidate, Ahmed Effendi, threatened to stand, his chances of election were swiftly torpedoed by the abolition of the cumulative vote in Cape Town (McCracken 1967, 96).

Despite this and the growth of segregationist measures and a predatory attitude to African labour resources (notably by Rhodes, among others), the non-racial franchise was valued by blacks and tolerated by most whites, if only as a 'safety valve', in John X. Merriman's phrase. It also became 'locked into position by the necessities of Cape political life' (Davenport 1987, 33). On the eve of Union nearly fourteen per cent of the Cape electorate were coloured and African, a factor that secured to them a degree of political leverage that was entirely absent elsewhere in South Africa.

While there is no doubt that the Cape delegates put up a fight for the entrenchment of the non-racial franchise, they caved in on two critical issues: the (hitherto purely theoretical) right of people of colour to be elected to Parliament; and federation.

Then, as now, most liberals have favoured a federal system for South Africa as a defence against an overweening central government. As Olive Schreiner put it, in a federation,

> [t]he walls of each self-governing State are so many barricades, each one of which must be broken down before any oppressive over-domination can absolutely succeed; and, behind any one of which a successful resistance may take place when others have fallen. (Schreiner 1960, 2)

Whether the South Africa Act of 1909 would have provided more defence against subsequent authoritarian government had it been genuinely federal, as opposed to pseudo-federal, is doubtful. A wider issue remains: then, as now, South Africa is a society that seems vulnerable to either authoritarian government or to government with hegemonial pretensions or, of course, to both. Whether federation would offer sturdier resistance than unitarism remains a live issue. Defence of the Cape common-roll franchise for African men became the fundamental issue for liberals, both black and white, as segregationist plans unfurled in the decades after Union. The franchise issue, of course, was not the only one to concern liberals. The Natives Land Act of 1913 was an indication of the temper of the times.

The formation in 1912 of what was to become the African National Congress (ANC) was a reaction to the progressive denial of rights. The early members of the ANC were essentially constitutional liberals in outlook. Peter Walshe writes of them:

> [They] were the products of missionary education – ministers, teachers, clerks, interpreters, a few successful farmers, builders, small-scale traders, compound managers, estate and labour agents. They were not trade unionists, nor were they socially radical ... they were setting out to attain what they considered their constitutional rights – equality of

opportunity within the economic life and political institutions of the wider society. They believed Western and
Christian norms to be closely interrelated, and accepted
the Cape qualified franchise as their ideal. (Walshe 1970, 34)

Then, as now, the ANC was a 'broad church', embracing various
ideological strands, unified around the common goal of ending
racial discrimination. At least into the mid-1940s the dominant
strand was one of 'constitutional liberalism'. This was insuffi-
ciently strong meat for the Youth Leaguers, who formed themselves into a distinctive ginger group in the ANC in 1943. Even
thereafter, when closer ties with the Communist Party were
forged and 'Africanism' became a significant force inside the
ANC, prominent members of the ANC remained firmly liberal in
their views. The scholarly Z. K. Matthews of Fort Hare University
College was one. Chief Albert Luthuli, leader of the ANC from
1952 to 1960, was another. Luthuli never called himself a 'liberal',
describing himself as tending towards 'the outlook of British
Labour, with some important modifications', and expressing
favourable views about the (South African) Liberal Party (Luthuli
1962, 154, 140). Some of Luthuli's admirers would no doubt resent
as an impertinence any posthumous recruitment of him to the
liberal cause, but a content analysis of his writings leaves little
doubt that however he may have categorized himself, his views
were well within the broad liberal spectrum, as the African
writer Lewis Nkosi acknowledged in an obituary (quoted in
Vigne 1997, 133).

    No good purpose, however, is served by retrospective dissec-
tion of an individual's putative ideological affiliations. The
point is that, contrary to the assumption made by some, South
African liberalism has never been a purely white phenomenon.
For the first three decades of this century liberalism among
whites was a diffuse force. There was no liberal party and liberals were scattered throughout civil society – in the churches (a

major source of liberal inspiration), the universities, the press, and the professions (notably the legal profession). Except for a tiny handful of more visionary employers, hardly any business leaders would have identified themselves (or have permitted themselves to be so identified) as liberals. Liberalism was alien to the major parliamentary parties, apart from glimmerings of cautious and paternalistic liberal views among some of the Unionists (who were absorbed into the South African Party in 1919). Liberalism, in short, lacked a focus.

To some extent this changed in 1929 when the South African Institute of Race Relations was formed out of the Joint Council system. The Institute had no political agenda and remained scrupulously independent of any party. Its constitution, adopted in 1932, read:

> To work for peace, goodwill, and practical cooperation between the various sections of the populations of South Africa. To initiate, support, assist, and encourage investigations that may lead to greater knowledge and understanding of the racial groups and of the relations that subsist or should subsist between them. (quoted in Hellmann 1979, 4)

The Institute's importance to liberalism is of such magnitude that it is not possible to do justice to it in the course of a few paragraphs. Suffice it to say that the Institute enabled some of the best liberal minds to deliberate together. Especially in its earlier years, it was an important meeting ground for white and black. While the United Party government was in power (1934–48), the Institute's lobbying of (distressingly few) sympathetic politicians and administrators achieved some modest success.

The Institute's strength, however, was its research. Ellen Hellmann (a formidable scholar who received a doctorate in social anthropology for research in the Reef squatter camp of Rooiyard) describes its agenda:

The Institute commenced its work with neither a preconceived programme nor ready-made policy. It believed in the pursuit of truth as a value in itself. It believed that the systematic seeking out of facts relating to the conditions which determine the quality of life of the disadvantaged groups in South Africa would increase public awareness and promote interracial understanding, an understanding without which there could be no peaceful future for South Africa. It recognized the inherent worth and dignity of every human being and his right to the full development of his innate potential. It affirmed the values of democratic society, with its accepted rights and duties, together with respect for the rule of law and the safeguarding of individual liberty. It pledged itself to pay due regard to opposing views sincerely held. (Hellmann 1979, 9)

The Institute gained (and retains) a reputation for meticulous research. Its factual inputs into all the major debates acquired the respect of even non-liberals. While avoiding any taint of party partisanship, the Institute never hesitated to enter the thickets of controversy.

These are well-known facts that bear repetition. What is less obvious is the spin-off that the Institute's activities had on the character of liberalism generally: South African liberals are well-informed about the nature of their society. To take one example: Helen Suzman has many estimable qualities, but perhaps one of the most important was the solid grounding in fact that characterized her speeches. If she did not have the information she required, she hounded the minister and his officials until she got it; when she had it, she used it to devastating effect. She was also indefatigable in carrying out on-the-spot investigations of issues.

Similar qualities appear in the parliamentary work of earlier liberals like Margaret Ballinger, Edgar Brookes, Donald Molteno, and J. D. Rheinallt Jones, all of whom were elected under the provisions of 1936 legislation that provided for a limited degree of separate representation for Africans. The tradition of well-researched speeches has continued to characterize the small liberal contingent in modern parliaments before and after 1994. 'Forward to freedom with facts and figures' was jokingly suggested as a slogan for the Institute by some of its younger members. The slogan would not do, but it was not an inaccurate pointer to the mindset of South African liberals. Many were intellectuals and academics for whom hard empirical data were the raw material for their thinking. Liberals were found in many disciplines: Alfred Hoernlé was a philosopher; W. M. Macmillan, C.W. de Kiewiet, and Eric Walker were historians whose writings collectively rescued South African historiography from the 'white-man-bringing-light-to-the-benighted-heathen' view that had previously been dominant; Monica Wilson and Winifred Hoernlé were social anthropologists; William Hutt, Ralph Horwitz, Herbert Frankel, and Desmond Hobart Houghton were economists; and Z. K. Matthews was an authority on African law and administration (as well as being vice-principal of Fort Hare).

Non-university intellectuals and writers were also important: Leo Marquard was a historian of note. His earliest book, *The black man's burden* (written under the pseudonym of John Burger in 1943), broke new ground in the sharpness of its critique of segregation. Alan Paton is most famous as a novelist, but his biographies of J.H. Hofmeyr and Archbishop Geoffrey Clayton, as well as his political journalism, are also highly significant.

A younger generation of liberal scholars carried on the tradition of engagé scholarship, as well as robustly contributing to the defence of intellectual freedom and university autonomy. It would be invidious to single out names, but the work of legal scholars like John Dugard and A. S. Mathews, who documented the abuse of human rights and the erosion of the rule of law, deserves mention. Michael Savage's painstaking analyses of the human cost of the pass laws and the economic costs of apartheid were also seminal efforts. Lawrence Schlemmer's regular analytical surveys have been full of brilliant insights.

The weakness of liberalism on the political front was nowhere better illustrated than in the vote in Parliament in 1936 on the bill to abolish the Cape African franchise. Only eleven voted against it; 169 voted for it. The voting showed that when white South Africa united, black South Africa invariably paid the price. Hofmeyr was a beleaguered man, but he took his courage in both hands and delivered what Alan Paton describes as 'one of the great speeches of South African parliamentary history'. He quotes Hofmeyr's Cassandra-like warning: 'By this Bill we are sowing the seeds of a far greater potential conflict than is being done by anything in existence today' (Paton 1964, 227).

In the 1930s and 1940s white liberals had little political alternative but to support the United Party (UP), which governed until 1948. The other option, for those who were appalled by the injustices of segregation, was to join the Communist Party of South Africa. There is little doubt that a number of white communists joined out of genuinely humane instincts – Bram Fischer is a case in point. But Stalinism and tight control by the Comintern ensured that for most liberals this was an unacceptable affiliation.

Many of Hofmeyr's speeches today sound at best paternalistic. His exposed political position trapped him into the language of white political discourse, which was intensely segregationist. Nevertheless, Hofmeyr possessed a strong sense of justice and a clear vision of individual dignity. Hopes that he might succeed Smuts and lead the United Party in a clear liberal direction were dashed by his early death in 1948. Although by far the most capable man in the Cabinet, Hofmeyr had powerful enemies among the conservative barons of his party. Many believed that his liberalism had cost them the 1948 election.

During the war years the UP had shown some signs of edging towards an acknowledgement that segregation had failed. Even Smuts, whose views on racial matters could most charitably be described as ambiguous, declared from an Institute of Race Relations platform in 1942 that 'segregation has fallen on evil days' (Smuts 1942, 10). The Social and Economic Planning Council, chaired by a stalwart liberal, Edgar Brookes, had been appointed by the government to advise on post-war policies. In successive reports that ranged over a variety of issues, the Council pointed in a direction that, if not overtly liberal, was at least reformist.

Hopes that the UP, now in opposition, could be persuaded to adopt a clear-cut liberal alternative to apartheid were to be dashed. Even the intake of bright and able young MPs in 1953 and 1958 (Colin Eglin, Helen Suzman, Zach de Beer, and Ray Swart, among others) could not budge the UP from its sterile course of vying with the Nationalists for the title of best protector of white interests. Its slogan, 'White leadership with justice', was not only a contradiction in terms, it was an absurdity.

In some quarters of the white English-speaking community, the demand for a clear, authentically liberal political voice had grown since 1945. Defeat of the UP in 1953, and the UP's fuzziness on racial issues, convinced them that the time was ripe for a new party. Thus was born the Liberal Party, with prominent names like Alan Paton, Leo Marquard, Oscar Wollheim, Gerald Gordon, Jordan Ngubane, Selby Msimang, and Margaret Ballinger among its founders. Special mention should be made of Peter Brown, a wealthy young Natal farmer, who epitomized the best of liberalism: principled, idealistic, and tough, the latter quality being demonstrated by his unflinching endurance of a banning order that lasted ten years.

In the fifteen years of its existence the Liberal Party never won an election in a white constituency, whether at national, provincial, or local level. It received minimal support from the press and much attention from the security police. Its demise in 1968 occurred as a consequence of the Prohibition of Political Interference Act, which outlawed multiracial parties; in truth, such had been the toll on the party of banning orders and other forms of harassment that by 1968 it was up against the ropes. In terms of membership the Liberal Party was small; 8 000 members, mostly African, was the highest number it ever reached. In those parts of the country where it was especially active, like Northern Natal and the Transkei, it received admiration, if not necessarily membership, from Africans whose causes the party had taken up (Vigne 1997).

In no sense could the Liberal Party be described as having detailed policies. It was remote from power, and the unceasing necessity of reacting from day to day to apartheid's latest abomination left little time for party leaders to spend long hours considering alternatives. This was especially true of economic policy. This writer recalls Alan Paton saying at a public meeting in Durban in 1961, 'The Liberal Party must make up its mind whether it is a capitalist or a socialist party'. The issue was never resolved, but it is reasonably safe to say that while the Liberals were staunchly anti-communist, most would have favoured some form of social democracy.

Much the same was true of constitutional policy. Donald Molteno, one of the country's leading constitutional authorities, had drafted the original policy, which was based on federalism, a strong commitment to the rule of law, and a qualified franchise, but it contained nothing like the detail which the Progressive Party's Molteno Commission featured. (Molteno left the Liberal Party and joined the newly-formed Progressive Party in 1959.[1]) Universal adult franchise was adopted in 1960, which prompted the resignation of a number of prominent white members.

The Liberal Party was more of a moral crusade than a party in a conventional sense. The point is encapsulated in the celebrated remark made by Molteno to Paton: 'The trouble with you, Paton, is that you think the Liberal Party is a church' (Paton 1988, 122). On the face of it, it achieved little, but the prominence of some of its members ensured that a liberal critique was injected into public debates, and that a liberal voice (usually Paton's) was heard abroad. In many respects the Liberal Party reconnoitred the way for the subsequent emergence of the Progressive Party.

Inevitably, the Liberals were in a kind of rivalry with communists, who operated through the Congress of Democrats (cod), a white organization with a membership of some three hundred, which was part of the Congress Alliance. Liberal suspicions of the Congress of Democrats reached a climax of sorts with the Congress of the People in Kliptown in June 1955, at which the Freedom Charter was signed. The Liberals at first cautiously agreed to participate, but they were deeply suspicious of cod's and the South African Indian Congress's involvement since they regarded both as communist fronts that were hostile to the Liberal Party. Attempts by Liberals to make the Congress of the People more fully representative, as well as other suggestions, were ignored. Peter Brown expressed the disillusionment of his colleagues (and, incidentally, cast some doubt upon myths that subsequently developed around the Freedom Charter), saying:

> The proposal for holding national elections, for marchers to converge from all corners of the country on a central point where they would discuss the draft of the Freedom Charter, which would contain a synthesis of their grievances and demands – both ideas were abandoned. Proper elections, even on a minor scale, were never held. A thorough canvass to collect grievances was never conducted. (quoted in Vigne 1997, 47)

Many Liberals believed – like Africanist members of the ANC who would subsequently break away – that the Congress of the People had been masterminded by communists, indeed, even that the Freedom Charter itself had been written by communists. However strongly circumstantial evidence supports these suspicions, the Liberal Party's ultimate refusal to participate in the

Congress damaged its relationship with the ANC, a fact that many Liberals subsequently came to regret.

A radicalized ANC was far more amenable to the message of socialism – and, subsequently, revolution – than the far less muscular offerings of liberalism. Indeed, throughout much of the Third World, nationalism embraced socialism. Apart from the Soviet Union's anti-imperialist stance (notwithstanding its own domestic form of internal imperialism and the vassal-like subjection of much of Eastern Europe), the Soviet model of 'democratic centralism' in a one-party state and forced industrialization offered the mirage of a quick fix. Moreover, after the banning of the ANC and the Pan-Africanist Congress (PAC) in 1960, and the ANC's subsequent decision to wage a war of liberation, the Soviet Union provided aid, training, and other forms of support to the ANC in exile. In comparison, the Western democracies did little until much later.

In the circumstances it was hardly surprising that many in the ANC turned their backs on liberals, especially if they were white. The rift was never absolute, and good interpersonal relationships between individual liberals and ANC members continued to prevail in many cases. The complex relationships between individual liberals (notably Patrick Duncan) and the PAC stemmed largely from a common visceral anti-communism (Driver 1980).

The emergence of the Progressive Party in 1959 marked a new phase in the development of liberalism. In contrast to the amiable eccentricity of the Liberal Party, the Progressives were slick, well-organized, and far better funded. Moreover, initially at any rate, they had a base of twelve MPs, many of them able people. That, of course, soon changed, because in the 1961 election only Helen Suzman was able to retain her seat. As the Liberal Party had learned, even moderate liberal views were unacceptable to the large majority of the electorate. Thirteen years would pass before Suzman was joined in Parliament by six more Progressive Party MPs.

Little purpose will be served by recounting subsequent developments in the Progressive Party, including the absorption of smaller splinter parties, and its reincarnation as the Democratic Party. This story has been well told in several accounts (see, for example, Swart 1991). Policy also shifted: the complex qualified franchise proposals were finally abandoned in 1979 in favour of universal adult franchise; proposals for a minority veto were also dropped in the 1980s.

The proposal for a minority veto was derived from recommendations made in a book entitled *South Africa's options*, co-authored by Frederick van Zyl Slabbert (leader of the Progressive Party from 1979 to 1986) and this writer. The book addressed the problem of creating and sustaining democracy in deeply divided societies, and concluded that modified consociational techniques offered the only hopeful possibility. The knotty point was that 'simple majoritarianism' has not achieved credible democracy in any deeply divided polity (a proposition that remains true). To this writer, at any rate, the implication of this finding was that a more consensual style of government which avoided the possibility of majority tyranny was needed for South Africa.

However, the insertion of the word 'veto' into Party policy immediately raised many hackles. It was construed as a fiendish, covert way of preserving white privilege. *South Africa's options* makes it crystal clear that the authors had no such intention and even explicitly warned that if a veto were used for such a purpose the entire system was liable to fail. The intention, perhaps poorly expressed, was to convey the idea that serious political differences should be the subject of negotiation and bargaining, rather than being resolved by the majority party's steamroller.

The point of this deviation into policy issues is to make the further point that liberalism, a doctrine of individual rights, does not yoke easily with collectivist phenomena such as nationalism and ethnicity. Whether the paradigm of the liberal-democratic state can cope with them and retain the credibility of its democratic character remains a moot point.

Throughout the apartheid decades, liberals (meaning here principally Liberals and Progressives) were buffeted from both right and left. Individuals suffered heavily for their views. Especially in the 1950s and 1960s, white liberals were commonly regarded as outcasts in their communities. Canvassing for candidates was a thankless task. The allegation, commonly made by supporters of the Black Consciousness Movement, that white liberals could retreat into the security and affluence of their communities was only half true.

In Parliament, Helen Suzman and those who joined her later were hated and reviled by the Nationalists for their persistent probing and their casting of light on dark places. Only people of exceptional courage and stamina like Peter Brown, Helen Suzman, and Colin Eglin (again, it is invidious to single out names) could have lasted the pace. The accusation that they were covert defenders of the status quo is not only absurd, it is insulting. True, they were not revolutionaries, but realists who recognized that the state could not be overthrown by the efforts of the armed struggle. South African liberals have always been reformist, seeking incremental change of a cumulative nature and, where possible, seizing opportunities that created additional political space.

Not only were they active on the parliamentary front, they also sought first-hand information from what were often literally battle-fronts. Confrontations between police and demonstrators, highly emotional funerals of activists, forced removals, and the hardships resulting from the pass laws were regularly monitored by liberals inside and outside Parliament. Special mention needs to be made of the Black Sash in this respect. Their activities deserve a separate paper, but space permits only the briefest acknowledgement of their sterling work.

In Helen Suzman's case, perhaps her finest extra-parliamentary work was her regular visiting of political prisoners. This could be done only by invoking her status as an MP. Apart from forming enduring friendships, she was able materially to improve the living conditions of prisoners (Suzman 1993, 137–169). (The writer recalls an episode in Lusaka in 1989 during a meeting with the ANC when Mrs Suzman was challenged by a young radical who insisted that such visits were 'useless'. She immediately turned to one of her ex-prisoner friends who is now a senior ANC cabinet minister and asked him if he thought this was true. He, a great bear of a man, answered the question by embracing and kissing her. A trivial episode, no doubt, but indicative of the respect in which she was held and the value placed on her intervention.) There were no votes to be derived from these activities. On the contrary, for many whites they confirmed the view that liberals were little short of traitors.

Apart from the critique from the left, which persisted into the 1980s and then faded somewhat as the Marxist-Leninist world largely collapsed, liberals, especially white liberals, experienced a sustained bombardment from the Black Consciousness Movement. Its most articulate exponent, Steve Biko, accused liberals of arrogance in assuming a 'monopoly on intelligence and moral judgement', of being 'self-appointed trustees of black interests' who 'set the pattern and pace for realization of the black man's aspirations', and who verbalize 'all the complaints of the blacks beautifully while skillfully extracting what suits them from the exclusive pool of white privilege'. Non-racial organizations like NUSAS (the National Union of South African Students) or the University Christian Movement were in reality not non-racial at all, since invariably whites would gravitate to most of the leadership positions. White liberals, said Biko, 'should realize that the place for their fight for justice is within their white society' (Biko 1987, 74, 75, 77).

These arguments were painful to white liberals, not least because there was some truth in them. Whites could – and many did – extricate themselves from the struggle even to the extent of emigrating and making highly successful lives for themselves abroad. At the core of Biko's analysis, but only as an unstated premise, was a subtle, insidious dynamic that shaped black-white relations, even in ostensibly 'non-racial' organizations. This dynamic derived from what Biko and others termed 'colonization of the mind' – that corrosive process whereby racist assumptions about black inferiority were unconsciously internalized by blacks. This phenomenon acted as a self-fulfilling prophecy, causing blacks to underperform in cooperative relationships with whites, including those who genuinely despised racism. Hence the strategy summed up in the slogan, 'Black man, you're on your own!'

Biko's other accusations – that white liberals assumed they held a monopoly on intelligence and moral judgement, and that they regarded themselves as trustees of black interests – may have been based upon his own experiences. In this writer's experience, however, which is a lifetime devoted to the liberal cause, any liberal who displayed such views in thought or deed would have been censured by fellow-liberals. White members of the Liberal Party and the Democratic Party were extremely sensitive to allegations of paternalism or of seeking to speak 'for blacks'. There may have been breaches of these self-imposed rules, but they were exceptions that proved the rule.

How, then, is the liberal record to be weighed? As the danger of a new attempt at intellectual hegemony increases, liberalism runs the danger of being written out of the script, except as a hindrance to 'real' change.

As was suggested at the beginning of this paper, an accurate assessment will not be easy to make. We are in any case too close to the times for dispassionate analysis. What follows is, accordingly, written with tentativeness. It is not an argument, but only the sketch of a possible one.

No liberal would claim that liberalism was the main driving force in South Africa's transition. The lesser claims that can be made are by no means unimportant, however. In one of his gentler remarks about liberals, Steve Biko said:

> ... the liberal must serve as a lubricating material so that as
> we change gears in trying to find a better direction for South
> Africa, there should be no grinding noises of metal against
> metal but a free and easy flowing movement which will be
> characteristic of a well-looked-after vehicle. (Biko 1987, 79)

Liberals played their part more or less to Biko's script: there was
little alternative. Their incessant nagging, their ability to expose
the human costs of apartheid, and their unceasing championing
of an alternative vision of society based on respect for human
rights acted like a form of water torture on the Nationalists. The
abuse endured by Helen Suzman, the Black Sash, miscellaneous
academics, clergy, and journalists was, in a perverse way, acknowledgement that the truth hurt. Alan Paton asked why it was that
the Nationalists resorted to such savage measures against people
who are so weak:

> And the answer is that the anger is not primarily directed
> against those who do not believe in the dream; it is primar-
> ily directed at the reality that will not take the form of the
> dream, and at the dream that will not become reality.
> (Paton 1988, 277)

Liberals can take some credit for removing the blinkers that
blinded so many Nationalists for so long. For a minority to have
yielded power to the majority without the devastation of a civil
war was a process with very few historical precedents. It could
not have happened unless significant numbers of the power-
holders had awoken from their dream and recognized that
unless a settlement was negotiated, rivers of blood would flow.

The Democratic Party (which at its apex won twenty per cent
of white votes), other organizations mentioned in this paper,

and significant elements in the business community served as a 'lubricating material', and prevented the conflict from degenerating into one involving substantially monolithic racial groups. (It would be unfair and churlish to deny that non-African communists also played an important part in inhibiting racial polarization, even if liberals continue to have suspicions about their precise role.) These are not inconsiderable achievements. With its roots in the Cape Colony of the 1820s, liberalism can validly claim a long pedigree, longer and more continuous than any of its modern competitors. In its long and chequered history it won few battles but it may claim, in a significant sense, to have won the war. Statutory racial discrimination was finally overthrown with the adoption of an interim constitution in 1993 and the installation of a new government in May 1994. The final constitution is by no means a perfect document: it is essentially unitary, though with federal fig-leaves, and it retains strong elements of the Westminster model, with its 'winner-take-all' proclivity. Arguably, neither of these qualities makes for durable democracy in a deeply divided society like South Africa.

Even so, the constitution enshrines core liberal principles: the protection of human rights and the rule of law. It is ironic that political organizations like the National Party and the ANC, neither of whom could be described as liberal, could agree on an essentially liberal form of state. Liberals have wisely chosen not to crow about this remarkable turn of events. Constitutions, as James Madison remarked, are 'mere parchment barriers': they may restrain or inhibit the abuse of political power, but on their own they cannot prevent it. Liberals' long experience in exposing and combating the misuse of power may yet stand them in good stead.

1

JOHN DUGARD

The new constitution: a triumph for liberalism? A positive view

CONSTITUTIONALLY, the liberal ideal has triumphed in South Africa. Both the 1993 interim constitution and the 1996 constitution reflect the hallmarks of liberal democracy: representative government, political accountability, proportional representation, an independent judiciary, a bill of rights, guaranteed press freedom and free speech, and a non-prescriptive approach towards economic policy. Despite this triumph of liberalism over other ideologies, however, there appears to be some discontent among liberals over our new constitutional order.

The reason for this, I believe, is to be found in the differences among approaches towards constitutionalism.

South African liberals have traditionally adopted an English approach towards the role of law in society. A. V. Dicey's notion of the rule of law has been their principal guide. While Dicey sought to advance individual liberties, due process of law, and independent courts, he was critical of constitutionally protected rights (on the grounds that such protection was often mere rhetoric) and special courts (particularly European administrative tribunals). For him, the rights of the individual were to be found in the common law and were best protected by ordinary courts. During the apartheid years liberals generally judged the arbitrary and discriminatory laws of apartheid by the rule of law. Helen Suzman's speeches are full of appeals to the rule of law, and it was Olive Schreiner's lodestar. Although Donald Molteno, Ben Beinart, and Tony Mathews appreciated the value of constitutional protection for human rights, it is clear that they too placed great trust in the rule of law.

The African National Congress (ANC) has a different constitutional tradition. Many ANC leaders believed that the rule of law was too vague and failed to spell out the rights of the individual, particularly in the social and economic spheres. They preferred, therefore, to draw on the United Nations Universal Declaration of Human Rights and the constitutions of socialist states for their inspiration. This different approach is reflected in the Freedom Charter of 1955, which includes both civil and political rights ('blue rights') and social and economic rights ('red rights'). While in exile, ANC members were exposed to developments in the United Nations and the Council of Europe on the protection of human rights by treaty – a development that was largely ignored by liberals in South Africa. Some exiles, such as Albie Sachs, spent considerable time in the United States, and inevitably the American constitutional experience made its mark too.

In South Africa, attitudes towards the rule of law began to change in the 1980s. Non-governmental organizations such as the Centre for Applied Legal Studies (at the University of the Witwatersrand), the Human Rights Centre (University of Pretoria), and Lawyers for Human Rights started to measure the laws of apartheid against the standards contained in international human-rights instruments. This new approach also appeared in the writings of academics and the pronouncements of some judges, such as Milne and Corbett. Appeals were now made for a bill of rights protected by a constitutional court. Some liberals preferred to advocate a return to the rule of law, but increasingly this was a minority position among constitutional lawyers.

During this period a number of meetings of ANC lawyers and
South African human-rights lawyers were held abroad, at which
there was consensus that human rights should be constitutionally protected. The rule of law *à la* Dicey was not mentioned.
When change came in the early 1990s, there was agreement
that the new constitution should include a bill of rights. The
ANC favoured such a course because of its historical commitment
to such an instrument, as shown by the Freedom Charter.
Furthermore, lawyers in the ANC who had spent many years in
exile – notably Kader Asmal, Penuell Maduna, and Albie Sachs –
brought with them the principles of international human-rights
law. The National Party (NP), which had vehemently opposed a
bill of rights while in power, now saw the advantages of a bill of
rights for the protection of the white minority. As it had never
understood the rule of law and had always misinterpreted or
denigrated it, the NP also turned to international norms. Here it
followed the recommendations of the Olivier Commission
Report on Human Rights of 1989, which paid little attention to
the concept of the rule of law.

Thus the interim constitution of 1993 was drafted by politicians and lawyers influenced by new developments in constitutional and international law. The constitutions of Canada,
Germany, and India, and the International Covenant on Civil
and Political Rights, the International Covenant on Social,
Economic, and Cultural Rights, and the European Convention
for Human Rights were the principal models to which the drafters
turned for guidance.

The drafting of the 1996 constitution followed a similar
pattern. Here the influence of international human-rights law
was even greater, as Constitutional Principle II (established in
1993 in negotiations towards the final constitution) directed
drafters to be guided by universally recognized human rights –
which was interpreted by the advisory committee (of which I
was a member) to mean generally accepted human rights.

The objections of liberals (including the South African Institute of Race Relations and the Free Market Foundation) cannot all be explained on the basis of different approaches to the protection of rights, but this does perhaps help to explain the following disagreements.

Social and economic rights

Civil and political rights – 'blue rights'- are the primary concern of liberals. 'Red rights' are seen to be of socialist origin (which undoubtedly they were) and therefore unacceptable to liberals. Liberal lawyers also object to such rights on the grounds that they are not justiciable, and some claim that they are not universally recognized.

Such objections fail to take account of the extent to which social and economic rights are recognized today. The International Covenant on Social, Economic, and Cultural Rights is supported by 135 states, and many constitutions include such rights. They may not be universally recognized, but they are generally accepted in today's world. As to justiciability, many civil and political rights are likewise dependent on the allocation of resources for their fulfillment (legal aid, for example).

Horizontal operation

Liberals tend to see a bill of rights as an instrument of a negative character that will do no more than protect the individual against the state. They therefore object to the extension of the bill of rights to relations between persons, both natural and corporate. This fails to take account of the fact that human-rights instruments are today largely seen as rights-conferring, that is, as instruments that confer rights on individuals in their relations with state and co-citizen. In the modern world the individual is often as much in need of protection against the large corporation as against the state.

Moreover, many countries today outlaw racial and gender discrimination practised by private clubs and schools. Surely South Africa's legacy of racial discrimination compels South Africa to respond, as the 1996 constitution has done, by making the bill of rights horizontal in its operation?

Freedom of speech

The 1996 constitution qualifies freedom of speech in respect of hate speech and the advocacy of war. Many liberals object to these restrictions. But again, they have their origin in the International Covenant on Civil and Political Rights.

Constitutional court

The South African Appellate Division was so tainted by its support for apartheid that it could not be used for the protection of human rights. A representative constitutional court with a clean record therefore seemed an obvious solution to the problem. Liberals (including ex-Chief Justice Corbett) object to such a court, presumably because in Diceyan terms it is a special court. This fails to take account of the extent to which constitutional courts are used today outside England. It also fails to take account of the circumstances which made the retention of the Appellate Division for the protection of the constitution impossible.

Apartheid as a crime against humanity

Both the 1993 and the 1996 constitutions give their approval to the controversial amnesty process which treats – at least in theory – the security forces of the previous regime and the ANC liberation movement forces in an even-handed manner. Inevitably, there are criticisms of this even-handedness from the ANC. Why, such critics ask, should those who committed crimes in pursuance of liberation be treated in the same way as those who committed crimes against humanity? After all, Nuremberg did not try both Nazis and members of the resistance movements in Europe.

This is a valid criticism, and one with which I agree, but the political realities of the South African settlement made it impossible to pursue the Nuremberg option. Still, I find it strange that Hermann Giliomee (as a former president of the South African Institute of Race Relations, does he automatically qualify as a liberal?) should reject the argument that apartheid was a crime against humanity on the basis that it was so declared by the 1973 Convention on the Suppression and Punishment of the Crime of Apartheid, which 'was sponsored by communist dictatorships' (Giliomee, 1997). His argument fails to take account of the fact that apartheid qualifies as a crime against humanity in terms of the Nuremberg Charter, the Statutes for the International Tribunals for the Former Yugoslavia and Rwanda, the International Law Commission's Draft Code of Crimes against the Peace and Security of Mankind, the 1968 Convention on the Non-Applicability of Statutory Limitations to War Crimes and Crimes against Humanity, the decision of the French Cour de Cassation in the Barbie case, and numerous resolutions of the General Assembly of the United Nations. Moreover, some ninety states are today parties to the 1973 Convention, and few of these could be described as communist dictatorships. Giliomee's refusal to consider international developments caricatures the liberal attitude that I have sought to describe.

Conclusion

Dicey's rule of law is no longer invoked in England today. Instead, those who seek protection for their human rights turn to the European Convention of Human Rights and the European Court of Human Rights in Strasbourg. South African liberals should likewise abandon their attachment to Victorian notions of the rule of law and look to international human-rights instruments for the protection of human rights. South Africa has signed and will soon ratify the International Covenants. The government has yet to sign the Protocol to the International Covenant on Civil and Political Rights which recognizes the right of individual petition to the UN Human Rights Committee. Wouldn't it be wiser for liberals to press for signature and ratification of the Protocol rather than to engage in attacks on the new constitutional order? Their criticisms show little understanding of the modern law on the protection of human rights.

2

ANTHEA JEFFERY

The new constitution: a triumph for liberalism? Some doubts[1]

Introduction

In assessing whether the new constitution represents the 'triumph of liberalism', the first step is to consider what liberalism means. There are likely to be as many views on the appropriate definition as there are liberals to hold them, and I can only describe my own perspective on the issue.

Liberalism, to me, embodies three core concepts:

- respecting individual civil liberties and the rule of law;
- limiting the power of the state as much as possible while at the same time promoting its effectiveness in playing its proper role; and
- preserving a 'zone of autonomy' which allows as much freedom as is appropriate to the private person, both natural and juristic.

In assessing the constitution, a further key issue is the choice of which terms to focus on. There are several, however, which are self-evidently so important that they warrant examination. These are:

- the guarantees of individual liberty in the bill of rights;
- the direct horizontal application given to the bill of rights;

- the extension of the socio-economic rights included in the bill of rights;
- the extent to which power is concentrated at the centre, or dispersed among the provinces; and
- the powers given to a new 'super' attorney general.

The guarantees of individual liberty within the bill of rights

The interim constitution of 1993, which came into effect on 27 April 1994, introduced into our law important guarantees of individual liberty. The bill of rights guaranteed the right to equality before the law; to freedom from torture and degrading punishment; to freedom of speech, assembly, and association; to fair and speedy trial in open court; to administrative justice; and to access to information held by the state concerning the individual. It also guaranteed the right to universal adult franchise, and to freedom of political choice.

All these important guarantees of individual liberty are carried forward into the new constitution, and this is undoubtedly its greatest achievement. Important caveats must also be noted, however. The first is that freedom of speech has been significantly curtailed by the prohibition of 'hate speech'. The definition of hate speech is complex, and the way in which it is likely to be interpreted commensurately difficult to foresee. The danger, however, is that its broad language could lend itself to a selective interpretation by the courts, which might allow 'racist' or 'ethnic' utterances by some but not by others. Double standards could also attend the related prohibition of incitement to violence, for inflammatory language used by the ruling party might be condoned, while equivalent language used by its opponents might be condemned.

The second important caveat is that emergency rule can now more readily be introduced. The criteria for declaring it have been broadened to include a 'catch-all' provision of no clear meaning, while the parliamentary endorsement that is necessary has been made easier to procure. In the interim constitution, the declaration of emergency rule would lapse after three weeks unless extended by a two-thirds majority in the National Assembly. Now the first extension of emergency rule requires only a simple majority in the assembly, while subsequent extensions require a sixty per cent majority of its members. The key difference is that the ruling party can secure a sixty per cent majority on its own, whereas a two-thirds majority (given the parliamentary make-up during the 1994–1999 term) would require the support of an opposition party as well.

Direct horizontal application of the bill of rights

The 1993 bill of rights, like almost every other bill of rights in the world, was vertical in its operation. That is, it shielded the citizen from the abuse of power by the state. The 1996 bill of rights, by contrast, allows for direct horizontal application. This means it can be enforced, on a horizontal basis, by one private person against another. It also means, in a complete inversion of the normal function of a bill of rights, that it can be enforced by state functionaries against the private person.

The Constitutional Court warned strongly against the dangers of direct horizontal application in a defamation case decided by it under the 1993 constitution in May 1996 (*Du Plessis and others v De Klerk and another*, 1996 (5) BCLR 658 (CC)). In this case, a majority of judges confirmed that the 1993 bill of rights was generally binding on the state alone. The majority judgments also sounded trenchant warnings about the implications of direct horizontal application of the bill of rights. It would, said Mr Acting Justice Sydney Kentridge, introduce a pervasive uncertainty into the law, while requiring the courts to 'strike down' the common law and replace it by new rules of their own devising. It would 'constitutionalize' the whole of common law, said Mr Justice Laurie Ackermann, and require conflicting guaranteed rights to be balanced against one another, with no indication as to how this should be done. It would also, he added, impose new legal *duties* on private persons, which was contrary to the purpose of bills of rights elsewhere. Mr Justice Albie Sachs said that it would turn South Africa into a 'dikastocracy'– a country ruled by judges – in which rulings of the Constitutional Court on what the bill of rights required would tie the hands of Parliament in effecting the piecemeal reform of common law which had always been its province.

Now that the 1996 bill of rights introduces direct horizontal application, these warnings are particularly apposite. Also disturbing is the vague test incorporated in the bill of rights for determining when a guaranteed right should operate horizontally. This vague wording could be used to confine direct horizontal applications within relatively narrow limits. It could also be used – as favoured by at least one of the judges on the Constitutional Court – to make the socio-economic rights of access to housing, health care, social security, food, and water binding on private persons as well as on the state.

Even if this particular outcome is avoided, direct horizontal application is still likely to generate a number of problems. In the United States, horizontality has generally been rejected, despite strong urgings for its adoption by those who claimed it necessary to combat race discrimination by private persons. Moreover, it was rejected for reasons which are as cogent here as they are in the US, and which may be summarized as follows. Firstly, horizontality serves to generate a clash between competing guaranteed rights; for example, between the right to free speech and the right to dignity. This, in turn, generates a hierarchy of rights in which some are recognized as winners and others as losers. Secondly, horizontality generates a constitutional framework 'in which the state is omnipresent'. It is, in the words of one

American author, 'disquietingly totalitarian' in its effects, and seeks to make virtually every aspect of individual behaviour subject to state control. In doing so, it contradicts the deep 'psychological need [of the individual] to believe that there are essentially some private realms, albeit circumscribed by state and society, in which actions are autonomous'.[2]

Horizontality has generally been rejected in Canada as well, for reasons which seem much the same. And in Ireland, where direct horizontal application has been most applied, its use has demonstrated two things in particular. First, horizontality can operate as a double-edged sword, for it has been used, in part, to promote gender equality – a goal that would doubtless be applauded in 'progressive' circles – and, equally, to curb the power of the trade unions (an outcome less likely to be welcomed in those quarters). Secondly, the Irish cases also demonstrate that horizontality was not necessary at all to reach an equitable outcome, for the same results could have been reached on established principles of common-law interpretation.

The extension of socio-economic rights

An assessment of the effect of extending socio-economic rights – which, in the 1993 constitution, were broadly confined to children's rights and the right to education – requires first an understanding of the difference between 'first-generation' and 'second- generation' rights.

First-generation rights are political rights – rights not to be detained, not to be prevented from expressing criticism or dissent, not to be tortured or arbitrarily killed, not to be unfairly discriminated against or denied equality before the law. The primary purpose of a bill of rights has always been to protect the individual against the abuse of these rights by an authoritarian state.

After the Second World War, however, the notion began to be

propagated that first-generation rights were meaningless without second-generation rights – rights to housing, to jobs, to health care, to education, to social security, and so forth. The argument was summed up in the question – what does the right of free speech mean to a person who is starving and has no shelter?

Bills of rights in various countries began to make some, usually limited, concessions to this view by including within their terms, for example, the right to free primary (and sometimes also secondary) education. Some countries, such as Scandinavian ones, also included limited guarantees of social security.

Other countries (such as India, Nigeria, and Namibia) went a different route. On assuming independence, they incorporated in their constitutions a 'traditional' bill of rights guaranteeing first-generation political rights, and a separate chapter of 'fundamental objectives' in terms of which the state undertook to strive for the provision of housing, health care, social security, and so forth. However, there was no attempt to make these provisions binding and justiciable rights.

Communist countries had earlier taken yet another route, and had included within their bills of rights both first- and second-generation rights. For example, the bill of rights in the constitution of the former USSR provided that citizens were entitled, inter alia, to employment, health care, housing, and education, to be provided through the 'socialist economic system' and the exercise of 'public control'.

South Africa's new bill of rights – having listed a number of first-generation rights – provides, in sections 26 and 27, that 'everyone has the right to have access' to adequate housing, to health-care services (including 'reproductive health care'), to 'sufficient food and water', and to social security. The state is obliged to take 'reasonable' measures, within its 'available resources', to 'achieve the progressive realization of these rights'. Those who have questioned the wisdom of including these provisions have generally been accused of seeking to retain white privilege, and the effect of this has been a chilling stifling of necessary debate. Within the limited debate that has occurred, proponents of the inclusion of these rights have generally said that there can be no harm in them because the right to 'have access' to housing, for example, is different from the right to 'have' a house. What precisely the difference is seems difficult to explain. What it appears to boil down to, however, is a view that a right to 'have access' is not really an enforceable right at all, but that the inclusion of these provisions is nevertheless required because it reflects a commitment on the part of the state to meet its citizens' most pressing socio-economic needs.

Critics of the inclusion of these provisions respond that there is little point in incorporating 'rights' that are meaningless, and that their incorporation may be far less innocuous than is generally supposed. This is for a variety of reasons, of which the most important are probably the following:

- These provisions could generate an enormous amount of costly litigation – much of it at taxpayers' expense – and could also bog down the delivery of housing and other resources while the Constitutional Court and the new high courts strive to decide what level of housing is 'adequate'; how much food or water is 'sufficient'; how many abortion and other clinics are needed, and where; whether a particular state policy is 'reasonable'; and what the state's available resources comprise, given the fact that it can always increase those resources by raising taxes or borrowing funds.
- These provisions will tend to increase the power of the state, because the state will tend to siphon yet more revenue from the private sector to meet these needs; new jobs, if any, will tend to be state jobs; and overall, the power of patronage of the state could increase significantly, for the state would then become the principal purveyor of employment, housing, health care, water, and even food.
- Second-generation rights could come to overshadow first-

generation rights, as has happened in communist countries. Political liberties could be eroded or suspended in the search for the delivery of material goods, and those who criticize the state's endeavours in this regard could be branded unpatriotic, reactionary, divisive, and dangerous. At minimum, 'advocacy' or 'good-news' journalism could tend to take the place of critical debate. And

- The bill of rights as a whole might tend to lose legitimacy as its provisions prove unenforceable. The danger is that it may come to be viewed as nothing more than a set of 'paper' guarantees, with no binding force or effect in either first- or second-generation spheres.

Finally, it must be queried why provisions of this nature should be considered necessary in our new bill of rights at all. A ruling party in a country characterized by widespread poverty must inevitably regard the provision of housing, health care, and so forth, as key priorities. It should not need a bill of rights to spur it into action. If it fails to meet expectations in these spheres, the remedy is not to take it to court for a judicial order 'forcing' it to govern more appropriately, but to vote it out of office at the next election. And, assuming for the sake of argument that some kind of constitutional provision is indeed necessary to propel state policy towards effective delivery, why should this not have been done (as in many other countries) through the inclusion of a separate set of directive principles?

The federalism issue

To what extent does the new constitution concentrate power at the centre, or disperse it to the provinces? The answer is that the combined effect of 'cooperative governance' and of other provisions setting out the powers of the provinces is to make it crystal clear that power, in the 1996 constitution, is concentrated at national level even more strongly than under the equivalent 1993 provisions.

The relevant sections are long and complex, and I can only sketch them in broad outline. At the outset, however, two aspects of cooperative governance merit particular mention. The first is that all spheres of government are now enjoined to 'coordinate their legislation with one another', and that this must inevitably reduce the scope for provincial variations on nationally determined policy. The second is that all spheres of government are also enjoined to 'avoid legal proceedings against one another'. The implication is that the jurisdiction of the courts in intergovernmental disputes has effectively been ousted, and aggrieved provinces will in future have to resort to new and more 'appropriate' mechanisms to be established for this purpose. These could be packed with supporters of the ruling party, in the same way as was the 'Senate' when it ruled on the 'coloured' vote in the 1950s. More germane to the 1990s is that rebukes to the national government administered by the Constitutional Court at the instance of the two non-ANC provinces might not be repeated if alternative mechanisms for resolving intergovernmental disputes must be used instead.[3]

Also important are the powers of the National Council of Provinces (NCOP), which replaces the Senate. These are particularly opaque, but their complexity cannot obscure the likelihood that the will of central government will always prevail. In most of the decisions taken by the NCOP, each province has a single vote, and all that is needed is the support of five out of nine provinces. In some instances (for example, an amendment to the bill of rights), the vote of six provinces is required. The two provinces not governed by the ANC in the 1994–1999 term, however, can always be outvoted.

Concurrent spheres of competence in which both central and provincial governments have power to legislate are very broad, and include key areas such as education, health, transport, development, welfare, and trade. This will not do much, however, to limit the power of central government. Legislation in these spheres can be introduced in either the National Assembly or the NCOP. If introduced in the National Assembly, a bill requires only a simple majority of votes cast for its adoption – and this in a situation where one-third of the members of the Assembly constitutes a quorum. It then goes to the NCOP, where all that is needed is the vote of five provinces out of nine. If, by unlikely chance, the NCOP rejects a bill, it can still be adopted by the National Assembly (following a complex mediation process by a committee likely to be dominated by the ruling party) by a two-thirds majority of its members. It is unlikely, however, that the National Assembly would often be compelled to take this route.

As if this were not enough to secure central domination, all legislation that falls outside these spheres and that does not affect the provinces can be enacted into law – irrespective of any opposition from the NCOP – by a second vote in the National Assembly, taken by a simple majority of votes cast. In addition, the exclusive powers reserved to provinces are indeed 'common for municipalities' and are limited to abattoirs, ambulances, archives, museums, libraries, provincial roads, and so forth. Furthermore, in the event of conflict between national and provincial legislation, national legislation prevails in broadly defined circumstances. It also prevails wherever doubt as to the correct interpretation makes it difficult for a court to decide the issue. Moreover, conflicting provincial legislation that is not overridden on this broad basis can prevail over national legislation only if it is approved by the NCOP, by five votes out of nine. The effect of these override provisions is best illustrated by reference to a provincial law, such as KwaZulu-Natal's legislation requiring its chiefs to be paid at provincial level. The central government's conflicting legislation is likely to prevail over the KwaZulu-Natal law under the broad override provisions. But, just to make doubly sure of this result, the KwaZulu-Natal law

cannot prevail over the national law unless it is endorsed by the
NCOP by five votes out of nine – a majority which the IFP-ruled
province would be highly unlikely to muster. In practice, accordingly, it is the national law that will prevail.

To ensure the dominance of central government still further,
other provisions of the constitution enable the cabinet to assume
responsibility for implementing legislation in any province, in
circumstances which are also broadly defined (but subject to the
endorsement of the NCOP). They also prevent provincial administrations from assuming responsibility for implementing
national legislation at all – even where the law falls within exclusive provincial competence – unless the province in question
has the 'administrative capacity' to do so. Disputes regarding a
province's capacity must be decided by the NCOP, by the usual
five votes to nine.

Introduction of a 'super' attorney general

The 1996 constitution differs also from the interim one in introducing a national or 'super' attorney general. The constitution
provides for the establishment of a 'single national prosecuting
authority', headed by a new 'National Director of Public Prosecutions', with wide-ranging powers to 'determine prosecution
policy', issue 'policy directives', 'intervene in the prosecution
process when policy directives are not complied with', and 'review
a decision to prosecute or not to prosecute' taken at provincial
level. The nine provincial directors of public prosecution are
made subject to the National Director in this way, while the minister of justice is given 'final responsibility' for the prosecuting
authority across the country.

Though calls for the introduction of a super attorney general
had been made earlier, the decision to include this provision in
the constitution seems to have flowed in considerable measure
from the dissatisfaction of the ruling party at the failure of the

attorney general in KwaZulu-Natal, Mr Tim McNally, to show
sufficient zeal in prosecuting the 'third force' for its role in
promoting political violence in the province (see also chapter 5,
'The rule of law since 1994'). The independence of attorneys
general is a vital ingredient in preserving the independence of
the judicial system. This provision in the new constitution
threatens that independence, while again serving to increase the
power of the central government at the expense of provincial
autonomy.

How liberal is the constitution?

Let us begin by recalling the key elements of the constitution
earlier identified. The guarantees of individual liberty are very
important – but they have also been constrained in significant
ways through the 'hate speech' and emergency provisions. How
these latter provisions will operate in practice remains to be seen.
What is noteworthy already – though this is not the fault of the
constitution in any way – is that guarantees of fair trial in particular are coming into disrepute for promoting the rights of the
perpetrator without any corresponding benefit for the victims
of crime. The result is not only a determination on the part of
government to exclude the right to bail for serious offences –
something the new bill of rights *should* but will not necessarily
prevent – but also an increasing resort to brutal self-help by people
grown impatient with ineffective governance in this sphere (see
also chapter 5, 'The rule of law since 1994').

Particularly disturbing from the liberal perspective is the fact
that the guaranteed rights have been turned into a code of *obligations* for individuals and the private sector. This stems, of course,
from the direct horizontal application of the bill of rights. This
could have disturbing implications in enforcing conformity to
new policies with strong ideological overtones. Worrying too is
the extension of socio-economic rights to include the rights of

access to housing, health care, and so on, for these will increase
the power of the state while undermining the free market and,
probably, the crucial first-generation rights. Moreover, if these
socio-economic rights are given direct horizontal application
the results could be even more disturbing.

Also ominous from a liberal point of view, which seeks the
dispersal of state power rather than its concentration at a single
point, is the fact that the powers of the provinces have been
significantly curtailed. Cooperative governance and the NCOP
will help ensure that the central government can always prevail
over provincial administrations, and that the provinces will
indeed become administrative agencies for the implementation
of national policy, rather than independent formulators of different and possibly more liberal policies.

Also disturbing from a liberal point of view is the introduction
of a 'super' attorney general. This will erode the independence of
the criminal justice system and could allow a politically appointed
National Director to substitute his or her own decisions on
prosecution for those of provincial attorneys general. This, too,
will help to build the power of the central state and ensure that
its own priorities regarding prosecution are implemented coun-
trywide.

The overall score card? The 1996 constitution is certainly not
a 'triumph' for liberalism, for it marks a retreat from the more
balanced and more liberal provisions of the 1993 constitution.
The 1996 constitution creates the framework for a strongly
centralized state, in which the emphasis could readily be placed
on enforcing a new ideology rather than allowing liberty to take
root and grow. If the aim of the ruling party is to implement a
new form of social engineering, this constitution gives it the
tools to do so. And whether the ruling party indeed embarks on
that path will depend not so much on the constraints placed in
its path by the provisions of the constitution, but rather on how
it straddles the conflicting demands of internal and international

constituencies. It is disquieting indeed that the new constitution *in itself* provides so inadequate a guarantee of individual liberty, and that it is likely to do little to encourage liberalism.

3

PATRICK LAURENCE

Liberalism and politics

AN ANOMALY UNDERLIES South Africa's contemporary
political situation: the new constitution adopted on 4 February
1997, like the interim constitution that preceded it, is firmly
based on liberal values, yet the word 'liberal' is conspicuously
absent from the nomenclature of all the major political parties.
The two main parties, the African National Congress (ANC) and
the National Party (NP), prefer to identify themselves as national parties. The remaining parties associate themselves with
freedom (the Inkatha Freedom Party (IFP) and the Freedom
Front), democracy (the Democratic Party), Africanism (the Pan
Africanist Congress), and Christianity (the African Christian
Democratic Party).

Of all the parties that contested the watershed April 1994 election, not one chose to describe itself as liberal, preferring instead
a variety of labels denoting commitment to federalism, peace,
women's rights, and workers, among others.

The anomaly cannot be coincidental. Essentially, it is the
product of a collective mentality forged in the struggle against
white minority rule, a mindset which, consciously or unconsciously, shies away from association with liberalism.

As Frederik van Zyl Slabbert has noted, South Africa during
the struggle was polarized by two competing 'redemptive

45

ideologies' (Slabbert 1993) associated largely but not exclusively
with the NP, as the self-proclaimed protector of the white minority
and guardian of law and order, and the ANC, as the champion of
the indigenous majority against exploitation. While there may
have been occasional nods in the direction of political tolerance,
the antagonists tended to assume that they had all the answers,
and that those who were not with them were against them.
Political forces which sought to promote an alternative more
often than not found themselves castigated as part of the
problem.

Van Zyl Slabbert, a former leader of the Progressive Federal
Party, which sought a way around the redemptive ideologies,
spoke from experience when he said, in mid-1993: 'To question
the reality of the *Total Onslaught* immediately got one defined as
part of it; to doubt any strategy of the struggle immediately made
you a willing or useful idiot of *The System*' (Slabbert 1993).

Helen Suzman, who was a lone liberal voice in the old whites-
only Parliament for thirteen years, recalls the immediate reaction of P. W. Botha after Prime Minister Hendrik Verwoerd's
assassination by a parliamentary messenger in September 1966.
As Verwoerd lay dying, Botha waved his finger at her and said:
'You liberals are to blame ... We are going to get you all' (personal interview – P. L.). Botha's reaction is clear evidence of the
anti-liberal phobia that existed in the ranks of the NP at the
time, for it is widely recognized that the origins of the murder of
Verwoerd most likely lay in the dementia that tormented his
killer, Dimitrio Tsafendas, and not in political conspiracy.

The Suppression of Communism Act codified the NP's
phobias; ostensibly fashioned to crush communists, it was also
used to silence and ban liberals (Peter Brown and John Aicheson
come to mind) and black nationalists (among whom Nelson
Mandela and Albert Luthuli are pre-eminent examples). The
Prohibition of Political Interference Act of 1968, which prohibited people of different race groups from belonging to the same

political organization, was also aimed in part at the Liberal Party, which had taken the radical step of proclaiming its belief in universal adult suffrage and was beginning to attract a steady stream of black recruits to its ranks.

On the other side of the political spectrum, the radical leftist Neville Alexander remarked upon his release from Robben Island in 1974: 'Liberalism is a greater danger in the long run to the struggle of the oppressed than fascism, for the very reason that it seems to speak with the tongue of the people' (quoted in Slabbert 1993).

Scepticism about liberals permeated the writings of Steve Biko, the charismatic founder of the black consciousness movement. In the early 1970s he wrote: 'The biggest mistake the black world ever made was to assume that whoever opposed apartheid was an ally.' Liberals, he continued, were intellectual dilettantes who identified with the cause of black liberation to ease the burden of guilt as they enjoyed the fruits of minority rule. 'Although he [the typical liberal] does not vote for the Nationalists (now that they are in the majority anyway), he feels secure under the protection offered by the Nationalists and subconsciously shuns the idea of change' (Biko 1978).

Biko's views echo those of Robert Sobukwe, the founding president of the Pan-Africanist Congress (PAC), who wrote in *The Africanist* of January 1959: 'We regard them all [whites] as shareholders in the SA Oppressors' Company (Pty) Ltd. There are whites, of course, who are intellectually converted to our cause but, because of their position materially, they cannot fully identify themselves with the struggle of the African people. They want safeguards and checkpoints all along the way, with the result that the struggle of the people is blunted, stultified, and crushed' (Sobukwe 1977, 508).

The heritage of the past lives on: liberals remain popular targets of attack. Liberalism as a consciously proclaimed philosophy has only one unashamed champion in the party political arena in the Democratic Party (DP), which won a tiny sliver of the vote (1.68 per cent) in the 1994 general election. Even the DP, however, chooses to identify itself as a democratic rather than a liberal party, possibly because of objections to the term liberal by two of its three founding leaders, Wynand Malan of the National Democratic Movement on the left and Dennis Worrall of the Independent Party on the right.

Despite these criticisms from both sides of South Africa's polarized political debate, liberalism has managed to survive and see its values incorporated in the new constitution. David Welsh has aptly observed that liberalism may have lost many battles, but it won the war (Welsh 1994). The reason for the paradox is that the two main political forces, the NP and the ANC, were forced to negotiate a compromise when neither was able to impose a settlement on the other. The NP, realizing belatedly that liberal values offered the best protection against a tyranny of the majority, strove to include them in the constitution; the ANC, weakened ideologically by the collapse of communism in Eastern Europe and the Soviet Union between 1989 and 1991, abandoned its flirtation – to put it kindly – with a communist-style people's democracy and opted for parliamentary democracy.

Though deeply suspicious of one another, the two sides have been able to reach a modus vivendi in a constitution that enshrines many classically liberal values: the rule of law, a justiciable bill of rights guaranteeing fundamental freedoms, and an independent constitutional court to protect the constitution from the ambitions of wilful politicians.

There are regrets in the DP, the IFP, and the NP that the constitution is not more definitely federal and that it has weakened rather than strengthened the power of provincial governments. This concern is reinforced by the fear that the new National Council of Provinces actually facilitates control by the ANC through its majorities in seven of the nine legislatures (in the 1994–1999 term) while ostensibly strengthening the hand of the provinces in central government. But neither of these reservations contradicts Nelson Mandela's contention that South Africa now has one of the most democratic – and, it can be added *sotto voce*, most liberal – constitutions in the world.

Liberalism in South Africa is thus buttressed by the new constitution, and in that sense may be stronger than it has ever been. Its weakness as an organized political force is, in part, counterbalanced by its strength in civil society, where liberal values are championed by a variety of institutions ranging from non-governmental organizations (such as the Institute of Race Relations, emerging as a strong voice in post-apartheid South Africa) to sections of the media and some of the universities. It would be a mistake, however, to underestimate hostility towards liberals and hence to liberalism in the new South Africa. 'Liberal' is used as an insult far more frequently than as a badge of praise. Neither of the two main political parties can be regarded as trustworthy defenders of liberalism: they are reluctant rather than genuine converts who have been forced to adopt liberal values by political exigencies. To argue for prudence, however, is not to deny that there are people of liberal disposition in the new NP and in the ANC.

Indeed, President Mandela is a liberal, and shows it in his commitment to racial reconciliation and his award of a gold medal for meritorious service to Helen Suzman, the doyenne of South African liberalism. A caveat needs to be added, however. His tendency to play the racial card and attack unnamed whites, as he did during the Sarafina II crisis when Health Minister Nkosazana Zuma came under fire, is worrying. Another leading ANC member with a strong commitment to liberal values of 'fair play' and open debate is Tourism Minister Pallo Jordan, although he would almost certainly be horrified to be described as a liberal.

It is perhaps pertinent to note here that the Rev. Stanley Mogoba, elected president of the PAC in 1997, impresses DP

leader Tony Leon as a liberal. Mogoba, previously the Presiding
Bishop of the Methodist Church of Southern Africa, is determined to revive the PAC's non-racial tradition, an objective
which is certainly compatible with liberal values. Though often
marginalized by malevolent racism, the PAC's non-racial tradition has survived the savage crimes committed against 'settlers'
in the name of liberation. The tradition is implicit in the slogan
'There is only one race, the human race' (Sobukwe 1959). Another
manifestation is found in Sobukwe's definition of an African as
a person, irrespective of colour, whose primary loyalty is to
Africa and its people. (Juxtaposed with his comment that all
whites are shareholders in the SA Oppressors' Company, this
definition illustrates the competing ideological forces within the
PAC.)

But, individual exceptions aside, anti-liberal sentiments still
swirl strongly in these two parties and underscore the need for
vigilance against possible future attacks on liberal values from
their ranks. In the ANC, there is an inclination to turn a blind eye
to zealots among its members. For example, Dan Mofokeng was
promoted to a top position in the Gauteng provincial government
after he had openly advocated making townships no-go areas to
whites during the 1994 election. With regard to the NP, there has
been increasing suspicion that former President F. W. de Klerk
knew of but turned a blind eye to the machinations of military
intelligence during South Africa's transition to democracy. This
places a question mark over his conversion to liberal values and
the durability of his commitment to them. The NP's use of
cartoons calculated to arouse fears of blacks among the coloured
community during the 1994 election is another cause for concern.

The dangers to liberals and liberalism are not confined to the
mainstream parties. South Africa is awash with hostility towards
and suspicion of liberals. These sentiments often emerge in the
context of pressure for the transformation of institutions in the
private and public domains to bring them into harmony with

the post-apartheid ethos. Liberals who dare to question the process are targeted for abuse. It matters little whether they resist wholesale Africanization in the racial sense of the word, raise questions about the substitution of one racial order for another, or express doubts about the wisdom of a particular appointment made in the name of black empowerment. For example, the antagonism roused against 'liberals' by the 'Makgoba affair' at the University of the Witwatersrand was remarkable. Senior academics who questioned the administrative competence and moral integrity of William Makgoba, then deputy vice-chancellor of the university and a prospective candidate to succeed Robert Charlton as vice-chancellor, were accused of resisting transformation per se; they were dubbed the 'gang of thirteen' and castigated with a range of abusive epithets which simultaneously managed to smear the professors as individuals as well as liberalism as a political philosophy. When Makgoba retreated from the fray, his defenders – including the vociferous Jon Qwelane and Thami Mazwai – did little or nothing to set the record straight. Though Makgoba's sudden docility disappointed them, the 'liberals' – not all of whom were happy with the label – still stood condemned for their impertinent questioning of Makgoba's past actions.

Liberals in post-apartheid South Africa are increasingly damned as stubborn defenders of privilege, as people who like to occupy the moral high ground by protesting against the iniquities of racial oligarchy while enjoying its benefits.

Water Affairs Minister Kader Asmal and his associate Ronald Roberts have written: 'Liberalism, worn down over the years, has become South Africa's last credible instrument of privilege. At its core is echoing space' (Asmal and Roberts 1995). The same article accuses liberals of siding with the National Party in their demonization of the 'liberation movement' as one which spawned 'Stalinist child-eaters'.

Criticism of liberals has also come from another quite unexpected quarter: men and women who define themselves as liberals or social democrats but who categorize the present generation of high-profile liberals as closet conservatives or neo-conservatives. In their view, these liberals are guilty of a 'slideaway' (to borrow the phrase coined by Jill Wentzel of the Institute of Race Relations for another type of apostasy) to the right. Thus Ken Owen, past editor of the *Sunday Times*, writes:

> South African liberalism has been wrenched from its historical base and dragged to the Right by a group of tough-minded young people who emerged from the fight against the revolutionary Left in the [19]80s. They are probably best described not as 'liberals' but as neo-conservatives ... Politically [they] are led by the Democratic Party's Tony Leon ... Intellectually, however, the mainspring of the New Right ... lies in the Institute of Race Relations where the formidable John Kane-Berman presides over a battery of intelligent, if zealous, young opponents of anything they can define, pejoratively, as socialism. (*Sunday Times*, 12 Nov. 1995)

In Owen's view contemporary liberals, a.k.a. the New Right, have abandoned concern for the individual for an obsession with the market.

The same theme is taken up by Margaret Legum, a long-standing opponent of apartheid. She sees the emergence of what she describes as 'liberal fundamentalism', a label she attaches specifically to the Institute of Race Relations and its parliamentary affairs manager, Colin Douglas. She writes: '... liberal fundamentalists reveal themselves as the essential conservatives among the political philosophies on offer today. They favour the status quo or, at best, a pace of change which contradicts the idea of transformation'.

Leading the attack from a different perspective is Thami

Mazwai, the managing director of *Enterprise* and the former chairperson of the Black Editors' Forum, who took up cudgels on behalf of Makgoba. Mazwai seems to see red whenever a (white) liberal appears on the horizon: he led the attack on the Freedom of Expression Institute (FXI) after it was mandated by the Truth and Reconciliation Commission (TRC) to prepare 'preliminary investigation documentation' for a proposed TRC hearing on 'the role of the media during the apartheid years'. Mazwai, a man of undoubted personal bravery and principled commitment to the struggle, believes 'liberals have arrogated unto themselves the right of deciding what shape post-apartheid SA must take' (Mazwai 1996). For that reason he opposed any role for the FXI in investigating, even for the purposes of initial discussion, 'the role of the media under apartheid'. The primary reason for his successful objection – the TRC withdrew its invitation – was that it amounted to an investigation of the media by 'our tormentors', by which he was referring to the presence on the FXI executive of two white liberals, Raymond Louw, former editor of the *Rand Daily Mail,* and Clive Emdon, director of the Independent Media Diversity Trust and former senior journalist of the *Rand Daily Mail.*

Apart from maligning the integrity of Emdon and Louw, under whose editorship the *Rand Daily Mail* exposed many apartheid brutalities and was accused by various National Party cabinet ministers of denigrating South Africa, Mazwai seems to have ignored the role of black notables and journalists on the FXI, including Enoch Sithole of the SABC, Nomavenda Mathiane of *Business Day,* and Tyrone August of the *Sowetan.* The presence of white liberals seems to have been enough to elicit his implacable opposition to the FXI, even if its role was limited to appointing an independent researcher to carry out the investigation on its behalf.

Mazwai's campaign against the FXI recalls allegations that the TRC is controlled by a 'white liberal clique'. The charge – dismissed forthrightly by TRC chairperson Desmond Tutu – again ignores indisputable facts: the chairperson of the TRC is black. So, too, are the chairpersons of its human rights, amnesty, and reparations committees (Tutu, Hassen Mall, and Hlengiwe Mkhize), and the head of its investigative unit, Dumisa Ntsebeza. Moreover, the six whites on the TRC (out of seventeen commissioners) are not homogeneous politically. Neither Chris de Jager, a former member of the Conservative Party, nor Wynand Malan, a former member of the NP and founder of the National Democratic Movement, fits the liberal mould; the remaining members – Alex Boraine, Richard Lyster, Mary Burton, and Wendy Orr – may be classified as liberal in the broadest sense of the word, though one suspects they might prefer the labels 'progressive' or 'democratic'.

The conclusion is that liberals cannot assume that the battle is won just because the constitution incorporates liberal principles. If in the past they were construed by the NP establishment as opening the door to besieging 'barbarians', today they are cast in the role of attempting to bolt it against the legitimate aspirations of 'the people'. If, in Welsh's metaphor, the ideological war of the past has been won by liberals against their communist and nationalist adversaries, a new war has begun in which liberals cannot be as assured of victory.

4

CHARLES SIMKINS

Must contemporary South African liberals be Thatcherites?

The forms and limits of contemporary liberal economic thought

The two major currents of economic thought which liberalism has had to accommodate in the twentieth century have been the Keynes/Beveridge package of the 1930s and 1940s on the one hand, and the libertarian critique of this package in the 1970s and 1980s on the other. It is tempting, but not accurate, to think of the two as a social-democratic revolution and a conservative counter-revolution. Many libertarians work selectively with the liberal tradition, sometimes describing themselves as 'classical' or 'nineteenth-century' liberals. But this concept is an *ex post* construction (of a liberalism uncontaminated by social democracy) rather than an accurate reference to an actual period of thought. In the first half of the nineteenth century, the dry Jeremy Bentham was balanced by a wet John Stuart Mill. In the second half, the Darwinian Herbert Spencer was balanced by the Hegelian T. H. Green. All these thinkers came to very different conclusions. Nonetheless, the liberal tradition is not infinitely elastic; a discussion of some of the difficulties on both the libertarian and the social-democratic fronts will indicate the boundaries of liberal economic thought.

Libertarians often look forward to the 'end of politics', at least as far as political intervention in the economic realm is concerned. Of course, for there to be an economic realm at all, the state has to guarantee a system of property rights. A considerable part of Friedrich von Hayek's work describes politics as a threat to a complex, but delicate, liberal economic and cultural order. In the United States, the end of political control over economic policy takes the form of a demand to constitutionalize important realms of economic policy, such as a balanced budget or the independence of the monetary authority, thereby taking these issues out of the realm of day-to-day politics.

The 'end of politics' is, of course, the major theme in anarchist theory, of which libertarianism is a part. But an understandable longing for an autonomous realm of the economic should not delude one into thinking it possible. The nearest available realistic strategy in the late twentieth century is to aim for the containment of illiberal elements in political life. Two ways of proceeding are available. The first is direct domestic political participation. Secondly, one may rely on, and emphasize, domestic and international economic structural factors which have a marked effect on government economic policy. Their political effect is indirect, but real. Certain kinds of illiberal political strategies will certainly alarm markets, and are therefore discouraged. Globalization – freer flows of capital as well as goods and services, and growing international economic integration – is a powerful force favouring liberal policies.

Nonetheless, the libertarian critique of social-democratic thought, with its central emphasis on the role of the state as an extensive regulator of the market, must be taken seriously. T. H. Marshall saw social democracy as guaranteeing social citizenship via full employment, a social safety net and extensive social services, and an egalitarian income distribution. This inevitably meant high rates of taxation.

But our understanding of the world has changed in important ways since 1945. Some examples:

- More is known about the theory of optimal taxation, which does not support high marginal rates of tax on income from employment.
- We are now inclined to see public policy less as a set of state commands imposed upon subjects, and more as a game between government and people. The new understanding of policy sees outcomes as a consequence of decentralized strategies at a number of levels rather than the simple result of state commands. Sensible public policy is therefore, if rational choice theory has any validity, more market-oriented. The state, rather than being seen as monolithic, becomes a series of related offices between whom there are principal-agent problems. There is no automatic alignment of the objectives of those in charge of policy and those who carry it out. Optimal contracts have to be worked out to create this alignment as far as possible, and these can take one far from traditional civil-service practices. If contracts between offices and between offices and the public are not optimal, avoidable inefficiency (including possible corruption) creeps in.
- Public choice theory suggests that, under many circumstances, the state may not be an efficient agent of the public it is meant to serve under democratic rule.
- Many welfare measures have come to be seen as partly or wholly self-defeating; a standard example used in introductory economic analysis is that of rent control. Analysts of income-maintenance measures often conclude that they collectively create a poverty trap by imposing a very high effective marginal rate of tax on incomes just above the poverty level.
- Outcomes are now understood to depend on the consistency and credibility of policy. Older views focused only on policy content.

If problematic state behaviour is one issue, state capacity is another. There are at least two other aspects to be considered. First, Joel Migdal has observed that the state may be incapable of formulating and consistently executing impersonal public policy, as political leaders struggle to placate constituencies, deal with local strongmen, and guard against challenges to their position from people within their own ranks. This phenomenon is, of course, to be found in every political system; the differences between advanced industrial countries and developing countries are ones of degree. Often the state is weaker in relation to the society it governs in developing countries than in developed countries. European development advisers who think within the Western European social-democratic tradition, for instance, have often failed to appreciate the marked differences between state capacity in their home countries and state capacity in the economies they think about. Their policy proposals, when adopted, have often led to radically different outcomes than those expected.

Secondly, historical experience defines the feasible range of forms of regulation of society by the state. Michael Mann has made the point that the welfare state and the warfare state are intimately connected; the extensive warfare associated with the emergence of the modern European state system has created a tradition of far more extensive state regulation than in the United States, for instance. A British example: one of the origins of the National Health Service was the discovery at the time of the Boer War and again in the First World War that only two in five working-class young men were fit for military service. Again, conscription and rationing in wartime accustom a nation to extensive state regulation. By contrast, Theda Skocpol has recounted how the United States between 1865 and 1917 developed only a limited range of welfare services (for mothers and soldiers, two groups generally agreed to be deserving) even though there were budget surpluses for much of the period.

The welfare state has also been founded on the immobility of factors of production. This is a crucial problem in a time when the trends are towards greater mobility. The Bretton Woods international economic dispensation was designed to promote international trade in goods and services by a series of agreed moves towards free trade. But it deliberately placed limits on international capital flows. It was in the wake of the collapse of the Bretton Woods system in the 1970s that the present high level of international capital mobility emerged, with major new consequences for the conduct of national macro-economic policy.

Changes in labour mobility have been slower and more limited. While population movement within Western Europe is easier than it used to be, the boundary between Western and Eastern Europe remains. Even within Western Europe, employees have to negotiate national barriers, and incentives to move are much diminished by non-portable social benefits. The European state system as a whole is in massive labour-market disequilibrium made possible only by restrictions on movement. This can be seen from the problems of integrating even the four Visegrad states (Czech Republic, Slovakia, Poland, and Hungary) into the European Union. These countries have a combined population of sixty million, half of whom are economically active, with wage rates one-seventh those in Western Europe. What would happen to the Dutch labour market if a million hungry Poles descended upon it? Small wonder that fear of instability in the East has re-emerged as a major factor in Western European consciousness.

What attitude should contemporary liberals take to cross-border mobility of capital and labour? One might learn from the divagations of Marxist theory. Marx himself described capitalism as transforming the world; in his view, only when the innovative possibilities of capitalism had been exhausted at the international level would there be opportunities for socialism. Some Marxists, however, have argued that capitalism underdevelops large parts of the world; capitalist stagnation then sets in before all countries are developed. Currently, the empirical evidence is against the latter view; in recent decades, the developing world has been growing faster than the advanced industrial world, and this pattern has been widely if unevenly spread. The innovative possibilities are far from being exhausted either at the extensive (greater use of inputs) or the intensive (technological change) margins.

While capital movements can be a real problem for developing countries that have not yet learnt to co-exist with them and manage them, they have also been instrumental in achieving high growth rates in countries that can generate and use them. In the early 1990s, Fortune magazine estimated that there were 1.5 to 2 trillion us dollars of capital in the hands of fifty million overseas Chinese – $30 000 to $40 000 for every man, woman, and child – available to move around Asia as opportunities for investment present themselves.

Population movements are more problematic. Two points need to be made, one philosophical and one political. The great systems of moral philosophy have been universal in orientation and the question is now being asked: if it is improper to regard only people of the same race or gender as oneself in ethical calculations, why should it be any more appropriate to limit the moral universe to those with the same nationality as oneself? Ethical problems concerning income distribution or poverty have been considered until very recently on a national basis – hence the welfare state – but should they be?

At a practical political level, it should be noted that some states have highly effective border controls; others, like the United States, do not, and have to make periodic adjustments to cope with the presence of illegal immigrants. In the us, this is not only a matter of geography; just as important are relations with Mexico (especially under the North American Free Trade Agreement (nafta)), and the existence of a group of employers for whom cheap immigrant labour is necessary or highly convenient.

Capital and labour movements reinforce the tendency of free trade to produce equality in factor prices between countries. Equality in factor prices is in turn a powerful means to the creation of international equality. Why factor prices are currently so different is a question at the heart of modern growth theory, one of the more influential developments in economic thought during the last decade. As answers become more apparent, policies to make factor prices more equal will follow. Also, it is becoming more common, and more appropriate, to think globally about developments that used to be conceptualized nationally. Thus:

- A global fertility transition is underway to which a number of African countries are contributing, and economists are starting to analyse income distribution and poverty around the world.

- Global poverty studies may be more important than national studies in shaping our sense of which policies are desirable. Estimates of global income distribution and poverty have been appearing for the past fifteen years.

- While politically the United States may seem dominant in the post-Cold War period, its contribution to world output has dropped from 50 per cent immediately after the Second World War to 20-25 per cent today, with a consequential diminution of its role in world finance, which now has three dominant currencies, rather than one.

- Closed economy analysis has steadily lost ground in macro-economic theory.

The impact of developments since the end of the 1970s on national policy options, particularly at the macro-economic level, is the subject of a large and controversial economic literature. Some analysts have stressed 'competitiveness', that is, the conditions for producing tradeable goods at low cost which can compete on world markets. Another group has considered the determinants of economic growth, dividing nations into winners and losers according to how they perform on a range of economic variables. A sceptical critique of this approach argues that impressive economic performance can be at least as much due to good fortune as to good policy; this decade's economic miracle can be the next decade's average or poor performer. Brazil saw rapid growth in the late 1960s and much of the 1970s, only to experience stagnation and retrogression in the 1980s. Even the *Wirtschaftswunder* now has an unemployment rate higher than at any time since 1933; Japan, too, has gone off the boil. A third current of opinion urges at least the larger economies to behave strategically as traders, rather than working with a free-trade model. To the extent that the world economy is divided into blocks, this will be a debated option.

Macro-economic theory and policy is now inherently controversial, and there can be no simple prescription for success.

Macro-economic stability is generally prized as a policy goal, but the optimal means to achieve it are not always clear.

Globalization tends to reduce the macro-economic policy instruments available to government, while introducing pressures not known in the Bretton Woods era.

The evolution of liberal economic thought in South Africa

Liberalism has much to say about both politics and economics; South African liberals, always a small political force, have had to choose at any given time a subset of possible themes around which to focus their energies. Thus, in the 1960s, Helen Suzman as the single Progressive Party member of Parliament was better known for her advocacy of civil rights and political freedoms, in a decade when both were being eroded by an illiberal National Party, than for her economic views. And, as the 1980s wore on, the energies of many liberals were devoted to thinking about how a political transition could be made to incorporate as many of the features of a liberal constitutional state as possible. This task has only recently come to an end with the adoption of the 1996 constitution.

By contrast, liberal thinking in the 1930s and 1940s was focused mainly around social and economic issues. There were political debates – around the edges of the franchise question, for example, with liberals unsuccessfully attempting to extend or defend the Cape tradition of a property-qualified common voters' roll for African men. But the major liberal intellectual innovation of this period was the concern with black poverty. This issue was put on the agenda by a number of talented social anthropologists and sociologists through academic publications and work through the South African Institute of Race Relations. In the Rowntree tradition, poverty datum lines were defined and policies assessed by their ability to keep as much of the population above them as possible. The influence of this work could be seen in the Native Economic Commission Report of 1932, and more strongly in the wartime reports of the Social and Economic Council. Mine wage policy, for instance, was discussed in the light of a basket of requirements necessary for survival. So was the setting of rentals for local-authority housing in urban townships.

This work continued to have real effects on government policy after 1948. The National Party certainly rolled back poverty alleviation programmes in the first decade of its rule, but it could never eliminate them. And in the end, the National Party removed racial discrimination in a way never contemplated by the old United Party governments. South African liberal thinking about poverty has always been unashamedly 'end-state' or consequentialist, rather than 'procedural' or deontological; that is, it has justified poverty policies by referring to their outcomes, rather than deducing them from first principles.

Of course, the strategic choice of themes to emphasize never boils down to a simple choice between politics and economics.

The best-known economic counterpoint to the political themes of the 1960s was the O'Dowd thesis, which took its cue from modernization theory. The core proposition was that continued economic growth would take South Africa beyond a racially restricted democracy, with sharp limitations on civil and political rights, to an inclusive and freer democratic system. The analysis was written in strictly positive terms, but there was an implicit normative message, similar perhaps to the reflections of the Vatican Secretary of State on the 1929 Concordat with Mussolini's Italy. Fascism, he mused, would be over in twenty years (a correct prediction), but Mother Church is eternal.

The O'Dowd thesis had limited resonance for two reasons. First, it appeared in 1966, when modernization theory was being challenged by dependency theory (a left-wing contender), which at the time seemed to offer exciting new intellectual perspectives. (In retrospect, modernization theory has worn better than dependency theory, and there has been a new round of work in the modernization-theory tradition in the last fifteen years. With this new work, and the collapse of communist systems because they could not offer a viable route to affluence, has emerged a degree of liberal triumphalism unknown during the 'short' twentieth century (1914-1991). To match the confidence of Fukuyama's 'end of history' idea, one would have to go back to a late nineteenth-century text such as Bosanquet's *Philosophical theory of the State*. By the end of the 1980s, South African Marxism was in a worse crisis than liberalism had been twenty years before. (Cosmopolitan liberalism is back in fashion.) The second, more subtle, problem had to do with the mixed reception of the thesis among liberals themselves. This was a *Sitz im Leben* problem: while large mining houses are disposed by the nature of their business to take the long view, liberals in a Black Sash advice office or, on occasion, on the tenth floor of John Vorster Square, found such a perspective harder to cultivate.

It was not long, however, before a political version of the

O'Dowd thesis appeared in the form of Heribert Adam's *Modernizing racial domination*. Adam started to make explicit what the O'Dowd thesis had not: the political route away from Verwoerdian apartheid. Its main audience was reformers within the National Party, a group identified by later American 'transitologists' as crucial to political change. Their influence opened up new opportunities for liberalization, which usually constitutes the early stage of a political transition. At the end of the 1970s, there was both an international shift of opinion towards rolling back the state in favour of the market, ushered in by Margaret Thatcher and Ronald Reagan, and a decline in the capacity of the South African state to regulate the lives of black people against their desires. By the early 1980s, the stage was set for the progressive dismantling of the pervasive state controls erected to serve National Party interests twenty or thirty years earlier. This was a programme with which most liberals could identify, and some of them had quite a lot of fun making a contribution to it. Specific South African circumstances meant that one could go with the dismantling flow, without necessarily having to subscribe to all the premises of the Thatcherite project.

A new phase began with the political unbannings of February 1990. It is one of the findings of the literature on political transitions that entry into the formal political system by previously excluded groupings is accompanied by their deradicalization. This is for two related reasons: (a) political exclusion leads to embittered radicalization, and (b) short of a revolution or an aborted transition, inclusion must mean that the establishment and its challengers come at least within debating range of each other. Like other aspects of political change, deradicalization does not drop from heaven, but needs to be the outcome of debate – quite a lot of debate in the South African case, as a few exhausted liberal economists could testify by 1994. One should not forget the length of the road travelled by intellectuals in the African National Congress (ANC) since the early 1990s. Debate played its role; experience in government since April 1994, however, has been a more effective teacher than any theorist.

A sensitive and important indicator of the orientation of economic policy is labour-market policy, including industrial relations. Deracialization and modernization of the industrial relations system was ushered in by the Wiehahn report in 1979. It fell to employers and unions to deal with each other by negotiation, just as political contestation between establishment and extra-parliamentary challengers started to increase sharply. In order to maintain a distinction between reasonably orderly shop-floor relations and the troubled world of politics throughout the 1980s, employers were prepared to make concessions. There was little resistance to union recognition and virtually no attempt to squeeze wage-push inflation. Equally, in the early 1990s, business was more concerned to promote economic policy dialogue than to push particular business interests too hard. It was only after April 1994 that the South African Foundation was reorganized as a big business association, producing its 'Growth for All' document in early 1996. This was a clearer and more focused announcement of business interests than had been seen for years, and it provoked a sharp debate, eliciting a statement by the Congress of South African Trade Unions (COSATU) on economic policy. More importantly, it was followed by the government's Growth, Employment, and Redistribution (GEAR) strategy, now more frequently discussed than the Reconstruction and Development Programme (RDP). This development is not surprising; as the new political system proves itself stable, it can expect to have to process sectoral demands that are more precisely and insistently formulated than they were during the transitional period.

It is in this context that four contemporary themes will play themselves out:

- *the political struggle between illiberal and liberal principles in South Africa*, as part of a global contest between Jihad and

MacWorld (to use the colourful title of a recently published
book). This struggle is, in fact, at the heart of debate within
the ANC, as well as in the tension between relatively affluent
minorities and the ANC's constituencies. MacWorld will win
if there is a broadly inclusive growth in per capita income;
stagnation or crisis will create opportunities for Jihad.

- *our relationship with the African hinterland*, particularly as far
as flows of capital and labour are concerned. Policy-makers
are finding it hard to come to terms with international migra-
tion in southern Africa. Pressures for an extensive welfare
state along European lines are pressures for closure of our
northern borders, but the capacity to stop determined immigrants does not exist and would be very expensive to construct.
Some of the proposed incentives for slowing immigration are
not convincing; indeed, they have a Tomlinson Commission
feel about them. The Maputo corridor, for instance, will help
develop southern Mozambique, but it will not thereby deter
Mozambican immigration. South African goods destined
for export will travel in one direction; Mozambicans intent
on developing business links with Johannesburg or finding
their way onto the Gauteng labour market will travel in the
other.

- *participation in the global economy*. This imposes conditions
on domestic macro-economic policy. The effect has already
been felt in pressures to liberalize capital flows, to reduce the
budget deficit, and to conduct an orthodox monetary policy.
All these measures are necessary to minimize South Africa's
vulnerability to external economic shocks.

- *the extent and nature of redistribution and poverty reduction*.
Some of the liberal arguments about this are contained in the
next section. The debate is not about whether or not redistribution and poverty reduction should take place, but about
the forms and limits of the enterprise. South Africa has the
capacity to become (and, indeed, already is) a 'residual welfare

state', but its present provisions are patchy rather than universal, and not as effective as they might be.

Liberal principles, economic policy, and redistribution

Liberalism is characterized by a strong preference for voluntary exchange over imperative coordination as a basis for social integration. This is so even within social-democratic versions of liberalism. It was Rawls's second principle in *A Theory of Justice* that excited most comment; it was less often noted that his first principle (that of maximum liberty, subject to equal liberty for all) was put forward as prior to the second.[1]

Liberals, even those of a libertarian tendency, usually acknowledge that some degree of imperative coordination is necessary; hence the reference to a 'nightwatchman state' in Nozick, for instance. Where rules have to be set, the preference is for them to be such that individuals can rationally submit themselves to them. An example of imperative coordination that satisfies this condition is the rule that people drive on one side of the road only (the left in some countries, the right in others). An example of imperative coordination that does not is the massive licence that the Red Guard was given to intervene in the lives of ordinary Chinese people at the end of the 1960s.

What of redistribution through the state? This is certainly a form of imperative coordination. Accordingly, some libertarians have argued that the only form of redistribution that is justified is through voluntary, private charity, and that redistribution through the state is illegitimate. Another view, popular in contemporary South Africa, is that redistribution through the state is appropriate as compensation for past injustices. The implication of this view is that redistribution would have to be dealt with by judicial or quasi-judicial processes. (And, insofar as injustice was imposed by a state policy of broad application, the problem of identifying victims is considerable.) On this view, there would be a time when redistribution through the state comes to an end, that is, when historical injustices have been rectified as far as possible.

A Rawlsian justification would have to argue that (a) redistribution through the state is necessary to ensure equal liberty for all, and (b) that it helps in maximizing the position of the least well-off. Social democrats have characteristically talked of participation, or, to use T. H. Marshall's well-known phrase, of 'social citizenship', the argument being that below a certain standard of living people cannot effectively participate in the life of their society. The latter two views might appear close, but there are substantial logical problems in tying up liberty, risk aversion (Rawls), and participation (Marshall).

There once used to be a utilitarian case for redistribution, on the grounds that the marginal utility of money to the poor is greater than to the rich, but this fell victim to theoretical work in economics which emphasized (a) that utility is an ordinal rather than a cardinal measure, and (b) that there are insuperable problems in aggregating it over individuals.

There certainly remains a pragmatic case for redistribution, as an easer of the social tensions that would arise if the distribution of income were purely market-determined. In an interesting study, De Swaan argues that the state has ended up with certain roles because more localized and private systems could not deal adequately with the problem of the poor. And there is a good argument for redistribution through the state in the fact that we are much more concerned with equality in education than with equality in car consumption or in the performance of horses, where it is inequality that counts.

Nietzsche once observed, after reviewing theories of punishment, that we cannot tell any longer why we punish. Different, even contradictory, theories are embodied in institutional practice. It seems appropriate to say the same of redistribution through the state. Actual practice reflects a current equilibrium of interests, and the interests themselves are conceived of in different ways. One might also add that it is very difficult to tell how much redistribution the state is doing. Current methodologies for measurement use best guesses about quantities we have little knowledge of (even in advanced industrial countries), such as the incidence of corporate taxation or the benefits from public goods. Usually, the results are presented as a best guess within a quite wide range.

The only work of this sort in South Africa was done by Michael McGrath, who concluded in the 1970s that the state redistributed between whites and blacks to a mild extent. Revisiting the issue in a recent paper presented to the Economic Society, he concluded that taxation by itself leads to a small increase in relative inequality, whereas the taxation and expenditure package leads to a substantial drop in inequality. Given the popular concern about redistribution, it is surprising that there is not more intellectual effort devoted to keeping a record of how we are doing.

It helps to disaggregate the problem for two reasons. First, it is easier to provide a rationale for a programme than for redistribution through the state as a whole. Secondly, one can more readily identify the increment of redistribution associated with a particular programme than estimate the extent of redistribution as a whole. Take housing policy, for instance. It is there because shelter is on the standard list of 'basic needs', the most important class of merit goods. The debate has been between proponents of mass housing provided by the state and proponents of a capital subsidy system which will help the poor purchase better shelter than they otherwise could have.

For the time being, the second approach is the dominant policy approach in housing, though all kinds of influential constituencies are unhappy with it. This approach has two key advantages over the first: it permits households to choose more freely what kind of housing they would like, and it enables the government to opt for a wide, rather than deep, approach to housing benefits. Any mass state housing programme, even at the traditional 'matchbox' level, would run out of funds well before meeting all needs, while the capital subsidy system is starting to create new incremental units at roughly the level of new household formation. Evidence available in the late 1990s suggests that it has reached households in large numbers. Critics claim that housing policy has been constructed according to the liberal agenda. So it has; it allows freedom on the part of its participants and it is well targeted. Some households might have got more under the alternative policy and can be expected to demand more redistribution, but many others would have got nothing.

Or take the currently controversial student financial aid system. Although students would clearly prefer grants to loans, the justification for a loan system is that, for the same outlay over a period of time, a loan system can finance two students for every one that a grant system could assist. Not more than two, alas, because there are so many risks to disadvantaged student survival in the higher education system and in entry to the labour market. Any loan scheme would do well to get half its money back. The optimal loan scheme would be one that provided every student accepted with just enough money to make the difference between being able to take up an offer and not being able to. Beyond that, state resources are better allocated to other uses. It should be remembered that the present loan scheme started small in 1991 with an Independent Development Trust (IDT) allocation of R25 million. It was clear that allocations had to grow, and they did. The 1996 allocation was R300 million, which was getting close to the amount needed. The decision to cut the 1997 allocation in nominal terms was a poor one, even in conditions of fiscal austerity. One could have increased it for inflation and for the increase in the number of students needing assistance, and cut the direct allocations to universities a little more.

Conclusion

Must contemporary South African liberals be Thatcherites? No; the Thatcher and Reagan programmes were products of their time and place and are inappropriate here and now. One should note that Thatcherism and Reaganism both fought on two fronts: corner-shop Methodism against patricians and consumers of school milk, and the Wild West against pointy-headed East Coast intellectuals and welfare queens. Here the struggle is more Hayekian, for the preservation and extension of liberal values, both important in themselves and needed in the search for growth and development, and against policies which would cut us off from both. Redistribution is necessary for social inclusion of large groups of people whose contribution is necessary to take development forward. But it must be as efficient as possible not to undermine the savings necessary for development. This framework has to contend with a demand for high consumption now, with pressures for substantial and inefficient redistribution towards small but influential groups, including strongmen, and with a generally ill-informed public susceptible to populism. It also has to deal with a stand-pat conservatism which denies any need at all for redistribution.

But South African liberals cannot be pre-Thatcherites either. Nostalgia for the 1950s and 1960s is no basis for the hard and hard-headed thinking that has to go into policy analysis in the conditions at the beginning of the fast-moving twenty-first century. The liberal defence of academic freedom is that it is the best framework for innovation. Intellectual innovation around mainly economic questions is what is most needed now; that, and the guile to get policies adopted in an environment where, too often, ignorant armies clash by night.

5

ANTHEA JEFFERY [1]

The rule of law since 1994

THE RULE OF LAW may be defined in a variety of ways. For present purposes, it connotes the following principles:
- that no punishment should be imposed without fair trial before an impartial and independent court for an offence clearly defined in law;
- that the proper administration of criminal justice should neither be impeded nor thwarted by the state;
- that respect for the criminal-justice system and its presiding judges should be upheld by the government; and
- that the criminal-justice system should operate effectively and expeditiously so that guilt can be determined or innocence confirmed without unreasonable delay.

The rule of law under the apartheid government

Under the previous government, these principles were widely abrogated.[2] From the early 1960s, detention without trial was sanctioned by the law for increasing periods of time: first for 14 days, then for 90 days, then for 180 days, and then indefinitely in certain circumstances. (This was in terms of the notorious Terrorism Act of 1967.) Detainees suffered assault and torture by the police, and some sixty died in mysterious circumstances in

the period from 1963 to 1984 (Motala 1987). The reasons given by
the police for their deaths in detention were unconvincing. Some
fell from high windows, some slipped on the soap while showering,
some fell against walls and incurred severe brain damage, while
many committed suicide. The record was disturbing and deeply
suspicious.

Under emergency rule, which applied throughout the
country from 1986 to 1990, tens of thousands of people were
detained, and many were alleged to have been tortured. Most of
these detainees were members and supporters of the United
Democratic Front (UDF) and the Congress of South African
Trade Unions (COSATU). Both of these organizations were allies
of the banned African National Congress (ANC) and South
African Communist Party (SACP), which had called on their
supporters within the country to make South Africa ungovernable and apartheid unworkable.

Many opponents of the government were penalized in other
ways. Many were 'listed' under security legislation, so that their
views could no longer be cited. Some were subjected to house
arrest. Newspapers and other publications were banned on a
number of occasions. Protest marches and gatherings were
routinely prohibited after the Soweto revolts of 1976, in which
some 575 people died within eight months. Of these, 451 died at
the hands of the police (Kane-Berman 1979; Jeffery 1997c, 28).

Controversy surrounded the administration of justice as well,
particularly from the late 1950s. The independence of the judiciary became compromised, for the National Party (NP) was
widely believed to have made a number of political appointments
to the bench. Some of the country's best advocates were passed
over for judicial appointment, while others refused on principle
to accept appointment as judges under apartheid's inherently
unjust law.

Capital punishment was a competent sentence for a number
of serious crimes. Some 1 100 people were executed in the 1980s,

giving South Africa the third-highest rate (behind Iraq and Iran) of capital punishment in the world (*South Africa survey*, henceforth referred to as *Survey*, 1995/96, 465). Most of those executed were black people, convicted either of common-law murder or of statutory offences under laws such as the Internal Security Act of 1982 and its predecessor, the Terrorism Act of 1967. Some judges were regarded as 'hanging judges', eager to impose the death penalty where a prison sentence would have sufficed. Many judges were believed to be biased in favour of the white population, and this was sometimes said to be reflected in the differential sentences imposed on white and black offenders.

Many common-law principles forming key elements of the rule of law were replaced by statutory provisions intended to make it easier to prosecute apartheid's opponents. Security legislation contained many provisions reversing the normal onus of proof, and was also often cast in such broad terms as to make it difficult to know what conduct was prohibited and what condoned. In addition, under the Criminal Procedure Act of 1977, confessions made to the police by detainees were presumed to have been freely and voluntarily made if confirmed in writing before a magistrate. Prosecutors were thus spared the common-law onus of proving that such acknowledgments of guilt had not been extorted under duress. Policemen were given a commensurate incentive to use torture as an investigative tool.

The NP government tended to extol the criminal-justice system as evidence of its commitment to the rule of law, while glossing over the ways in which its key principles had been undermined. It took pride in the fact, for example, that inquests were always held into the deaths of detainees. Their results, however, were often inconclusive – generating concerns that important evidence had been covered up rather than revealed. The most notorious example of this was probably the inquest into the death of Steve Biko, a key leader of the growing Black Consciousness Movement (BCM) in the 1970s (Kane-Berman 1979, 44–46).

Biko was detained in the Eastern Cape in September 1977 and died in detention some days later, security police alleging that he had fallen during interrogation and hit his head against a wall. He was then driven, naked and unconscious in the back of a police van, from Port Elizabeth to Pretoria – a distance of more than a thousand kilometres. He died soon after his arrival at police headquarters in Pretoria. The response of the minister of justice, Jimmy Kruger, was to state, 'It leaves me cold'. An inquest was held but concluded in a three-minute verdict – as was often the case – that no individual could be held criminally liable for his death (*Survey* 1977, 164).

The Eastern Cape remained a centre of political resistance after Biko's death and the banning of nineteen black consciousness (BC) organizations in October 1977. In the 1980s, when the ANC's campaign to make South Africa ungovernable began, the area was soon in ferment. Security police cracked down, and a number of anti-apartheid activists died in mysterious circumstances. Among these some of the most prominent were the Cradock Four[3] and the Pebco Three[4], whom security policemen have now confessed before the Truth and Reconciliation Commission (TRC) to having killed (see 'The granting of amnesty' below).

Progress in the post-apartheid era

Progress has been made in restoring the rule of law since 10 May 1994, when a new government assumed power under a new interim constitution. This was the product of negotiations in the early 1990s and provided for a government of national unity reflected in a multiparty cabinet. It took effect on 27 April 1994 – the date of the country's first non-racial election – and provided for a further constitution to be drawn up by an elected Constitutional Assembly (comprising Parliament's two houses sitting together) within a two-year period.

The 1993 constitution (Constitution of the Republic of South Africa of 1993, Act No. 200 of 1993) marked a profound departure from the past in many ways. In the context of the rule of law, its most significant contribution was to include within its provisions an entrenched and justiciable bill of rights. This was particularly important in guaranteeing the right to due process and providing important safeguards for detainees.

The 1993 constitution has since been replaced by a further constitution (Constitution of the Republic of South Africa, Act No. 108 of 1996), signed into law on 10 December 1996 and brought into operation, in general, on 4 March 1997. This is different from the 1993 constitution in a number of important ways (see chapters 1 and 2 in this volume). Its guarantees of due process are, however, generally similar.

Constitutional guarantees of due process

Under the initial interim constitution, every detainee was given the rights to be informed of the reasons for his or her detention; to be treated humanely; to consult with a lawyer of his or her choice; to be visited by family members and a private doctor; and to challenge the lawfulness of the detention in court (Section 25 (1)).

In addition, every person arrested for an alleged crime was accorded the rights of a detained person as well as the rights to remain silent; to be brought before a court within 48 hours and to be either charged or released, or informed of the reason for continued detention; not to be compelled to make a confession; and to be released on bail 'unless the interests of justice otherwise required' (Section 25(2)).

Further, every accused person was given the right to a fair trial. This was defined as including the right to a public trial within a reasonable time; to be informed of the charge; to be presumed innocent and to remain silent; to adduce and challenge evidence;

not to incriminate her or himself; to be represented by a legal practitioner of his or her choice; to be provided with legal representation at state expense 'where substantial injustice would otherwise result'; not to be charged or punished on a retrospective basis; not to be tried again for the same offence; to have court proceedings interpreted into, or conducted in, a language which she or he understood; and to be sentenced within a reasonable time after conviction (Section 25(3)).

The equivalent provisions in the 1996 constitution are essentially the same. This is important in continuing to safeguard the rule of law. It also has a practical significance in that judicial decisions interpreting the due process requirements of the interim constitution remain apposite under the new dispensation.

Impact of constitutional guarantees on the criminal-justice system

Guarantees of due process have buttressed the rule of law and have had a significant impact on the criminal-justice system in a number of respects. Provincial divisions of the former Supreme Court – renamed High Courts under the 1996 constitution – have played an important part in interpreting the right to fair trial (Jeffery 1997a). They have ruled, for example, that an accused must be:

- given proper notice of his or her rights, not merely a 'mechanical recitation' of these (*State* v *Melani and others*, 1996 (2) BCLR 174 (E)); and
- warned of her or his right to remain silent before being questioned by the state as to whether he or she admits all elements of an offence to which he or she has pleaded guilty. (Such questioning – in derogation from common-law principles – had earlier been sanctioned under the Criminal Procedure Act of 1977.) (*State* v *Maseko*, 1996 (9) BCLR 1137 (W))

These courts have also shown a reluctance, on occasion, to over-turn established rules facilitating criminal investigation and prosecution. Thus, they have also:

- ruled that the consent of an accused is not necessary for the holding of an identification parade or the taking of finger-prints (*Msomi* v *Attorney General of Natal and others*, 1996 (8) BCLR 1480 (N)); and

- affirmed the long-established rule that an adverse inference may be drawn against an accused who says nothing to disturb the prima facie evidence of guilt presented by the prosecution (*State* v *Scholtz and another*, 1996 (11) BCLR 1504 (NC); *State* v *Brown and another*, 1996 (11) BCLR 1480 (NC)).

The Constitutional Court, first established under the interim constitution, has also played an important role in interpreting the right to due process and upholding the rule of law. Thus, the court has:

- declared unconstitutional provisions in the Criminal Procedure Act of 1977 presuming a confession to have been freely and voluntarily made (*State* v *Zuma*, 1995 (2) SA 642 (CC));

- invalidated provisions of the Arms and Ammunition Act of 1969 presuming anyone occupying premises in which illegal weapons have been found to be 'in possession' of these (*State* v *Mbatha*; *State* v *Prinsloo and others*, 1996 (3) BCLR 293 (CC));

- struck down provisions in the Drugs and Drugs Trafficking Act of 1992 placing the onus on an accused to counter various presumptions (See, for example, *State* v *Bhulwana*; *State* v *Gwadiso*, 1995 (12) BCLR 1579 (CC); *State* v *Julies*, 1996 (7) BCLR 89 (CC); *State* v *Ntsele*, CCT 25/97, Constitutional Court, 14 October 1997);

- declared unconstitutional provisions of the Gambling Act of 1965 creating presumptions which could result in conviction despite reasonable doubt as to the guilt of the accused (*Scagell and others* v *Attorney General of the Western Cape and others,* 1996 (11) BCLR 1446 (CC));

- accorded trial courts a discretion in allowing an accused access to the state docket and to prosecution witnesses (*Shabalala and others* v *The Attorney General of the Transvaal and another,* 1995 (12) BCLR 1593 (CC));
- abolished juvenile whipping and imprisonment for civil debt (*State* v *Williams,* 1995 (7) BCLR 861 (CC); *Coetzee* v *The Government of the Republic of South Africa and others; Matiso* v *The Commanding Officer, Port Elizabeth Prison and others,* 1995 (10) BCLR 1382 (CC)) ;
- allowed unrepresented prisoners leave to appeal in person (*State* v *Ntuli,* 1996 (1) BCLR 141 (CC)); and
- invalidated a provision in the Companies Act of 1973 allowing self-incriminatory answers given in the course of inquiry into a company's affairs to be used in evidence in subsequent criminal proceedings (*Ferreira* v *Levin NO and others; Vryenhoek and others* v *Powell NO and others,* 1996 (1) SA 984 (CC)).

On the other hand, the Constitutional Court has upheld the validity of provisions:

- obliging the director of a company in liquidation to answer questions regarding its financial affairs (*Bernstein and others* v *Bester NO and others,* 1996 (4) BCLR 449 (CC)); and
- compelling a person who has been subpoenaed to provide information regarding a crime to answer the questions put to him or her (*Nel* v *Le Roux NO,* 1996 (4) BCLR 592 (CC)).

The court has made these rulings on a basis, however, that preserves the individual's right to remain silent. In both instances, it has indicated that an examinee cannot be compelled to answer questions if the answers would be self-incriminating.

The interim constitution also helped to restore the rule of law by limiting the circumstances in which emergency rule could be declared. It further provided protection for those detained at such times, and prohibited certain fundamental rights from being suspended under emergency regulations. The 1996 constitution is similar in its terms, save that it reduces the parliamentary majority required for continuing emergency rule once it has been declared from a two-thirds majority to sixty per cent, and makes the circumstances in which emergency rule is justified significantly broader (Jeffery 1997a, 134).

The Constitutional Court has also found the death penalty contrary to the rights to life and human dignity contained in the interim constitution. (*State* v *Makwanyane and another*, 1996 (3) SA 391 (CC)) (It left open, however, the constitutionality of capital punishment for treason in time of war.) In response to its judgment, the death sentences imposed on some 440 prisoners – whose executions had been stayed under a moratorium on capital punishment introduced in 1990 (*Survey* 1995/96, 465) – were commuted to imprisonment for varying terms. (These terms are still in the process of being decided.) In 1997, legislation was enacted removing references to capital punishment from various statutes.

Constitutional provisions, however – important as they are – do not provide a comprehensive picture. The progress made in this respect has not always been matched in other spheres.

A faltering criminal-justice system

Crime has been increasing for many years and is widely perceived to have escalated sharply since 1994 – though police statistics show a reduction in certain categories of crime, including murder, in recent years. Other crimes, particularly robbery and truck hijackings, have shown a significant increase. The total number of crimes reported from January to September 1994 was some 1 480 000. The total number reported in the equivalent period of 1997 was approximately 1 520 000, reflecting an overall increase of some 2,8 per cent. The accuracy of police statistics in this regard is difficult to gauge and is also limited by the fact that many crimes are seemingly not reported (Potter 1998).

An overburdened prosecuting system

Convictions, by contrast, have shown a sharp fall. The figures show that police catch fewer than one in four criminals, that only half of these are prosecuted, and that only about half again are convicted.

The rate of conviction dropped from 1 611 per 100 000 of the population in 1972 to 1 145 in 1992 – a drop of 29 per cent in twenty years. The crime rate, however, increased by 35 per cent over roughly the same period (from 1975 to 1993). The fact that statistics have not been kept fully since then suggests that the situation has become even worse. The odds of a perpetrator of a serious crime being convicted were estimated in mid-1997 at about one in twenty (Schoenteich 1997d, 6–7).

Reasons for the low conviction rate include a lack of resources, a shortage of personnel, and inadequate experience and training among the police and the prosecution services. Almost one-third of all prosecutors resigned between January 1994 and December 1996 – some 520 out of a total of 1 620. This was primarily because of bad pay, poor working conditions, and falling morale. Vacancies were filled by graduates with no prosecuting experience; in 1996 the average experience of district court prosecutors was 1.6 years. Among regional prosecutors, who are responsible for prosecuting serious crimes including murder and rape, average experience was 2.2 years (Schoenteich 1997d).

Statistics from 1995 illustrate the dimension of the problem. 'On average, for every 1 460 crimes investigated by the police during that year there was only one prosecutor'. Prosecutors were also burdened with clerical and administrative responsibilities and by a dearth of equipment and support staff. In 1997, moreover, there were more than 150 vacancies among prosecutors, state advocates, and state attorneys – and a waiting list of 1 600 law graduates waiting to fill those positions. Many posts were left vacant, however, because of the department's determination to fill them with affirmative-action candidates. In addition, a number of experienced white male state attorneys were passed over for promotion for affirmative-action reasons. Though they won a case for unfair discrimination in early 1997, the justice minister, Dullah Omar, immediately appealed against the judgment (Jeffery 1997b, 2). This has done little to encourage experienced white prosecutors to stay in the service (Schoenteich 1997a, 1).

An under-resourced police force

Within the police force the picture is largely the same. The South African Police Service (SAPS) is understaffed, with one police officer for approximately every 350 civilians. This figure is low by international standards, especially given the country's high crime rate, geographic size, and relatively youthful population. Specialized crime units are particularly understaffed, and in August 1996 the organized crime unit had the resources to investigate only 32 of the country's 481 identified crime syndicates. Poor pay and difficult working conditions have helped to undermine morale among police officers, while a significant number of new recruits are functionally illiterate. Some 30 000 police officers have passed their tenth grade of schooling (previously Standard Eight) or less. A survey conducted by the SAPS showed that 100 police officers and 764 civilians working in support posts had passed their sixth grade (previously Standard Four) or less; 4 873 police officers and 2 978 civilians had passed either their seventh or eighth grade (previously Standard Five or Six); and 6 284 civilians and 26 056 police officers either their tenth grade (previously Standard Eight) or less (*Survey* 1997/98). Most detectives have no specialized training, and only a quarter have been on a detective's course (Schoenteich 1997d, 6–7).

Prison overcrowding

The faltering criminal-justice system has important consequences for the rule of law. The first is that justice has been delayed – and commensurately denied – in many instances. It has also resulted in horrific prison overcrowding.

Of the 140 000 people in the country's overcrowded prisons – intended to accommodate only some 95 000 prisoners – about 40 000 are currently awaiting trial. The Department of Correctional Services estimates that the prison population will reach 156 000 by the end of 1998. Its budget for 1997/98 caters for a mere 118 000 prisoners and thus entirely ignores the needs of at least 20 000 inmates (Schoenteich 1998a, 24–25).

Prison overcrowding is a serious issue. 'Far from rehabilitating criminals, prisons are rapidly becoming the epicentre of the country's crime problem. The recidivism rate is extremely high and only one in eight prisoners does not commit further crimes after his release' (Schoenteich 1998a, 24). Part of the overcrowding has been caused by a slow-moving criminal-justice system. Awaiting-trial prisoners spend an average of five months in prison before their trials are finalized. For complicated cases, the waiting period can be far longer. In some areas, moreover, the problem is even more acute. In November 1997 in KwaZulu-Natal, for example, some 220 awaiting-trial inmates refused to go to court in protest against undue delays in their trials. According to the president of the South African Prisoners' Organization for Human Rights, Miles Bhudu, some prisoners had been awaiting trial for more than two years. 'They have been waiting so long it is as good as if they are already serving a sentence', he said (Schoenteich 1998a, 24–25). Such instances make a mockery of the constitutional right to trial within a reasonable period.

A recent Constitutional Court judgment on the issue seems far removed from reality. In *Sanderson* v *Attorney General (Eastern Cape)* (CCT 10/97, Constitutional Court, 2 December 1997), the Constitutional Court was asked to consider whether a two-year delay in bringing an accused to trial had contravened his right to trial within a 'reasonable time'. It responded that, in deciding what constitutes a reasonable time, a court must make a value judgment, considering such factors as the kind of prejudice suffered by the accused, the nature and complexity of the case, and the lack of state resources which hamper the investigation or prosecution of the case. Pre-trial delay, it warned, should 'not become a form of punishment'. Its strictures are likely to remain meaningless, however, so long as the criminal-justice system remains so overburdened and so under-resourced.

The right to bail

The increase in the number of awaiting-trial prisoners can be attributed, in part, to a tightening-up of bail law in 1995. In addition, many prisoners have been granted bail but cannot afford to pay the amount set – usually less than R1 000 and often less than R500 (Schoenteich 1998a). The content of bail law has also been controversial for some time, and the government has seemingly tried to effect a 'quick fix' for the crime problem by making bail more difficult to attain.

The 1996 constitution guarantees the right to bail (as did the interim constitution), but makes this subject to 'the interests of justice'. In 1995 legislation was first enacted to tighten up conditions for the granting of bail. The Criminal Procedure Act of 1977 was amended to provide that the refusal of bail is in the interests of justice if the accused might interfere with witnesses, hamper police investigation, fail to stand trial, or endanger the safety of the public or of any other individual. Courts are expected to play an inquisitorial role in inquiring into these factors. In addition, where an accused is charged with a particularly serious offence – such as murder, rape, violent robbery, or hijacking of a motor vehicle – bail must be refused unless an accused can discharge the onus of showing that 'the interests of justice do not require his detention in custody' (*Survey* 1995/96, 493–494; Jeffery 1997a, 90–92).

High rates of violent crime continued thereafter, however, and the government sought to tighten bail laws yet further. President Nelson Mandela said in August 1996 that such legislation would indeed be enacted despite threats by 'idealists' to take the government to court on the issue (Jeffery 1997a, 92). In 1997 the department of justice proposed the enactment of new legislation providing that any person accused of a wide category of serious crimes should automatically be denied bail. Though this proposal was in time abandoned, Omar then put forward two further disturbing provisions to govern the granting of bail.

First, the courts would be obliged to refuse bail where 'there was a likelihood that the release of the accused would disturb the public order or undermine public peace or security'. Such a provision would hold grave implications for the rule of law, for it would 'oblige the courts to grant or refuse bail not on the merits of the accused's case, but on the basis of mob rule. Thus, if any group vocal and large enough to "disturb the public order" or "undermine the public peace" were to threaten mayhem and civil unrest should an accused not of their liking be released on bail, then a court would be obliged to refuse it' (Schoenteich 1997c, 32).

The second proposal was that for certain specified offences, including treason, a court would have to refuse bail if it were 'convinced that a reasonable suspicion existed that the accused committed the offence'. This would be tantamount, however, to 'a blanket refusal of bail as a person can only be arrested and charged if the arresting officer has a "reasonable suspicion" that the suspect has committed an offence'. Also disturbing was the inclusion of treason, a political offence, within provisions

'ostensibly aimed at fighting violent and serious crime'. This
would make it possible for a government in the future to 'incar-
cerate political opponents on a charge of treason for weeks and
even months before the finalisation of their trials' (Schoenteich
1997c).

Ultimately, the most disturbing elements in these proposals
were removed. The 'mob rule' proposal was modified to provide
that a court would be entitled to deny bail only where 'in exceptional circumstances, there was a likelihood that the release of
an accused would disturb the public order or undermine the
public peace or security'. The second proposal was amended to
remove any reference to treason and thus make it clear that bail
could still be granted in relation to this crime (see Criminal
Procedure Second Amendment Act of 1997).

Limiting judicial discretion in sentencing

The rule of law also came under threat from the department of
justice when it warned in 1997 that it would seek to counter
crime by stipulating minimum penalties for a number of
serious offences. This would have removed a necessary judicial
discretion and tied the hands of the courts in determining
sentence irrespective of the surrounding circumstances. Again,
this proposal was ultimately abandoned by Omar. Instead, an
amendment to the Criminal Procedure Act of 1977 lays down
the minimum penalties to be imposed for various crimes but
also makes it clear that lesser sentences may be ordered where
'substantial and compelling circumstances exist' to justify this
(see Criminal Law Amendment Act of 1997).

An impetus towards self-help

Other threats to the rule of law have also arisen, but are difficult
to quantify. One of the most disturbing trends is an increased

impetus towards self-help. While the police are now constrained by the constitution as to the methods they may use in crime-detection, vigilante groups are not. There is anecdotal evidence – but no incisive study – suggesting that such groups have been formed in some former black 'townships', and that they are viewed by residents as more effective than the police at solving crime because they have no hesitation in breaking down doors and brutally assaulting suspects in order to obtain confessions and recover stolen goods.

The best-known vigilante group is People Against Gangsterism and Drugs (PAGAD), which operates in Cape Town, Durban, and Gauteng. It asserts that the police are ineffective against drug cartels, and has resolved to take the necessary action itself. In a notorious incident in August 1996, a mob of its members set alight and shot dead an alleged drug lord, Rashaad Staggie, saying they could no longer wait for the police to act (Jeffery 1997a, 70). (The principal suspect in the matter was brought to trial in February 1998, but the case against him was withdrawn after contradictions emerged in the testimony of a key prosecution witness.)

In August 1997 a police superintendent in the Western Cape – where PAGAD is most active – said that the patterns of the vigilante group were changing. He reported that in the last eight months of 1996 PAGAD had staged some 110 marches to the homes of alleged drug dealers and gangsters. It had also carried out some 38 acts of urban terrorism, including drive-by shootings, and petrol-bomb and hand-grenade attacks. In the first six months of 1996 the campaign of urban terrorism was increased with 71 attacks recorded (*Survey* 1997/98).

In October 1997 the national commissioner of the SAPS, George Fivaz, granted extraordinary policing powers to those dealing with the conflict between PAGAD and alleged gangsters. Powers of search and seizure without warrant were thus granted to the police for operations on the Cape Flats (see 'Search, seizure, and surveillance' below). Fivaz said the powers had not been granted for an indefinite period, but would be used on an ongoing basis to deal with continued violence in the area (*Survey* 1997/98).

New vigilante groups also emerged. One, comprising black business, is known as the 'Mapoga-a-Matamaga' (meaning the Colours of the Tiger). It was formed in August 1996 following the killing of six businessmen in Mpumalanga. According to its leader, John Malolego, membership of the group increased to 3 000 in both Mpumalanga and the Northern Province by late 1997. 'In May 1997 the group reportedly admitted to murdering at least five people whom they alleged the police had been either unwilling to arrest, or incapable of arresting.' In July 1997 the police reported that most leaders and some eighty members of the group had been arrested and were facing charges of murder, assault, attempted murder, and public violence (*Survey* 1997/98).

Also in May 1997, a group calling itself the 'Soldiers of Islam', and having the same aims as PAGAD, petrol-bombed the house of a suspected drug dealer in Lenasia, Gauteng. A spokesman for the group said they would continue such attacks until the drug trade stopped.

Kangaroo courts have also been convened by communities on a number of occasions. For example, in July 1997 a 'people's court' was reported to be operating in Boipatong, Gauteng. The court – comprising about a hundred elders from the community – allegedly presided over cases ranging from rape, murder, and hijackings to assaults, robberies, and family disputes. Punishment consisted mainly of whipping, with each member of the court being entitled to administer a maximum of six lashes. Cases such as murder and rape, it was said, were normally referred to the police (*Survey* 1997/98). In a number of incidents, however, alleged murderers and rapists have not been handed over to the police, but have instead been caught and executed on the spot.

Detention, torture, and deaths in police custody

Detention of illegal immigrants

Detention and torture of political opponents by the state has generally come to an end, save possibly in KwaZulu-Natal (see 'A partisan police and army in KwaZulu-Natal?' below). Illegal immigrants have allegedly been detained for varying periods pending deportation, but little information is available in this regard. The provisions permitting detention in these circumstances are essentially the same as those applied by the previous government, but the incidence of detention has accelerated as the number of illegal immigrants has increased.

Police torture

Allegations of the use of torture by the police in order to obtain confessions have continued. Few of these accusations have been tested in court, however, and it is difficult to ascertain how many of them are properly substantiated. In some instances, however, evidence of assault or torture appears indeed to have been established (Jeffery 1997a, 45–47). Thus:

- in March 1996, seventeen former policemen were sentenced to a total of 156 years' imprisonment for their part in the killing of Sammy Magano, who was tortured to death in Mafikeng in July 1995 following a robbery at the Molopo Sun Hotel (*Star* 15 March 1996);
- in November 1996, four policemen from the Vaal Triangle were convicted of assault with intent to do grievous bodily harm for having administered electric shocks to a suspect in August 1994;
- in the same month, an electric shock machine was found on the premises of the Middelburg Murder and Robbery Unit after an accused had complained of torture; and

- in December 1996, two police constables from Brixton (Johannesburg) were convicted of assault with intent to do grievous bodily harm and each was sentenced to a fine of R10 000 or one year's imprisonment.

An Independent Complaints Directorate has been established within the SAPS to probe allegations of torture and other misconduct by the police. In October 1997 it stated that in the preceding six months more than 370 deaths in police custody or as a result of police action had been reported to it. Another 236 reports of serious criminal offences, allegedly committed by the police, were received over the same period. These included 55 complaints of torture. Neville Melville, chief executive of the Directorate, expressed concern about the apparent high incidence of torture as well as deaths during arrests. 'It is disappointing to see the allegations continue', he said. 'We would have hoped for some changes in policing techniques, especially in interrogation methods' (*Business Day* 31 October 1997).

Torture in 'C-Max' prisons?

Controversy surrounded the question of whether conditions in a new high-security prison, dubbed 'C-Max', constituted a form of torture. The introduction of C-Max was announced by the government in late 1997. The first such facility was constructed in a revamped section of Pretoria's maximum-security prison, and was able to accommodate about a hundred prisoners.

Inmates of C-Max are locked alone for 23 hours out of every 24 in cells three metres square with wire-mesh ceilings that allow constant surveillance. They may not smoke, and are not allowed television, electrical appliances, money, or contact visits. They may not leave their cells without cuffs, and may exercise in four-metre by two-metre cages for an hour a day. They may talk to prisoners in adjacent cages during this time. Prisoners leaving the jail (for a court appearance, for example) must be shackled to a 'stun belt' with a remote-control device capable of shocking them into temporary paralysis should they try to escape. Prisoners are to be kept in C-Max for a minimum of three months, pending psychological evaluation that may result in further detention or their rejoining the general prison population (Wentzel 1998, 21–23).

The C-Max facility was visited by veteran anti-apartheid campaigner Helen Suzman in her capacity as a member of the Human Rights Commission of South Africa. She described it as a 'horrific place', in which electric lights burned practically all day and night, and in which there were no direct windows – only tiny slots at the top of each cell. Conditions in C-Max, she stated, came close to torture. Prisoners were kept in what amounted to solitary confinement, and their rights under the United Nations Standard Minimum Rules for the Treatment of Prisoners were clearly abrogated (Wentzel 1998, 21–23).

According to the government, C-Max has been established 'for the most difficult, unruly, and dangerous prisoners in our prison system'. It allows prison authorities to clamp down on gangs, and safeguard other prisoners from rape or murder. The first prisoner to be sent to C-Max, however, was Eugene de Kock – a former police 'hit-squad' commander based at Vlakplaas (near Pretoria), who was sentenced in 1996 to life imprisonment on various counts of murder and many more of fraud. He had been upgraded to category A, the status accorded model prisoners, the day before his transfer to C-Max. Whatever atrocities he had committed while in the police, he had clearly not been a dangerous prisoner.

Three of the eighteen other people who were inmates of C-Max in October 1997 had been convicted not of violent crime but of fraud. Another was a known gang leader, but had no record of violent conduct while in prison. Overall, stated a spokesperson for Lawyers for Human Rights, the government itself seemed unclear as to the criteria for sending people to C-Max. Prison authorities had also contravened the Correctional Services Act of 1959 in consigning prisoners to the high-security facility. The statute made it clear that prisoners could not be stripped of privileges – as consignment to C-Max implied – without a prior hearing by a prison committee. No C-Max inmate, however, had been accorded this right (Wentzel 1998, 21–23).

Concern has been expressed that C-Max may be abused by the government to impose inordinately severe conditions of imprisonment not only on unruly prisoners but also on perceived political opponents of the ruling party. The choice of De Kock as the first prisoner to be sent to C-Max lends support to this view.

Search, seizure, and surveillance

Privacy now guaranteed

Unauthorized and illegal searches, seizures, and surveillance were widespread in the apartheid era. Under the interim and present constitution, however, the right to privacy has been guaranteed. Section 14 of the 1996 constitution declares that 'everyone has the right to privacy' and states that this includes the rights not to have one's person, home, or property searched, not to have possessions seized, and not to have the privacy of communications infringed (Jeffery 1997a, 50–56).

Police powers

The police, under the Criminal Procedure Act of 1977, have long had extensive powers of search and seizure to prevent and investigate crime. A search warrant is normally required, however, and cannot lawfully be issued unless the police can satisfy the presiding judicial officer that incriminating evidence is likely to be found. Failure to comply with this requirement formed the basis for a successful application by Winnie Mandela, then deputy minister of arts, culture, science, and technology, in March 1995 to invalidate a warrant under which police had searched her Soweto home and seized certain documents. Judge P. E. Streicher said the test had not been satisfied and ordered the return of the documents seized (*Star* 23 March 1995).

In May 1996 the Cape of Good Hope Provincial Division of the Supreme Court in Cape Town was called upon to rule on the admissibility of evidence found by the police in the course of a search not authorized by warrant or consent. The issue arose when police searched the home of an accused with the latter's consent and found a bag containing stolen goods. However, the bag belonged to another person, who had not consented to its being searched. The investigating officer had been told this, but had nevertheless continued with the search.

The court found the continuation of the search in these circumstances a 'deliberate and conscious violation' of the right to privacy guaranteed by the constitution. This violation gave the trial court a discretion as to the admissibility of the evidence. In general, such evidence would be 'absolutely inadmissible' unless 'extraordinary excusing circumstances' were present. In this instance, such circumstances had not been demonstrated – and the evidence could therefore not be admitted. (*State* v *Mayekiso en andere*, 1996 (9) BCLR 1168 (C))

The Constitutional Court has since cast doubt on this ruling, stating that evidence obtained as a result of an unconstitutional search does not automatically become inadmissible in subsequent criminal proceedings. 'Depending on the circumstances, fairness might require that such evidence be excluded.' However, 'fairness might in certain circumstances require that such evidence be admitted'. The admissibility of such evidence was thus, in each instance, to be decided by the trial court in the light of the surrounding circumstances. (*Key* v *Attorney General, Cape of Good Hope Provincial Division*, 1996 (6) BCLR 788 (C))

Under the South African Police Service Act of 1995, the police also have extensive powers of search and seizure. Any member of the S A P S may search any person or premises where this is 'reasonably necessary' to prevent illegal immigration or the illegal importation of goods. In addition, the national (or a provincial) commissioner of police may order the cordoning-off of any area, for not more than twenty-four hours, where this is 'reasonable in the circumstances to restore public order or the safety of the public'. Any member of the S A P S may, within this area, search any person or premises without a warrant 'where this is reasonably necessary'.

The *Sunday Times* (16 July 1995) described the powers thus given to the S A P S as 'breathtaking in their disregard for established legal procedures'. They were reminiscent of apartheid emergency rules, and would give the police 'vast powers of search and seizure without the irritation of having to obtain a warrant from a magistrate'.

Telephone taps and other surveillance

Telephone tapping and other means of surveillance have also proved controversial. In April 1995 Omar disclosed in Parliament that the security forces had made 386 requests in 1994 to tap telephones or intercept mail. Of these, 378 had been granted, and 65 remained in force in 1995. In terms of the Interception and Monitoring Prohibition Act of 1992, such requests must be approved by a judge, who must be convinced that an actual or impending serious offence cannot be investigated in any other way, or that the security of the state is threatened. Noting the high approval rate reflected in these figures, *Business Day* (20 April 1995) commented: 'Some assurance is needed that the judiciary is giving strong cognizance to individual liberties.' In 1996 the security forces made 410 requests to tap telephones or intercept mail, and 350 of these were approved. (*Hansard* (S:Q) col 182, 22 February 1996)

In January 1996 Fivaz said he had found evidence of systematic spying on himself and other senior police officers (Johnson 1996, 1–9). The home telephone of a senior police officer had been found to be tapped, while a listening device had also been found in the office of the Gauteng provincial commissioner of police, Sharma Maharaj. Other provincial commissioners had also reported that they had been the targets of surveillance by unknown agents (*Citizen* 5 January 1996). In the same month, it was also revealed that a sophisticated tracking device had been found in the official vehicle of the minister of land affairs, Derek Hanekom, while the chairperson of the board of the South African Broadcasting Corporation (SABC), Ivy Matsepe-Casaburri, alleged that her telephones had been tapped and her home watched (*Star* 23 January 1996). It was also claimed that the private telephone of Magnus Malan – a former minister of defence, then on trial on charges of murder and conspiracy to murder in relation to the KwaMhakutha massacre of 1987 (see 'Undermining judicial authority' below) – had been tampered with and was possibly being tapped (*Citizen* 26 February 1996). (Moreover, these reports followed earlier allegations of spying. In July 1994 there had been reports of a bugging device found in the bedroom of President Mandela. Another had been found in the office of the minister of telecommunications, Pallo Jordan, while the de-bugging of Omar's office had been accompanied by an illicit search.)

In February 1996 it was alleged that the National Intelligence Agency (NIA) – charged with internal security and intelligence gathering – had been responsible for spying on senior police officers, as revealed the previous month. A report by the investigative unit of Independent Newspapers claimed, in addition, that 'thousands of international as well as local telephone calls and fax communications were being intercepted – many unlawfully and unconstitutionally – by the South African intelligence community from a top secret facility' (*Star* 21 February 1996).

An NIA spokesperson, William Theron, claimed that such measures were taken only against 'enemies of the state', but declined to answer whether such action was constitutional. He also left open the issue of how the 'enemies of the state' had been identified, and whether interceptions had indeed been implemented with the requisite judicial authority (Johnson 1996, 9).

A judicial commission of inquiry into the matter was promised by both Omar and deputy president Thabo Mbeki, but was never in fact appointed. Instead, the joint parliamentary standing committee on intelligence was mandated to investigate the allegations. It reported in March 1996 that there was no evidence that the NIA had 'bugged or spied upon senior police officials'. It suggested that criminals might instead have done so (*Citizen* 30 March 1996). This explanation was endorsed by Mbeki, who said the bugs could have been placed by 'drug smugglers, car theft syndicates, money launderers, or the perpetrators of the KwaZulu-Natal violence' (Johnson 1996, 3).

There is much scope for surveillance in the new South Africa, for the intelligence community in the country is considerable – comprising not only the NIA but also the police Crime Intelligence Service (CIS), the army's Military Intelligence (MI), and the South African Secret Service (SASS). The SASS is responisible for gathering intelligence abroad, but the other three agencies all work internally. They report to different ministers, and coordination and control is the responsibility of a National Intelligence Coordinating Committee (NICOC) under Mo Shaik, which in turn reports to the cabinet's Coordinating Committee on Security. 'The only integrating thread in this rather muddled picture is the extremely dense network of SACP cadres it involves' (Johnson 1996, 5). Dr Sizakele Sigxashe, the NIA director-general, was earlier trained in East Germany and the USSR. Joe Nhlanhla (deputy minister for intelligence in the President's office) and Sydney Mufamadi are both SACP members, while the deputy minister of defence, Ronnie Kasrils – who plays an important role in relation to MI – is an SACP executive member and the former head of intelligence for the ANC's erstwhile armed wing Umkhonto we Sizwe (MK, or Umkhonto). It is generally assumed that Mo Shaik and Azhar Cachalia, the secretary for safety and security (who has equal status within the police with Fivaz) are also members of the SACP.

The intelligence community has also grown considerably under the new order. It now includes not only members of the former National Intelligence Service (NIS) and earlier Security Branch, but incorporates some 900 ANC intelligence agents, as well as the security service earlier established by the Pan-Africanist Congress (PAC), and the intelligence services of the former 'independent' homelands of Bophuthatswana, the Transkei, and Venda. 'The new NIA now has almost three times as many staff as the old security apparatus had even at the height of the "total onslaught"' (Johnson 1996, 6). The intelligence services budget, moreover, witnessed a 66 per cent increase from R427 million to R710 million in the 1995/96 financial year. Its budget in the 1996/97 financial year was much the same at R724 million (Pereira 1997a).

This exponential growth in the intelligence budget – effected at a time when health and teaching jobs were being cut in the cause of economy – seems to have been justified by the ANC on the basis, among other things, that the NP was conducting a 'surreptitious destabilization strategy' and was using 'networks built within and outside the country' for this purpose. An ANC discussion document, *One Year of GNU*, warned of 'counter-revolutionary mobilization' and emphasized the need to 'guard against the Allende syndrome', in which 'problems within the country were orchestrated with the involvement of international anti-democracy forces' (Johnson 1996, 6).

The ANC's concern regarding counter-revolution did not abate. In February 1997 Dr Sigxashe said 'foreign secret agents were flooding into the country and some of them appeared bent on subverting the government' (*Citizen* 20 February 1997). At the ANC's fiftieth national congress in Mafikeng in December 1997, Mandela devoted a significant portion of his five-hour address to lambasting 'counter-revolutionary' forces in the media, among political parties, and among non-governmental organizations (*Citizen* 17 December 1997). In addition, an article by prominent SACP leader Dr Blade Nzimande (1997) in the ANC's mouthpiece, *Mayibuye*, was handed out to delegates at the conference and also warned against counter-revolution.

Opening a joint headquarters for the NIA and SASS outside Pretoria in December 1997, President Mandela stated, 'There are forces that are bent on reversing our democratic gains, who have chosen to spurn the hand of friendship that has been extended to them, forces that do not want reconciliation, indeed forces that wish of us to apologise for destroying apartheid' (*Citizen* 4 December 1997). Opposition parties, especially the Inkatha Freedom Party (IFP), queried the need for the new headquarters, and expressed concern that it could be used to target political opponents of the ANC. The building cost some R166 million, and is a luxurious and sophisticated complex which has been dubbed the 'spy palace' (*Rapport* 2 March 1997). Some insight into the equipment it incorporates was provided when it was revealed that a telephone-fax intercepting machine worth R1.8 million and capable of intercepting thirty calls at a time had been stolen from the building in November 1997 (*City Press* 23 November 1997).

NIA activities have generally remained shrouded in secrecy. What little information has come to light gives cause for concern, however. It was revealed, for example, that the NIA was devoting 'much of its resources to investigating gang warfare in the Western Cape and the causes of violence in KwaZulu-Natal'. These two provinces are, of course, the only two the ANC does not control. The NIA has also played an extraordinary and generally unreported role at the University of Durban-Westville

(UDW). NIA agents 'became openly active on the campus' and a bug was discovered under the desk of the chairperson of the Combined Staff Association (COMSA), whose endeavours to take control of university affairs had become the subject of contest and controversy (Johnson 1996, 7–8). There are also unanswered questions regarding the death of Muziwendola Mduli, the NIA head of security, who was found dead in his car by a mysterious jogger who disappeared from the scene and could not later be traced. The police declared his death a suicide, while Joe Nhlanhla proclaimed it murder. Both the police and the NIA began their own investigations – and it is possible that the bugging of senior police officers formed part of the latter (Johnson 1996, 8).

In November 1997 the Afrikaans newspaper, *Rapport*, revealed that President Mandela had personally instructed the heads of the four intelligence services to investigate the possibility of a violent insurrection in the country. Particular attention, the president said, was to be paid to investigating generals from the former security forces as well as various businessmen. Mandela expressed special concern about 'economic sabotage' and the possibility of a conspiracy in this regard. There were many businessmen, he continued, who were sabotaging South Africa by taking large quantities of money out of the country and by discouraging foreign investment. The intelligence heads were thus instructed to find out precisely who was involved in this and how great the range of sabotage had become. Concern was also expressed that generals in the former police and army were conspiring to take control of the country by force – and the intelligence services were thus required to investigate. The possible role of large security companies as front organizations for the generals was also to be investigated. *Rapport* (30 November 1997) stated that a thorough and comprehensive investigation into these matters had been launched, and that it included 'monitoring and observation'.

Under the previous government, it was common knowledge that surveillance was widespread and that 'neither letters nor telephones were secure'. Despite the guarantee of privacy that has now been included in the constitution, there is reason for concern that the 'bad old ways are still in place, with agents merely reporting to a new set of political bosses' (Johnson 1996, 3).

A partisan police and army in KwaZulu-Natal?

Allegations and evidence of partisanship in the past

Tensions between the ANC and the IFP have long been high in the province, which has witnessed the deaths in a low-key civil war of some 12 000 people since 1984. Fatalities have declined significantly since the general election in April 1994, but the killing has undoubtedly continued. A peace process which began in May 1996 – shortly before local government elections were to be held in the province – has helped to reduce tensions but has witnessed little concrete progress in almost two years. The underlying differences between the parties remain strong despite recent rumours of their impending merger, and the legacy of bitterness and revenge engendered by a decade or more of low-key civil war remains to be resolved (Johnson and Johnston 1998).

The role of the security forces in the province has long been controversial. Before the change of government in 1994, elements within the former South African Police (SAP) and South African Defence Force (SADF) were widely believed to have acted as a sinister 'third force' in stoking violence between the ANC and the IFP. There was evidence of this too, especially in the Trust Feed massacre of 1988 (Jeffery 1997c, 257–263). Limited further evidence regarding the role of the third force emerged from the trial of Eugene de Kock, while the evidence presented in the Malan trial proved flawed and was found to be inconclusive (Jeffery 1997c, 755–766, 741–755). The KwaZulu Police, which operated in the former KwaZulu homeland until 1994, were also widely alleged to have constituted the IFP's own 'private army' and to have played an important part in hit-squad attacks on ANC leaders and activists.

The IFP, for its part, disputed these allegations and accused some members of the police and soldiers in both the KwaZulu and South African forces of being in cahoots with the ANC. It pointed, for example, to the involvement of a policeman in the killing of thirteen Inkatha Youth Brigade members in KwaShange in the Midlands in 1987. It cited, too, the role of an SADF member in the execution of an induna and his family at Patheni, near Richmond, in 1992. The IFP also charged the ANC with responsibility for the deaths of some 400 of its leaders in the course of the war, and alleged that many of these had been killed in professional assassinations carried out by members of Umkhonto and self-defence units (SDUS) armed and trained at the ANC's behest (Jeffery 1997c, 162–163, 368, chapters 6, 8).

Further allegations and evidence in the post-election period

Following the April 1994 election, a number of Umkhonto cadres and SDU members were incorporated into the new SAPS and South African National Defence Force (SANDF). The IFP has alleged that the enmity of these former combatants towards it has continued in the post-election period, and that they have used the cover provided by the new security forces to harass and attack the IFP with impunity.

The ANC has denied this, and has stated that the continuing conflict in the province has been sustained by the third force which 'has kept its head down but its work up' in the democratic era. This was particularly evident, it stated, on the south coast of KwaZulu-Natal, where local police had helped the IFP attack an ANC supporter in Gamalakhe near Port Shepstone in July 1995.

Police were also alleged to have participated in the killing of an
ANC leader and former Umkhonto cadre, Joseph Nduli, in
Durban soon thereafter, and to have embarked in conjunction
with the IFP on a 'campaign to kill influential ANC leaders'. In
December that year, moreover, police were implicated in the
killing of nineteen ANC supporters at Shobashobane on the
south coast. The ANC said the attack had been a 'joint venture'
between the police and the IFP. Witnesses alleged that police
had done nothing to stop the killing, but had instead assisted the
attackers by escorting them out of the area. Police bias towards
the IFP, said Mufamadi, had created a 'culture of impunity' in
the province, and national intervention was needed to bring this
to an end. For this purpose, a number of special investigation
units were established in KwaZulu-Natal. These were able to
bypass normal police channels and to effect a number of arrests.
Violence dropped thereafter, and the ANC said this proved the
security forces could put an end to political deaths provided
they had the will to do so (Jeffery 1997c, 556–571).

By contrast, the IFP complained on a number of occasions
about partisan and illegal searches of its members. In August
1995, for example, the IFP threatened legal action against the
minister for safety and security, Sydney Mufamadi, following a
raid on the north-coast home of one of its leaders, Khayelihle
Mathaba. Mathaba said police and troops, ostensibly looking for
illegal weapons, had 'thrown stones on his roof, burst into his
house without a warrant and caused extensive damage to his
property'. Thereafter, police at a nearby police station 'refused to
register his complaint about the raid', telling him there was 'no
reason' to open a docket. The secretary general of the IFP, Dr
Ziba Jiyane, said there was 'an organised campaign within the
police and defence force to intimidate, harass and murder IFP
leaders' (*Citizen* 26 August 1995).

In 1996 the IFP alleged that security forces had continued to
abuse their powers in conducting searches in KwaZulu-Natal. In

the aftermath of the Shobashobane massacre Commissioner Fivaz said that the 'use of extra powers granted by the South African Police Service Act of 1995 was being considered. These would allow the cordoning off and searching of an area without a warrant, as well as other powers' (*Sunday Tribune* 6 January 1996). The IFP said the police and army were already conducting searches without warrants, and had also damaged property and assaulted residents. The IFP further alleged that searches had been conducted in a biased manner, and had primarily targeted IFP-supporting enclaves in KwaZulu-Natal while ignoring those supportive of the ANC.

In late April 1996 the IFP alleged in addition that some of its members who had been arrested on suspicion of involvement in the Shobashobane massacre had been assaulted and tortured by the police. The SAPS denied this, and said minimum force had been used in making the arrests. Soon thereafter, one of the accused died in Durban-Westville Prison from what police described as an asthma attack. A state pathologist who subsequently conducted a post mortem said Mr Nyawose had died of 'bronchial asthma'.

In May 1996 the IFP called for the suspension of Capt. Mandlenkosi Vilakazi, the head of a special investigation unit operating in northern KwaZulu-Natal. The party's call followed the death in police custody of one of its supporters, Ngiyane Mhlongo, on 28 April 1996. An independent pathologist, Dr Reggie Perumal, said Mhlongo's injuries could have been caused by 'a heavy blow or a twisting motion which had broken his neck'. A spokesperson for the IFP, Ed Tillett, said five witnesses had signed affidavits alleging that policemen had assaulted Mhlongo at the time of his arrest. He added that nine cases of torture and assault involving members of Capt. Vilakazi's team had been reported to local police stations over several months. An IFP MP, Hugh Lee, said that in one of these a seventeen-year-old youth had had a rope tied around his neck and a plastic bag put over his face by members of the unit, who had then tried to drown him in the Tugela

River. Lee added that 'brutal methods of interrogation were being used to force IFP members to confess to crimes they had not committed, and to have them implicate other IFP members' (*Business Day* 22 May 1996).

An editorial in *Business Day* (22 May 1996) commented that police had offered 'three different versions' of how Mhlongo had sustained injuries: 'in a car accident, in a fall from his bunk, and in a fall "while standing"'. These, it continued, were 'disturbingly reminiscent of police explanations for deaths in detention during the apartheid era'.

Capt. Vilakazi, who was also alleged to have organized the release of an ANC member arrested in connection with the murder of an IFP supporter, was subsequently removed from his post by provincial police headquarters on the basis that his unit should instead be headed by a superintendent (as were three similar units in the province). The ANC said that Capt. Vilakazi was the victim of a 'vilification campaign', and called for his reinstatement. This was subsequently ordered by the Durban and Coast Local Division of the Supreme Court in Durban, on the grounds that the police captain had not been afforded a proper hearing before action had been taken. The Complaints Investigation Unit of the SAPS said its investigations indicated that Capt. Vilakazi and his unit had not been responsible for the death of Mhlongo. Dr Perumal also stated, following an inspection of the prison in which Mhlongo had died, that he could have sustained his fatal injuries in a fall from his bunk.

The IFP also alleged that a number of its members had been shot dead by security forces in the province in various incidents. An IFP leader, Thulani Ndlovu, was alleged to have been beaten and shot dead by five SANDF members in November 1994. Another IFP leader, Jabulani Khumalo, was allegedly shot dead by a police officer in the doorway of his home in Wembezi, Estcourt, in September 1995. The IFP also accused the police of complicity in the killing of another of its members, Zeph Sibiso, in Wembezi in January 1996. It added that a prison warder who was a member of the ANC-aligned Police and Prisons Civil Rights Union (POPCRU) had organized an ambush near Impendle (KwaZulu-Natal Midlands), also in January 1996, in which another IFP member had been killed (Jeffery 1997c, 510, 642–643).

Further disturbing allegations regarding abuse of power by security forces in KwaZulu-Natal arose in February 1998, in the early stages of the trial of Sifiso Nkabinde. (Nkabinde, a former ANC 'warlord' and SDU leader in the Richmond area, had been expelled from the party in 1997 for allegedly spying for the former government. He was subsequently arrested and charged on various counts of murder.) The presiding judge in his trial, Judge Jan Combrink, said there were indications that the ANC had interfered in the police investigation. A suspect had been taken away from the police by MI officers from the SANDF, who were 'former Umkhonto operatives attached to the ANC'. Their action had been unlawful, moreover, for the SANDF had no jurisdiction to investigate crime. Moreover, a senior ANC leader and the MEC for health in the province, Dr Zweli Mkhize, had ordered a particular policeman removed from the investigation, again without authority to do so. In addition, there was convincing evidence that the telephones of the accused had been bugged, and that confidential communications between Nkabinde and his lawyer had been monitored in this way (*Sowetan* 18 February 1998).

Obstructing justice in the Shell House shootings?

The Shell House killings on 28 March 1994 raise key questions regarding the ANC's apparent obstruction of justice in order to protect its followers. The killings took place in the aftermath of a 'bloodless coup' in Bophuthatswana which had witnessed the ouster of President Lucas Mangope on 12 March 1994 and the fall, a few days later, of the Ciskei's Brigadier Oupa Gqozo. Both homelands had allegedly been targeted for destabilization by the ANC, which had also sworn to bring down the KwaZulu home-land in which the IFP held sway. The ANC's intent in this regard was summed up in Joe Slovo's phrase: 'Two down, one to go' (Laurence 1998, 24). Against this background, a Zulu protest march was held through the streets of Johannesburg 'to display to the country at large, and the ANC and the [NP] government in particular, the strength which the IFP could muster' (Laurence 1998, 24).

During the march, nineteen people were killed. Nine were killed in clashes near the ANC's regional headquarters in the city and eight were shot dead outside the ANC's national headquar-ters, Shell House, when ANC security guards opened fire on the marchers.

The ANC said its guards had fired in self-defence and in res-ponse to an attack on Shell House. The Democratic Party (DP), the IFP, and the police denied this, and said security guards had opened fire on the marchers without provocation. The police tried to gain entry to Shell House to search the building, but were denied access by ANC security guards. 'No weapons were seized, no guards tested for gunpowder residue, no ballistic tests made, no lists of people in the building compiled, no statements taken.' Police returned next day with a search warrant, but Nelson Mandela refused to allow them to execute it. Instead, he promised full ANC cooperation in the police investigation and his assurance was accepted by Koos Calitz, police commissioner for the Wit-watersrand (Jeffery 1997c, 488–489).

Subsequent investigation was, however, marked by broken ANC promises. ANC weapons were handed over to the police in dribs and drabs, and at the end of December 1996 – almost three years after the shootings – approximately a hundred remained outstanding by the ANC's own admission (*Rapport* 1 December 1996). The first batch of some forty weapons was handed over by the ANC only in July 1994, and did not include the assault rifles which witnesses said had been used. By October that year, a further hundred weapons had been handed over – but no meaningful ballistics tests could be conducted, nor could the necessary link be made between a particular weapon and any individual present in Shell House at the time. The ANC provided four witnesses to the police, but these allegedly refused to disclose even their names – relying on their right to remain silent under the constitution (Safro 1995, 8–9). Further suspicions arose when a number of Umkhonto operatives were reported to have been present in Shell House on the day of the march, and to have been spirited away to the Wallmannsthal military base (Northern Transvaal) the same day. The ANC said, however, that the Umkhonto cadres had simply constituted an 'advance team' for military integration and had been expected by the SADF.

The ANC admitted to the Goldstone commission, which investigated the killings, that it had fired the first shots. It was only in July 1995, however – long after the Goldstone commission had concluded its inquiry – that Mandela acknowledged in Parliament that he had instructed the ANC's security guards to protect the building against IFP attack. 'I gave instructions to our security that if they attacked the house, please you must protect that house – even if you have to kill people.' Mandela's statement to the police in this regard was submitted only in February 1996 – almost two years after the massacre had taken place (Jeffery 1997c, 701, 622, 543, 624).

An inquest was finally initiated into the shootings in 1997. It ruled in December that year that no individual member of the police, the ANC, or the IFP – nor the three organizations as a whole – could be held criminally liable for the eight deaths outside Shell House (Citizen 10 December 1997). The inquest was presided over by Judge Robert Nugent, who noted that his task had been complicated by the failure of the authorities to conduct a thorough and prompt investigation into the killings when the trail of evidence was still intact, or before it had been deliberately obscured.

He also berated all three of the principal protagonists in the shootings – the ANC, the IFP, and the police – for negligence and/or obstruction. The police, he said, had failed adequately to investigate; the ANC had frustrated investigation by withholding information; and the IFP had seemed 'simply to have washed its hands of any responsibility for the conduct of its members'. Dissemblance during the inquest was 'quite extraordinary', he added, and he and his assessors had been confronted with 'a morass of evidence but little in the way of established facts' (Laurence 1998).

Thus, relying primarily on video footage to reconstruct events, Judge Nugent rejected the ANC's contention that the protest march had been organized to 'unleash an orchestrated campaign of violence and destruction'. He also rejected the ANC's key argument that the march was intended as a pretext for a premeditated attack on Shell House. Mandela's warning on the eve of the march of an impending attack on Shell House (given to the then President and police commissioner) was 'at best unspecific', he said. Other evidence from ANC leaders was equally vague, or contradictory. Overall, the court concluded, the ANC's evidence regarding the planned attack had been contrived. 'It was fabricated after the event so as to bolster the explanations that had been put forward for the shooting which occurred at Shell House' (Laurence 1998).

Evidence given by the ANC's security guards that they had opened fire only after they had been shot at from the crowd was also rejected by Judge Nugent. 'The overall weight of the evidence points prima facie to the conclusion that the shooting was initiated by heavy firing by the ANC guards.' He added (Laurence 1998):

Prima facie the evidence does not show that Shell House and its occupants were about to come under attack, nor could it reasonably have been believed at the time that it was about to come under attack.

Prima facie there was no justification for shooting at the crowd at all.

Moreover, the barrage of fire was in any event grossly excessive. We do not accept that any warning was given … It was clear, too, that when the shooting started the crowd immediately disintegrated and fled. To have continued firing at them went far beyond what would be permitted in legitimate defence.

Any endeavour at criminal prosecution has long been delayed by the ANC's seeming obstruction of justice, and seems now to have been finally precluded by the inquest finding. Civil claims for compensation, running to millions of rands, are being brought against the ANC and the minister for safety and security. These claims may not succeed, however, for some of the security guards involved in the shootings have applied for amnesty from the TRC. If this is granted, it will exonerate both the guards and the ANC itself from any civil liability as well.

Addressing a rally in Gauteng on Freedom Day, 27 April 1996 – almost two years after the Shell House killings – an IFP spokesperson said the ANC was proving, in many ways, to be 'merely a successor to the repressive apartheid government'. Particularly important was the ANC's conduct regarding the shootings. 'In our new country,' he stated, 'where justice is supposedly for all and all are equal before the law, we find that the ANC and its killers are more equal than others.' If the ANC ultimately escapes civil as well as criminal liability for the Shell House shootings, this perception is likely to grow.

Undermining the independence of the criminal-justice system

There are various disturbing indications that the independence of the criminal-justice system is being compromised. Some of these concerns have been sparked by the minister of justice himself, particularly in his seeming support for 'struggle book-keeping' and 'struggle murder'.

Support for 'struggle' crimes

In 1997 Dr Allan Boesak returned from the US to South Africa to face trial on some thirty charges of theft and fraud involving some R8 million. The charges arose from his alleged role in diverting funds donated by a Danish agency to his Foundation for Peace and Justice – formed to assist the victims of apartheid – to his own personal use (*City Press* 3 August 1997). Boesak was greeted on his arrival at Cape Town International Airport by Omar, who was then also the ANC's chairperson in the Western Cape. Omar expressed strong support for Boesak, who played a key role in the founding of the UDF in 1983, as a stalwart in the struggle against apartheid. He added that neither Mandela, Mbeki, the cabinet, nor himself had been consulted about the prosecution, implying that they might not have sanctioned it if given the opportunity (*Business Day* 7 March 1997). He also said it had been difficult to maintain full records in the struggle years, when anti-apartheid organizations were constantly being monitored by security police. Opposition parties accused him of having abused his position as minister of justice in thus expressing understanding and tacit support for 'struggle bookkeeping' (*Mail & Guardian* 27 March 1997).

Seeming support for 'struggle murder' followed. In November 1997 Winnie Madikizela-Mandela, the former wife of the president, appeared before the TRC to answer questions regarding the role of the 'Mandela United Football Club' in Soweto in the late 1980s. The 'club' had comprised a number of young men who had been her 'bodyguards' at the time and were alleged to have played a key part, among other things, in kidnapping and assaulting four youths suspected of being informers for the former government. One of the four, fourteen-year-old Stompie Seipei, was killed. Winnie Mandela had been convicted in 1991 of kidnapping Stompie and sentenced, on appeal, to a fine of R15 000. Her alibi – that she could not have played a part in the death of the youth because she had been in Brandfort (Free State) at the time – was apparently accepted.

Madikizela-Mandela's hearing before the TRC took place in public, at her request. She was accused by the witnesses before the commission, among other things, of having herself killed Stompie by stabbing him with a knife, of having assaulted and tortured the other youths as well, and of having stubbornly refused to heed appeals by leaders of the UDF and ANC to release the youths and disband the club. Her alibi was also cast into doubt when Albertina Sisulu contradicted a statement on the issue she had earlier made in a widely publicized BBC interview (*Citizen* 3 December 1997).

Against this background, Omar came out in strong support of Madikizela-Mandela, emphasizing that the murder allegations against her could not be compared with the crimes of apartheid.

The *Citizen* commented that given his earlier condoning of Boesak's alleged 'struggle bookkeeping', his remarks suggested that 'barbaric practices such as "struggle kidnapping" and "struggle murder" could be condoned if they were perpetrated by someone on the side of liberation'. The newspaper added that Madikizela-Mandela had suffered grievously under apartheid and had also been a rallying point in the struggle against it. Support for her in Omar's personal capacity was thus understandable. It continued: 'But Omar is the minister of justice, and in that role he should not be seen to be taking sides. This is a far more important issue than his faux pas about Boesak's funny bookkeeping. If the minister is seen to be condoning murder, for whatever reason, that is a devastating blow to the shaky image of justice in this country' (*Citizen* 20 November 1997).

Particularly significant, however, are two further threats to the independence of the criminal-justice system. These come not merely from ill-advised comments by the minister but from proposals for new laws which hold serious implications indeed for the legitimacy and independence of the administration of justice.

A new 'super' attorney general

In 1992 the NP sought at last to put the country's attorneys general beyond the reach of politicians. Until then, the attorneys general were subordinate to the minister of justice who could reverse their decisions. The legislation was changed in that year to make them accountable to Parliament instead. The Attorney-General Act of 1992 was intended to ensure that attorneys general could institute and conduct prosecutions 'in a professional and objective manner without being pressurised from any source whatsoever' (*Frontiers of Freedom* 1995, 10).

In late 1994, however, the National Association of Democratic Lawyers proposed the appointment of a 'super attorney general' who would be a member of the cabinet and be given authority over all provincial and local attorneys general. Omar backed the proposal, saying: 'Many people saw the attorney general as an instrument of the apartheid state. The independence of the attorney general's office was introduced in the dying days of apartheid. I am not opposed to independence ... [But] I cannot escape the conclusion, as an individual, that this independence was introduced not so much to guarantee independence as to entrench the status quo.' He also expressed concern that an independent attorney general might argue against the unconstitutionality of the death penalty, for instance, and would fail to 'bow to the wishes' of the government on the issue (*Frontiers of Freedom* 1995).

The Association of Law Societies (ALS) expressed disquiet at the proposal, as well as concern that the appointment envisaged would be 'purely political'. The independence of attorneys general was particularly important, for they were responsible for deciding who should be prosecuted for contravening the laws of the land. They acted as 'custodians for the entire population and should therefore be free from interference from politicians'. Moreover, said the ALS, given the extent of broad popular support for the retention of the death penalty, why should an attorney general not argue against its abolition – even if this contradicted the views of the government of the day? (*Frontiers of Freedom* 1995).

When the 1996 constitution was first adopted by the Constitutional Assembly in May that year, the ALS opposed its certification on a number of grounds, including the role it envisaged for a 'super' attorney general. Section 179 of the constitution provides for a 'national director of public prosecutions', to be appointed by the president and answerable to the minister of justice. The national director would be entitled to issue 'policy directives' to govern the prosecution process. He would have ultimate control in this regard and would be empowered to instruct his provincial counterparts – the present attorneys general – to institute or halt a prosecution. He would further be able to intervene in the conduct of any prosecution if he so wished.

The ALS objected to section 179 on the basis that it would infringe, among other things, the separation of governmental powers which the constitution was enjoined to reflect. Giving judgment in September 1996, however, the Constitutional Court dismissed this objection.

The pressure previously placed by the ANC on the attorney general of KwaZulu-Natal, Tim McNally, underscores the dangers of subjecting prosecutorial decisions to political control. The

ANC has long been displeased with McNally, alleging him to be reluctant to prosecute the 'third force' which the ANC believes responsible for fomenting political violence in the province. The matter came to a head in late 1995 when McNally declined to prosecute a number of IFP leaders implicated in hit-squad activities against the ANC. The ANC reacted angrily, saying that the attorney general should be brought before a judicial committee to account for his conduct, and should also resign 'in the interests of justice'. Six attorneys general from the other provinces defended McNally, saying the various allegations against him were 'of a generalised nature and completely unsubstantiated, making it virtually impossible to respond meaningfully to them' (Jeffery 1997c, 739–740).

Towards the end of September the attorneys general from all nine provinces, including McNally, were called before a special parliamentary justice committee chaired by Johnny de Lange, a senior ANC and SACP leader. De Lange accused McNally of 'lacking a sense of urgency' in prosecuting political murders. McNally responded that his office fulfilled its duties 'professionally and speedily' but required sufficient prima facie evidence before it could act. He had only been provided with two 'hit-squad' dockets, and one had resulted in prosecution while the other had lacked such evidence.

McNally was cross-examined for seven hours by the committee, led by De Lange. The DP described the hostile cross-examination of McNally as an 'inquisition which far exceeded permissible bounds'. It warned that the independence of the judicial system and its capacity to function without fear or prejudice was a cornerstone of the country's legal system, and that the ANC's conduct in relation to McNally placed South Africa 'on a slippery slope towards the eventual loss of judicial independence'. The ANC said the hearing emphasized the need to act swiftly in introducing an 'independent national attorney general able to coordinate policy on prosecutions' (Jeffery 1997c, 740).

The National Prosecuting Authority Bill was tabled in Parliament soon thereafter. The bill echoes the constitution in giving a new national director of public prosecutions the power to control prosecuting policy in all provinces. It also provides for the national director to be appointed by the president and to hold office for a limited fixed term, renewable once only. It states that the national director need not possess any minimum legal qualification – though this will be required for the provincial directors – and this, of course, increases the danger that a political appointment may be made. In addition, the bill gives the current attorneys general very little security of tenure. All will automatically become provincial directors when the act takes effect, and will be deemed to have been appointed as such from the time when they initially took office as attorneys general. They will hold office for a fixed term only and can be re-appointed for a further specified period once thereafter – but they have no right to this.

All the existing attorneys general will thus be placed under pressure to perform to the ANC's satisfaction in order to qualify for a second term of office. Those who have already incurred the party's wrath – such as McNally – are unlikely to be re-appointed. Moreover, the fact that appointment as a provincial director will be retrospective in its operation will mean that their fixed period of initial appointment could rapidly expire. Under the 1992 act, by contrast, attorneys general were accorded security of tenure and were entitled to hold office until retirement at age 65 (Schoenteich 1997b, 5).

The introduction of lay assessors

In February 1996 it was reported that 'magistrates, prosecutors and members of the legal profession were up in arms' about a bill providing, among other things, for the introduction of lay assessors. This was viewed 'as turning the South African legal system into "people's courts" where the magistrate would be retained as the presiding officer to give some degree of credibility' to judgments. The assessors, however, would effectively decide all criminal cases except for minor traffic offences. Fears were expressed, in addition, that they might be 'almost illiterate people', who would be called to sit in judgment, for example, in complicated fraud cases requiring analysis of sophisticated forensic audits (*Citizen* 15 February 1996).

When the first draft of the 1996 constitution was adopted, it called for the enactment of legislation introducing lay assessors. The ALS objected to this provision as well, but this too was rejected by the Constitutional Court on the basis that many legal systems make provision for the participation of lay people. In January 1998 Omar sought cabinet approval for a bill making the use of lay assessors compulsory in the magistrates' courts in criminal trials involving crimes against a person. (This means the vast majority of criminal trials.) Such matters are to be heard by a magistrate and two lay assessors, who will be able to overrule the presiding judicial officer on any factual dispute. Most criminal trials held in the lower courts are decided on fact, however, rather than legal argument (Schoenteich 1998b).

The lay assessors will thus be able – if they believe an accused's denial of guilt is credible – to acquit him over the objections of the presiding magistrate. Untrained lay people, however, lack 'the theoretical knowledge, training and practical experience' needed to weigh conflicting evidence and reach a considered verdict. Worse still, lay assessors could decide to convict where 'a presiding officer with years of courtroom experience would acquit' (Schoenteich 1998b).

It is also doubtful what useful contribution lay assessors could offer in sentencing. There is no need for their input in this regard, for existing rules of criminal procedure allow any relevant witness to present evidence on the feelings of a community to assist a court in determining a sentence (Schoenteich 1998b).

The department of justice says the assessors will be selected on the basis of their 'representativeness in the community'. But South Africa is a racially and politically divided society, in which selection is likely to be contested where accused and victim come from different socio-economic and ethnic backgrounds or from rival political parties (the ANC and the IFP especially). Requiring an assessor to recuse her or himself will, however, be a time-consuming process which will exacerbate the already unacceptably slow delivery of justice (Schoenteich 1998b).

Getting two lay assessors to attend court when required will add to the logistical nightmare that already besets the magistrates' courts. At the Johannesburg Magistrate's Court alone, some 7 000 trials are standing over from 1997 – to which are added over a thousand new cases every month. 'It is a mammoth logistical task for the police to subpoena all the state witnesses involved in these trials. Assuring the attendance of lay assessors will further stretch limited state resources' (Schoenteich 1998b).

Omar's justification for the lay assessor system is that the judiciary in general lacks legitimacy and that the problem can be addressed by securing community participation in the lower courts at least. However, both the legitimacy and the independence of the magistrates' courts could be fatally eroded by the proposed new system. What is needed is not a new form of 'people's courts' but 'a system which processes cases rapidly and ensures a consistent and reliable application of justice' (Schoenteich 1998b).

The role of the Truth and Reconciliation Commission

The 1993 constitution spoke, in its 'postamble', of the need to create a 'historic bridge' between the past of a 'deeply divided society characterised by strife, conflict and injustice' and a 'future founded on the recognition of human rights and democracy'. It also emphasized the importance of promoting national unity, reconciliation, and the reconstruction of society. It added that the purpose of the constitution was to transcend the divisions of the past as well as 'the transgression of humanitarian principles in violent conflicts'. This required an emphasis on understanding rather than vengeance and on reparation rather than retaliation. To this end, the postamble stated that amnesty was to be granted for all acts and offences 'associated with political objectives and committed in the course of the conflicts of the past'. It concluded by enjoining Parliament to pass a law providing for the mechanisms and procedures through which this could be done (Jeffery 1997a, 78).

Pursuant to these provisions, Parliament enacted in 1995 the Promotion of National Unity and Reconciliation Act, providing for the Truth and Reconciliation Commission (TRC) and its various structures. To encourage perpetrators of human rights abuses to reveal the truth about the past, the act allowed for an extensive amnesty encompassing both civil and criminal liability.

The TRC is widely believed to have been modelled on a similar Chilean commission established in the early 1990s to probe the killing or 'disappearance' of thousands of people under the military rule of General Pinochet and his armed forces. According to Omar, the 'core ideas' for the TRC 'come largely from the Chilean model' (Myburgh 1996, 27–28).

There are, however, various key differences between the Chilean commission and the TRC. Most relevant for present purposes is that the Chilean body was strictly bipartisan in its composition, with four of its eight commissioners coming from 'the Left' and four from 'the Right'. Moreover, the Chilean body eschewed any notion of moral relativism: the view that the evils perpetrated by the regime justified or excused the crimes committed against it. As the Chilean commission stated:

'The human rights violations that took place must not and

cannot be excluded and justified on the grounds of previous actions by those whose rights were violated' (Myburgh 1996, 28).

In addition, the Chilean commission took the view that full protection of human rights in the future was 'conceivable only within a state truly subject to the rule of law'. Thus, the re-establishment of the rule of law was central to the structure and approach of the Chilean body. It was decided that in no case was the commission to take on legal functions proper to the courts or to interfere with cases already pending. Perpetrators were not to be named because to do so would violate their rights to fair trial and due process (Myburgh 1996, 28).

These important principles have all been abrogated by the TRC. Controversy has surrounded the composition of the commission since its inception, for the seventeen commissioners as well as their supporting staff are widely viewed as coming primarily from the side of the ANC (*Survey* 1996/97, 638). Moreover, key leaders within the ANC – including Omar himself – have continually put forward the view that apartheid was a 'crime against humanity', equivalent to Hitler's rule in Nazi Germany. Hence, any human rights violations perpetrated by those who sought to overthrow it in a 'just war' could not be equated in any way with the evils committed by those who sought to perpetuate it (Giliomee 1995, 23–24).

Casting doubt on judicial findings

A key element underpinning the rule of law is respect for the judiciary and for the system of criminal justice. Should this be lost, the impetus towards self-help is accelerated. Moreover, where judicial independence and integrity are significantly challenged, there is a danger that a beleaguered judiciary will respond by becoming more executive-minded in its decisions.

Judicial decisions should never, of course, be above searching scrutiny and considered criticism. There is a difference, however, between such assessment and sustained attack on judicial integrity – especially where the latter emanates either from the ruling party or from significant individuals and organizations seemingly close to it.

The strictures of the Chilean commission regarding the need to uphold the rule of law are thus particularly important. They have also, however, been ignored by the TRC. A number of earlier trials and judicial commissions of inquiry have been revisited, and substantial doubt has been cast not only upon their outcome but also on the probity of the judges responsible for the relevant rulings. Examples include the following.

Revisiting the 'Sharpeville Six'

In September 1984 violent protest broke out in the black township of Sebokeng in the Vaal Triangle. Black local councillors were particular targets of attack, and in the neighbouring black township of Sharpeville, the deputy mayor, Khuzwayo Dlamini, was 'stoned and set alight near his burning car'. His death was described by the judge in the subsequent murder trial of six accused as 'gruesome, medieval and barbaric'. The six were convicted of murder under the common-law doctrine of 'common purpose', the court accepting that the six had participated in the attack and shared a common purpose with the rest of the mob to kill Dlamini. Evidence proffered by the defence to show that the accused had not participated in the murder was rejected. The six were sentenced to death in December 1985, and the Appellate Division of the Supreme Court (renamed the Supreme Court of Appeals in the 1996 constitution) upheld the conviction and sentence at the end of 1987 (*Weekly Mail* 5 February 1988).

A national and international campaign was mounted against the conviction of the Sharpeville Six. The 'common purpose' doctrine was rejected as an outrage, and the judgment condemned as a travesty of justice. The UDF, which effectively served as the internal wing of the banned ANC in this period, was particularly vociferous in its condemnation of the verdict, while the ANC itself urged the international community to plead for clemency for the Six. Their death sentences were subsequently commuted to terms of imprisonment by former state President P. W. Botha and they were released in 1991, as part of the steps taken to prepare for constitutional talks (*Survey* 1991/92, x1).

When the TRC began its work in 1996, it heard evidence from one of the Sharpeville Six, Mr Duma Khumalo, that he had been wrongly convicted. The trial court, however, had accepted testimony that Khumalo had stoned Dlamini's house, made petrol bombs, burnt the deputy-mayor's house, and pushed Dlamini's car out of his garage. It had also found that though Khumalo had thereafter been absent from the scene for a period, he had rejoined the crowd and participated in the killing of Dlamini (*Weekly Mail* 5 February 1988). Khumalo told the TRC, by contrast, that he had been wrongly convicted because the trial judge had failed to hear the testimony of a key defence witness. The chairperson of the commission, Desmond Tutu – who was a co-president and key leader of the UDF in the 1980s – responded that some judges had 'colluded [with the apartheid government] when they should have been the last bastion of those few rights people still had'. He added that these judges ought to 'come and tell their story' to the commission. Their conduct would not 'be held against them' but it was important to 'clear the air' (*Survey* 1996/97, 642).

(By contrast, the use of the doctrine of common purpose to convict members of the IFP of the murder of nineteen ANC supporters at Shobashobane was welcomed by the ANC. In March 1997, eighteen IFP members were convicted of murder in relation to the massacre – five on the basis of common purpose. The trial judge explained it thus: 'Although five of the accused had not been seen attacking any of the victims, by joining the estimated 2 000-strong impi [armed force] they had shown a common objective with those who were armed and shooting at their fleeing victims.' The ANC responded that 'the judgment would restore confidence in the judicial system' (Survey 1996/97, 602).)

Rejecting the acquittal of Malan

Also instructive is the ANC's reaction to the acquittal of Malan on all charges of murder and conspiracy to murder arising from the KwaMhakutha massacre of thirteen people in KwaZulu-Natal in January 1987. Malan and his nineteen fellow accused – mostly senior SADF and MI officers – were alleged to have trained 200 IFP supporters in the Caprivi Strip of Namibia to act as hit squads against the ANC and UDF in the province. The massacre was alleged to have been perpetrated by some of these trainees and to have been directed by MI operatives. (The thirteen people killed were, in fact, IFP supporters, and not the UDF activist allegedly intended to be targeted.)

The state's case was flimsy from the start, however. It unravelled under cross-examination when a number of inconsistencies in the prosecution's evidence were revealed. The trial judge also rebuked Superintendent Frank Dutton, the investigating officer in the case, for 'probably deliberately misleading' the court. It further indicated that the statements of witnesses had been tampered with and said the police investigation team appeared to have coached witnesses and 'cut and pasted' their statements. As a result of the weaknesses and inconsistencies in state testimony, Malan and his co-accused were acquitted in October 1996.

ANC officials in KwaZulu-Natal, who had predicted that the trial would conclusively establish 'third-force' culpability for violence in the area, reacted with outrage to the acquittal. 'In the eyes of our people', it warned, 'this verdict may not be acceptable. It is doubtful whether our people will ever have confidence in the judicial system if it remains the same.' The Human Rights Committee – many of whose trustees seemingly have links with the ANC – responded that the judgment had generated a crisis in the justice system and 'the ability of the courts to handle such cases'. Desmond Tutu, in his capacity as chairperson of the TRC, said his commission constituted a better vehicle than the courts for finding 'the real truth'. His sentiment was echoed by the deputy chairperson of the TRC, Alex Boraine, who added that the TRC was a 'better vehicle for establishing facts of this nature than courts of law' (Pereira 1996, 6).

Tim McNally, the attorney general of the province, who had prepared and presented the prosecution's case, 'came under fire from various commentators for not securing the conviction of Malan and the other generals. He had been placed under enormous political and media pressure to prosecute the case and, when the accused were acquitted, was attacked by the TRC and various newspapers' (Pereira 1996).

President Mandela's response was different and commendable. He said of the verdict: 'We were not in court and did not have the benefit of hearing the evidence and cross-examination. The judge had all these opportunities and I fully accept the decision.' His office added that confidence in the courts was essential to prevent society 'degenerating into private vengeance and extra-legal activities' (Pereira 1996). His valuable comments were largely drowned out, however, in the general expression of outrage.

The TRC, moreover, has since effectively re-opened the case by initiating an investigation into the role in the KwaZulu-Natal violence of the IFP's Caprivi trainees. Key evidence in the Malan trial regarding the allegedly offensive nature of the training provided the Caprivi group has been raked over once again. The shaky evidence regarding the KwaMhakutha massacre itself, however, has seemingly been ignored. It would thus not be surprising if the TRC were to reach a different verdict regarding the generals' culpability and to hail this as 'the real truth'.

Re-opening the 'Kimberley' case

In 1997 an ANC member and former Umkhonto commander,

Laurens Mbatha, applied to the TRC for amnesty for a 1993 hand-grenade attack on the Bophuthatswana consulate in Kimberley. He told a TRC amnesty committee that the 'two ANC activists sentenced for the attack knew nothing about it'. The grenade – which killed a policeman and injured 39 others – had been thrown at his instruction, he averred, by another ANC member and Umkhonto operative, Walter Smiles (*Business Day, Citizen* 28 October 1997). The two convicted prisoners then in turn applied for amnesty, and a witness who had earlier implicated them in the attack was reported to be 'prepared to say that he had lied during their trial' (*Sowetan* 30 October 1997). The *Sowetan's* political correspondent commented: 'The plight of the two prisoners raised questions about whether the police and justice system manipulated evidence – and even events – to procure convictions in cases involving cadres of liberation movements before the 1994 election' (*Sowetan* 1 August 1997).

What most newspaper reports omitted to mention, however, was that the testimony of Smiles – claiming responsibility for the attack – had earlier been considered and rejected as untrue by the trial court. One of the TRC commissioners, Denzil Potgieter, who had been defence counsel in the earlier case, knew this but failed to bring it to the TRC's attention. The attorney general of the Northern Cape, Charl du Plessis, commented that Potgieter had thus knowingly allowed false testimony to be given to the commission. This was highly improper, and 'the obvious intention was to prove that the original conviction had been wrong' (*Survey* 1996/97, 640–641).

Re-trying the Eikenhof Three

Similar developments have occurred concerning the 'Eikenhof Three'. In 1993 a mother and two teenage children died in a hail of AK-47 bullets while driving along a motorway near Eikenhof (south of Johannesburg). Three ANC members were identified as responsible for the attack by an unnamed informant, who in turn received the advertised reward of R250 000. The three were convicted by Judge David Curlewis on the basis of confessions made by two of them as well as the testimony of four eyewitnesses. In July 1997, however, a PAC member by the name of Phila Dolo, who was serving a prison sentence in the Eastern Cape for another murder, claimed responsibility for the attack, and stated that the three had been wrongly convicted (*Citizen* 13 August 1997).

Tokyo Sexwale, then premier of Gauteng, visited the three prisoners and told the press that the jail sentences were 'a profound injustice to the men and their families'. He called for an immediate investigation into the witnesses who had pointed them out, the police who had investigated the case, the prosecutors who had 'cooked evidence', and the judge who had sentenced the three to seventeen years' imprisonment. He wondered, he continued, how many other people had been wrongly hanged or sent to jail under the justice system of the past. He assured the three that 'all that now kept them in prison was paperwork' and that they would be freed once the evidence of their innocence had been compiled by the TRC and handed to Omar and President Mandela (*Citizen* 26 July 1997).

Cheryl Carolus, the ANC's deputy secretary general and a prominent SACP leader, said she would ask Mufamadi to launch an investigation into how the police had 'concocted and falsified evidence' to get the three convicted. This would include an inquiry as to whether the police had shared the reward money among themselves. The ANC would encourage the three prisoners to bring civil claims for wrongful arrest against the police, and would also press for an investigation into Judge Curlewis (*Citizen* 6 August 1997). She urged all 'good' judges to come forward and cooperate with the TRC in its investigation of the apartheid-era judiciary (see 'Calling the judges to confess' below).

The ANC also said it had traced three witnesses whose evidence had been relied upon during the trial. These were 'cooperating' with the party's truth and reconciliation desk, and were 'willing to testify that they had falsely implicated the three' (*Business Day, Sowetan* 6 August 1997).

Doubts were subsequently expressed as to whether the matter was as clear-cut as the ANC alleged. While the ANC claimed that the three accused had been tortured to extract confessions, and that the judge had erred in accepting these, the reality was far more complex. Two of the three accused had made confessions and had alleged at the trial that these had been extracted under duress. Judge Curlewis rejected their testimony, however, describing them as 'appalling witnesses' who had given 'absurd' evidence and 'lied maliciously'. Though their confessions were thus admitted, the most telling testimony against them came not from these statements but from four eyewitnesses. These included a passenger in the car attacked, a schoolboy who had spoken to one of the accused shortly before the attack, a passing motorist also wounded in the shooting, and the owner of the vehicle used to perpetrate the attack, who had been coerced into driving the car at the time (*Star* 1 August 1997).

Weaknesses and inconsistencies also emerged in the PAC's statements about the attack. Dolo himself subsequently said that though the attack had been carried out under his orders by three cadres (all of whom had since died and thus could not testify), he had not personally taken part in it. The PAC's secretary general, Mike Muendane, initially stated that five cadres of the organization's former armed wing, APLA (Azanian People's Liberation Army), had carried out the attack. He subsequently retracted this as incorrect, but refused to say how many men had indeed been involved. Dolo refused to identify the three APLA cadres allegedly responsible for the killings, or to give any further information unless he was first freed from prison (*Star* 1 August 1997).

As the ANC's ire mounted, a journalist on the *Star*, Robert Brand, warned (14 August 1997) that it was not for the ANC, the

PAC, or the newspapers to decide whether there had indeed been a miscarriage of justice and, if so, who was to blame. It was for a court to decide the issue after further investigation and a full hearing, accompanied by a proper testing and evaluation of the evidence. 'I am making this point', he continued, 'because I believe one of the cornerstones of our democracy is the rule of law. And the more we undermine the integrity of the judicial system – as opposed to pointing out the flaws and seeking solutions – the more we undermine the rule of law'. He pointed out that the publicity surrounding the case had placed the new investigation under pressure, and had the potential to undermine public confidence in the judiciary. 'The scene has been set to discredit the ruling if it goes against what certain parties expect. If the court, after consideration of the evidence, old and new, comes to the conclusion that the original conviction was correct, would the ANC and PAC be able – or willing – to turn around to their supporters and persuade them to accept the judgment?'

Re-opening judicial commissions of inquiry

A judicial commission of inquiry had been held to probe police shootings at Langa township near Cape Town on 21 March 1960 (Jeffery 1991, 25–26). Judge Diemont found that two people had been killed by police, and that the order to shoot had been justified. (The police had opened fire after they had virtually been surrounded by a crowd of 10 000 people and when they were slowly being compelled to retreat under a barrage of missiles. The judge also criticized the police commanding officer for failure to communicate with the organizers of the march before resorting to violence, and for having given an inadequate warning of impending fire.) The TRC, however, was told by a witness that she had counted 175 graves of protesters mown down by police in the incident (*Survey* 1996/97, 640). Professor Tom Lodge of Wits University warned thereafter that the TRC risked becoming a 'commission of untruths', for there was no mechanism through which false testimony could be exposed. 'There should be some screening of witnesses', he said, 'failing which the truthful witnesses will be discredited by the untruthful ones' (*Star* 24 April 1996).

Similarly, a judicial commission of inquiry had been conducted by Judge Kannemeyer into police shootings at a different Langa township (on the outskirts of Port Elizabeth in the Eastern Cape) in July 1985. Judge Kannemeyer had found that some twenty people had been killed when police, who had not been equipped with adequate riot control equipment, opened fire with live ammunition on an advancing crowd. The TRC was told, and accepted without demur, that 34 people had been killed, that police had tried to conceal some of the deaths, and that a baby had been among those shot. Much of this testimony had previously been tested and rejected as inaccurate by the commission, but was now regarded as the truth (Survey 1996/97, 641).

A further judicial commission of inquiry by Judge Louis Harms into alleged 'hit-squad' operations within the police was particularly criticized by and before the TRC. The Harms commission was appointed in 1989 after a convicted murderer and former policeman, Almond Nofamela, had confessed to having participated in 1981 in the 'hit-squad' execution of a prominent anti-apartheid activist, Griffiths Mxenge, in Umlazi (Durban). The work of the Harms inquiry was significantly impeded, however, by the mysterious disappearance of a number of key police documents.

Judge Harms concluded that no police hit squad existed at the Vlakplaas farm (outside Pretoria), as had widely been alleged. He also, however, delivered a scathing indictment of the Civil Cooperation Bureau (CCB), a covert arm of the former army, and said there was evidence linking it to various abuses, including 'two and possibly three attempted murders' (Jeffery 1997c, 241–242). The evidence was insufficient, however, to identify those responsible for the deaths of various anti-apartheid activists, including David Webster, who had been gunned down outside his Johannesburg home in 1989 (Survey 1988/89, xxx). Judge Harms added that the CCB was probably involved in more crimes of violence than the available evidence showed. He criticized the disappearance of the relevant CCB files as 'unpardonable'. He added that there was 'a general probability' that members of the police had committed violent crimes for political ends, especially as the ANC and PAC had earlier 'declared war on the SAP and SADF' (Jeffery 1997c, 241–242).

At a TRC hearing regarding Webster's assassination, the activist's former partner, Maggie Friedman, accused Judge Harms of having ignored important evidence so as effectively to exonerate the police from culpability for his murder. Dr Alex Boraine, the deputy chairperson of the TRC, said it might be necessary to call Judge Harms before the commission and ask him to reconsider his earlier conclusions. The judge would have to do so, he indicated, not only in relation to Webster's death but also as regards the wider question of police hit squads and the role that these had played in attacking and killing opponents of apartheid.

Calling the judges to confess

Following the TRC's re-examination and uncritical acceptance of new testimony regarding the Sharpeville Six, Desmond Tutu stated that some judges should come before the TRC to 'clear the air' about their role in the apartheid era. In August 1996, in its first submission to the TRC, the ANC urged that 'judges, magistrates and prosecutors involved in gross travesties of justice' should appear before the TRC. Judges, stated the ANC, had 'condoned the barbaric practices of the security police and given terrorism laws a "veneer of legal responsibility" ... Judicial commissions had promoted the goals of the apartheid state or covered up its culpability in cases of gross human rights violations'. These included, in particular, the Kannemeyer commission into the Langa massacre in 1985 and the Harms commission into hit squads (see 'Re-opening judicial commissions of inquiry' above). Mbeki, addressing a special panel of the TRC, added that 'selected judges had in many instances been put in charge of political trials and were responsible for the judicial murder of people fighting against apartheid' (*Citizen* 23 August 1996).

During 1997 a number of special hearings were convened by the TRC to probe, among other things, the role of business, the churches, doctors, the legal profession, and the media in supporting apartheid and thus aiding the commission of gross human rights violations. Judges were also called upon to make submissions, and to appear in person before the TRC.

A written representation was made to the TRC by the chief justice and his deputy, the president of the constitutional court and his deputy, and a former chief justice. (These were Judge Ismail Mohamed, Judge H. J. O. van Heerden, Judge Arthur Chaskalson, Judge Pius Langa, and Judge Michael Corbett.) The five stated that it was important to 'acknowledge the role of the legal system in upholding and maintaining apartheid, and the injustices associated with it'. Apartheid in itself had constituted a gross abuse of human rights, and it was not surprising that the police and the administration of justice had lost legitimacy in the eyes of most South Africans. Criminal trials had not met minimum standards of fairness in democratic countries, while detention without trial and repressive laws designed to curtail political dissent had been greeted 'with only muted protest from some of the judges and members of the legal profession'. On occasion, too, 'justice was done and was seen to be done – and in this way values central to the rule of law were not entirely lost' (*Business Day* 30 October 1997). (A number of other judges, including Judge Harms, also made individual submissions to the commission.)

No judges appeared to testify before the TRC, however, concerning the role they had played in human rights violations in the apartheid era. Tutu responded that the TRC would be engaging the judges in due course and 'hoped that it would not be necessary for the commission to drag them to the TRC'. Tutu said he was distressed that no judges had appeared, and said this showed that they had 'not yet changed a mindset that properly belongs to the old dispensation. We should not pretend that judges are not human and not fallible. They have made mistakes in the past and there is no reason to believe that they will not again' (*Sowetan* 24 October 1997). The Black Lawyers Association and the Human Rights Commission, a statutory body empowered under the 1996 constitution to investigate and rule on human rights abuses, berated the judges for their failure to appear (*Sowetan* 28 October 1997).

Judge Harms responded: 'The constitution guarantees the independence of the bench. If judges now have to account before a commission, what prevents the government from appointing another commission next year to call judges to account?' An editorial in the *Citizen* commented that judges had not made the law under the previous government, and had been duty-bound to apply it. If they were now subpoenaed to appear before the TRC, their judicial independence would be challenged and their status undermined. Judicial findings should, where appropriate, be subject to review and appeal as well as to informed comment.

But judges should not be called upon to 'answer to a body like the TRC, which has its own set of rules, does not grant people who stand accused by others the right to question the witnesses, and seems to be a law unto itself'. It warned Tutu not to 'meddle with the judiciary', for to do so would be to destroy the impartiality and independence of the bench (*Citizen* 7 August 1996, 30 October 1997). Moreover, since many 'apartheid' judges remained on the bench, any attack on them by the TRC could make it untenable for them to continue in office (*Citizen* 30 October 1997).

Paula McBride, the wife of Robert McBride, who had ultimately been reprieved from execution for his role in the Magoo's Bar bombing in Durban in the 1980s, attended the hearing and delivered a stinging attack on the judiciary. McBride accused the country's judges of having made 'a bigger contribution than all the state's assassins in shoring up the system'. She continued:

> They presided over commissions of inquiry that whitewashed security force excesses and corruption. They upheld the grand theft of the homes and land of black people. They punished opponents of their system (for theirs it was) with the harshest array of cruelties, including banishments, house arrests, hard labour, lengthy jail sentences and, wherever they could find any pretext, death.
>
> Yet even up to now they have managed to preserve and propagate the absurdity that they were somehow above it all – impartial. They gave the system a veneer of respectability which the state could flaunt to the outside world and at the same time added steel to the hand that crushed so many of the people of this country.

She demanded that judges be subpoenaed to appear before the TRC and answer for their conduct (*Mail & Guardian* 31 October 1997).

Judge Chaskalson responded to this and similar criticisms by saying that generalizations about the role of judges in the apartheid era were 'neither fair nor accurate'. 'In dealing with complex problems such as the assessment of the role of the judiciary under apartheid, rigorous analysis was called for rather than broad and emotional generalisations.' The courts had been given a central role under the new dispensation to transform society and sustain the new democratic order and had generally shown a 'commitment and a sensitivity to this task'. Moreover, the majority of the present judiciary had been appointed before 1994, and their skills and experience were needed. He added that the judiciary under apartheid had included 'moral judges' who had helped to place limits on arbitrary action, thus 'preserving important principles of fairness and justice in the law' (*Citizen* 1 November 1997).

Naming perpetrators of gross violations of human rights

The Chilean commission decided not to name individual perpetrators. Wrote one commissioner: 'To name someone who has not defended himself and was not required to do so would have been the moral equivalent of convicting someone without due process.' The T R C, however, has shown no such scruples. The act empowers it to name 'perpetrators of gross human rights violations' and it has exercised this power often.

When it first began its hearings into human rights violations in the Eastern Cape, two former police officers sought an order postponing the hearing of evidence that would implicate them in the poisoning and disappearance of an activist, Siphiwe Mtimkulu, in 1982. The two contended that they had a right to know of what they stood accused well in advance of the hearing, so that they could timeously respond to the allegations against them. An order to that effect was granted, overturned on appeal, and ultimately restored on further appeal to what is the Supreme Court of Appeals. The then chief justice, Judge Michael Corbett, ruled that the commission must give alleged perpetrators 'timeous and reasonable notice' that they were to be named, as well as details about the allegations (*Survey* 1996/97, 640).

Though this ruling has provided limited protection for alleged perpetrators, it remains inadequate. The T R C must give 21 days' notice to those who are to be named, but 'the accused have no means of defending themselves, or clearing their reputations'. Naming by the T R C results in an effective presumption of guilt. The T R C also has full – and seemingly arbitrary – discretion in deciding which cases will be heard and thus which perpetrators will be named. Most of those named have been former security force members charged with assaulting, torturing, and killing anti-apartheid activists. Little has been heard, by contrast, about those who planted limpet mines and land mines that killed and maimed a number of civilians, or about the SDUS, which the TRC acknowledged had moved beyond its control and initiated a reign of terror in certain areas (Myburgh 1997, 37).

The granting of amnesty

The TRC's capacity to grant amnesty from civil and criminal liability for crimes committed with a political objective also holds grave implications for the rule of law. It is likely to breed contempt for the system of criminal justice by seeming to place a section of society above the reach of the law.

In 1988 the amnesty process was far from ended and it is too early for full analysis of its implications. Already, however, amnesty has been granted to Brian Mitchell, the former police officer responsible for the massacre of eleven people in Trust Feed in KwaZulu-Natal in 1988, and to Dirk Coetzee, another ex-police officer, for the brutal murder of Griffiths Mxenge in Durban in 1981.

Amnesty hearings have provided graphic details regarding a number of horrific incidents of torture and murder. The TRC has been told of various atrocities committed by the former security forces: of activists shot dead by police and left in shallow unmarked graves (Natal Witness 15 March 1997); of how the Pebco Three, for example, were abducted, interrogated, and shot dead, and their bodies dumped into the Fish River (Business Day 4 November 1997); of how a police officer shot dead two activists who had been injured in a shootout with police and were being taken by police van to hospital (Citizen 28 June 1997); and of how security police used the 'wet bag' method of torture to suffocate activists and thereby induce them to talk.

The TRC has also been told of how APLA cadres in 1993 attacked the Heidelberg tavern in Cape Town with the intention of killing 'anything that lived' (*Citizen* 28 October 1997); of how an American student, Amy Biehl, was killed in Guguletu, Cape Town, for 'being white' (*Business Day* 10 July 1997); and of how other APLA operatives threw grenades and mercilessly shot at a mixed-race congregation at St James Church in Cape Town killing eleven people and injuring fifty-eight (*Sowetan* 14 July 1997).

The granting of amnesty to those responsible for such outrages offends all sense of justice. It also holds grave implications for the rule of law in future. It makes it clear that a 'political' motive can justify the most brutal of killings and allow the perpetrators to escape scot-free. It cheapens the sanctity of human life and could encourage those accorded amnesty, who have killed for political reasons in the past, to kill for criminal advantage in the future (Myburgh 1997).

The Chilean commission, it seems, was wiser than our own in this regard as well. 'For the sake of national reconciliation', it said, 'and preventing the recurrence of such events, it is absolutely necessary that the government fully exercises its power to mete out punishment.' For the Chilean commission 'the sanctions contemplated within criminal law, which should be applied to all alike, should thereby be applied to those who transgress the laws safeguarding human rights'. By contrast, 'granting amnesty to those who apologise to the victims of their crimes (or "mistakes"), while depriving the victims of legal recourse, does nothing for justice and even less for reconciliation' (Myburgh 1997).

There are other problems with the amnesty process, too. Much of the evidence provided to the commission has not been fully tested or corroborated. Assertion has often been accepted as the truth. Moreover, a differential standard of 'full disclosure' has been and will continue to be applied, it seems. For those on the 'right' side of the TRC – such as Dirk Coetzee – the requirement has readily been found to have been met. For those on the 'wrong' side – such as the murderers of the ANC and SACP leader Chris Hani – a far stricter standard is likely to be imposed. For the ANC's senior leadership the requirement of full disclosure· appears to have been abandoned entirely. The amnesty committee, in December 1997, granted amnesty on a collective basis to thirty-seven ANC leaders, including Mbeki and other cabinet ministers. No details were provided, however, of the human rights violations for which amnesty was sought or granted. The legislation according the TRC its amnesty powers makes no provision for granting amnesty either on a collective basis or without full disclosure. The TRC was told by senior counsel that the amnesty granted to the ANC leaders did not accord with legislation, and the commission resolved to review the matter. The TRC did nothing further, however, until the NP brought suit. The TRC then instituted proceedings as well, and tried to persuade the NP to withdraw its action. The NP refused to do so, stating that it did not trust the TRC to pursue the case with vigour. It noted in this regard that the chief executive officer of the TRC, Dr Biki Minuku, was himself among the thirty-seven ANC leaders granted amnesty. The matter proceeded in May 1998 to the High Court in Cape Town, and the granting of the thirty-seven amnesties was set aside as invalid. The amnesty applications in issue were then referred back to the TRC for further consideration.

The gruesome testimony that has been seared into public memory thus far is mainly that implicating the former security forces in atrocities. Few details have emerged of other gross violations of human rights – of the black policemen and councillors killed as collaborators; of women forced to drink detergent bought at white shops during consumer boycotts; of conflict between UDF and PAC supporters in Soweto in the mid-1980s; of the killing of hundreds of IFP supporters and leaders in the larger conflict in KwaZulu-Natal; of the victims of torture and other abuses in ANC camps in Angola and elsewhere; of the necklace executions of some 500 people.

If these incidents are not examined by the TRC – as seems increasingly likely to be the case – then the public will never be given an opportunity to weigh security force outrages against those perpetrated on the other side. Moreover, 'the TRC will not provide a vehicle for truth, justice, or reconciliation. More than anything else, it will emerge as a mechanism for washing the blood off the hands of South Africa's new political masters' (Myburgh 1997).

The consequences for the rule of law could also be severe:

> Whatever the political outcome of the commission's work, the effect of its *modus operandi* will be to damage our perceptions and experience of justice. Unlike the centuries-old tradition of adversarial justice (that allows both sides to be heard), the truth commission allows for only selected cases to be heard, and for people to be accused of crimes without being given the opportunity to defend themselves ... By denying accused persons the opportunity to cross-examine their accusers, and by effectively exonerating all manner of human rights violations because of the cause in whose name they were committed, the commission sets a precedent for how certain crimes could be dealt with in the future ... At worst we could see special investigative task units dealing with certain crimes and, since the precedent has now been set, special tribunals with rules of procedure different to those of courts of law set up to deal with certain cases. This is something that anyone interested in protecting the rule of law will have to watch for in the years ahead (Pereira 1997b, 7–10, 8–9).

Conclusion

Much has been gained in the transition to a democratic order, particularly in the adoption of a constitution that guarantees due process, and in the establishment of a Constitutional Court empowered to uphold fair trial. Much is also, it seems, in the process of being lost.

The criminal-justice system is crumbling under the pressures placed on it, and the impetus towards self-help is growing. There is evidence that the ANC has obstructed the administration of justice in relation to the Shell House shootings. There are disturbing indications of security-force partisanship in KwaZulu-Natal. There is reason for concern about extensive and unconstitutional surveillance. There are threats to the independence and integrity of the judicial system, especially in the introduction of a 'super' attorney general and of lay assessors in criminal trials.

The truth commission, in particular, is making a mockery of the rule of law by its selective hearing of untested evidence, by its failure to uphold the principles of *audi alteram partem* and *nemo judex in sua causa*, and by its exoneration from all liability of the perpetrators of horrific acts of violence. Also disturbing is its erosion of respect for the judiciary and its undermining of the principle of equality before the law. Through the work of the TRC, shifting standards of justice are being given a new sanctification, while the ANC and its supporters are emerging as 'more equal' than others.

Unless these disturbing trends can be arrested and reversed, there is a danger that the rule of law will be eroded in increasing measure, and that the country's important new constitutional guarantees of justice will prove commensurately ineffective.

6

R W JOHNSON

Liberal institutions under pressure: The universities

IN 1957 THE NATIONAL PARTY (NP) government, with its infamous Extension of Universities Act, stamped its own narrow-minded and already long-discredited ideology on South Africa's higher education system. Racial segregation, by then under terminal attack in the American South and long since banished elsewhere, was to be made the organizing principle. Black, coloured, and Indian students who had for years formed an important minority at the English-speaking universities of Cape Town (UCT), Natal, Rhodes, and the Witwatersrand (Wits), were henceforth to be relegated to specially established 'tribal colleges'. Indian students would attend the University of Durban-Westville, coloureds the University of the Western Cape, Zulus the University of Zululand, Xhosas the universities of Fort Hare and Transkei, and so on.

The 1957 Act was a calamitous step. It took thirty years for the system it inaugurated to collapse, first when non-white groups were allowed to attend one another's universities, and then when 'white' campuses were integrated as well. To understand how much damage the Act did, one has merely to ask what would have happened if, instead, the NP government had done nothing: a great deal of money would have been saved, and the country would have been spared the bitterness of a generation of black and coloured students who were pushed into clearly inferior (and in many cases still non-viable) institutions. Instead, a generation of graduates well educated at Wits, UCT, Natal, and Rhodes would today form a professional black middle class, determined that its children should receive the same quality higher education that it did.

In 1997 the government, led by the African National Congress (ANC), passed its own Higher Education Act. Again, the intent was to force on higher education a narrow-minded, debunked ideology. The Act not only provided for overweening central control – the Minister of Education was given power to change any institution or merge one with another, and to close down any university or technikon he or she wishes with only six months' notice – but also prescribed to every institution that it should run itself on a model of 'cooperative governance' including, notably, so-called transformation forums in which students, workers, and (often politicized) representatives of 'the community' tend to marginalize or drown altogether the voice of academics on the campus. It goes without saying that none of the world's leading universities are run in such a manner, that such strong centralized control runs counter to all notions of university autonomy and academic freedom, and that everywhere else it has been tried – in central and Latin America and, more spasmodically, in various European institutions in the wake of the 1968 protest wave – this model of worker-student power has been disastrous to academic management.

The ostensible motive for the Higher Education Act – and, indeed, the entire thrust of ANC education policy – is the need for 'transformation' of the nation's universities and technikons. (For simplicity's sake this article will confine itself to the dominant institutions within the higher education system, the universities, though much that is said here is applicable to the technikons and colleges of education as well.)

Liberal academics and students at the universities, battered by decades of turmoil and somewhat dazed by a new set of demands that often casts them as the villains, have not defended academic freedom and university autonomy with the same vigour that they showed against the old NP government. They have tended to go along with the new mantras of 'transformation', although many of those involved find it difficult to say exactly what transformation entails. More confusingly still, no one seems able to point to a university, either in South Africa or anywhere else in the world, that has been successfully 'transformed' and thus represents the final end state of this process. Even worse, those campuses where transformation activists have been longest in the ascendant are almost invariably scenes of great strife and, often, lower educational standards than would be acceptable elsewhere. These facts are far too easily dismissed. If one asks where else in the world universities are run on the lines now proposed for South Africa, one is liable to be told – with pride – that the design is unique. One is reminded of the mother who proudly points out her uniformed son in the army march-past: 'There he is – and what's more, he's the only one in step!'

Five types of university

When Margaret Thatcher was first told of Francis Fukuyama's *The end of history and the last man*, she is said to have exploded: 'End of history? Beginning of nonsense!' And certainly, if we are to avoid talking nonsense about South Africa's universities, we have to have a little history, for they have had very different starting points and records: there is no point in regarding them as all the same. There are, in fact, five different models.

English-speaking liberal universities

These universities were very much the cultural possession of English-speaking whites and enjoyed a genuinely liberal culture in which there was room for the expression of a wide variety of views. Their liberalism had its limits – although they resisted racial segregation, even their pre-apartheid history saw a fair amount of hypocrisy over hidden but real racial quotas and a less than total commitment to the liberal principles they preached. (For instance, while serving on the University of Natal SRC in the early 1960s, I was threatened with expulsion by the 'liberal' vice-chancellor, E. G. Malherbe, for refusing to organize a segregated graduation ball.) Nonetheless, their tolerance was real, and they did nothing to inhibit a flourishing left subculture which produced several generations of leaders and cadres for the SACP and a number of black graduates.

They were constructed very much on the British model, with syllabi to match. Even in the 1960s students studied more British than African history, and English literature courses typically featured not a single African author. The point, simultaneously true in Australian universities, was to retain strict compatibility with the British system, since many of the faculty had been trained there and many of the students hoped to do a further degree either in Britain or in the USA. Thus there was great emphasis on maintaining international currency for the universities' degrees and scholarship, with faculty conducting research and producing publications intended to keep them connected to an international academic world beyond South Africa.

Afrikaans universities

These were the cultural possession not just of white Afrikaners but of a National Party-Dutch Reformed Church-Broederbond nexus which stressed a notion of Christian National Education that was at sharp variance with the culture of the English-speaking campuses. The atmosphere was considerably more authoritarian and it was taken for granted that student leadership (organized in the Afrikaanse Studentebond) would accept the dictates of their NP elders. Thus the ethos closely resembled that of a high school, with SRCs playing the role of blazer-wearing prefects and strict rules governing the behaviour of women students in particular (no jeans, no smoking, no male guests, curfew hours, etc.).

This in turn reflected the defensive and anti-colonial thrust of Afrikaans culture. English-speakers, though a minority without political power, conducted themselves with the confidence of a traditional ruling class, enjoying open debate and disagreement, tolerance of division within its own ranks, and so on. Afrikaans culture, despite its ruling status, lacked confidence and retained the more closed, parochial, and unity-enforced character typical of a minority group.

While a few of the faculty of these universities might have done a degree at Leyden or Amsterdam, the overwhelming majority inhabited a cultural world bounded by South Africa. They invented a great many prizes and awards which they gave to one another, but it was a closed circle. There was no concern about the maintenance of an entrée into an international academic world, and accordingly far less stress on publication and research. Essentially, such universities were giant teaching factories – often at a very reasonable, though locally set, standard.

Fort Hare

A class of one: a black university founded within a white English-speaking missionary tradition. As a result, liberal standards of tolerance and pluralism applied and several generations of black students – including Nelson Mandela, Mangosuthu Buthelezi, Robert Mugabe, and Robert Sobukwe – benefited from an education far superior to that found in the tribal colleges. Fort Hare produced serious African intellectuals, such as Z. K. Matthews and his son Joe, and brought them into contact with the likes of Edgar Brookes. Although a hotbed of political discussion, the atmosphere at Fort Hare was tolerant and open. Some of its graduates went on to study or teach at universities in Britain and the UK, though few returned to Fort Hare to feed this international experience back into the system. The university attracted blacks from all over southern Africa and thus had no particular ethnic coloration. Although now assimilated into the category of 'historically disadvantaged universities', Fort Hare's liberal history gives it a distinctive character.

The tribal colleges

These have now been rechristened as historically disadvantaged universities (HDUs), the change in nomenclature telling a remarkable political story. When they were founded by the apartheid government in the 1960s, these universities (Turfloop; Medunsa; Venda; UWC; UDW; Zululand; Transkei; and Bophuthatswana, now the University of the North West) were vilified by the ANC and the PAC as illegitimate, ethnically defined, and third-rate institutions not worthy of the name of universities. But as the number of their graduates grew and the ANC penetration of their campuses progressed, they were redefined as victim universities and thus in the vanguard of history. Originally controlled by Broederbond and homeland administrations, some (most notably UWC and UDW) have set out to be 'universities of the Left', while Africanism of one variety or another tends to dominate in the others. Typically, the HDUs have been severely disadvantaged by lower levels of funding, chronic non-payment of fees, the poorer educational background of most of their students, and a mixture of student unrest and administrative problems: by 1998 some were clearly near the point of collapse. Ironically, while their connection to the international academic world is tenuous, an increasing number of their graduates hold important positions in government.

Distance education

The University of South Africa (UNISA) is the largest correspondence university in the world, and its success led to the creation of
the federal university of Vista, with campuses around the
country. Vista's students are almost entirely black and UNISA's
now predominantly so, though UNISA otherwise belongs to the
world of the Afrikaans universities, headquartered in Pretoria
with a largely Afrikaans faculty and administration. Only the
physical distance between faculty and students prevents the
clash between these two cultures from being even sharper than
it already is.

Transformation: some home truths

Clearly, any attempt at transformation that fails to take these
very different histories and characteristics into account will fail.
Equally, any strategy aimed at somehow melding these extremely disparate institutions into the same end-state will fail. Large
differences between these institutions will always remain and it
is even desirable that this is so, just as it is in other countries, for
a diverse mix of universities can better cater to varying needs.
But that is not to say that there is no need for change.
    Most protagonists of transformation want five things:
1   the decolonization of university culture, with courses and
    syllabi made more relevant to
    African realities;
2   more equal resources for universities, thus remedying the
    underfunding of the HDUs;
3   the admission of more black and brown students to make
    the total student body more representative of the country's
    demography;
4   the creation of a comprehensive student loan scheme
    in order to fund (3); and

5 the appointment of more black faculty and administrators,
   especially at senior level.

It is important to realize that these demands (numbers (1) and
(5) in particular) make full sense only in the context of the
historically white universities (HWUS), for there has been no
internal resistance to such changes at the HDUS for some time.
While the rhetoric of transformation may be heard at some of
the HDUS, it generally signifies a political battle of a quite
different kind[1].

Moreover, to a degree that is seldom acknowledged, there is
nothing new about such demands within the HWUS either: in
practice, most of these changes have been under way for some
time; many began even in the apartheid era. Thus courses and
syllabi have been thoroughly decolonized and reformed: in
most cases there is little left to do. The funding discrepancy
between the HDUS and others has been reduced by the simple
(and disastrous) expedient of reducing state funding for all
universities. The intake of black and coloured students has been
hugely increased and is growing year by year. A national loan
scheme has been set up. And there has been a strong push to
appoint black faculty and administrators ever since the late
1980s, with strong affirmative-action policies in place at most
HWUS.

What has stopped these processes going further than they
have has not been a lack of will so much as three practical problems. At the Afrikaans universities both the language and the
predominant culture have acted as a barrier to black entry at
both faculty and student level, though this has been overcome to
some degree by the provision of parallel English-language
courses. Secondly, the demand for a comprehensive loan scheme
must be viewed in light of the poor prevailing rate of loan-
repayment and the frequent demand by the South African
Students' Congress (SASCO) for education to be wholly free.

In practice, this means a demand for very large amounts of money which are unlikely to be paid back at all. Funds are simply lacking for this. Thirdly, affirmative-action hiring, even at pay rates far in excess of those which comparable white staff can expect to earn, has been stymied by the sheer lack of suitable candidates and the speed with which the most promising black academics are picked off by business and government.

As it is, it is by no means clear that this strategy is working. Large numbers of disadvantaged black students have been admitted, but the handicap imposed by the poor level of schooling available in black areas has doomed many of them to poor results or outright failure, this despite the effective emergence of two-track standards and such devices as 'affirmative marking'. Faculty, particularly at the HDUS, complain that many of their students are barely literate, and even at the HWUS (which tend to receive the cream of the crop) the intense efforts made at remedial education merely attest to the size of the problem. If the pressure continues for more and more under-prepared students to be admitted, the result can only be falling standards and higher rates of academic failure.

The fact is that much of the money now being spent on higher education would be far better spent on setting up a series of intermediate remedial colleges whose sole purpose would be to compensate disadvantaged students for their poor school education by intensive remedial tuition aimed at bringing them up to minimum university standard. In effect, the government is now trapped by decades of its own rhetoric ('The doors of learning shall be thrown open ...' etc.), and particularly by an all-inclusive human- rights rhetoric which has seen almost everything proclaimed as a right, including, not least, education. Inevitably, Sasco proclaims that even higher education is a right and that it is therefore wrong to charge for it, let alone to exclude from universities those who do not pay their fees.

The government does not concede this case but it is successfully bullied by it. It has formally accepted the goal of 'massifi-cation' – of hugely increasing student numbers on all campuses – not for any discernible educational or personnel-planning reason but because that is what the rising cohort of black youth demands. To this end the government has set aside ever larger sums to fund student grants and loans and continually badgers foreign donors and private business to add to the amount. Yet nothing is more destructive to the existing higher-education system than massification – which essentially means that the universities are being overrun by huge numbers of ill-educated, often ineducable, and assertive black youths who are destined to become a new generation of unemployable and often barely literate graduates. In the end, the government will have to bite the bullet, accept that the collapse of the black schools (which has worsened since 1994) makes a nonsense of massification at tertiary level, and set up remedial colleges to save what it can. The real question is how much damage it will inflict on universi-ties before it acknowledges this.

Some of the rhetoric of transformation is so heady that it is important to be quite frank about what can and cannot be ach-ieved. The example of the historical handicap of the Afrikaans universities is an important one to note in this respect. From 1948 on, National Party governments made strenuous efforts to ensure that any gap in standards between Afrikaans and English schools was closed, and they also gave heavily preferential financial treatment to the Afrikaans universities. Fifty years later, the annual university league table reflecting academic research and publication still puts the University of the Witwatersrand and the University of Cape Town at the top, Pretoria third, and the University of Natal and Rhodes University still ahead of most of their Afrikaans peers. Of course, in those years the Afrikaans universities have produced many individually brilliant scholars and researchers, but at the collective, institutional level even two generations of effort under favourable conditions have not been sufficient entirely to close the gap between the Afrikaans and English HWUS.

The lesson is that there is no reason to believe that the HDUS will be able to overcome their far greater heritage of handicap any more rapidly than Afrikaans institutions did, and something of the same is bound to apply to many individual black and brown South Africans as well. There is some discomfort in acknowledging such unpalatable truths as these, but in the long run the pain that stems from ignoring them will be greater.

The politics of transformation

The cry for transformation is not emitted in a vacuum but comes from campuses that have been the scene of intense political activity for a generation. South Africa's campuses have always been over-politicized compared to what passes as normal in most other countries, but this process of politicization reached its peak in the 1980s when both the HDUS and the English HWUS were the scene of permanent and enthusiastic mobilization behind the UDF. The fact that the ANC, the PAC, and the South African Communist Party (SACP) were banned meant that the student movement, like the trade union movement, achieved a heightened significance as a de facto surrogate, especially since campuses were able to afford effective bases to these banned movements. Many of the student activists forged in this atmosphere went on to attain high office in the government, the ANC, non-governmental organizations (NGOS), and elsewhere.

The unbanning of the ANC, the PAC, and the SACP robbed student politics of much of its significance at a stroke. The parties set up their own offices and had no further need of a campus base or of surrogates. But this period left behind an aura of excitement and drama, as well as the memory of the extraordinary upward mobility achieved by the earlier generation of activists. The result today is a class of 'struggle wannabes', determined to enjoy the adrenalin of the 'struggle', this time for an impossible-to-define, indeed almost metaphysical, transformation. What adds bite to this demand is the fact that radical black students in the 1980s, despite being a minority on campus, found that over and over again they were able to win their point by dint of their 'legitimacy' and by the hard-edged politics of mobilization – strikes, littering campaigns, sit-ins, damage to property, and physical intimidation. In the end, this worked because campus authorities quailed at the thought of the confrontation required to defeat 'legitimate' minorities willing to use such methods.

Today's radicals, knowing the weakness of the authorities, naturally deploy the same methods, usually with similar success.

What they have realized is that by such means a minority can exercise majority power – provided it can maintain a quasi-permanent state of mobilization. But if mobilization is to be permanent, then it cannot be for practical, realizable goals – for these would be quickly conceded. It has to be for impossible objectives ('pass one, pass all' or 'no exclusions no matter what').

This impossibilism is often quite nakedly apparent, as in SASCO's campaign against the Report of the National Commission on Higher Education in early 1996, when SASCO demanded that the universities support their demand for the report to be withdrawn – before it had even appeared and before they knew its contents. The quest for a 'transformation' that no one can quite define – the pot of gold at rainbow's end – fits perfectly into impossibilist politics.

The politics of permanent mobilization

This politics of permanent mobilization in turn feeds on several sources. The first is strictly material. Education, particularly a university degree, is seen as a pathway to a good job and thus to middle-class status. Once admitted to a university, many black students feel that such an outcome is more or less guaranteed, and that that is the meaning of liberation – that their time has come. Inevitably, a strong sense of entitlement overwhelms any notion that a degree is conditional on the fulfillment of various academic tasks and tests. A university administration that attempts to insist on the validity of those tasks and tests is thus affronting a potent force: hence, too, the demands for 'no exclusions', 'pass one, pass all', and so on. The point to be grasped here is that while the struggle thus unleashed is fought under the slogans of the radical left, the battle is actually one for the 'right' to a middle-class status and income.

Secondly, campus battles are to some extent being orchestrated. In the early 1990s, NEHAWU (the National Educational, Health, and Allied Workers Union), under outspokenly communist leadership, made its appearance on campuses and rapidly enrolled many manual and administrative workers, almost immediately making itself a force to be reckoned with. At the same time, SASCO – which gets its funds from the Congress of South African Trade Unions (COSATU), the whole of whose top leadership belongs to the Communist Party – has clearly come under strong SACP influence, to the point where SASCO has been helping communist youth organizations to get started on campuses in potential opposition to the ANC Youth League. The strong SACP influence within both NEHawu and SASCO means that the SACP is in a strong position to push its own agenda on campuses. It is important to realize that the implicit current model being imposed on higher education – all-out 'transformation' with worker-student control – has been supplied by the SACP, which is preoccupied with using the universities to forge the new organic intelligentsia which will carry the national democratic revolution through to its second, socialist phase. It is far from clear exactly how the SACP's higher education strategy works in detail, but it should be recognized that its influence with NEHAWU, SASCO, and academics who are in or close to the party has given it enormous leverage on many campuses. In 1997 this alliance

was able to select one of its own, Dr Colin Bundy, as the new
vice-chancellor of the University of the Witwatersrand, South
Africa's largest English-speaking university with a proud liberal
tradition. Perhaps nothing symbolized this changing of the guard
better than Dr Bundy's cheeful admission that at his previous
university he had been in the habit of addressing all students as
'comrade'.

Thirdly, the political struggle at universities is effectively
encouraged by the general over-politicization of the campus
and by the fact that many educational 'progressives' see that
politicization as normal or are ideologically still convinced that
angry students are, in some hard-to-define way, the representatives of the masses, of legitimacy, and of the struggle. On top of
that, they are plain scared of taking them on. This sort of thinking was perfectly reflected in the recommendation of the government's National Commission on Higher Education (mirrored
in the Higher Education Act) that the roles appropriate to the
student-worker-led transformation forums should include:

- involvement in selecting candidates for top management
  positions;
- identifying and agreeing upon problem areas to be addressed;
- interpreting the new national policy framework;
- setting an agenda for change;
- providing a mediating forum;
- participating in restructuring governance structures;
- developing and negotiating a code of conduct; and
- monitoring and assessing change.

In other words, such forums can do whatever they want. And
whereas university administrators have to juggle financial pressures versus faculty demands versus policy pressures versus
donor requirements and a host of other factors, these forums
will be free simply to opine away. Such forums have no duties,
no competing pressures to reconcile – they have, in the famous

phrase, power without responsibility. As such, they are a recipe for certain trouble.

But the problem goes further than that. Students and campus unions (read: SASCO and NEHAWU) are also represented on Senates, so that there can be no decision-making body in the university where they are not present. SASCO will run the SRC, sit in the forums, on Senate, on Council, on a new national Higher Education Forum – and on just about everything else. There runs through such recommendations the belief that campuses are and must always remain theatres of intense political activity. Students will have to act as full-time politicians, playing endless representative roles, becoming, as it were, professional 'stakeholders'. The notion that students are at university essentially to study and that SASCO activists are typically among the academically weakest students on the campus, wholly unable to spare the time for such full-time political careers, is simply foreign to such conceptions. It is more or less bound to happen that such activists will fail their exams, will become candidates for exclusion, will become the rallying point for further 'no exclusion' struggles, and so on and on ... Somewhat similar points may be made about the gardeners, cleaners, cooks, and clerical staff organized in NEHAWU.

The false microcosm

Underlying these political struggles is a conception to which Deputy President Thabo Mbeki gave voice in an address to the University of Natal in Durban in 1996. The transformation of universities was important, he said, because the university was 'a microcosm of the wider society'. This is, of course, quite untrue: in no country are universities really representative of the whole society – the children of the middle classes were as over-represented at Sussex, where Mbeki studied, as they are at Wits or UCT. The faculty represent a peculiar and rather bohemian section of the middle class themselves, while campus workers are equally atypical of the working class as a whole. Universities are, indeed, rather odd and special places – large villages dedicated to a single set of activities with the emphasis on unforced compliance by thousands – sometimes tens of thousands – of young men and women co-existing closely in a way they would never be expected to at home, on the factory floor, or anywhere else.

Nonetheless, Mbeki's mistake is a common one, widely shared by activists who, transparently, believe that just as we now have a black president and government, so this change must be replicated on every campus. This symbolic identification lends further intensity to campus struggles – it allows activists to see themselves as carrying through the struggles of 1990–1994. This is the reason SASCO activists at both Wits and Pretoria at first objected on principle to the idea of the vice-chancellorship going to a white candidate and attempted to prevent a white candidate from standing at all at Wits. (Ironically, in the end the only candidate acceptable to SASCO and NEHAWU proved to be white.) The same reasoning gives a special importance to the appointments to other senior administrative posts – the black campus president must, so to speak, be seen to be backed by a black cabinet. The argument, the tactics, the objectives are all racial, even racist. So strong is this identification that if transformation means any one thing, it is this. Naturally, this interpretation is gleefully encouraged by the handful of possible candidates for such affirmative-action appointments.

The ancillary notion is that demography equals legitimacy. South Africa's long denial of majority rule gives this equation its special force, but in the university context it is peculiar. At the University of the Western Cape, for example, black students, in the era when they were still a minority on that campus, attempted to justify their dominance of the SRC by arguing that they enjoyed legitimacy because there was a black majority in South Africa. Their coloured opponents sought to justify their own position by arguing that while that might be true, coloureds were the true bearers of legitimacy in the Western Cape because there they had the demographic majority. The one thing on which there was agreement – that universities were all about demography – is actually quite foreign to the functions and raison d'être of a university.

The politics of cultural capture

This last argument gives pause for thought, however. While it may be phrased in terms of demographics, the real crux of the matter is that certain campuses are perceived by certain population groups as their cultural possessions. Nelson Mandela reportedly told black intellectuals that they must not push their claims too hard at UWC: Africans had many universities but UWC was the only coloured university. As so often, the President showed a shrewder grasp of underlying ethnic realities than his followers. For the fact is that Afrikaners see Stellenbosch as 'their' university just as English-speaking whites see UCT as 'theirs'. These cultural possessions are precious. Father and mother, son and daughter went there; these institutions are worth fighting for.

And a fight it is. For what we are witnessing is the politics of cultural capture – and this is bitter stuff. In the case of Wits, for example, by pressing for affirmative-action appointments and a large increase in black student numbers, claiming that only an all-black SRC is 'legitimate', and demanding no exclusions, the SASCO-NEHAWU alliance is demanding that Wits be taken away from its white, English-speaking constituency and turned into a giant Turfloop. This is why, in white upper-middle-class circles of Johannesburg, one can hear that Wits is 'gone', that it is 'lost'; this is the bitter commentary of cultural dispossession. Equally, statements by black radicals that it is not 'acceptable' that Stellenbosch should have a white Afrikaner as rector and that there must be no bias towards the Afrikaans language are the prolegomena of cultural capture and are bitterly understood as such. What is going on is a struggle for the cultural capture of one campus after another. Thus far only one group has irretrievably lost – UDW has entirely ceased to be an Indian university at student level, though even there a desperate rearguard action is being waged by Indian workers in the university administration, albeit under a radical flag.

It is this struggle for cultural capture that has made the battle of the campuses so fierce. Given the long history of group struggle in South Africa and the tremendous sensitivities that exist over the survival of different cultures and languages, it is tempting to call for a degree of cultural protectionism – to say that Stellenbosch must be left as an Afrikaans-medium university, that UWC should be seen as a predominantly coloured campus, and so on. But this doesn't solve the problem – there are so many more Afrikaans-medium universities than can be justified by the fifteen per cent of the population to whom this is a first language, and it hardly deals with the questions faced by English-speaking HWUS.

The destruction of the African university

The real context for any discussion of the future of South Africa's universities has to be the destruction of universities elsewhere in Africa. Wherever one looks on the continent one can see the wreckage of once fine institutions – at Makerere (Uganda), Algiers, Lusaka, Kinshasa, Accra, Ibadan, Nairobi, Dar es Salaam, Addis Ababa: it is a terrible roll call. These universities have been ruined by a combination of government interference, over-politicization, funding cuts, massification, and often quite dramatic maladministration. All these factors may now be found in South African education too, and anyone who is mindful of what has happened in countries to the north cannot but worry that the first democratic government could well preside over a similar collapse.

Already many of the HDUs are in a state of such turmoil and delapidation that they are universities in name only, and the contagion clearly threatens to spread to a number of other institutions too. With the best will in the world it is impossible to prevent standards from falling if these institutions are inundated by large numbers of semi-literate students and their administration is paralysed by continuous disturbances, funding cuts, and the blocking power of highly politicized worker-student coalitions.

This crisis is undeniably real, and it makes the politics both of cultural capture and of cultural protectionism seem almost petty. For what is at stake in South Africa is enormously greater than was the case in Ghana or Uganda. The collapse of universities there was a tragedy for those societies, robbing them of the possibility of institutional renewal, but at the end of the day the economies of those two countries depend on a large subsistence sector plus the cultivation of cocoa and coffee cash crops – activities that continue irrespective of what happens on a university campus. South Africa's situation is very different. With its large industrial economy, growing service sector, high-tech agriculture, and modern infrastructure, the country relies utterly on a continuous supply of well-educated graduates. Already the major HWUs are dangerously dependent on a group of middle-aged white academics who will vanish from those institutions before long and who are most unlikely to be easily replaced by teachers of similar quality: their low salaries, difficult conditions of work, and a dearth of suitable black replacements more or less guarantee that. That is, even if government policy were not so damaging to universities as it is, there would be a real danger of institutional degradation in the next decade.

Standing up for the liberal ideal of the university runs counter to strong currents in South African society, particularly in the curious period of cultural revolution through which it is currently passing. To take an obvious example, it is close to accepted parlance on many campuses that white males should be the least-considered group for jobs, student places, awards, and so on. But if we really mean what we say about wanting to build a non-racist, non-sexist society – and if we want to remain true to the liberal university ideal that all that matters is academic study, research, and achievement – then the corollary is that a white male can be as good or as bad as anyone else. It cannot be right to treat white males as a pariah group, particularly when one is looking at a university system in which this group still accounts for the bulk of the faculty. No one doubts that it is important to have more black and women professors, administrators, technical staff, and students – but if we make racial or gender targets our main objective we are not only undermining the whole ideal of what a university is, but we could also be undermining the key functions such institutions have to play.

That is to say, the ANC-led government will soon be forced to choose whether it really wishes to impose a set of political, ideological, and parochially racial criteria on higher education. If it does, it will most assuredly destroy its universities at horrendous cost to the country's economy and future. Alternatively, it may realize in time that universities, to be worthy of the name and to do their job properly, have to be intrinsically free and meritocratic institutions, best left alone by government, best governed if their administrators and academics have the decisive say in how they are run, and producing the best results if race, colour, religion, and political affiliation all come far behind the natural hierarchy of intellect and academic achievement. If only for functional, economic reasons, in other words, the government may ultimately have to allow the universities to be run as the liberal institutions they should always have been in any case.

7

CHARLES VAN ONSELEN

Closer to home: student unrest and the welfare function

SOUTH AFRICA'S TERTIARY education institutions are plagued
with apparently endless unrest. This constitutes a major crisis,
not only for those institutions but for the country as a whole:
we cannot do without properly functioning universities and
technikons.

But the phenomenon is also a puzzle. The government quite
clearly believes that while student struggles had a part to play in
the broader liberation struggle of the 1980s, in the face of continuing unrest and campus trashing it is inclined to say, 'It's time to
stop such antics now – we must get on and build the country'.
Patently, this has no effect.

There is, in fact, a real question mark over why student unrest
continues. No doubt the causes are many and complex. What we
need, I would suggest, is a new way of seeing this phenomenon.
Let us first examine the conventional political analysis of contemporary student unrest. Let us then revisit the same phenomenon
from a slightly different historical and sociological perspective
to see whether this does not offer us another 'way of seeing' and
understanding contemporary student behaviour, which often
appears as mindlessly violent as it is poorly directed.

Massification: wave of the future?

The conventional wisdom – which I think holds sway in government circles, in most non-governmental organizations, many development agencies, and among left-of-centre academics and sections of the English press – is that the problems currently experienced in the South African tertiary education sector are, in the main, a direct consequence of our racially tortured past.

To overcome the inequities caused by apartheid policies, there is a need, first, for financial redress – redirecting resources away from the privileged 'historically white universities' to the much neglected 'historically black universities'. Secondly, the state must help right the historic wrongs of Bantu education by rapidly increasing access to an integrated system of tertiary institutions which are themselves simultaneously developing policies to overcome the deficiencies of an appalling secondary-school system.

The daunting quantitative dimensions of this task are outlined in the government's 1996 green paper on higher education transformation:

> While it endorses the major elements in the case [made by the 1995 National Commission for Higher Education] for a 'massification' of higher education, the ministry believes that the report's suggestion that the participation rate of the 20- to 24-year cohort should be increased from 21% to 30% over the next ten years (a rise in student numbers from about 800 000 to about 1 500 000 in 2005) should be treated as provisional until more detailed demographic and labour market analyses are available.

In addition to the call for the so-called 'massification' of tertiary education, there is also widespread agreement that the sector should become more firmly rooted in the social, economic, and political realities of the continent. In order to do so, institutions of higher learning must demonstrate greater cultural sensitivity by paying closer attention to the issue of 'Africanization', which should, in turn, be coupled with a thorough-going reform of curricula and syllabi.

Furthermore, existing structures of governance that were shaped by the old and discredited order need to make way for 'models of cooperative governance' which would not only seek to involve a wider range of stakeholders in tertiary education, but by so doing, would also deepen and strengthen democratic practice at every level of the system. All these elements taken together constitute what in the current debate is characterized quite correctly as the process of 'transformation' in higher learning.

At first blush, this programme of transformation – which reflects some undeniable political, social, and cultural forces at work in contemporary society – has more in it to laud than to lament. It is precisely because of these underlying realities that most of us have come to adopt its ultimate goal as a broadly desirable educational outcome, and confined our criticism to the means that are used to achieve it. But even the public criticism that does emerge is often muted – more in sorrow than in anger – precisely because much of the activity is directed towards a desirable educational outcome.

Thus, most of the criticism is based on the assumption that what we are currently confronted with is simply a local manifestation of age-old methods of student protest and riot, and that if it were not for the impatience of youth and a lamentable shortfall in state financial resources, the instability in South African tertiary education would probably fall within broadly acceptable parameters.

Students, migrancy, and the extended family

We may need to abandon conventional wisdom, however, and try to see the problem in a slightly diverent way. In particular we have to examine the following three propositions, which flow from adopting a slightly longer-term historical and sociological perspective and a much closer analysis of the forms of supposedly 'anti-social' behaviour that current student unrest takes:

1 that what we are currently witnessing is not so much a classical manifestation of 'student unrest' released by unrealistic expectations coming in the wake of a largely peaceful and successful political revolution, but an insistent plea for the alleviation of acute rural (and urban) poverty and distress via a youth cohort which is acutely aware of its responsibilities to the extended family, and which senses that it can most readily articulate its demands in educational rather than social terms;

2 that in accommodating economic demands which seem to come from ordinary students struggling to survive in the tertiary sector, but which in reality derive more from a youth cohort deeply scarred by the ravages of apartheid schooling and poverty, the current government is in danger of confusing its welfare and educational responsibilities to the detriment of both;

3 that seen in this light, the current disturbances in the tertiary education sector are both less irrational and less 'anti-social' than they seem; nevertheless, the short-term and shortsighted accommodation of problems that manifest themselves primarily as 'student' demands might also hold longer-term political and even potentially revolutionary consequences for society as a whole.

These propositions are perhaps easier to accept once we place them in their broader historical and sociological context. In this regard there are two points which South Africans do not reflect on often enough when they debate economic development and social dislocation.

The first of these has to do with the nature of the industrial revolution that we are still experiencing: we hardly qualify as an industrialized nation, let alone as a 'post-industrial' one. The South African industrial revolution – only some 135 years old and unlike that of Europe, for instance – is taking place in a society that has not passed through a protracted feudal period. Feudalism produced some of the political, social, and cognitive structures that served as precursors to industrialization elsewhere. But the South African industrial revolution, which was precipitated by primary industry in a colonial context, was built on a foundation of communally held African values which – for better or worse – have long been underwritten by the system of migratory labour.

An unintended consequence of this has been to prolong notions of social commitment to and responsibility for the extended black family, and to frustrate the emergence of the smaller and more self-contained social units that characterize modern first-world economies.

Simply put, most of our planners – including those in the field of tertiary education – simply do not take sufficient cognizance of the fact that in South Africa we are more often dealing with extended black families than with the nuclear or single-parent families that form the social building blocks of most contemporary first-world economies. Black South Africans – including most, but admittedly not all young black South African students – are extremely serious about their social and economic commitments to their grandparents, their parents, and their siblings.

The youth avalanche

It is, moreover, a far more central fact than is often realized that the South African population as a whole includes an unusually large number of young people. Statistics show that in 1993 over 37 per cent of our population was younger than fourteen years of age, and it may be reasonably safely assumed that nearly 50 per cent of our population is under twenty years of age.

When these two facts – the preponderance of young people, and their social commitment to the extended family – are inserted into a context of acute rural poverty, low economic growth, an unemployment rate of more than 35 per cent, large-scale under-employment, and a rapidly changing education system, there are consequences which extend well beyond the mere quantitative dimensions envisaged in the proposed 'massification' of tertiary education. Some of these problems are already becoming evident in many institutions of higher learning.

Viewed from this perspective, it becomes easier to understand why many young black South Africans see access to a college of education, a technikon, or a university as assuming an importance that far transcends the intrinsic value of a tertiary education qualification per se, and why many are willing literally to fight for the right to enter and stay in the sector regardless of how well or how badly they have been prepared for it by their secondary schooling.

For thousands of black South Africans, access to tertiary education has become the difference between having a roof over their heads and being homeless, between being fed for a part of the year or starving, between owning some clothing or being decked out in rags, and between meeting their social commitments by sending home small amounts of cash to their families, or joining the ranks of the unemployed.

In the absence of universal conscription to the armed forces, significant youth employment schemes, or the dole, the tertiary education sector becomes, in effect, a sponge which the state – perhaps unwittingly – uses to absorb thousands of unemployed youth who still seethe with a revolutionary anger that derives from the injustices of the recent past.

Higher education's welfare function

The other side of this rather depressing picture is that over the past decade our universities, technikons, and colleges of education have had to earmark an ever-increasing proportion of their financial resources – which are in any case declining in real terms – for financial aid to needy African students.

These intra-institutional budgetary re-allocations to accommodate an almost insatiable demand for bursaries and loans have produced a set of highly visible outcomes.

Tertiary education institutions first of all cut back on their building and maintenance programmes. This results in physical decay, which produces an environment characterized by filth and neglect – conditions that do nothing to diminish the propensity to riot. The next part of the budget to absorb cutbacks is research, which in the hierarchy of educational needs is perceived by some to be elitist and certainly less important than undergraduate instruction. Finally, the instruction budget itself is cut back. The consequence is a worsening of staff-student ratios, which in turn results in a further falling-off in educational performance, higher failure rates, a renewed set of complaints about culturally inappropriate or insensitive teaching, the need to use only basic English, and the demand to 'Africanize' ever more rapidly.

The physical decay on most South African campuses is very visible, and those who doubt it may quickly enlighten themselves by touring their nearest tertiary institutions. What is less visible is the extent to which this process of earmarking funds for undergraduate bursaries and loans, coupled with declining state subsidies, has eroded the core activities – research and teaching – at some leading universities.

I give but two examples. Even at two of our most prestigious 'historically white' universities, the amount of funds devoted to bursaries and loans over the past five years has outstripped the amounts allocated to research. At Wits, for example, the research budget for 1996 was R9 124 000, while R12 787 060 was allocated to bursaries and loans. In addition, the allocation to Wits students from the National Student Financial Aid Scheme amounted to R13 138 128.

Imperceptibly, we are thus turning many of our universities, technikons, and colleges of education into institutions with a fundamental responsibility for accommodating, feeding, clothing, and transporting – as opposed to simply educating – some of the nation's poorest and most underprivileged young citizens.

The point comes home even more starkly when it is learned that at one university in the Western Cape the annual cost of catering, in residences, already exceeds the university's entire research budget. At Wits things have not yet reached that point, but the catering budget in residences now stands at R6 670 000 (much of which is funded through the university's financial aid scheme since many of the students living in catering residences are on financial aid), which is already over two-thirds of the university's research budget.

It maybe argued, of course, that the increasing assumption of a quasi-welfare role by tertiary education institutions, although not desirable in itself, at least helps dedicated, committed, and focused students to see through their programmes of instruction without jeopardizing their performance or physical well-being. This is often the case, but not nearly often enough.

There is already a significant amount of qualitative if not quantitative data which shows that many hard-pressed black undergraduates divert large proportions of their loans and bursaries to the maintenance of their extended families. They do this by foregoing either their own meals or other needs so that they can make cash remittances to their extended families – a sort of ghostly parody of the migrant labour system in which financial responsibilities devolve upon the village youth rather than upon the village men.

In short, economic necessity dictates that too many of our students from underprivileged backgrounds use bursaries and loans that emanate from either the public or the private sector for purposes other than education.

The reality: closer to home

A few illustrative examples should suffice. The dean of students at Wits has reported that in dealing with the cases of students facing 'financial exclusion', approximately one in four admits in interview that part of his or her bursary has been spent on meeting social commitments at home. Since students know that such expenditure might be regarded as illegitimate, the true figure is certainly not lower than this and could be higher.

Moreover, the dean has reported that similar trends are evident in the rollover loan programme, which gives financial aid to those who have met the minimum requirements to avoid academic exclusion but cannot re-register because of outstanding account balances. Between 1993 and 1997 both the number of students and the amounts involved more than doubled. Many students admitted that despite such help and part-time employment, they still could not re-register for the next year because they had to meet financial obligations at home.

Thus in a roundabout way students were borrowing from the university – effectively their banker at preferential rates of credit – to support families at home. Sometimes this happens simply because students are holders of ready cash at opportune moments and are asked to lend to family members – and later such 'loans' prove to be unrepayable.

But the dean of students has also reported that at least one in three of the students he interviews claims that they cannot leave residence because they cannot now accept going back to live in small rooms which they share with multiple siblings. This is particularly true of students in self-catering units. It is not just that to such students their residence room is their home: they are also relieving pressure on their family's housing and often providing accommodation for family members arriving in Johannesburg to look for work.

Bread-and-butter issues such as bursaries

One might add two further illustrative examples, one drawn from the realm of personal experience and close to home, and the other structural, drawn from the *National teacher education audit* (a report for the department of education sponsored by the Danish International Development Agency in 1995).

The new vice-chancellor of the University of Cape Town, Professor Mamphela Ramphele, addressing the Ernest Oppenheimer Memorial Trust last year, began her talk by noting that she had been the recipient of an Ernest Oppenheimer Memorial Award while she was a student at the Natal Medical School during the period 1968 to 1972. There can be no doubt about Ramphele's ability to focus on her studies, and hers is an undoubted success story. But she also went on to say:

> That bursary award made it possible for me to support
> my mother and siblings during the very difficult period
> following my father's death in 1967. It was a modest
> amount by today's standards, but it made an enormous
> difference to my life and that of my widowed mother.
> (Ramphele 1996)

A clearer example of the hidden linkage between bursary use and rural poverty would be hard to find.

Secondly, Rosamund Jaff, Michael Rice, Jane Hofmeyr, and Graham Hall, authors of the *National education teacher audit*, detected some of the horrid welfare-bursary-alienation malaise that plagues many colleges of education, which are often situated in remote rural areas beset by high unemployment rates, when they noted:

> The most disturbing finding in the audit of the college sector was the large proportion of students who are not committed to teaching and merely want a tertiary qualification as a means to further study or a job outside teaching ... Generally, students showed little awareness of and interest in wider educational and societal issues outside political flash points and bread and butter issues such as bursaries. (Jaff et al. 1995, 236)

It would seem from this and other evidence that important parts of the education sector have already come to assume as much of a quasi-welfare as an educational role in our low-growth economy.

Put another way, it would seem that for many of our poorest and least-prepared undergraduate students, the short-term economic imperative of gaining entry into the post-apartheid tertiary education sector has become at least as important as the longer-term educational objective. Moreover, this process is often most advanced in the least developed parts of our tertiary education system – in our 'historically black' universities, technikons, and colleges.

The economic imperative

Once this is conceded, it becomes easier to understand student behaviour and militancy. Admission to or exclusion from an institution of higher learning often means – quite literally – the difference between life and death for the poorest of poor black students and their families. Academic progress alone ensures continued access to a bursary or a loan and, like the removal or reduction of the dole in more developed societies, has consequences that extend well beyond the confines of certification or graduation.

Seen from this perspective, it is easier to understand why the process of student admission and re-admission is so often accompanied by violence, why there is a populist tendency to exert pressure downward on academic standards (pass one, pass all), and why all exclusionary processes – but more especially those involving so-called 'financial exclusions' – are vulnerable to challenge by riot.

Nor is it surprising that amidst so much apparently mindless student rioting, canteens and kitchens should become such frequent and specific objects of attack and looting: what one is seeing is the spectre of medieval bread riots rather than modern manifestations of student unrest.

In these struggles one hears much of the 'worker-student alliance' on campus, which generally means a concerted NEHAWU-SASCO front (the National Educational, Health, and Allied Workers' Union, and the South African Students' Congress). This is now accepted as an ordinary feature of campus life when in fact it is not: try getting trade unions and student associations to concert in this way on, say, British or American campuses and you will see that such alliances are not unproblematic.

But in South Africa, campus cleaners, cooks, security guards, janitors, and lab assistants are often older-generation migrants to the city, coming from the same rural and small-town communities that their slightly younger brothers, sisters, and cousins have come from to enrol as students. One can often find a real sociological basis for such alliances in precisely the same considerations of migrancy and the extended family that do much to explain the character of campus struggles.

The quasi-welfare function of the tertiary sector and the hidden class struggle of our most economically deprived citizens and voters continues to be poorly understood by the state and an increasingly urbanized middle-class public. In this context, the government's proposal to give priority to the 'massification' of tertiary education over a better integrated but significantly diverse system of higher learning is alarming. As the French and many other governments in Europe discovered to their cost in 1968, systems of tertiary education that neglect their core functions of teaching and research can, in the fullness of time, come to exact an awful price from society.

The government urgently needs to think again about how it intends to incorporate its newly enfranchised, unsettled, and predominantly youthful population. In particular, it needs to give careful thought as to where it wishes to draw the line between the right of access to tertiary education for adequately prepared scholars, and the legitimate social welfare needs of its rural (and urban) poor. Failure to distinguish clearly between these competing demands could bring about a dramatic increase in the number of poorly educated, unemployed graduates in an economy characterized by a high degree of unionization and low economic growth. It is a mixture that has created a painful history of political instability in, among other places, post-colonial West Africa.

If one takes such factors into account, campus disputes can no longer be reduced to a question of whether one is for or against 'transformation', or indeed for or against any of the above processes. We have to understand things as they really are if we are to have any chance of accommodating or managing – let alone changing – them.

8

KEN OWEN

Liberal institutions under pressure: The press

OF ALL THE LIBERAL institutions in South Africa that engaged in some sort of struggle against apartheid, the English-language newspapers and the journalists who worked for them were probably the most self-congratulatory. They saw themselves as shock troopers in 'The Struggle', on the front lines of one of the great moral battles of the twentieth century, and it did not matter that few of them actually did much in it.

Liberal parliamentarians like Frederik van Zyl Slabbert or Alex Boraine might fall into doubt and abandon the parliamentary arena; the Progressive Party, like the Liberal Party before it, might agonize about the wisdom of open support for a universal fran-chise; the Bar might be split between advocates like Sydney Kentridge who spurned appointment to the Bench, and those like John Didcott who made the more difficult moral decision to administer bad law with good intent; the universities might drift into political correctness and suppression of speech; the Black Sash and the Institute of Race Relations might be torn by internal strife as the struggle continued from decade to decade; but the English-language press, by and large, did not waver in its right-mindedness: it was in the vanguard, and it was free of doubt.

So it came as a special shock for journalists of what was called 'the opposition press' to discover, soon after liberation, that

public hostility towards them was more widespread and more
intense than they had imagined, and that it extended to key
elites whose support was necessary to the survival and functioning of a free press.

Prominent among these elites were the judges who, led by the
Chief Justice, slid easily into the role of censors, subjecting
newspapers to prior restraint – in effect, forbidding publication
– in a series of cases. The tone was set in the notorious Sage case
in which Mr Justice Corbett, apparently taking his cue from a
British case involving Queen Victoria's private letters, forbade
publication of information obtained from stolen documents;
gentlemen, he sniffed, did not read other people's mail. Anyway,
he argued insultingly, newspaper editors (unlike judges presumably) could not be expected to distinguish the public interest
from their own. Coming from the Chief Justice, it was perhaps
the most damaging comment ever made about the South African
press.

And it was surely no accident that soon afterwards Mr Justice
Gustav Hoexter, who had come to prominence in the 1950s as
one of the lawyers prosecuting Nelson Mandela, delivered a
landmark opinion, as brilliant as it was devastating, that effectively restated and confirmed the illiberal South African common
law on the press. Information, it transpired, was not necessarily
to be viewed as a public good, and often it was a private asset. In
the eyes of the courts, it seemed, the reputation of a gentleman
ranked higher than the crude processes of a modern popular
democracy. The attitude contrasted starkly with that in Australia
where the judges of the higher courts were using ingenuity and
wit to stretch the definition of free speech in preparation for the
democratic twenty-first century.

This made a depressing start to the new era. It also augured ill
for the future. Whatever the deficiencies of the South African
press – and they were many – the newspapers did keep South
Africa and the world broadly informed of the progression of

apartheid; no South African could say afterwards, like Germans of Nazism, that 'we didn't know'. Neither judges nor parliamentarians, both classes possessed of greater freedom to speak out than the newspapers, did nearly as much to tear away the mask of apartheid as had the press. And indeed, that service to the nation had been achieved, very often, by reading other people's mail, by using stolen documents, and by trashing private reputations. The latest interpretations of the law, had they been faithfully enforced under apartheid, might well have had a more inhibiting effect on the press than many of the cruder restrictions imposed by the National Party (NP) government.

Nor, after liberation, did the new constitution-makers take a much more benign view than the judges. They did, it is true, lay the basis for greater press freedom than the country had ever known, but they baulked at entrenching free speech or giving it anything like the weight which it enjoys under the First Amendment of the American constitution. They did not trust either the newspapers or the idea of free speech, so they brushed aside the modest request of the Conference of Editors for full entrenchment of free speech, and instead assigned to that right a lesser status and a lesser protection than they gave to other rights. In effect, they put into the hands of legislators and judges the power to decide how much freedom would be 'reasonable' in the new democracy. This reluctance to relinquish control of discourse was, given the centrality of free speech to both democracy and to the wider search for truth, revealingly ominous.

For the time being, it hardly matters; we have a greater degree of press freedom than Britain. But it rests insecurely: the temper of the times, the interests of politicians, and the prejudices of judges might at any stage be brought to bear on the definition of 'reasonableness', and cause the noose to tighten. The constitution, like a broken umbrella, may be found to suffice only when it is not needed.

There have been other shocks, some major, some minor.

Among the minor shocks was the realization, quickly driven home by people like Thami Mazwai and Jon Qwelane, that so-called 'liberals' were thoroughly detested by black journalists who had spent the apartheid years at the nether end of the newsrooms, both patronized and distrusted. The brunt of the criticism was directed at the former Argus company, whose editors had never thought to define themselves as liberals, but South African Associated Newspapers (saan), later Times Media Limited (tml), did not escape. The debate quickly degenerated into a listing of the petty grievances of former staff members, but some editors were drawn into demeaning and pitiful protestations of their own political correctness. During the apartheid era the status of editors had steadily declined; the end of apartheid saw that status all but demolished. Even journalists began to put forward other ways of directing a newspaper, such as 'representative' editorial boards or committees.

The attack on past editors had a thinly disguised, if unadmitted, agenda: it was an attempt, generally successful, to disqualify liberal journalists (with the word 'liberal' serving often as a racial code term for 'whites') from claiming the top jobs in the newspapers of the new society. The message was plain enough: 'mainstream' journalism would in future be the province of apartheid's erstwhile underclasses. Liberation had brought both a shift of status and a chance to settle old scores, and the Truth Commission offered a handy instrument. Interestingly, there was no attempt to investigate the record of past 'liberal' parliamentarians, whose access to information and freedom to speak out had always exceeded the powers of the press, though there was some guarded discussion of the role of judges who had enforced apartheid law and who, like MPs, had made little use of their privileged position to speak out against apartheid.

These double standards, too, were revealingly ominous. More serious, and less self-serving, was the criticism by Deputy President Thabo Mbeki that the newspapers failed as a medium

of public information. In particular, they failed to give their
readers a fair assessment of the policies, intentions, and actions
of the new government. Total war against the Nationalists was
understandable, and indeed necessary; but was total war appropriate when the government was popularly elected and carrying
out the will of the people? Confused and petulant, the newspapers fell back on learned responses, complaining of an attack on
press freedom; in fact, it was more serious. It was an attack on
the pretensions of the press.

Mbeki had touched a raw nerve. What he was saying, of course,
was that the press was failing its role as the fourth estate, and this
criticism was surely justified. The level of journalism was, by the
end of apartheid, quite appalling. As the returned exiles were quick
to note, the English-language press especially had fallen into decay,
becoming steadily shabbier, less reliable, and more gimmicky as
its performance fell. For decades, the 'fight against apartheid'
had served as a justification for every kind of malpractice, including reckless use of 'sources', manufactured 'quotes', refusal to
hear the other side if that side was politically hostile (whether
the African National Congress (ANC) or the NP), and so forth.
Gradually, as the disciplines of good journalism decayed, the
journalism itself decayed. Perhaps not everybody would agree
that the alternative newspapers that sprang up in the last decade
of apartheid had outperformed the mainstream newspapers as
those alternative newspapers themselves claimed, but they had
shown up deficiencies in the mainstream press, and those
deficiencies centred not on lack of moral conviction, but on lack
of competence. The mainstream newspapers were simply not up
to the job.

By the 1990s there was hardly a public figure who, in private
conversation, did not have some horror story to tell of an ignorant, incompetent, unprepared reporter asking for child's guidance on some matter of public concern, and then failing to grasp
or report that guidance. There was hardly a public figure who

had not been misreported, recklessly if not maliciously. Behind that experience lay an industry in disarray, falling apart. For example, when SAAN (later TML) moved to a new building, nobody thought what to do about the library. In the confusion that followed, some vital records went to universities, where they may be retrievable, but a vast treasure-house of information was plundered by journalists and sold off to American academics (one of whom told me so). The library has since been partially rebuilt, but the habit of research has been lost; most reporters go to interviews with no more preparation than a glance at the morning paper. The result, as one might expect, is shallow reporting and persistent inaccuracy. As an editor I repeatedly tried to warn my staff that anything printed in a South African newspaper was likely to be wrong; they assumed I was being liverish.

Inaccuracy, of course, is the most visible but also the most trivial of newspaper sins. The major function of a newspaper – its greatest power – is to set the agenda for the nation by its selection of news, and by the prominence given to that news. Good judgment, consistency, and a profound knowledge of public affairs is necessary to perform this function, so it is a serious indictment, altogether true, that few English-speaking journalists in South Africa follow the news with any diligence. I have known senior journalists, aspiring to become editors, who readily confessed that they knew nothing of sport, did not understand business, and were bored by politics. Their sole qualification was an ability to manufacture cliched 'faction' in the curious style of the British popular papers in the 1950s and 1960s.

I do not greatly admire British newspapers (my formative experience was American) but they are redeemed by wit and intelligence, by sophisticated judgment, and superb writing; South Africa has entered an era in which lightweight editors cannot, or dare not, write. Lesser staff take their cue from the editors, and reporters are an object of scorn among sub-editors and office politicians, some of whom have made successful careers without ever venturing into the society which they profess to interpret. The spirit is tabloid, but it lacks the vigour and resourcefulness of good tabloids.

These points, I confess, are generalizations. There are exceptions and I shall come to some of them shortly, but the poor quality of the newspapers is not in dispute, and Thabo Mbeki is stating no more than the obvious when he says that the newspapers are well-nigh useless as instruments of democracy.

What is seldom discussed (because it is deemed dangerous to do so) is the reason South African newspapers have become so bad: the blame falls on the editors, but the fault lies almost entirely with the owners and managers who appoint those editors and control the resources. They have allowed the institution of the press to decay over a period, not of years, but of decades. However inadequate the editorial performance of the newspapers, their management is worse. Like the mining men who controlled them, the managers of the industry judged themselves entirely by the speed and ruthlessness with which they could extract profit.

For years I nurtured the naive fantasy that one day Harry Oppenheimer, the godfather of the industry, might express the wish to have a good South African newspaper at his breakfast table every morning. That alone would have caused a revolution in the industry; but the call never came, so managers who were themselves incapable of either producing or judging a good newspaper escaped into the mere pursuit of profit. In this pursuit, editorial considerations were deemed marginal or irrelevant, and journalists were seen as flighty creatures to be humoured and stroked lest they raise awkward obstacles to profit-making. I usually sum up my own experience by recalling that, at the end, I helped make a crude trading profit of more than R80 million in a year – out of only a hundred-odd journalists – but I could not get budget approval for three extra training positions.

Lack of training, exploitative salaries, disdainful treatment of journalists, crumbling infrastructure, ageing plant and equipment, excessive profits, and a total lack of democratic vision explain, in very large measure, the sorry condition of the English-language press. The treatment of staff caused unending staff shortages, lasting over a period of thirty or forty years, as journalists constantly fled the profession, or fled abroad. Staff turnover was ruinous and demoralizing but it did not disturb the managers, one of whom had notoriously remarked that he could pick up sub-editors whenever he needed them – in the gutter. When I took up the editorship of *Business Day* (for the second time) I was handed a staff list of seventy-three names, including secretaries, messengers, and darkroom assistants, and on my desk I found the resignations of fourteen journalists, most of whom were emigrating.

That was in 1986, after the closure of the *Rand Daily Mail* and the *Sunday Express*. In the following year one-third of my staff emigrated, and five years later I was still shaping the newspaper around the inadequacies of the staff rather than the needs of the society. Since then, matters have improved somewhat at TML, thanks mainly to Stephen Mulholland's enlightened staff policies, but training has still not made up the losses. In the industry as a whole, I would estimate, more than half the senior staff have been promoted to levels of their own incompetence.

Journalism is a calling; it attracts idealistic young people. Management is not. So while the editorial staff struggled to produce good newspapers, the managers of the industry worked to maintain the cartel, a near-monopolistic comfort zone in which they could maximize profit and minimize effort. The markets were rigged to eliminate most competition. Even the South African Press Association (SAPA), which might have become the basis of a good, cheap news service such as Mbeki craved, was systematically starved of resources by mindless cost-cutting. The distribution system, centrally controlled, was a nightmare of incompetence and unreliability. The printing plants were overworked, under-maintained, and subject to perpetual breakdown; in one twenty-four-week period the *Sunday Times* had nineteen major breakdowns in its printing or information technology departments. Training, where it existed, was exploitative, aimed at locking young people into jobs for two or three years at minimal cost. Many then left the profession disillusioned.

Worse, circulations were rigged. The managers assumed, on primitive cost calculations, that the price of a newspaper did not cover the cost of its production. Hence every newspaper was perceived to be sold at a 'loss' that had to be covered by advertising revenue. Every manager's ideal was to sell enough newspapers to keep advertisers happy, and not a copy more. Once a newspaper achieved an 'ideal' circulation – say, 200 000 for the *Star*, or 500 000 in the case of the *Sunday Times* – circulation was restricted by under-supplying the market. 'Sell-outs', which sometimes afflicted 85 per cent of the distribution points, required centralized control of the system. Hence, more effective systems like Australia's (where newspapers are sold and delivered by independent franchised agents) could not be introduced: they might sell too many newspapers! Not even at the *Sunday Times*, where huge economies of scale were possible, were managers willing to contemplate changing either their archaic assumptions or their archaic practices. Attempts to change their thinking were interpreted, correctly, as attacks on their comfort zone, and were fiercely resisted.

Beneath all this lay the question of power. If any newspaper were to produce a profit from the sale of newspapers, or even break even, it would decisively shift power from advertising to editorial departments, from managers to editors. It would force the newspaper to serve readers (and Thabo Mbeki's constituents) as well as it served advertisers, and the managers were not about to permit that to happen. For a very good reason.

At the heart of the industry lay a cosy relationship between the managers and the advertising industry, a relationship cemented by a pernicious system of kickbacks: the ad agencies were paid 16 per cent of the revenue received for every ad they placed on behalf of their clients. (Whether this arrangement was in the interests of the advertisers themselves is open to question: the system creates intense pressures on advertisers from their agents to use big, expensive, full-colour ads.) One result was to reduce the number of potential advertisers to a handful of cash-flush corporations whose executives had to be wined and dined on golf courses around the country. For advertising salesmen, life was a social whirl of expensive jaunts to Sun City and the Wild Coast, elaborate 'promotions', golfing weekends, and mutual entertainment that verged on corruption.

Virtual corruption sometimes passed into actual corruption. For years I struggled to keep pornographic ads out of the news-paper (my conviction that the level of smut had become offensive to readers earned me the nickname 'Attila the Nun') but somehow the porn and prostitution ads always came back. Many years later I got the explanation from a disgruntled ex-wife who confes-sed she had acted as 'bag lady', collecting bribes for her husband in return for placing the ads. When I gave her letter to the man-agement, it was brushed aside with embarrassment: the husband was not even questioned, and so far as I know still works in his old job.

The conflicting demands of advertisers and readers are common to all newspapers; in South Africa, the balance has been upset. As the demand for more profit grew relentlessly, year after year, the search for ways to maximize profit grew. To detail the strata-gems used would require a great deal of boring technical discus-sion, but three categories of method were used: staff quality, including staff training, was allowed to decay and editorial quality was sacrificed; infrastructure and back-up services were reduced, usually at the expense of editorial quality; and finally, unrelenting pressure was exerted to make editorial matter serve the needs of advertisers, not readers.

This last category of pressures, which threatened to undermine the credibility and therefore the political and social utility of the newspapers, was bound to lead to severe clashes over editorial quality and editorial independence, and it did, but the pressures were merciless. More and more, commercial 'supplements' displaced ordinary news pages. These supplements promised advertisers a certain kind of editorial coverage – whether or not it interested the readers was immaterial – in return for their advertising. So disproportionate amounts of space were given over to motoring, or to computers, or to commercial exhibitions, or to pseudo-news about minor industries, and less and less of the available resources of staff, space, and money was given to news coverage. In extreme cases, where editorial staff baulked at providing the necessary propaganda, the advertising staff hired their own mercenaries (at rates which the editorial departments could not afford) to fill the space with commercial lies.

Advertising supplements and so-called surveys led to cruder devices, such as 'sponsored news', a euphemism for commercial propaganda presented in the guise of independent editorial matter, or 'success stories' about businesses, written by the owners of the businesses themselves but published in the guise of independent editorial matter. Readers could hardly know which parts of the newspaper to believe, and which to dismiss as commercial lying. So the products grew shabbier, and the journalists, lapsing into cynicism, set out to exploit the system by writing endlessly (and inexpertly) about restaurants or foreign travel in return for free meals or air fares or wine or loaned cars. For editors, life became an endless, futile struggle to preserve the integrity of the newspaper, and as the quality of editors declined, so did their ability to resist the pressure.

In effect, the newspapers were converted into advertising media. Politically and socially, they became well-nigh indefensible, and in the end the readers, who were not fools, began to drift away. The flight of readers from the English newspapers is frightening, far exceeding the normal decline of newspaper readerships in the modern world. Perhaps two million readers have been lost, and the various explanations for the flight have in common a refusal to acknowledge that most English newspapers in this country are now hardly worth reading.

English-language editors in South Africa have always had to toil in an unpromising environment. The community of English -speaking whites whom they primarily served and from whom they sprang, was simply too small to sustain major newspapers. The problem was overcome by building a constituency from diverse elements, rather as a New York politician does: something for the Jews, something for the blacks, something for the Afrikaners and the Indians, all of it set in a WASP cultural matrix. This formula, intended to serve commercial rather than political interests, was made possible by powerful support from abroad in the form of British and American lifting rights and skilled journalists and by the status of English as a lingua franca. But it was a delicate balancing act requiring great skill and sufficient space and resources. When more and more space was diverted to commercial propaganda, the balancing act became impossible. Whole classes of readers were ignored and lost.

Political tension made matters worse, unleashing powerful new forces on the market. As conflict sharpened, it became more difficult, if not impossible, to hold both white and black readers, or both Afrikaans and African readers, and in trying to compromise, most newspapers lost at both ends. African readers in Johannesburg, for example, abandoned the *Star* for the *Sowetan*, which soon became the country's biggest daily, and a powerful voice for views that were neither Anglo-Saxon nor liberal. The end of apartheid had the perverse effect of legitimating ethnic interests, so Afrikaans readers (including coloured people in the Cape) reverted to newspapers that best expressed their emotions and served their needs: *Die Burger* overtook the *Argus* in sales. Except for the niche publications like *Business Day* and the *Mail & Guardian*, almost all English newspapers found themselves in decline. The interesting exception – one which casts light on the weaknesses of the rest of the English press – is the *Citizen*, which has held its circulation quite well. Having displaced the *Rand Daily Mail*, it now barks at the heels of the *Star* (which makes a virtue of disaster by defining itself as a suburban newspaper serving the interests of advertisers interested in the northern suburbs of Johannesburg, just as the *Argus* defines itself as a suburban newspaper serving the Peninsula; both rationalizations are transparent). The *Citizen*, politically disreputable, needs no such sophistries. The question is, why?

Years ago, Mr Justice Goldstone, who is after all a liberal of international repute, told me he read the *Citizen* because it was the only newspaper that kept him informed. That remark still holds true. The *Citizen's* eccentric editor Johnny Johnson has followed old-fashioned rules of good journalism, dutifully separating the news from his own conservative comment. His news sense is superb, as is his instinct for the lowest common denominator of white readership. Of course, he woos readers from all communities, and shrewdly, but his newspaper and his values are firmly rooted in the conservative church-going sports-mad English-speakers of Johannesburg's southern suburbs and the East Rand. Interestingly, that used to be the territory of the *Rand Daily Mail* when I worked for it in the late 1950s before it became trendy.

Johnson is also an extraordinarily powerful editor able to protect his editorial space against the demands of both advertising and profit-seeking. He owes that power to his unique position within Perskor, the Afrikaans publisher of the *Citizen*, and he has managed to retain sufficient space to cover the news. He has kept his costs down by shrewd use of SAPA copy, and has avoided the trap of substituting entertainment (including dubious weekly 'scoops') for a basic news service. (Mbeki should be pleased with the *Citizen*, though I suspect he is not; Johnson, unlike Mbeki, is not a European sophisticate.) The *Citizen* is not to be emulated or copied, but it does offer lessons.

If the picture I have sketched seems bleak, then I have succeeded in capturing something of the reality: the old mainstream English press in South Africa is sickly, and its sickness will, in at least some cases, be terminal. The new African nationalist publications (I use the term loosely to suggest newspapers that meet the needs of the mainly African mass market) have already captured the future. The Afrikaans newspapers, devoted to the language and to the interests of Afrikaans-speakers, have seized the lion's share of white readership. The English newspapers, which might have staked out non-racial turf for themselves by offering all communities an excellent product, have instead gone down-market in pursuit of a quick buck. They serve a boring diet of random 'drama' and phoney scandal, topped with silly puns and other half-forgotten devices from the Fleet Street of the 1950s. I do not see how they can survive except as suburban newspapers (in which role they face fearsome rivals from the free sheets). Anyway, South Africa does not have (as Independent Newspapers discovered) the resources of management, or the vision, to devise and execute a rescue operation.

So where will the liberal cause find expression? Or, to put it differently, where will the new democracy find its fourth estate? The mass newspapers, under African editors, are bound to respond to the pressures from their readers: working-class people, newly urbanized, looking to government for social security and advancement. They will not be comfortable with the liberal emphasis on liberty, and they will certainly not tolerate the elitist libertarian free-market theory that has lately displaced the former liberal concern for the common individual. Nevertheless, the survival and health of South African democracy depends on the willingness and ability of these newspapers – the *Sowetan, City Press,* and the like – to take up the role of opposition. There have been some encouraging signs of a tough-minded independence among some prominent black journalists, but there is reason to doubt that it extends very deeply into the profession. There is little reason to think that black journalists have escaped the debilitating effects of mismanagement that has so damaged their white colleagues.

For the old English-language publications, the only discernible role is subsidiary. The *Mail & Guardian* and *Business Day* are effective niche publications, but the *Sunday Times* is struggling to hold its multiracial readership and may, if things go wrong, decline very rapidly. The Independent stable of newspapers, if one disregards the boastful style of its chief executives, offers little comfort: the dailies have been reduced to suburban reach, while the new Sunday paper is quintessentially a colonial product, its settler attitudes painfully evident in its choice of news and in its ingratiating attitude towards government.

As for liberals, they are back in the environment of 1968, when not even the *Rand Daily Mail* would overtly back the Liberal Party. (Laurence Gandar, the paper's legendary editor, thought Liberals too radical, and threw his support behind the qualified franchise of the Progressive Party.) So liberals must survive as they can, opportunistically, using whatever means an unsympathetic or indifferent press may offer. If that leads to a revival of something like the old banned liberal newspaper *Contact*, it may be no bad thing. As an 'alternative' to the mainstream press, *Contact* always outperformed the much-praised 'alternatives' that followed.

9

MARTIN WILLIAMS

The press since 1994

ONE MAY WELL DISPUTE to what extent the South African press, or even sections of it, can truly be described as liberal, either in the past or in the present. Many newspapers supported apartheid, while others were complaisant or browbeaten. Sadly, few South Africans would regard the press as a generous-spirited champion of freedoms. There were, of course, pressures on the press. During National Party rule more than a hundred laws affected the media. Some journalists were detained, some banned. Some newspapers were closed. Emergency regulations were used to censor news. Subpoenas were brandished to intimidate journalists into disclosing their sources. These formal pressures have been dealt with extensively elsewhere (Tyson 1987). I should like to discuss the less formal, but equally repressive, insidious pressures.

There have been references, favourable and otherwise, to the 'liberal press' in South Africa for many years, and some editors have indeed regarded themselves as champions of liberal causes. But, as with so many issues in South Africa, the shadow of racial politics added significant complications. It is fantasy to believe that any mainstream newspaper was a tireless or consistent champion of human rights for the oppressed during the apartheid era. From time to time newspapers did take up campaigns on issues such as prison conditions, detention without trial, or forced removals, but coverage of such issues was neither extensive nor sustained. They were, at best, stories to be covered.

The Afrikaans press supported the National Party and apartheid to the end, as did one or two English papers. Even when the mainstream English press abandoned the far-from-liberal United Party in the late 1960s and early 1970s, it was merely to support politicians with such conservative ideas as a qualified franchise for blacks.

This history was not without its price. Frene Ginwala, Speaker of the National Assembly, was merely expressing the long-standing hostility of many black South Africans towards the 'liberal' press when she addressed the *Sowetan* newspaper's Media Freedom Day in Johannesburg in October 1997:

> [South Africa's] liberal tradition ... may have its roots in the struggle for press freedom by British settlers against a colonial governor in the early part of the nineteenth century ... But by the end of the century, this liberalism was imbued with racism.
>
> The ideas promoted by this liberalism, often found in the rhetoric of colonial governors and viceroys of the British Empire, were not implemented when it came to its black subjects.
>
> The experience of this liberalism for the majority of South Africans was of conquest and appropriation of the land and natural resources of the country. Its advent on South African soil stopped black economic development rather than enhanced it, and eventually reduced African men to being migrant workers. Notwithstanding the lofty statements about equality for all subjects of the British Empire, black franchise rights were bartered in exchange for control of mineral wealth. (Ginwala 1997)

Some would take issue with the historical accuracy of this statement. To look at South African history and see there a genuine test of liberalism is hard indeed. As George Bernard Shaw said of socialism, it was an idea that was talked about but never tried. Beyond that, to condemn the 'liberal' press bell, book, and candle is to ignore the courageous work of Laurence Gandar's *Rand Daily Mail*, Donald Woods' *Daily Dispatch*, the *Weekly Mail* of the 1980s, and the efforts of many principled individuals. Nonetheless, the point remains that there is a deep-seated dislike of the English-speaking 'liberal' press among many blacks, who feel, rightly or wrongly, that it has never acted in their interests. It does not help much now to point out cases where the press took up the cudgels on their behalf.

Given this less than heroic background, it was somewhat surprising to hear the strong professions of apparently liberal values from a number of newspaper people at the Truth and Reconciliation Commission (TRC) hearings into the media, where there were not a few distorted retellings of the past. Peter Sullivan, editor of the *Star*, for example, claimed he had originally started in journalism in order to fight apartheid. John Battersby of the *Sunday Independent* apologized for not having done enough to oppose apartheid. His boss, Independent Newspapers' chief executive Ivan Fallon, told the TRC that his company and its chairperson, Irish baked-beans magnate Tony O'Reilly, were 'significant friends of the new South Africa' (Brand 1997, 6). Fallon, for years an extreme right-wing Thatcherite columnist on the conservative *Sunday Telegraph* (London), has, indeed, made an effortless move towards a new form of political correctness. In this he is far from alone. All too many journalists who toadied to the apartheid government to the end quickly re-set their sail and toadied to the new government instead.

The new African National Congress (ANC) government was not easily satisfied, however. In its view, the duty of the press had been to oppose apartheid, and now that apartheid had been overcome, its duty was to support the new government. Even the reporting of embarrassing news was suspect, and despite the almost desperate fawning of most of the 'liberal' press, ANC displeasure grew apace. Before long, President Nelson Mandela was accusing the press of being run by embittered, conservative whites.

Fallon, far from defending even the muted independence of the press, tried to downplay any conflict with the government. He told the Johannesburg Press Club, '... I don't want a crossfire situation which could result in the situation we're trying to avoid' (Hunter 1997, 6). No one asked him to explain 'the situation we are trying to avoid', but his subtext was clear: we don't want to rock the boat with the ANC government. This effectively pulled the rug from under the editors and journalists working for Fallon's company, the largest in the English-language press in South Africa. Even the straight reporting of news – such as corruption in government or the ANC's failure to deliver on its election promises of more jobs and a million houses – was not straightforwardly defended by senior management: clearly, the cultivation of a warm relationship with government came before all else. How could journalists in that group act as liberal watchdogs when their seniors behaved in such an obsequious, ingratiating, and approval-seeking way?

President Mandela's reference to control of the media by 'conservative whites' was symptomatic of a continuing focus on the racial composition of newspaper ownership, management, and staff. Cyril Ramaphosa is chairperson of the company that owns the Times Media Limited newspapers, and Nthato Motlana is chairperson of New Africa Investments Limited, owners of the *Sowetan*. These are significant holdings; nevertheless, they were dismissed as insufficient by Ginwala in her Media Freedom Day speech, and President Mandela has openly held black journalists up to scorn as mere tools of whites. There is no doubt that the acid test of black empowerment in the government's mind is that the press should be supportive of government. President Mandela summoned many leading black journalists and made it very clear to them that this was how he saw the matter.

Ramaphosa assured the TRC that 'black empowerment at boardroom level would be accompanied by empowerment in the company's newsrooms' (SAPA 1997, 7). Draft and existing legislation envisages incentives to encourage all employers to advance black employment, and black journalists have formed their own racially exclusive forum to promote their interests. Deputy President Thabo Mbeki, a supporter of the black journalists' forum, has expressed puzzlement that the media should say unkind things about the new government. His belief is that while it was correct to oppose the apartheid regime, the ANC government has legitimacy and should therefore not be subject to such critical scrutiny.

Clearly, when a government starts to consider itself above criticism, warning bells should sound for the functioning of open democracy. Among editors, however, Mbeki's persistence has paid dividends. Following his attack, more and more newspaper centimetres were devoted to articles in support of the new order, and there was a general toning down of criticism. Despite this, President Mandela returned to the attack in his valedictory speech to the ANC conference at Mafikeng in December 1997, slating the 'white' press together with the 'white' parties and certain non-governmental organizations as agents of counter-revolution and destabilization. For the first time, these gravely illiberal sentiments reached a wide international audience and brought the first really tough criticisms of President Mandela in the foreign press.

Meanwhile, the press has done little enough to deserve such criticism or even to earn its spurs at all. Perhaps the perceived inadequacies of the liberal press in the past, particularly on racial issues, have inhibited today's journalists from pursuing their proper critical and liberal role. Indeed, in order to avoid

labels such as 'racist' or 'conservative', which have become associated with liberalism, some journalists have distanced themselves
from the very idea of a liberal press.

The ANC has sometimes said it is 'under siege' from the press
– but there is a misunderstanding here. It can never be right for
journalists to cease to challenge abuses of power. That, surely, is
a central pursuit for the liberal media if freedoms are to be safe-
guarded. Yet while the new elite gives every indication of being
just as susceptible to the corrupting influences of power as rulers
anywhere, the truth is that the press is soft-pedalling – but even
this has not softened the antagonism of the new rulers towards
the press. Unfortunately, few have drawn the obvious moral that
one might as well be hanged for a sheep as a lamb.

The new campaign of pressure on the press even has its allies
within the press. For example, in his submission to the TRC,
journalist Jon Qwelane charged 'all mainstream newspapers –
English and Afrikaans – with collusion with apartheid and
having a hand, directly or indirectly, in the subsequent murder
of tens of thousands of black people by the apartheid army and
police', adding, not without need, that 'I'm not off my rocker'
(Masipa 1997, 7).

Qwelane and his fellow polemicist Thami Mazwai have been
rewarded by the government for such tirades with the publishing contract for South African Airways' flight magazine,
Sawubona. In the climate generated by this type of hyperbole,
where racism is imagined in every crevice, journalists are
undoubtedly discouraged from sticking their heads above the
parapet. Preferment goes, quite visibly, to the praise-singers.
The leading journalist Newton Kanhema, who wrote a report of
an interview with Winnie Madikizela-Mandela that the ANC
leadership disliked, has found himself facing deportation – at
the same time that he won an international journalism award.

One notices this caution in a distinct lack of vigour in the
pursuit of controversial stories that could seriously rock the

boat. For example, Winnie Madikizela-Mandela, ex-wife of the president, leads a charmed life in the press. Although she is often out of favour with the core of the ANC leadership, the media still handle her gently. In September 1997, in response to detailed allegations of murder, assault, and kidnapping, she held a press conference, flanked by five 'witnesses' who she said would testify on her behalf. Bizarrely, for a press conference of this nature, no questions were allowed. At issue in this and ensuing encounters with the press were the deaths of at least eight people – several of them children – widely laid at the door of Madikizela-Mandela and her 'football team' of thugs. Also in question were the roles of many leading ANC personalities from the President down who had, at one time or another, apparently sought to protect Madikizela-Mandela from justice – in some cases by suppressing key reports of evidence, in one case even by allegedly kidnapping a key witness. In the course of the proceedings there were further reports of intimidation of witnesses – a commonplace whenever Madikizela-Mandela comes to trial.

Yet the media neglected to pursue any of these multiple leads. Instead, there were flippant references to Madikizela-Mandela as a 'feminist extraordinaire', and 'champion of the oppressed'. Fred Bridgland, British journalist and author of the book *Katiza's Journey* which implicates her in several heinous crimes, understandably expressed concern at the reluctance of the South African media to follow up the issues raised by his investigations (Bridgland 1997, 27). Throughout the TRC proceedings on this matter the international press was far more willing than the local press to ask unpalatable questions.

One result of this lack of investigative vigour by journalists has been to make the English newspapers in South Africa insufferably boring. In terms of genuine news or keen insights there is precious little to read. This is undoubtedly one of the reasons most English newspapers in South Africa have lost circulation precipitously in recent times. This in turn has put further pressure on the press, to which it has responded by resorting to gimmicks and competitions to boost flagging sales figures. Nobody, apparently, has thought that the remedy might be to report the real news more tough-mindedly.

While the English press has become increasingly bland, much of the more aggressive and critical role has, ironically, been assumed by the Afrikaans press. The Afrikaans press, for most of its history, could never have been described as liberal, nor would it have wanted to be. Some of the Afrikaans newspapers were official mouthpieces of the National Party at its zenith, and were formally thanked for their efforts at National Party congresses.

However, loss of power has given Afrikaners a different perspective on liberal values. Some have come to see benefits in the freedoms and rights which a broad liberalism advocates. Thus the Afrikaans press, which in general enjoys a buoyant circulation, is now giving sympathetic treatment to liberal arguments, and to liberal spokespersons who would previously have been regarded as enemies.

The journalists and editors of these papers frankly admit that they now regret their years of subservience to the National Party. At last they are free of that mould and much happier for it. 'All those years when English-speaking newspapers lectured us on the proper role of the press, to be the critical watchdogs of government', they say, 'they were right. And now at last we are fulfilling that role. It feels so much better; we are proper newspapermen at last. The only thing is, what has happened to the English-speaking press? They won the argument but they seem to have lost all heart for the role.'

10

RACHEL TINGLE

What role for the churches in the new South Africa?

ACCORDING TO THE 1996/97 *South African Christian hand-book* (Froise 1997), there are almost 30 000 Christian churches in South Africa belonging to 130 denominations, and the 1990 census showed that 78 per cent of South Africans identify themselves with a Christian church. Obviously by no means all these people are active and committed Christians as opposed to merely nominal church members; nevertheless, these figures are an indication of a fact which rapidly becomes obvious to any visitor to the country – that active church membership and real Christian belief in South Africa are very high, particularly compared to that in European countries.

For many Christians, allegiance to their church is much stronger than their allegiance to any particular political party. So the strength of Christian adherence means that South Africa's churches are, in the terms of American sociologist Peter Berger, influential 'mediating structures' – that is, social institutions that stand between individuals and other large-scale collectives, particularly the state (Berger and Neuhaus 1977). Because of this, South Africa's churches could act as a bulwark against political totalitarianism, and constitute a key component of a liberal, pluralistic society.

To what extent this is so in practice, however, depends upon the degree to which the churches are able and willing to act independently of the state, and this in turn depends to some extent on the teachings of the churches and the degree to which they counteract or complement the policies of the governing political party. Any student of recent South African history will quickly appreciate that although the churches have played a significant role in South African politics, this role has been a highly complex one: in the past the churches have by no means spoken with one voice, or taken up one particular political position.

It is well known (because it has been so widely criticized) that the Dutch Reformed Church (DRC) provided theological support for the advocacy of apartheid by the National Party (NP). (At the same time, the decision of the 1986 Synod of the DRC to declare that 'racism is a sin' which 'must be rejected and opposed in all its manifestations' was certainly a contributing factor in the NP's decision to reform the apartheid system.) On the other hand, it is also fairly well known that much of the liberal opposition to apartheid stemmed from the biblical sense of justice, as did the idea of the equality of all in the sight of God that was kept alive by some other denominations during the darkest years of apartheid oppression. Less well known outside South Africa itself, but no less contentious than the DRC's support for apartheid, was the degree to which some church organizations came to support some of the less attractive aspects of the liberation struggle, and became quite uncritical of the African National Congress (ANC) in particular (De Gruchy 1986).

Since the ANC is now South Africa's ruling party (and looks as if it will remain so for the foreseeable future), the degree to which the churches will act as 'mediating structures' and aid political liberalism will depend upon the degree to which the various churches and church organizations remain (or become) independent of any ANC alignment. For if they do not do so, they will almost certainly be guilty of the same kinds of mistakes as those perpetrated by the DRC during the apartheid years, possibly giving moral sanction to questionable government actions and helping to silence what might otherwise have been healthy criticism from certain sections of society. This analysis will, therefore, look particularly closely at the stance of those church organizations which in the past aligned themselves with the ANC and ask what position they are likely to adopt in future, before looking in rather less detail at other sections of the church.

Those church bodies which during the 1980s identified closely with the aims of the liberation movements found that gaining Christian support for the revolutionary process, which in practice in South Africa included revolutionary violence, was no easy matter given that this appeared to directly contradict Christian teaching to 'love your enemies' and 'do good to those who hate you'. Indeed, the ANC itself recognized this as a major problem in its attempts to radicalize black Christians, and for this reason regarded the church as a 'site of struggle' – a section of South African society that needed to be targeted to bring it fully on side in the liberation struggle. As former Methodist minister and ANC activist Cedric Mayson wrote in the November 1983 issue of the official ANC magazine *Sechaba*, 'some have the task of taking the struggle for liberation into the church and establishing guerrilla bases in enemy-occupied territory' (Mayson 1983, 25).

Two of the most prominent organizations which, intentionally or otherwise, might be regarded as such 'guerrilla bases' within the church were the South African Council of Churches (SACC) and the Institute for Contextual Theology (ICT), for they were major players in attempting to overcome the stumbling block to the revolutionary process represented by traditional Christian teaching. The essential tool in this process was the development of a specifically South African version of liberation theology, created largely by fusing elements of North American 'black theology' (developed in the 1960s as a theological justification for the American Black Power movement) and Marxist-inspired Latin American liberation theology (Tingle 1992). This found most prominent expression in *The Kairos document* ('kairos' is a Greek word used in the Bible to mean God's appointed time) which, although it was signed by 150 clergy and theologians, was produced under the auspices of the ICT and promoted by the SACC and World Council of Churches (WCC).

Published in 1985 when black-on-black township violence (often of a quite horrific nature) was beginning to escalate, *The Kairos document* (1985) quite specifically rejected a moderating and peace-making role for the church. Seeing the situation in South Africa as a simple two-sided conflict between the white oppressor and the black oppressed, it argued that the church must avoid becoming a moderating force between the two. Thus it not only rejected the 'state theology' of those who supported the apartheid status quo, but perversely also attacked what it called the 'church theology' of many of the English-speaking churches in particular which favoured non-violent reform and reconciliation between all racial groups. Using a favourite motif of liberation theology – that is, the 'liberation' of the Israelites from the oppression in Egypt – it argued that God did not bring His justice through reforms introduced by 'the Pharaohs of this world'; rather, true justice could come only from the oppressed themselves. Thus it declared that the conflict and struggle would have to intensify in the months and years ahead and that 'Christians, if they are not doing so already, must quite simply participate in the struggle for liberation and justice' (para. 5.2). This is called 'prophetic theology'. The most disturbing aspect of this supposedly Christian document, however, was that it dismissed black moderates as 'collaborators' and argued that activities such as 'throwing stones, burning cars and buildings, and sometimes killing collaborators' ought not to be called 'violence' at all, since only oppressors can accurately be said to use violence, and most of the violence used by black political activists should be seen as 'self-defence' (para. 3.3).

To get the message across, thousands of copies of *The Kairos document* were distributed internationally (in Britain, for instance, it was distributed jointly by the British Council of Churches and the Catholic Institute of International Relations), as well as in half-a-dozen local languages within South Africa. Its influence, therefore, should not be underestimated. As one of South Africa's leading liberation theologians, Prof. Charles Villa-Vicencio (1992b), has written:

> The 1980s saw people engaging in the social revolution on the basis of their religious ideals. *The Kairos document* became a material force. It was owned by the masses in the religious sector as a means of legitimating their engagement in the struggle for revolutionary change.

Subsequently, 'Kairos action' events (including training in civil disobedience) and 'Kairos liturgies' (which suggested, for instance, that Easter Sunday sermons should see the uprisings of the people 'as the resurrection of Christ in South Africa today') were developed (Tingle 1992, 111–114). In effect, according to these new liturgies, the struggle itself had become the new God; what was right or wrong could be determined only in relation to its effectiveness in furthering the struggle.

The cause of South Africa's liberation movements was also greatly assisted by the wcc. Through its Programme to Combat Racism (PCR), over the period 1970 to 1991, it gave the ANC $1.3 million and the PAC $700 000.[1] Furthermore, in May 1987 a meeting organized by the PCR in Lusaka issued a declaration, subsequently supported by the South African Council of Churches, stating that the nature of the South African regime 'compels the [liberation] movements to the use of force along with other means to end oppression'.

It was because of initiatives like these, as well as a further document, *The road to Damascus: Kairos and conversion,*[2] issued by the Institute for Contextual Theology in 1989, which argued that all Christians needed to experience a Pauline-type conversion to various forms of liberation theology, that some observers were led to conclude that some of the churches in South Africa were actually contributing to the spiralling black-on-black political violence in the townships. Former Archbishop of Cape Town (and an early general-secretary of the SACC), Bishop Bill Burnett, stated in December 1990, for instance:

> We have fiddled the scriptures for ideological ends, and it may be we must bear some responsibility for the awful breakdown of authority and random killings among young people, including policemen. (Kane-Berman 1993)

Similarly, John Kane-Berman, executive director of the liberal South African Institute of Race Relations, has stated that despite the part played by many churches in reconciliation, 'the role played by some South African churches in creating a climate in which people feel they could use violence, free of moral restraint, has probably been greatly underestimated'. More recently he has argued that since 'South Africa's liberation theologians endorsed violence, attacked reconciliation, and stigmatized those who disagreed with them', their activities should be probed by the Truth and Reconciliation Commission (Kane-Berman 1993, 61; Kane-Berman 1997, 1).

Throughout the 1980s, a select group of church agencies – primarily the SACC and the ICT, and to a lesser extent the Southern African Catholic Bishops' Conference (SACBC) – came to the forefront of the liberation struggle. The SACC itself devoted little of its energies to evangelism or the more traditional forms of Christian missionary activity.[3] It concentrated instead on the struggle against apartheid and was seen increasingly by other black political parties as being specifically aligned to the ANC – indeed, at the SACC's annual conference in July 1992, then SACC president Dr Khoza Mgojo admitted that the SACC was often viewed as the 'ANC at prayer'. Its very considerable funds for such activities were derived mainly from European and North American church organizations and aid agencies, the WCC, and the European Community, peaking in 1989 and 1990 at just under R24 million per annum (Tingle 1992, 258–264). In this way the SACC grew to be the largest national ecumenical council in the world and a major player in South African opposition politics.

It is highly questionable, however, to what degree the activities of the SACC reflected broad Christian opinion within South Africa. There are two reasons for this. In the first place, since membership fees and donations from member churches account-ed for less than 0.3 per cent of SACC income, SACC officials were essentially able to develop policies and programmes with little reference to the church denominations which theoretically they represented. Secondly, certain major denominations were not members of the SACC. These included the two largest church groupings in the country: the white Dutch Reformed Church and the vast majority of the black African Independent Churches (with around eight million members), as well as significant denominations including the evangelical Church of England in South Africa (CESA), the Pentecostals, the Salvation Army, and the Baptist Union. In fact, the theological and/or political radi-cals connected with the ICT, SACC, SACBC, and 'progressive' theological faculties or departments, like the University of Cape Town's, were a relatively small number of people compared with the millions of Christians in South Africa, but for a while they were able to take centre stage because of commitment, organiza-tion, international support, and overseas funding.

How do they see their work today, now that their objective of eliminating apartheid and securing political change has been achieved?

The SACC and related organizations would themselves admit that the past several years have not been particularly easy ones for them as, with the unbanning of the ANC and the Pan-Africanist

Congress (PAC) in 1990, their relative importance in the liberation struggle diminished and international funding began to be
diverted to the political groups themselves and, after the 1994
election, to the government. Overseas grants and donations to
the SACC fell from R24 million in 1990 to R18.8 million in 1995
(*Ecunews* 1996), and was expected to be only R14 million in
1996.[4] This reduction in overseas funding is likely to continue
(indeed, it would already appear worse still were it not for the
effects of the fall in the overseas exchange rate of the rand), and
because of this, in 1994 the SACC went through a major retrench-
ment and reorganization exercise in an attempt to shift the main
focus of operations to the provincial level. In the short term at
least this has obvious consequences for its effectiveness. As the
SACC's general-secretary Brigalia Bam stated in an interview
with myself in January 1997: 'In 1988 the SACC had a staff of 600;
today we have one of one hundred. There are now only nine
regional offices; there used to be fourteen. This severely limits
what we can do.'

Undoubtedly, the effectiveness of the South African Council
of Churches and the Institute of Contextual Theology has also
been affected by the loss of the leaders of these two organizations
to government posts. For instance, Fr Smangaliso Mkhatshwa,
general-secretary of the ICT from 1988 onwards (and before that
general-secretary of the SACBC) was elected as an ANC MP and
subsequently became deputy education minister, whilst the Rev.
Dr Frank Chikane, general-secretary of the SACC since 1987,
became an adviser to Thabo Mbeki. A number of other former
staff members of radical church organizations have also moved
into important government or quasi-government positions
since the elections. Sister Bernard Ncube and Saki Macozoma
(formerly connected to the ICT and SACC respectively) were
elected as ANC MPs; Archbishop Desmond Tutu was appointed
chairperson of the Truth and Reconciliation Commission;[5] and
the Rev. Barney Pityana (who played a key role in the liberation

struggle as director of the WCC's Programme to Combat Racism) was appointed chairperson of the Human Rights Commission.

The central problem for the SACC and other radical church organizations, however, has been to reorientate themselves to the new political situation and to redefine their theology and mission in this new context. To some extent this challenge was anticipated by Prof. Villa-Vicencio in his book, *A theology of reconstruction*, published in 1992. Continuing to employ the methodology of liberation theology, Villa-Vicencio looked forward to the change of government, which he referred to as a 'post-exilic' situation (drawing the parallel between the return of South Africa's political exiles and the Biblical account of the return of the Israelites from exile to begin the task of reconstructing Jerusalem), and asked what new form of 'liberatory theology' this new situation would give birth to (Villa-Vicencio 1992a, 7–8; Villa-Vicencio 1993). He saw it as a 'theology of reconstruction', which would be 'committed to enthusiastic participation in the constitutional debate, the establishment of a society governed by the rule of law, the affirmation of human rights, and the creation of law designed to produce justice now'. In other words, he says, the church is obliged to promote 'the next steps that our generation must take in order to attain social justice' (Villa-Vicencio 1992a, 13, 15).

In the same year and in similar vein, Nelson Mandela also looked forward to the change of government and outlined his view of the role of the church 'as an agent of change and transformation ... acting as midwife to the birth of our democracy'. In a speech at the centenary celebrations of the Free Ethiopian Church of Southern Africa, he sketched out an eight-point programme for the church to this end: to warn church members against superficial changes in society which would actually leave power and privilege in the hands of whites and a sprinkling of affluent blacks; to design strategies to deal with the legacy of apartheid; to act as the conscience of society; to be involved in education

for democracy programmes; to be involved in national reconciliation programmes, underpinned by confession and restitution;
to be involved in the 'war on violence'; to be active in 'nation-
building', particularly the reconstruction of the family and
'democratization of the economy'; and to be actively involved in
the education of children (Villa-Vicencio 1993).

The SACC itself sought the help of old international allies to
plan its way forward. In March 1995 it organized a consultation
on *Being the church in South Africa today* which, in addition to
representatives from the SACC itself, brought together the
general-secretaries of the WCC and the All Africa Council of
Churches, and well-known radical church activists from America
(Jim Wallis of *Sojourners* magazine), Britain (David Haslam,
long-time leader of the 'End loans to South Africa' campaign,
and Ian Fraser, a specialist on Latin American liberation theology),
and the Philippines (liberation theologian Edicio de la Torre).
Prominent delegates from South Africa included Barney Pityana
and Saki Macozoma, and radical theologians Fr Albert Nolan,
John de Gruchy, and Charles Villa-Vicencio. Given this line-up
it is hardly surprising that the papers from this consultation
display a continuing commitment to the methodological approach
of liberation theology: the central mission of the church is seen
as social activism rather than a gospel of spiritual salvation, with
this activism inspired and prompted by a special concern for the
poor and oppressed. Hence De Gruchy argues that 'A concern
for economic justice is not an addendum to the mission of the
ecumenical church, but central to that task ... one of the chief, if
not the chief criterion whereby we must evaluate the mission of
the church is whether or not it "proclaims good news to the
poor"'. This, he says, 'is the permanent test of the authenticity of
Christian witness, and the basis upon which critical theology
must evaluate all social and political structures' (De Gruchy
1995, 24, 18).

Because of this, although the consultation assumed the radical church must be in solidarity with the new government, 'giving its support to those initiatives, and especially the RDP (Reconstruction and Development Programme), which may lead to the establishment not only of a new but also a just social order', it agreed that this should be a critical solidarity in which the radical church remains 'prophetic', reserving the right to judge government actions and policies as to whether they truly help the poor and promote 'economic justice' or not (De Gruchy 1995, 19, 166). The new mission statement of the SACC was summarized by general-secretary Brigalia Bam in her 1995 General Secretary's Report:

> The churches are committed to stand in critical solidarity with the government, participating in and supporting those aspects that uphold justice, that bring new dignity, and create greater opportunities for the people; but challenging the government when it forgets the marginalized, the needs of the poor, and its responsibility to all sectors of society.

The possible scope of the radical church organizations to challenge the government should not be underestimated. Firstly, because these organizations were themselves actively involved in the political struggle that brought the new government to power, they feel they have earned the right to criticize if need be. In this they have a considerable advantage over the more moderate church organizations which, if they wish to criticize the government, are quickly silenced by taunts such as 'Where were you when we were taking to the streets to fight for justice?' Secondly, since a number of people in government previously held key positions within the radical church organizations, they are aware of the potential power (particularly as regards the influencing of international opinion) of opposition from the church.

As Brigalia Bam has stated, 'We know these people, and they

know us. And because some of them were previously in church structures and know the power of church structures, they are to some extent scared of us' (Personal interview, January 1997).

As regards the SACC's relationship with the current government in practice, however, there seems to be far more emphasis on solidarity than on criticism at present. The programme of initiatives of the SACC is very similar to the eight-point plan for the church outlined by Mandela, and what criticism there might be is conveyed privately, behind closed doors and among friends. At present, then, the SACC can best be viewed as working in partnership with the new government, trying to make the new dispensation work. But in this they face an almost overwhelming task, not only in setting up development projects to attempt to bring jobs and incomes to poor communities, but also in attempting to 'enter into moral reconstruction', re-instilling values that will help make the new democracy work and that will help overcome South Africa's enormous problems of crime and violence.

Although one is bound to have enormous sympathy for such aims, at the same time it might help if there were some recognition within the SACC and related bodies of the degree to which they themselves must take some of the blame for the situation. Prof. John de Gruchy has admitted that 'a respect for free speech as well as tolerance for the views of others became casualties of the liberation struggle. State violence not only killed, but it also evoked violence against the police, and we are now paying the consequences for this' (1995). This is an almost unique statement amongst radical churchmen, however, since there has still not been any recognition within radical church circles of the degree to which, by promoting a theology which justified revolutionary violence and failing to criticize the liberation movements' use of children for political ends, they themselves may have contributed to the present climate of violence in South Africa. If the SACC genuinely wants to engage in 'reconciliation, healing the nation, and nation-building' as Brigalia Bam has stated, then an honest assessment of the past can hardly be avoided – and yet it is as if certain issues and questions are still beyond the bounds of polite discourse.

The SACC also has to face up to the problem of how exactly moral values are instilled in a nation. In Christian societies this has traditionally been the work of the church, in preaching the gospel and teaching from the Scriptures. But this is work which the SACC abandoned for the political liberation struggle, and even now, despite Brigalia Bam's statement that 'evangelism is important; ultimately it has to be top priority', there is little evidence that this commands the SACC's energies or finances. In the SACC's projected budget for 1997, the Faith and Mission Department (which would deal with such matters if any would) was expected to spend only just over 4 per cent of the total budget, the vast bulk of which continues to be devoted to socio-political projects (SACC 1995). Nor is there much evidence that the SACC shares the concerns of the vast majority of South Africa's lay Christians (of all races) over the government's liberalization of abortion, secularization of the constitution, and related issues. Indeed, Bam's report to the November 1996 meeting of the SACC executive committee contains at least a partial defence of the government's new termination of pregnancy bill, which, upon its enactment in February 1997, has provided the new South Africa with one of the most unrestricted abortion laws in the world.

The role set for itself by the ICT is very similar to that of the SACC. It defines itself and its work as 'an independent Christian organization which promotes and develops a liberating theology to empower people in the work of social transformation towards justice, as a witness to the gospel in the everyday life of Southern Africa' (ICT Review 1995). As this mission statement suggests, it has played a central role in developing and promoting liberation theology in South Africa, and, like the SACC, virtually all the finance for this has come from overseas. Critics of liberation theology in South Africa have drawn parallels between the use of liberation theology in South Africa and the way in which it was used during the overthrow of the Samoza regime in Nicaragua to justify revolutionary violence to the otherwise theologically and politically conservative Catholic masses. They have also noted how subsequently some of the most prominent liberation theologians moved into the Sandinista government, continuing to help legitimize the regime in international church circles, even in the face of quite severe persecution of more traditional Nicaraguan Christians (*Signposts* 1994).

The ICT itself is not unmindful of these parallels, and has specifically studied the Nicaraguan experience to attempt to understand why the Sandinistas lost power in 1990 and what lessons this holds for the radical church in South Africa. The lesson, as spelled out in 1990 at the ICT's annual general meeting by former ICT general-secretary Smangaliso Mkhatshwa, was that 'they [the radical churchmen] had such a friendly and pro-gressive government they had stopped conscientizing the people'. Mkhatshwa therefore stressed the need in South Africa for 'an ongoing programme of conscientization and theological reflection', a policy which was adopted at the 1992 ICT Annual General Meeting with the decision to set up Contextual Theology Units (CTUs) around South Africa. CTUs can best be seen as the South African equivalent of the Latin American Basic Christian Communities (BCCs), groups in which liberation theology is 'done', where people at base level are taught to read the Bible in such a way as to enable them to reflect on their economic and/or political situation and decide on some form of action. According to the ICT's 1995 report, the initial programme of CTUs included education for democracy, a spirituality of struggle in the church, and the question of economic justice.

More than 200 delegates from local CTUs participated, with other South Africans and international delegates, at a conference organized by the ICT in September 1995 to celebrate the tenth anniversary of the original *Kairos document* and to ask whether there was a 'kairos' – a critical moment of truth or crisis – in South Africa today. The conference concluded that 'our focus was on the economic injustices still suffered by the vast majority of our people, despite the political changes in the country', and decided that 'economic liberation is the next battle' (*Kairos '95* 1996, 87, 8). As for what this should be liberation from, the consultation argued that 'the prevailing laissez-faire economic system will inevitably perpetuate and increase poverty and suffering' and pleaded 'with the Government of National Unity to protect its people from the effects of developed and liberalized trade'. So both at national and international level, the consultation showed a marked hostility to market-oriented or growth-based solutions to the problem of poverty. Specifically, the consultation argued that 'the growth-based market model has failed ... it aggravates rather than alleviates the serious crisis which the masses in our country experience' (*Kairos '95* 1996, 87, 15).

This essential hostility to the market economy had also been displayed at the March 1995 SACC conference mentioned earlier. Here, Villa-Vicencio had argued that the church must be engaged in a struggle to create a new form of 'social realism'. Because this 'is a realism committed to the liberation process, it cannot seek to preserve the socio-economic order that is inherited from the past. It must have as its ultimate goal the transformation of the existing order to the benefit of the poor', and he concluded that 'the quest for an economic alternative to exploitative capitalism constitutes the point of continuity between the theological agenda prior to the 1990s and that of the present' (Pityana and Villa-Vicencio 1995, 59, 69).

It is against this background of a commitment to fight for 'economic justice' and a hostility to the market economy that one should probably view the establishment of the Ecumenical Service for Socio-Economic Transformation (ESSET) in August

1996. Initially a project of the SACC, supported by the SACBC and the ICT, ESSET is now an independent body financed primarily by organizations in Norway with additional support from Canada, Germany, and Switzerland. It is headed by the Rev. Dr. Molefe Tsele, previously of the ICT. According to him, the original idea for ESSET came from Frank Chikane. As in the Kairos '95 consultation, Chikane argues that the 'prophetic witness' of the church in future will be in developing a 'theology of economic justice' and helping the government to resist the 'international forces which might lead it to make compromises' (Nolan 1994/95). Tsele has stated that 'political democracy will fall short and will be undermined unless we now enter into the new struggle for the democratization of the economy. What we now have to strive for is a just and equitable distribution of wealth in our country' (*Challenge* 1996b).

Although Tsele told the author in January 1997 that ESSET does not subscribe to any one school of economic thought and he is aware of the fact that churches need to be more informed about economics, all indications are that the radical church networks plan to campaign within the churches, and to keep up pressure on the government, to move away from a market-oriented economic system to a redistribution of income and resources in favour of the poorest of the poor. It is clear that many in such circles are concerned, for instance, about the government's new macro-economic strategy and apparent abandonment of the Reconstruction and Development Programme (RDP) (*Challenge* 1996a), and while some will not criticize the government too openly because of their old loyalties to the ANC, nevertheless, according to Tsele, he represents 'a very mixed constituency within which there are some very angry people'. Again, while one cannot but share the concern of the ICT, the SACC, and ESSET for the plight of the poor, and their impatience for things to improve, it has to be asked whether these organizations have learned anything from the experience of many countries elsewhere in Africa, as well as in the old Eastern bloc, where socialist and redistributive economic policies merely led to economic stagnation, the impoverishment of the bulk of the population, and an excessive concentration of power in the hands of the state. None of the papers at either the Kairos '95 conference or the SACC's March 1995 international consultation showed any real assessment of the South African economy or any grasp of the conditions needed to create sustained economic upliftment.

This, then, is the current stance of the church organizations that were previously highly supportive of the liberation movements. It is a position that might be summarized as 'radical critical solidarity' with the ANC government. But what of other church groups in South Africa?

Apart from the radical church leaders who supported the liberation movements, and the Dutch Reformed family of churches which had in the past supported apartheid, by far the largest group of Christians in South Africa are those of all races from all denominations – including Catholics and denominations belonging to the SACC – who see the main work of the church primarily in spiritual terms, with traditional Christian charity and social work as an important but secondary activity to preaching the gospel. In the past, such people have either tended to favour reformist political change, or ignored politics altogether. However, whether they are fully aware of it or not, attempts are now being made to draw some of them into the radical church orbit and thus, even if only in very subtle ways, their freedom of action in the public sphere is being diminished.

Significant in this respect was the decision of the International Fellowship of Christian Churches (IFCC) to join the SACC, initially as observer members in 1992, but with the intention now of becoming full members.[6] The IFCC is a network of charismatic /pentecostal churches presently made up of approximately 600 independent churches, with 1 500 ministers and 400 000 members. The decision is thought to have been largely the responsibility of present IFCC president Ray Macauley, pastor at the enormous Rhema Church in Randburg, Johannesburg. At the time, it caused something of a furore amongst those IFCC member churches (who were not consulted by the IFCC leadership prior to the decision) who had been deeply opposed to the theology and politics of the SACC.[7] There has been heated discussion as to whether the SACC is most likely to influence the IFCC or vice versa. Time alone will tell, but in spite of the size and resources of the IFCC, the political experience and commitment of those in radical church circles suggests that the line of influence will most likely be from the SACC to the IFCC, and it is therefore hard to see what the IFCC stands to gain by the move, other than a certain amount of political correctness in the new environment. Indeed, critics of the move say it displays nifty footwork by one who was close to the former white government. At the end of 1996 the IFCC itself underwent a reorganization, prompting some more resignations from member churches worried that the IFCC was moving in a 'socio-political direction'.[8]

Recent events within more evangelical church circles also appear to be pulling them in a similar direction. Until recently, most of the significant evangelical denominations that chose not to be members of the SACC belonged instead to the Evangelical Fellowship of South Africa (EFSA). In 1995 EFSA had a membership of twenty-two church denominations (including the Apostolic Faith Mission, the Baptist Union of South Africa, and the Church of England in South Africa) and thirty-three national Christian service organizations, representing around 1.75 million people (*EvangeLENS* 1995). Unlike the SACC, however, EFSA had virtually no administrative structure or outside funding. It was multiracial, and while not ruling out Christian involvement in politics, most EFSA churches concentrated on preaching the gospel and traditional forms of Christian social/welfare work.

A very different trend within evangelicalism was represented by Concerned Evangelicals (CE), an organization established in 1985 as a project of the ICT involving a group of 'concerned evangelicals' whose aim was to reflect on the 'kairos' facing evangelical Christians in South Africa at that time. In 1988 it emerged as a separate body under the leadership of the Rev. Caesar Molebatsi, one of the signatories to *The Kairos document*, describing itself in a publicity leaflet (in terms highly reminiscent of the liberation theology of the ICT and SACC) as working for an 'evangelical mission that is contextual, transformative, and empowering'. The most significant initiative of CE was its publication in 1986 of *Evangelical witness in South Africa*, a booklet that is best described as a more subtle, evangelical equivalent of *The Kairos document*, written apparently from the perspective of the churches, which, while not actively supporting apartheid, wished to change the system through moderate reformist means. 'The problem', stated the booklet, 'is that Jesus was radical, always geared to turning the world upside down ... He was committed to a radical change and we are committed to moderation, to reformist liberal tendencies which leave the system intact'. It therefore called on whites to confess their 'sin' of wishing to work for power-sharing and reform, and, in effect, called for blacks to confess their sin of not being more active in the liberation struggle.

Without doubt the theological stance of Concerned Evangelicals is very much at odds with most EFSA member churches, which would question if it is in any sense correct to say that Jesus was 'committed to radical change' in the usual secular political meaning of the phrase, as opposed to the radical change of life offered through the Atonement to any individual who is prepared to repent of sin and commit their lives to Him. But in spite of this theological chasm between the two organizations, CE and some EFSA leaders gradually became convinced that it was not God's will that there should appear to be such a division within evangelicalism in South Africa. This led to talks between the two

organizations, and in 1993 Concerned Evangelicals proposed
that the two should amalgamate.

By 1995, CE claimed a membership of about 800[9] (many think
this is an exaggeration, but even if it should be accurate it could
hardly be compared with that of EFSA), but in November of that
year, in a quite extraordinary process that has been described
by one commentator as 'a mouse swallowing an elephant'
(*Signposts* 1996), and by a member of the former EFSA executive
as a 'take-over', CE and EFSA joined together as equal partners
(with Africa Enterprise and the IFCC) to form a new organization, The Evangelical Alliance of South Africa (TEASA), with
former CE general-secretary Moss Nthla as general-secretary.
Although a professing evangelical, Nthla is close to the ICT,
having for some years been a director of Contextual Publications,
the company that produces *Challenge* (formerly the ICT magazine
and now an independent offshoot which, under editor Fr Albert
Nolan, acts as the main mouthpiece of the radical church movement within South Africa). The drawing of TEASA within this
orbit is perhaps further indicated by the coverage given to the
merger in issues of *Challenge*, as well as by Frank Chikane's
prominence at the TEASA launch, and subsequent TEASA public
prayer meetings.

According to the TEASA constitution, its aim is not only to
provide a fellowship through which evangelicals in South Africa
can work together in mission and evangelism, but also to provide
the means for them to speak 'when necessary with one voice on
public issues'. The dominance of the former CE constituency
within the TEASA structure, however, suggests that political concerns and programmes similar to the radical church network
will come to dominate TEASA too. Indeed, TEASA's first main
political initiative – its launch, in February 1997, in collaboration
with the Truth and Reconciliation Commission (TRC), of a
million-Rand reparations campaign for victims of human-rights
abuses – suggests this is what is happening. The reparations

campaign is seen by some as a way in which the churches which now feel they did not oppose apartheid vigorously enough can ease their conscience; but hard questions need to be asked about exactly who will benefit and to what extent and for what purpose. For instance, in addition to victims of state or police brutality, will the families of victims of necklace murders, or the families of black police officers killed in black-on-black violence, be eligible for compensation? And if not, why not?

The internal contradictions between the executive and member churches of TEASA may mean that it fails to get off the ground properly – the Church of England in particular seems rather lukewarm about the whole initiative. In the meantime, however, its very existence and particular focus of concern may be enough to silence or prevent what might otherwise have been a very vociferous campaign by the evangelical churches on a range of quite different public policy issues.

For there is no doubt that many of South Africa's lay Christians are exceedingly concerned about the direction the new government has taken over the secularization of the constitution, and the liberalization of legislation relating to abortion, pornography, gambling, and so on. In the main, these concerns over 'moral issues' are not being articulated either by the radical church groups, or at all adequately by many of the mainstream denominations (although there is no doubt that the Catholics and the Dutch Reformed Church feel extremely concerned about such issues), or by groups like the IFCC or TEASA.

However, there also exists what might be identified as a fourth stream of Christian groups in South Africa – a number of small and poorly-funded grass-roots pressure groups made up of theologically-conservative Christians who previously opposed the activities of the radical church organizations on largely theological grounds. These include United Christian Action, *Signposts* magazine, and the Gospel Defence League. Such groups see their role now as educating and mobilizing Christians in the struggle for traditional Christian values in society. In attempting to do this they are not afraid to stage public protests. In these, they admit, they have 'learned from the methods of the liberation theologians'. In May 1995 and again in May 1996 they organized marches on Parliament in Cape Town to protest against planned abortion legislation and against pornography. The numbers involved in such marches (20 000 in 1995 and 10 000 in 1996) far exceeds the numbers involved in marches staged by the radical churchmen. Although such demonstrations have had little discernible impact on the course of legislation, the 1996 demonstration, staged by an umbrella group calling itself Christian Voice, prompted President Mandela to request a meeting with the leaders because, as he said, Christian Voice represented an important constituency and he wanted to be seen to be open to its concern.[10]

Christian Voice and United Christian Action together have a mailing list of approximately 5 000 people, many of whom are pastors of churches and can hence spread the message even more widely. The president of Christian Action, Ds Soon Zevenster, a minister in the Evangelical Reformed Church, established a Christian radio station, Radio Tygerberg, in 1992, which is now on the air twelve hours a day and has an estimated daily audience of 250 000 people in the Cape Peninsula, with particular support from the coloured community. The influence of Radio Tygerberg is such that it is thought to have been largely responsible for the fact that the African Christian Democratic Party (ACDP) won one seat in the 1996 local government elections in the Tygerberg substructure (covering the black township of Khayelitsha), thereby holding the balance of power between the ANC and the NP.

Another influential grassroots Christian pressure group, now with an associated radio station, Radio Khwezi,[11] is 'Christians for Truth' (CFT), based at the mission station KwaSizabantu in KwaZulu-Natal. KwaSizabantu stands unashamedly for what might be called old-fashioned, traditional Christianity, with an emphasis on preaching and teaching of the Bible and prayer and repentance, and has quite specifically rejected the 'politicized' gospel of the radical churches. However, literally tens of thousands of people (including people 'outside' mainstream Christianity, such as African traditional healers) have flocked to KwaSizabantu to hear this message, and many have found a living faith in Christianity and come to a complete change in their lives as a result. Consequently, KwaSizabantu is a base not only for Christian evangelism, but also for very real black upliftment. Through numerous self-financing projects – including farming, market-gardening, a dairy, building and metal work, bread and cake-making, and a jam factory – the people who come and live on the mission station for weeks, months, or even years, acquire marketable life skills. From a farm of approximately 300 hectares, 1 400 people are fed every day, rising to 5 000 a day when they hold youth conferences. Their school, which has been integrated racially from its inception, has obtained a one hundred per cent matric success rate for the past eight years (several of their pupils have obtained the best results in South Africa); and more recently a small teacher-training college has been established, again with excellent results.

In 1990, concerned about the escalating black-on-black violence and reports of intimidation of black Christians by political activists, some of the Sizabantu leaders placed an advertisement in the *Sowetan* and other primarily black papers, asking Christians who were being intimidated in any way to contact them. This was the beginning of Christians for Truth (CFT); CFT concerns have now widened to embrace what is viewed as another form of anti-Christian persecution – the erosion of Christian values in society. CFT has grown rapidly since its inception seven years ago and it now mails a bi-monthly newsletter to approximately 65 000 people in South Africa (approximately half of whom are black) and a further 10 000 people in associated CFT groups in Europe. CFT groups have been active at local level in

South Africa, forming 'life-chains' to protest against the liberalization of abortion as well as organizing various forms of
demonstration against pornography and gambling. Interestingly,
in view of the stance taken by the radical church, CFT also quite
specifically states its commitment – based on biblical principles
– to 'the right of private ownership, free enterprise, and economic
progress'. The influence of CFT/KwaSizabantu within the South
African church (particularly the black church) is also spread by
the annual KwaSizabantu 'Ministers' Conference', attended by
roughly one thousand church ministers from various denominations.

To summarize this rapid and necessarily selective overview of
the present political stance of the South African church, it is
clear that many of the pre-1994 divisions remain. The radical
church organizations remain close to the ANC, are wedded to
liberation theology, and are most concerned to see a change in
social and economic structures so as to achieve 'economic liberation' for the poor. However, without doubt, they have lost the
old momentum and clear vision of the days of the liberation
struggle and seem almost overwhelmed by the task of 'nation-
building' they have set themselves. Paradoxically, for a group
which claims more than any other to be concerned for and close
to 'the people', it is questionable how much these groups really
represent grass-roots South African Christianity, and if, as
expected, their international funding gradually dries up, their
influence will almost certainly diminish.

In the meantime, however, the leaders of many of the theologically conservative and politically moderate denominations
and church groups are subtly being drawn into this camp –
largely because of guilt about not having been more actively
opposed to apartheid in the past – and do not have a distinctive
voice on public policy issues; at the same time, their main concern
remains what it always has been – the preaching and teaching of
the Christian gospel.

The small pressure groups which in the past actively opposed the radical church, however, have found a new agenda and a new momentum. This is the fight, as they see it, against the de-Christianization of South African society via legislation on moral issues introduced by the 1994–1999 government. This is finding a real resonance with many lay Christians of all races and denominations, and any political party seeking to attract votes would be foolish to ignore them. Indeed, there are some indications that many black people will not vote for the ANC again because of its stance on abortion.[12] As South Africa moves further from the apartheid era and from the 'national liberation' election, so such concerns may become more apparent, and black politics, in particular, may become more fragmented. Certainly there seems to be a political vacuum in South Africa in the sense that, with the possible exception of the African Christian Democratic Party (which currently has two MPs in the national Parliament, but has been suffering from organizational problems), no existing political party is fully representing the concerns of a large number of theologically orthodox Christians. Thus, as time goes on, those churches or Christian organizations prepared to voice these concerns publicly might become a focus of dissent and a force for pluralism in South African society.

11

MONICA BOT

assisted by DEE WINGATE

Freedom of education: a privilege or a right?

EDUCATION is an integral part of the way a community express-
es its cultural/philosophical outlook. The nature of schooling
tends to be controversial in many heterogeneous countries (for
example, where ideological content differs from a particular
community's convictions), and in some countries it has become
a source of conflict. In industrialized countries with substantial
immigrant populations, the question of how to accommodate
different language, religious, and/or cultural groups has exercised
the minds of policy-makers and educators alike.

South Africa's population is diverse in many respects; there
are eleven official languages and numerous different religions
and cultures. The public education system accommodates
language choice, but at secondary schools the medium tends to
be either Afrikaans or English. In the past, in respect of broader
philosophy, the system was differentiated according to race:
'Christian national education' in the case of whites, and 'Bantu
education' in the case of Africans. In general, it is a non-diversified
schooling system in the sense that there is only one type of secondary school, with a strong academic focus. (There are some
technical schools but their enrolment is relatively insignificant.)

Religious, philosophical, and pedagogical diversity has traditionally been accommodated in the private schooling system.

This sector, especially where it serves poorer communities, is heavily reliant on partial state funding. However, many private schools are accessible only to the financially better-off.

It may be especially useful in evaluating these circumstances to explore educational policies from the viewpoint of choice, to examine the ways in which other countries have approached these issues, and to compare their policies with the new policies that are being applied in South Africa.

The accommodation of choice: an international perspective

Both the form and the content of schooling are closely linked with a community's philosophy of life. This linkage underlies debates over issues such as the place and nature of moral and religious education within national curricula, and the accommodation of demands by cultural and religious minorities, and it is an important factor in shaping education systems (Dijkstra and Peschar 1996). A local expression of this is the current debate about the need to Africanize educational institutions and content, especially at tertiary level.

For this reason, freedom of education is acknowledged as a basic right by United Nations (UN) declarations (though not by the African Charter on Human Rights and People's Rights). For example, Article 29 of the Convention on the Rights of the Child, which was adopted by the UN General Assembly in 1989 at New York and signed by more than a hundred countries, states:

> ... the education of the child shall be directed to: ... (c) The development of respect for the child's parents, his or her own cultural identity, language values, for the national values of the country in which the child is living, the country from which he/she may originate, and for civilizations different from his or her own.

Individuals and bodies, it continues, should be free 'to establish and direct educational institutions', subject to the observance of certain principles and to the requirement that 'the education given in such institutions shall conform to such minimum standards as may be laid down by the State'.

Most declarations include the right of parents to establish or choose schools other than those provided by the public authorities. In a leading case in Europe regarding the respect of parental rights as enshrined in the European Convention for Human Rights (*Kjeldsen, Busk Madsen, and Pedersen* v. *Denmark* (1976)), the court described the philosophical basis of this right as follows: '... parents may require the State to respect their religious and philosophical convictions'. It furthermore said: 'The State is forbidden to pursue an aim of indoctrination that might be considered as not respecting parents' religious and philosophical convictions', and emphasized that 'the possibility of pluralism in education is essential for the preservation of ... "democratic society"'.

Numerous authors have stressed the importance of freedom of choice and variety for the preservation of democracy and individual liberty in pluralist societies (see, for example, Foon 1988). Another reason for allowing choice in heterogeneous countries is the lack of success in achieving social or political integration by means of education. In Pakistan, for example, Islamization has had a devastating effect on the Pakistani educational system. 'The emphasis on ideological education has intensified cultural and religious differences, resulting in communal conflicts and resentment of other cultures and other areas of knowledge' (Talbani 1996). Public resistance has taken the form of an exodus to Western-model and private English-medium schools.

In respect of South Africa, international educationist Theodor Hanf (1980) pointed out that attempts to achieve social and political segregation by means of education were equally unsuccessful: 'The more educated an Afrikaner is, the more likely he is not to believe in the teachings of [the National Party]... The better educated a black South African is, the more outspoken and militant is his refusal to accept government policy'. The reason is that 'factors preceding or running parallel to the formal educational system, such as ethnic group, social stratum or class, religious affiliation, or identification with a certain religion, are more strongly correlated with political attitudes than all educational variables ...'.

Hanf concludes:

> The less schools are used intentionally to socialise, to indoctrinate, to integrate, the less education will be subject to conflict. And since education in plural societies is closely related to issues like language, religion, and cultural identity, its political neutralisation can constitute a major reduction of conflict potential.

Accommodating choice in the public school system

Different countries have responded in a variety of ways to the need to accommodate philosophical, language, religious, or cultural diversity in education.

Within the public sector, three broad trends can be identified: decentralization, increased school autonomy, and curriculum diversification. These approaches are not mutually exclusive, of course, and often decentralized systems, for example, will also allow greater school autonomy and curriculum choice. School autonomy, on the other hand, need not be accompanied by decreased state control over education; state control may rather be exerted at other levels.

Decentralization

Switzerland has no national education department; each group has the school and language of instruction of its choice. In Belgium and the Netherlands, 'school covenants' granted cultural and religious communities a very high degree of autonomy. As a consequence, 'Political conflict over educational issues has practically disappeared ... All segments of the population have roughly equal access to education, and all the segments have got the kind of education they want' (Hanf 1980).

Decentralization cannot really be found in Africa, however. 'Even where national leaders stress the integration of schools into their local communities, curriculum, textbooks and other materials, major exams, and teacher selection, training, and promotion are all to be set nationally' (Samoff 1987).

Internationally, there is substantial interest in decentralization, especially since the collapse of Eastern European socialism. Jon Lauglo (1996) notes that this collapse has undermined the credibility of alternatives to the market mechanism. As a consequence, he anticipates that decentralization is likely to persist as a policy trend for education, together with an interest in mechanisms that attempt to reconcile decentralization with egalitarian goals.

Greater institutional autonomy

Another response has been to allow greater institutional autonomy, so that parental choice can be catered for. For example, schools can offer different subject choices, and define their own mission and character.

An additional rationale for increased autonomy is improved effectiveness. A comprehensive review of literature on effective schools concluded that they share certain characteristics, including an emphasis on school site management, with considerable autonomy given to school leadership and staff; curriculum articulation and organization aimed at achieving agreement on goals and developing a purposeful programme of instruction across grade levels; and a strong sense of community (Purkey and Smith, quoted in Cohn and Rossmiller 1987).

Possible risks of school autonomy are that schools try to attract (and enrol) the most able pupils only; that it undermines cooperation among schools; and that middle-class parents will benefit more than others. It also assumes that most options will be available within reach of customers.

A number of these risks are associated with a system that is uneven in terms of quality to begin with, while others could be addressed by policies similar to those applied to ensure equality between public and private schools. In other words, competition does not 'let the government off the hook' in terms of uplifting disadvantaged schools and ensuring certain standards across schools. It has been noted in respect of England that 'parental pressure through market-place competition may be leading to greater uniformity between schools: perhaps that was one of government's aims' (Welton and Rashid 1996).

Similarly, an article in *The Economist* on school autonomy in England argued that:

> ... the mere threat of parental choice should be enough to persuade poor schools to improve.
>
> And the government has created safeguards to stop schools from falling too far – a national curriculum and an inspectorate with the power to take over or close failing schools. Whatever the weaknesses of parental choice, it cannot be as bad as allowing bad schools to remain as local monopolies ... The Japanese, South Koreans, and Singaporeans have proved that a highly competitive schooling system can improve standards at the bottom as well as at the top. The Germans have demonstrated that selection need not

involve stigma if a variety of schools are provided for less-
academic children. (3 February 1996)

The Labour Party has also come out in support of this system, and
its leader, Tony Blair, has pledged to sack substandard teachers and
close poor schools (*Citizen* 29 Jan 1997).

Curriculum diversification

In many industrialized countries with substantial immigrant
populations, attempts have been made to adapt the curriculum,
either by adding to the syllabus or by adapting the content of
existing subjects. The motivation for multicultural education,
as it is commonly called, is twofold: the often poorer educational
performance of immigrant children, and the rejection by immigrant parents of assimilation of their children into the dominant
culture of the host country.

There is much debate about the aim of multicultural education,
which can vary from assimilation to consciousness-raising to
social reconstruction. In South Africa, a form of multicultural/
ethnic education was the national policy at all levels, but as
Sanza Clark (1993) points out, it was used not to empower but to
marginalize various cultural and ethnic groups. More generally,
in highly stratified societies where subordinate groups lack
controlling influence in the schools, diversity in the curriculum
and educational objectives may actually hinder rather than
facilitate a conscientization process among subordinate groups,
whereby these would be enabled to effect change in their
circumstances. An example is agricultural schooling offered to
rural children in many developing countries.

A problem in Africa is that both the structure and the content
of education have a strong European orientation, and a European
language is often used as the official medium of instruction.
Content changes have generally been limited to revisions of the

geography, history, and civics syllabi in favour of a stronger consideration of local problems. Radical structural or curricular reforms have been attempted only in Tanzania (ruralized education) and Rwanda. Most of these have failed, however, because they were not accompanied by coherent changes in the overall socio-political framework (Hanf et al 1975).

Another difficulty is the varied success, if one can call it that, of different curriculum approaches. Hill (1987) writes that in Germany, for example, where states have different systems and curricula, 'no system seems to have worked, and there seems to be no consensus about policy among German politicians and educators'. The author points to the difficulty of settling such questions owing to the fact that 'no ethnic or racial group is truly monolithic' in any region.

More generally, there is substantial support for the establishment of a core curriculum that reflects certain common needs and values and provides equal opportunities to all children, complemented by content that responds to different cultural, religious, or local needs. Even the differentiated content should be very flexible in order to accommodate different needs within ethnic groups (Bot 1991).

Accommodating choice outside the public school system

Another way to accommodate parental choice is to allow the establishment of private or independent schools. Public support for private education has grown in a number of countries recently, reflecting a demand for greater freedom of choice. There are two main areas of debate regarding independent schools, which are closely interrelated: that of educational equality, and that of government funding.

In countries such as the United States and Britain, independent schools are perceived to be of a higher quality than public schools;

this is in fact the main reason for their existence. In other countries, however, independent schools were established in order to accommodate choice, and their quality is often the same as that of public schools (examples include Denmark, the Netherlands, New Zealand, and Australia).

Many governments attempt to maintain educational parity between the public and private sectors. In Australia, for example, the funding of non-government schools was enacted as part of a more comprehensive programme to upgrade the general quality of education. In other words, the goals of quality and equality were pursued simultaneously (Foon 1988).

In the Netherlands, where some 65 per cent of primary and 83 per cent of secondary pupils attend private schools (Karsten et al 1995), the state prescribes educational goals and guarantees equal standards (all written final examinations are set and administered by the state).

Government funding of independent schools ranges from almost nothing in some countries to full state funding in others. The Netherlands, for example, has provided in its constitution for the public financing of private schools, and there is equal government support for public and private schools.

An interesting ruling was made in this respect in the Danish court case mentioned earlier. The court held that allowing for private schools 'was not an adequate response to the parents' concerns, as it would lead to the unacceptable result that only the rights of wealthy parents would be "respected". Thus, such options do not automatically relieve the state of its responsibilities to fulfil its obligations ... within the public school system'.

Private-sector growth and increased government subsidization of private schools usually go hand in hand. In a number of countries, there is a perceived need to increase the levels of funding for non-government schools and to actively promote the private education sector. The British government has recently proposed that parents and teachers be allowed to establish their own schools with state funding, something which already happens in the United States. Such schools would have to stick to the prescribed curriculum, but would be able to use other teaching methods and develop their own ethos (*Rapport* 5 January 1997).

In New Zealand, lack of funds forced Catholic schools to integrate into the state system about twenty years ago. However, the church agreed to integration only on condition that 'the religious or philosophical character of the school was not disturbed; and that ... the school would retain the right to reflect in its teachings its special character'. Moreover, the church would retain ownership of the buildings, and all expenses would be paid by the state. The partnership has deepened the Catholic character of the schools, and quality has been maintained (*Star* 20 May 1996).

In Lebanon, all schools that do not charge school fees receive a per capita state subsidy. This has resulted in a system in which there are schools of various Christian and Muslim denominations, Jewish schools, non-denominational schools, and state schools. 'None of these schools is exclusively for one community ... So schools are open, but people tend to go to their own schools'. French-medium schools increased after the per capita subsidy was instituted. 'All kinds of groups interested in the promotion of a particular language started ... to compete for clients from various groups' (Hanf 1980).

Foon (1988) concludes that the best way to meet the twin challenges of quality and equality in education is for government and non-government school systems to collaborate and complement each other's efforts. She points out that independent school systems appear strongest in those nations that have allowed secular and sectarian interests to be integrated into a unified body. In other words, the onus is on the government to ensure parity between schools and equality of opportunity, as well as excellence and choice in education.

The role of government in education:
public funding versus public supply

There is a common perception that governments should not only fund education but also be responsible for supplying and managing it. This obviously does not need to be the case; whether a pupil receives education at a school provided and run by the government or at a school funded by the government but run by another organization, the end result is the same. In terms of costs and efficiency, the second option may in fact have certain advantages.

As Luis Crouch (1996), a senior economist presently seconded to the Department of Education and the Education Foundation, points out, 'The traditional solution – publicly funded, publicly supplied, and centralized education – may have succeeded to a considerable degree in expanding mass access to education, but at the cost of increased inefficiency, bureaucratization, over-centralization of some functions, and a probable drop in quality'. Some of the reasons he gives for public-sector failure are the lack of incentives to allocate resources efficiently; the absence of competition; a tendency to make politicized appointments; and a lack of quality control in respect of outcomes. Crouch argues that the mix of private and public roles needs to be guided by the real comparative advantages of each sector, and that 'the public sector's key role is to improve the way the market for education services operates, regardless of whether the supplier and funder are public or private, for-profit or non-profit'.

The basic point is that it is the state's responsibility to provide financing to ensure that each child receives a certain amount of education of a certain quality or standard. Who can best provide the education or ensure standards, however, depends on a number of factors, including capacity both inside and outside the public sector. It is important to stress this, as in South Africa private schooling is generally perceived as elitist, while it need not be. There are many local examples of the latter: private involvement in pre-primary education is a case in point, as are mission schools in rural areas.

Prospects for freedom of choice in South Africa

As already mentioned, South Africa is a heterogeneous country in respect of language, religion, culture, and philosophy. At the same time, it does not have a tradition of choice or diversity in its extremely uniform and centralized schooling system. There is also no history of strong parental or communal involvement in education.

New education legislation has been passed, however. Both the constitution and national education legislation (the National Education Policy Act, 1996 and the South African Schools Act, 1996) support the right to education in the language of choice and single-medium institutions, where practicable.

Schools may be based on a common culture or religion, as long as there is no discrimination on the grounds of race and attendance at religious observances is free and voluntary. Independent schools may also be established, based on a common language, culture, or religion, with the possibility of state subsidization.

This section assesses the new policies in terms of the options for choice discussed above.

Decentralization

In terms of the National Education Policy Act, the minister of education has the power to determine national policy in respect of, *inter alia*, management, governance, and programmes of the education system. This includes curriculum frameworks, core syllabi, language medium, and admission policies. While the national department sets norms and standards, the provinces are responsible for the executive and administrative functions.

According to Blade Nzimande, education spokesperson for the African National Congress (ANC), the Act tries to achieve a balance between effective decentralization and central coordination, and emphasizes cooperative governance and partnerships. He said that provincial departments have wide discretionary powers within their areas of jurisdiction, so long as their decisions are in line with national norms (Interview, Cape Town, 6 November 1996). Gauteng's education minister, Mary Metcalfe, agreed that 'national powers are rightfully theirs' (Interview, Johannesburg, 3 March 1997), and a departmental spokesperson felt that 'as long as the national department focuses on policy issues and consults the regions, there should not be a problem' (Interview, Pietermaritzburg, 4 December 1996).

Some opposition parties felt, however, that central government has too much control vis-à-vis the provinces, and a departmental spokesperson believed that as a consequence, there was potential for conflict (Interview, Durban, 10 December 1996). An African Christian Democratic Party (ACDP) spokesperson said that 'exactly as the Nats [National Party members] have done, their [the ANC's] desire is for national and central control' (Interview, Cape Town, 7 November 1996). A Democratic Party (DP) spokesperson also said that 'the central government is attempting to hold the reins too tight on the provinces with the ultimate sanction of the budget' (Interview, Cape Town, 7 November 1996).

Various reasons were given for this, including the fact that there are strong forces to perpetuate the old, centralized system. Other factors are that 'the more inexperienced the new functionaries are, the more they need to do what their predecessors did', and the desire by bureaucrats to run schools themselves for reasons of patronage – 'they have an enormous payroll to dispose of' (Interview, Johannesburg, 24 October 1996). A reason cited by the ACDP spokesperson is that the main thrust at present is to reverse the legacy of apartheid, and that therefore 'the attention

is not on a new education model which is the ideal model'
(Interview, Cape Town, 7 November 1996).

Although parties such as the ACDP and the DP support more
extensive decentralization, most interviewees felt that because
of the enormous disparities between communities in terms of
capacity and infrastructure, a highly decentralized system such
as Switzerland's was not suitable here other than for non-educa-
tional matters such as school buildings or health and safety
matters pertaining to schools (Interview, Durban, 1 December
1996). In this regard, Andrew Donaldson has pointed out that
'the dangers of decentralizing into an uncompetitive and unac-
countable institutional vacuum have to be taken seriously'
(Donaldson 1996).

In respect of the devolution of power within provinces, opinions were generally positive. MECs are free to devolve powers as
they see fit, and can tender out certain functions or areas of
responsibility to private or non-governmental organizations
(NGOS). This already happens in the fields of pre-primary and
adult education, for example, and could be extended to the
provision of materials, books, training, and information technology support. 'We realize that a lot of expertise ... [is] located
outside government', said Nzimande. 'We need to harness that
expertise and capacity, especially in areas where government is
weak' (Interview, Cape Town, 6 November 1996).

Some interviewees doubted that this would happen on a wide
scale, though, in part because it could be viewed as 'not politically
correct' or as a dereliction of duties (Interviews, Johannesburg,
20 and 17 February 1997). Also, departments would need to set
up a tendering section and a section to manage such a system –
to assess compatibility, test outcomes, approve differences from
the norm, etc. (Interview, Johannesburg, 20 February 1997).
It is expected that the extent to which MECs use their powers will
differ from province to province, and that this will affect the
extent to which decision-making is devolved within provinces.

Gauteng has gone the furthest in its attempts to devolve management to local districts and shorten the chain of command, as evidenced by the fact that there are more senior management posts outside the department than inside (Interviews, Johannesburg, 20 February 1997 and 3 March 1997). There are problems, however, one of which is that districts are tending to shy away from responsibility, in part because they do not have confidence in the capacity of their offices. A problem mentioned by Metcalfe was that only about 40 per cent of management posts in Gauteng are filled (Interview, Johannesburg, 3 March 1997). As a result, the province is having to retreat slightly in respect of the devolution of control (Interview, Johannesburg, 20 February 1997).

All the provinces face capacity problems. In its report to the Department of Education, the Task Team on Education Management Development highlighted the following areas of concern in respect of the bureaucracy: dysfunctional structures; a shortage of appropriately skilled personnel; insufficient clarity on roles and responsibilities within and between levels of management; inadequate systems and procedures; inefficient and ineffective delegation; and crisis management (Report 1996). If decentralization is to be achieved, these issues need to be addressed as a matter of urgency.

Another constraint is the general shortage of funding for education, which limits what can be done. As Nzimande put it: 'How can you ensure that they [the provinces] meet the national norms and standards out of a budget with a given amount of money?' (Interview, Cape Town, 6 November 1996) All that the legislation stipulates at present is that the provinces must address backlogs and inequalities; how this is done is up to provincial legislatures.

It is extremely difficult for the provinces to raise additional funds for education, since they are excluded from using income tax, value-added tax, general sales tax, or property and customs duties, and provincial taxes must not prejudice national economic policies. In other words, provincial fund-raising seems largely confined to vehicle licences and gambling revenue (*Financial Mail* 7 March 1997), and possibly donor funding.

The shortage of funding is likely to have a negative impact on attempts to devolve authority, as it is evident that training programmes will be required for staff at all levels.

While there is thus theoretically the possibility of a more extensive decentralization of power within provinces, this is unlikely to occur because of the absence of capacity at lower levels, and a shortage of funding to establish and monitor a more decentralized system. However, cooperation with outside agencies, whether in the private or non-profit sector, is very likely to continue and possibly increase, given the capacity problems faced by the departments themselves.

School autonomy

In general, schools will have greater autonomy than in the past, although the powers of former Model C schools have been reduced somewhat, especially in terms of the admission of pupils and the hiring and firing of teachers.

Governing bodies on which parents constitute the majority were to be elected during the course of 1997. The functions of these bodies, as laid down in the South African Schools Act, 1996, include the development of the school's constitution, mission statement, religious policy, and admission policy (although in order to 'ensure equity and access', no admission tests are allowed). They must administer and control the school's property, buildings, and grounds, and recommend the appointment of educators and non-educators to the head of the department.

School fees may be charged once a resolution to do so has been adopted by a majority of parents attending a general meeting. The resolution must also provide for equitable criteria and procedures for the total, partial, or conditional exemption of parents who are unable to pay. The governing body may by process of law enforce the payment of school fees.

They must also prepare an annual budget, and establish and administer a school fund into which all money received by the school must be paid. This includes school fees, but by early 1998 there was no certainty as yet as to whether this includes state funding.

One interviewee pointed out that should this occur, provincial departments would have to improve their financial capacity and planning, as this would need fairly sophisticated financial control, such as electronic links between schools, districts, and the department. Only Gauteng and the Western Cape were seen as capable of developing this capacity in the near future (Interview, Johannesburg, 20 February 1997).

Functions which may be allocated include determination of the school's language policy, the choice of subject options in terms of provincial curriculum policy, and the purchasing of textbooks, educational materials, or equipment for the school.

Finally, the MEC may determine that some or all governing bodies may exercise certain functions depending on their capability. A governing body may serve more than one school if the head of department so determines (RSA, South African Schools Bill, as amended by the Portfolio Committee on Education (National Assembly) (B 58B–96)).

Too much or too little?

There were conflicting views on whether schools have been given adequate decision-making powers. Some interviewees felt that school governing bodies will be mere executive organs, while others were concerned that schools in disadvantaged areas would be negatively affected because of a perceived lack of capacity.

Several interviewees felt that the state is primarily interested in control. One educationist commented: 'What's happening in schools is not about outcomes, it's about control, and it's a very centralist agenda' (Interview, Johannesburg, 2 November 1996).

Those who thought that schools' decision-making powers should be extended cited the fact that a number of decisions taken by a school have to be ratified by the department (this applies to school registration, admissions, exemption from school fees, medium of instruction, and the hiring and firing of teachers, for example). As a National Party (NP) spokesperson said, 'They pull all the strings up to the MEC and take decision-making away from the communities' (Interview, Cape Town, 6 November 1996). Both the ACDP and DP spokespeople cited the abolition of corporal punishment as one of the issues that should have been decided not centrally but at school level. They would prefer a situation in which the state provides basic infrastructure and funding to schools and leaves decision-making to parents (Interviews, Cape Town, 7 November 1996).

There are two basic arguments for not giving schools more powers: one is that the government needs to ensure the provision of a basic level of education, and the other is that many communities lack the necessary skills to manage these powers. Nzimande argued in 1996 that 'our society is not mature enough; one is dealing with the effects of apartheid'. In addition, he viewed the powers demanded by some, especially regarding the admission of pupils, as a 'ploy to perpetuate inequality' (Interview, Cape Town, 6 November 1996).

Capacity problems were also mentioned by an educationist, who said: 'It is one of the evils of democracy that people have to make decisions about areas for which they are not adequately informed and cannot cope and we are being unfair about it in this country ... Democracy presupposes commitment, knowledge, and a capacity to do things. What we are doing is a contradiction: we have disadvantaged communities because of apartheid but, despite this, they are running schools and are being empowered to do that'. As a consequence, he expects that some people will be over-extended or that structures will be chaotic (Interview, Durban, 3 December 1996).

That a lack of capacity is a problem is borne out by the fact that in KwaZulu-Natal, only 200 out of 2 400 schools in the school feeding scheme were able to supply audited statements to show that they had delivered. A DP spokesperson concluded that 'Autonomy will need to be accompanied by high levels of training and monitoring' (Interview, Durban, 1 December 1996).

Problems found in many disadvantaged areas are the generally poor communication between schools and people in their locality; the low status of teachers and principals; the perception of lack of power among school staff, parents, and others in the community; the rurality and illiteracy of a large proportion of the population; and a concern that despite training programmes for governing bodies, involvement may continue to be poor (Coombe, in Coombe and Godden 1996).

Adele Gordon also found high levels of tension between teachers and parents during visits to schools in the former homelands, and a sense of alienation among parents at farm and community schools. While the devolution of decision-making to the school level may change this, she says that training governing bodies will not be enough, because of the lack of facilities in many areas. She believes that 'administrative support and funding for schools will have to be an essential part of the capacity-building package' (Gordon 1996).

Another commonly voiced concern is that governing bodies in disadvantaged areas will not be able to function independently. It is expected, for instance, that teacher unions will interfere, pupils will be manipulated by teachers or political parties, power blocs will form, and there will be continued corruption. It is clear that for decision-making at school level to be effective, schooling must be depoliticized and school communities must be able to organize freely around purely educational issues.

A final area of concern was that governing bodies have too

much power vis-à-vis the principal; one interviewee felt that their powers will undermine the role of the principal in determining the way a school functions (Interview, Johannesburg, 2 November 1996). Another feared that 'school boards will think that they have the functions of the principals ... and the principals will be running around not knowing what to do next' (Interview, Durban, 3 December 1996).

These are all very real concerns. However, what is the alternative? As Nzimande pointed out, effective community participation in governance is vital for restoring the culture of learning and teaching in schools. If this occurred, 'you could improve output by at least fifty per cent without having to spend more money' (Interview, Cape Town, 6 November 1996).

This view is supported by experiences in Chile, which showed that 'there is only an indirect link between improving resources to disadvantaged schools and their performance, especially in poorer rural schools'. Instead, clear operational procedures need to be 'implemented through a programme of management capacity-building at local level' (Coombe, in Coombe and Godden 1996).

The above underlines the importance of training and extensive capacity-building in respect of school governance. One study on improving the quality of primary schools concludes: 'The most urgent task is probably simply to make the school more welcoming for its users. Once the cultural gap separating parents and teachers has been bridged, more elaborate forms of participation become possible, and in particular more active involvement of parents in the school's management and control' (Carron and Châu 1996).

This would point to a flexible and incremental approach to the implementation of school-based management, related to capacity. In instances where governing bodies are not seen to be capable, one governing body may serve more than one school, or management will be provided through the inspectorate. One rough estimate is that this may apply to almost two-thirds of schools. While governance training will occur, it is a matter of concern that some departments have a limited capacity to do so in terms of funding as well as human resources.

A final point is, however, that one should not underestimate disadvantaged communities or illiterate parents, a number of whom will stand up and participate, and have in fact already done so.

In this regard, it is useful to cite some of the characteristics of schools in South Africa that operate well under difficult circumstances, or 'resilient schools', as Mark Potterton and Pam Christie (1997) call them. These include a sense of responsibility for themselves and their functioning; good leadership structures and principals who are strong managers and leaders; teaching and learning being viewed as the primary purpose of the school; the provision of a safe and orderly space for teachers and pupils; disciplinary actions linked to educational purposes; a culture of concern within the schools; and working relationships with the community. Interestingly, parental involvement in the schools studied tended to be limited.

It is clear that schools are likely to develop at very different rates as a consequence of their differential capacity, and the onus will be on school communities first and foremost to make what they can of the new policies.

Let us now examine school autonomy in respect of two issues which have received a lot of media attention, those of language and culture.

The issue of culture

Here as elsewhere, the issue of culture is a sensitive one, and widely differing viewpoints have been expressed. Hermann Giliomee has argued that with its deep racial and cultural divisions, South Africa has never been a nation-state, yet ANC spokespeople 'demand to build a homogenized nation' (1996). He points out that if there is one policy that has failed, particularly in Africa, it is the nation-building policy of newly independent states during the 1960s and 1970s. Western states, on the other hand, realize that assimilationist policies are not the answer to ethnic diversity, and regard the protection of minority rights as essential to stability and as a vital element of a constitutional democracy.

However, some educationists have warned against emphasizing cultural differences. Joe Muller points out that our past 'makes it very difficult to accept a curriculum which re-validates the politics of difference ... apartheid education used cultural difference as its ideological foundation' (Muller, quoted in Naidoo 1996b). Similarly, Wally Morrow 'warns against a schooling policy that is deliberately designed to respect cultural differences as it is highly likely to create differences which might not otherwise have existed and to accentuate and perpetuate the differences that already exist in our society' (1989, quoted in Naidoo 1996a).

These statements refer more to a policy at national level that seeks to enforce certain cultural or ideological views. In respect of individual schools, however, there is substantial support for allowing them more choice in this regard, thereby fostering a sense of ownership among communities. The Task Team on Education Management Development stated in its report: 'The approach we are advocating emphasizes that everything is driven by the values and mission of the school ... A true culture of teaching and learning ... can only thrive in a school where the major stakeholders feel ownership of the school's mission and ethos' (1996).

Provisions in the South African Schools Act are very positive in this respect in that they allow for more choice than in the past. Governing bodies must develop the mission statement of the school and establish rules for voluntary religious observances. In addition, the school policy must develop respect for South Africa's diverse cultural and religious traditions.

The Act also provides for public schools on private property 'in terms of an agreement between the MEC and the owner of the private property'. Where the owner is a religious organization, an agreement between the owner and the MEC 'must recognize ... the distinctive religious character of the school'. In 1997 Catholic, Adventist, Muslim, and some Anglican schools were negotiating an agreement in which they hoped to include freedom of conscience, life orientation, and input and veto powers on key appointments. About three-quarters of the Catholic schools, for example, were state-aided and could not continue without their previous level of funding. All wanted to become public schools under this agreement, as did some of the roughly hundred Catholic private schools (Interview, Johannesburg, 17 February 1997). This arrangement would be fairly similar to the one referred to earlier made in New Zealand with Catholic schools.

In principle, therefore, public schools may become Muslim or Catholic or Montessori, subject to the constitutional requirement 'if numbers warrant' and approval by the head of the department. The departmental response to such requests can be expected to vary from province to province. Metcalfe said that a decision to become a Montessori school, for example, would be consistent with the new professional leadership envisaged for schools and the new curriculum proposals. However, where specialist teachers, facilities, or equipment are required, the school would have to provide the necessary funds (Interview, Johannesburg, 20 February 1997).

The extent to which school communities will take advantage of these options is another issue. According to several researchers, for example, the degree to which our schools have focused on culture in the past has been fairly limited. Denys Schreiner (1997) wrote recently that 'our public schools, with the possible exception of the better Indian schools, kept general cultural education at a very low key ...'. This view is supported by an Afrikaans principal, who asked, 'What is Afrikaans culture? It's a South African culture. We all have braais, we go to movies, and so on' (Interview, Johannesburg, 5 February 1997).

In a study of racial integration in South African schools, Jordan Naidoo (1996b) found that 'many schools claimed to have a particular ethos but were unable to identify it clearly or say whether it would change as a result of desegregation'. Following integration, school staff were 'unable to make adjustments in their attitudes and everyday school and classroom practices to address the diversity that now exists in their schools'. Nor did most teachers see a need for significant curriculum change. He recommends that 'key curriculum elements should be choice, diversity (according to individual and community needs), relevance, learner interest, and community involvement'.

Among African families, Stonier (1996) did find a strong desire for schools 'to be concerned with family values and "culture"', the latter referring to such things as arts, weaving, sculpture, design, food, history of culture, and rituals. He concludes that 'if efforts are not made to accommodate the expressed needs of parents and the community, parents will continue to be alienated from the school'. In order to reduce the separation between school and home, he argues, active steps should be taken to involve parents in school matters, and to ensure 'that the world-view that obtains in the school has clear links with the main ingredients of the world-view that exists at home and in the community'.

Schools will also have to learn how to deal with a range of specific, day-to-day issues. Some interviewees expressed concern about the lack of clarity and direction from government as to how schools should deal with cultural and religious issues. Examples mentioned include religious holidays such as Eid, or Muslim girls wearing pants which are not part of the school uniform. A DP spokesperson commented: 'The government tends to downplay the differences but it doesn't actually work out like that in real life ... schools may make decisions which don't relate to the sensitivities of the environment' (Interview,

Durban, 1 December 1996).

As a consequence, a provincial education department spokesperson foresees 'a huge increase in minorities precipitating test cases on a wide range of issues', especially as he did not think 'any independent or government policy unit can effectively come up with a set of guidelines which will say "if you have 51 per cent it must be so" – things will have to be worked out on the ground' (Interview, Pietermaritzburg, 4 December 1996).

Some departments have set rules, however. For example, the KwaZulu-Natal education department enforces a policy that if the majority of students in a school want to take a certain holiday, such as Divali, they can do so but must make up the time. Similarly, teachers must make up the time or take leave.

Whether or not the lack of guidelines is a shortcoming is debatable, however; one could argue that flexibility or a lack of direction is preferable to rigidity. Independent schools have had to tackle such issues as well. A Catholic school, for example, which now has a majority of non-Catholic pupils emphasizes basic universal values, and aims to evolve an authentic South African culture. Concepts used to describe this include interculturation (where pupils and their cultures connect with each other) and inculturation (an Africanization of hegemonic cultures) (Interview, Johannesburg, 2 November 1996).

Independent schools have two advantages, however, compared with public schools. The first is that they can be selective in their admissions whereas public schools cannot. Freedom Front leader Constand Viljoen said therefore that 'Enforced admission would make diversity of language and religion taboo ... [and] force all children into multi-cultural schools, in the hope of achieving "a new national hallucination"' (*Citizen* 25 October 1996).

The second advantage is that they are free to express their own world-view, or to celebrate diversity, whereas in the public schools the government is perceived to want to downplay differences in all respects. The reason for this is that as apartheid overaccentuated differences, the counter-reaction by the government is to promote a simple South Africanism: 'commonality rather than diversity', as a DP politician put it (Interview, Durban, 1 December 1996).

An ACDP spokesperson was concerned about the fact that 'government has expressed itself as a secular government and will be pushing for secular practices at schools ... If you have religious freedom, you should be able to promote any kind of religion' (Interview, Cape Town, 7 November 1996).

On the other hand, one commentator felt that diversity was being over-emphasized. 'The basics of education ... and the bulk of the curriculum have nothing to do with diversity. However, one aspect of diversity is relevant – the aspect of religion, but this can be taught in the home environment and that is sufficient as long as what happens at school does not contradict what is taught at home' (Interview, Durban, 3 December 1996).

The issue of language

As mentioned, both the new constitution and education legislation in principle support home-language education. As Hermann Giliomee has pointed out, however, single-medium or home-language schools are not guaranteed (*Rapport* 26 January 1997).

There are sound educational reasons for supporting home-language instruction, as 'the use of the home language as the language of instruction in the early years of education has proven advantages, especially where the development of cognitive faculties is concerned. Conversely ... classroom use of a language which is not the language already spoken by the child results in cognitive and pedagogical difficulties' (*ADEA Newsletter* 1996). In Nigeria, it was found that pupils taught in their home language for the six primary years not only scored higher than their counterparts in regular schools, both academically and cognitively, but that their English skills were the same as those who were taught in English during the last three years of primary school. In South Africa, it has been found that bilingual programmes 'in which a language other than the students' mother tongue is used before a certain age or a certain "cognitive level" is achieved are not likely to be successful' (*ADEA Newsletter* 1996).

Afrikaans language groups such as the Afrikaanse Eenheids-groep view the availability of Afrikaans schools as a precondition for spontaneous cooperation in the interest of a broad South African nation. It has warned that the constitution will not gain broad acceptance and legitimacy if single-medium schools with a certain cultural and religious character are not provided for satisfactorily (*Mondstuk* 1996). A Freedom Front spokesperson said, 'We can only survive within our own culture if our language survives' (Interview, Cape Town, 7 November 1996). In October 1996, Freedom Front Youth leader Kallie Kriel called for the creation of a more militant Afrikaner umbrella organization to seek home-language education in Afrikaner schools (*Citizen* 24 October 1996).

Among Africans, home-language education has long been an issue, but not always because it was what they wanted. A language expert pointed out that the importance of language to people varies tremendously: 'There has been debate around the protec-tion of Afrikaans for a long time but the discussion around African languages is incredibly complex'. He found that 'in Soweto, parents will choose a school for proximity reasons, not language, and the school has to accommodate the languages of the children'. In Daveyton, schools on the outskirts were all poorer and single-medium, while towards the centre they were more middle-class and many languages were accommodated (Interview, Durban, 30 October 1996). However, this usually happens by using one language as the official medium of instruct-ion – usually English – and occasionally using another language which pupils understand better (Bot 1993).

According to research done by John Stonier among African

families in the Witbank area, 'Great store is placed on the mother tongue being taught as one of the languages'. Because language is seen to be linked to culture, 'it seems that instruction in the vernacular is required at least to the end of the primary phase' (1996).

As Hanf (1975) has pointed out, a problem is that in most African states, the abundance of local languages allows a foreign language to dominate. Arguments in favour of a European language are the need to maintain cultural contact with the outside world, the need for a common linguistic instrument for national integration, and, where there is a shortage of qualified teachers, the possibility of using foreign instructors. Counter-arguments are that using a foreign language could result in socio-cultural alienation, and that it is easier to become literate in one's home language. The cost of supplying teaching materials in different languages is also often cited as a problem in multi-lingual countries; however, these costs could be reduced by computer-assisted publishing (*ADEA Newsletter* 1996).

Others believe that it is important that different language groups go to school together as this is expected to improve relationships. This view is held by K. Skinner, national media officer of the South African Democratic Teachers' Union (SADTU), who said that 'A South African nation can only be built if pupils from different language groups mix' (*Rapport* 26 January 1997). A language expert mentioned that the dual-medium system, for which South Africa is internationally famous, 'accommodates relationships – you could not tell if people schooled in that system were English or Afrikaans. When the Nats came in and you got single-medium schools, bilingualism deteriorated and so did relationships – there was far less marriage between cultures' (Interview, Durban, 30 October 1996).

Nevertheless, there is most certainly a problem of educating children unfamiliar with a medium of instruction (MOI) together with children who are fluent in it. A DP spokesperson commented, 'Schools have problems of effective delivery where children do not have an absolute command of the language ... As a general rule, attempts to accommodate those who lag behind must not jeopardize the chances of others' (Interview, Cape Town, 7 November 1996).

In view of the undisputed advantages of home-language instruction and parental and official support for it, policies should as much as possible aim to facilitate it. In this respect, the legislation stipulates that schools may determine their language policy. At the same time, however, there are certain constraints on their choice of instruction medium: it must be approved by the MEC, schools cannot use language tests as an admission criterion, and MECs can override a decision by a school concerning non-admission of a child.

Certainly some provincial education departments have not gone out of their way to facilitate home-language instruction. When several Afrikaans-medium schools in small towns decided to amalgamate in order to maintain their language policy, they were opposed by the provincial MECs. This places a question mark around the commitment to home-language education. The MECs' opposition stemmed mainly from their perception that the schools had racial motives for their decisions. Such motives did play a role in certain instances, but in others they did not.

For example, two Afrikaans-medium schools in Mpumalanga amalgamated for academic and financial reasons, and to keep an Afrikaans high school in the area. They informed the department of their decision, but the department opposed it. It said that every school in the province should maintain a multicultural teaching situation and reflect the composition of the rainbow nation. The MEC for education, David Mabuza, told ten teachers that they must return to the now empty school or face dismissal (*Rapport* 23 February 1997).

An Afrikaans principal in Gauteng said, 'The department keeps phoning to say you have space so, according to them, there is a class empty and we can take in an English class from the township. But it is very difficult to do this and for kids to travel in [to our school]. On top of that, there are empty classes in the townships, so why make kids come here?' (Interview, Johannesburg, 11 February 1997).

More generally, there is a perception that the government does not want language diversity, but favours English-medium schools. According to the publication of the Transvaalse Onderwysersvereniging (the teachers' association for Afrikaans-speaking teachers in the former Transvaal) *Mondstuk* (1996), ANC members of the Parliamentary Portfolio Committee on Education have little understanding of Afrikaans-speakers' insistence on single-medium Afrikaans schools. Some members accused them of ulterior motives such as hidden apartheid, language imperialism, and a lack of identification with the building of a new South African nation and a new nationalism.

As a consequence of these factors, as well as the fact that 'the numbers game counts against us', as a Freedom Front spokesperson put it, some feel that the future of Afrikaans-medium public schools is bleak. As he felt that nothing could be done within the formal education system, 'the alternative therefore is to create private schools' (Interview, Cape Town, 7 November 1996).

Several independent Afrikaans-medium schools have now been established. However, support for the 'Volkseie' schools is questionable. An Afrikaans principal attacked them for their 'typical laager mentality', in the sense that 'they keep kids away from life'. He said: 'Most Afrikaans people love their language, but they are also not stupid – the language of business is English'. Educational quality was seen to be of primary importance to parents (Interview, Johannesburg, 5 February 1997). Another Afrikaans principal said that while parents feel very strongly about home-language education and regard it as their right, they are not prepared to provide any funding in order to ensure that their children continue to receive their education in Afrikaans (Interview, Johannesburg, 11 February 1997).

While the 'numbers game' may not be in their favour, it is expected that Afrikaans-medium schools will continue to exist. In larger urban areas, single-medium institutions are more likely to survive because of their larger feeder areas. In small towns and rural areas, however, it is accepted that many schools will have to choose whether to become dual- or parallel-medium. As a spokesperson for the South African Foundation for Education and Training commented: 'When a school is partly empty, you can't expect to keep the less privileged out' (Telephonic interview, 4 February 1997).

A committee was established in 1996 to investigate possible guidelines for the implementation of home-language education, comprising departmental officials, academics, and one teacher association representative. According to an agreement reached in late 1997, Afrikaans governing bodies will be allowed to refer children who wish to be taught in English to English-medium schools, and Afrikaans-medium schools will be allowed to keep their language medium unless forty-five children in a particular standard wish to be taught in English. In such instances, the school will have to switch to dual- or parallel-medium, whereby it will have to offer both Afrikaans and English instruction, either within the same classroom or in separate classrooms.

Hennie van Deventer, chairperson of the Federation of South African Schools, has wondered whether this agreement would be applied retrospectively. He said that certain decisions by provincial departments had prejudiced Afrikaans-medium schools, and that unless these were nullified, this agreement meant nothing. He was referring to those Afrikaans-medium schools, especially in the Northern Province, which have had to change their medium policy since 1994 (*Rapport* 16 February 1997).

We will have to see what the final recommendations are, and hope that ways are found in practice to meet parental concerns and wishes satisfactorily. Otherwise, the constitution's support for home-language education will be fairly meaningless. For educational reasons alone, the utmost should be done to facilitate home-language education, especially at primary level.

Curriculum diversification

New curricula are to reflect outcomes-based education and an integrated approach to learning, and were to be phased in from 1998. According to Dr G. Niebuhr, Chief Director of Quality Assurance, Department of Education, there will be an integrated approach in the early years of general education. In further education, up to matric level, the emphasis will be more on specialization (*Sunday Times Metro* 23 February 1997).

The National Qualifications Framework and outcomes-based education are expected to facilitate content and methodology choice. About sixty per cent of the curriculum framework will be set nationally, while about forty per cent will allow for provincial (and district) variation. Provinces can develop learning programmes, and determine how much flexibility there will be. Schools will have choice within those frameworks. Independent schools are also legally obliged to implement the system.

Schools could thus opt for an agricultural or entrepreneurial focus, specific cultural content, or a Montessori methodology. The main constraints appear to relate to funding, as departments are not in a financial position to provide the resources if specific equipment is needed, for instance. In principle, if the school has the resources and if the outcome is within the national framework, there would seem to be no problem.

Private provision

Legislation provides that 'any person may, at his or her own cost, establish and maintain an independent school'. They must be registered with the department, their standards must not be inferior to the standards in comparable public schools, and they must have a non-racial admission policy. State subsidies are also allowed for, subject to compliance with certain norms and minimum standards. Spokespersons for the independent school sector said that there are no particular limitations in the Act for independent schools.

This option has been described by some as a protection against the absorption of any minority's culture, language, or religion (*Die Volksblad* 9 April 1996). Most interviewees in fact view this option as a way to reduce the potential for conflict. As mentioned earlier, the Freedom Front sees it as a way out, and several 'Christelike Volkseie Skole' have been established which are 'very focused on culture' (Interview, Cape Town, 7 November 1996).

Several independent Afrikaans-medium schools have also been established in recent years, but for financial reasons this is not an option for many public schools. As an Afrikaans principal at a public school said, 'We do not have a resource base to tap into' (Interview, Johannesburg, 11 February 1997).

Enrolment in independent schools has been increasing rapidly, and one departmental spokesperson described independent schools as 'probably the biggest growth industry in South Africa to date' (Interview, Pietermaritzburg, 4 December 1996). According to Mark Henning, national director of the Independent Schools Council (ISC), there are about 600 independent schools teaching about 230 000 children (*Sunday Independent* 2 February 1997).

Another growing area of independent provision is that of home schooling. According to one department official, many applications for home schooling are coming from Christians who 'do not have faith in the state school system but cannot afford private schools' (Interview, Pietermaritzburg, 4 December 1996). While the South African Schools Act allows for home schooling as an option, it has been criticized for granting excessive discretionary powers to the heads of provincial education departments concerning registration.

In an article for *Indicator SA*, Kate Durham argues that a 'genuine outcomes-based educational system will have no interest in whether a child was educated at school or at home'. She concludes: 'Greater school choice and parental involvement would be in line with international educational developments' (1996).

As in a number of other countries, the debate in South Africa has centred on the quality of and government support for the independent sector. Growth in these schools has in fact resulted more from a concern over educational quality than anything else. The principal of an independent Afrikaans-medium school said that this also applied to his school; religion, language, and culture were all of secondary importance to parents (Interview, Johannesburg, 5 February 1997).

Growth is expected to continue if public schools cannot maintain their former standards. In large part, this is seen to be related to problems raising fees from parents. An educationist said that 'the lack of resources means that the state is reducing all schools to a common denominator. This will give rise to an elitist, dual system where the only quality schools will be provided by the users of education. Schools in Soweto are not working – who wants to go to those schools?' (Interview, Johannesburg, 2 November 1996)

One principal has solved the fee problem by getting parents to pay in kind by doing work for which the school would have had to pay – such as driving the school mini-bus, painting, or cleaning (Interview, Johannesburg, 11 February 1997).

Non-payment by some parents has resulted in disgruntlement among paying parents. As one departmental spokesperson commented: 'If parent A has to carry the cost of parent B, they will rather choose their own school where they don't have to pay double' (Interview, Pietermaritzburg, 4 December 1996).

Continued advantages of private schools were seen to be that they can respond more quickly to changes in the market-place; there is direct accountability (if they do not deliver, pupils walk out); they employ their own teachers (who can be fired if they do not deliver); they can apply admission tests; and, a more recent argument, that they can write the examinations of the Independent Examinations Board, which is perceived to administer examinations of a more acceptable standard than the new provincial examination authorities.

Some interviewees expressed a concern that because of their fee structure, independent schools are becoming whiter than before. However, a Pan-Africanist Congress (PAC) spokesperson expected black enrolment to increase as a consequence of the growing quality gap between public and independent schools. He was especially concerned that this would happen if the culture of non-payment for services were extended to education (Interview, Cape Town, 6 November 1996).

In general, politicians and education department officials were positive about the possible role of independent provision in areas where government is weak (especially in disadvantaged areas), largely because the state is not seen to be able to deliver quality free education to all in the foreseeable future.

There is still considerable debate about the funding of independent schools. Norms and standards to regulate the payment of state subsidies to independent schools are still being drafted. Legally, however, there is nothing to prevent an MEC from deciding to fund independent schools fully. Some organizations, such as the Congress of South African Students, have insisted that independent schools fund themselves or become public. The South African Democratic Teachers' Union later proposed that independent schools that provide quality education to underprivileged communities should continue to receive subsidies (*Sunday Times* 8 September 1996).

The most common rationale for continued subsidization of independent schools is that parents pay tax and are thus entitled to at least a basic subsidization. Alternatively, (partial) tax rebates could be considered. Spokespeople for independent schools also feel that the government should continue funding them in view of their past opposition to apartheid. Moreover, many are involved in outreach programmes. An option that is supported by a number of school principals is that the funding of disadvantaged children might be weighted to provide an incentive to private schools to admit them, although one principal felt that it was inadvisable on psychological grounds to have disadvantaged children on bursaries together with privileged children (Interview, Johannesburg, 10 February 1997). Departments seem to recognize that it would cost more to do away with subsidies, as a number of independent schools would be forced to close down or become public schools.

Henning believes that independent schools should be subsidized according to a different scale from public schools. 'Part subsidization represents a bargain to the state – education in accordance with the core curriculum at satisfactory scholastic standards and at half the price of educating a child in a public school' (*Sunday Times* 8 September 1996). He argues for a certain amount for basic education for each child, with the option of additional assistance for schools serving poor communities where the state is unable to provide because of financial or other constraints (Henning 1996).

There is thus substantial support for a higher level of funding for independent schools in disadvantaged areas, such as the former African mission schools, and also for continued support of the non-profit sector.

Several interviewees believed that independent provision could play a role in achieving the government's aims in the field of education (i.e. access, equity, redress, and quality), subject to its being state-funded. As such, a Dutch system (whereby all schools, public and independent, are funded on the same basis and the state ensures equality of standards) could be considered.

As mentioned earlier, this is the only way in which the government can ensure that there is parity between public and independent schools in terms of quality and access.

Conclusion

I have focused on the extent to which choice is accommodated in our schooling system. An advantage of choice, whether it concerns a particular curriculum, a specific teaching methodology, or a certain religious or linguistic focus, is that it brings parents closer to the schools and eliminates the risk of alienation which could arise if these needs are not accommodated. In recognition of this, the constitution and education legislation contain several positive provisions.

The governing bodies of schools, in which parents constitute the majority, can determine the mission and ethos of their school, and will have more choice in respect of the medium of instruction, curriculum, and methodology. There is also more scope for schools to cooperate or cluster, and to seek out alternatives. One school, for example, has introduced an International Baccalaureate. The fact that legislation has provided for public schools on private property, and for home schooling and independent schools, also augurs well in terms of choice and diversity. Finally, legislation is not excessively detailed or prescriptive, and this allows for 'room to move' or flexibility.

However, a number of constraints operate on public schools, in that most of the policy choices made by their governing bodies need to be approved at provincial level. Furthermore, they can only make recommendations regarding staffing, and cannot apply admission criteria. In other words, MECs have the final say over a number of crucial matters pertaining to schools. Independent schools will therefore continue to have certain advantages, which are seen to be directly related to their ability to maintain quality.

If the government is truly committed to involving and empowering schooling communities, allowing more choice, and increasing quality output, it should consider encouraging public schools to function more like independent schools. By the same token, it should consider providing maximum subsidization to the independent sector, especially where such schools operate in disadvantaged areas.

If, on the other hand, the government's agenda is basically one of control (an opinion held by many interviewees), there could be costly consequences in terms of the quality of the public education system and its output. As a DP spokesperson commented: 'Because of the apartheid legacy, the present government is insisting that everything must get better equally, and this is just not possible. You will end up without excellence' (Interview, Durban, 1 December 1996). Moreover, there is a lack of capacity to run the education system, in part because many newly appointed officials have little experience, and in part because departments are understaffed.

The consequence could be a dual-quality education system, either in terms of a good independent and poor public sector, or within the public education system itself. This has happened in Zimbabwe, for example, where 'low-density' multiracial and multicultural schools are found in middle-class suburbs, while 'high-density' schools of a low standard are found in African areas (Van Rensburg 1996).

How can South Africa avoid this and achieve its ultimate aim of providing quality education for all children? A number of suggestions have been made.

Encouraging competition between schools is generally thought to be one way of improving their quality. However, there are constraints on competition in that schools are not always within easy walking distance of each other. It also assumes that people will choose a school for educational quality and not because it has good sports facilities, for example. Nevertheless, some interviewees believed it could work if carefully monitored by the state, provided that children were not compelled to attend schools outside their communities (Interviews, Durban, 3 December 1996 and Johannesburg, 10 February 1997). Another potential problem is that competing schools may refuse to share resources. However, the fact that schools can now start diversifying in a number of respects is likely to address this problem.

Another possible way to improve school quality is to tie funding to enrolment. This already happens to a certain extent, as enrolment determines the number of teachers the state will pay for. Tied funding puts pressure on poorly performing schools to improve or face possible closure.

However, this option has received mixed support. Metcalfe commented that it 'assumes that schools have the wherewithal to improve but only lack the will' (Interview, Johannesburg, 3 March 1997). The Gauteng department has established a scheme whereby disadvantaged under-performing secondary schools will be given a certain amount of money to use on any project in order to improve their results. Targets will be set which must be met (Interview, Johannesburg, 6 February 1997).

It is clear that no funding policy can be applied simplistically or unilaterally, and that there is an important role for the state in guaranteeing certain egalitarian goals. A policy rewarding excellence, for example, would need to be supported by a range of other measures. The state will have to be responsible for ensuring adequate facilities and teaching standards, and defining and testing educational outcomes. As to actual provision, it should seriously consider using all available outside expertise and infrastructure in order to achieve its educational aims.

12

M W MAKGOBA

Oppositions, difficulties, and tensions between liberalism and African thought

IN DISCUSSING OPPOSITIONS, difficulties, and tensions between liberalism and Africanist thought in contemporary South African society, one needs first to define or describe liberalism, and to identify and define who the liberals or the champions of liberal values are in the new South Africa. Secondly, one needs to demystify the notion that Africanism, in particular Africanist thought, is incompatible with liberalism in contemporary South Africa. Thirdly, one needs to tease out the notion that liberalism is incompatible with racism. Fourthly, one needs to examine the behavioural pattern and practices of latter-day liberals in conjunction with the social experiences of the previously oppressed to seek clues to underlying tensions. And finally, one needs to analyse liberalism worldwide in a comparative fashion, to see how it has faced or risen to the challenges of racism.

When I explore these issues, I find I can make five assertions: (1) there are two types of liberalism in South Africa, the conservative English-speaking type and the African-rooted type; however, only conservative whites are perceived to be liberals; (2) there are many unrecognized African liberals; (3) Africanist thought is incompatible with conservative English-speaking liberalism but compatible with social-democratic-type liberalism; (4) while liberalism is incompatible with racism, liberals in

South Africa are not: they are cloned products of their social environment, that is racist South Africa, and are racist; and (5) liberalism on the whole has never successfully tackled racism in any society.

The challenge between the two types of liberalism lies in clear definitions, mutual accommodation, and the removal of the racial agenda. There are no inherent tensions, oppositions, or for that matter difficulties between Africanist thought and genuine liberalism, save that Africanist thought is but one version of liberalism; these tensions exist only between the disciples of the two polar forms. The tensions are thus not in the philosophies but in the messengers and their current context and historical experiences. The tensions are generated by race, different conceptions of society, the way in which racism has induced differing perceptions of the world, and the meaning of liberalism in our context, that is, which liberalism are we to choose? The universal failure of liberalism to confront the basis of racial conflicts in any society remains worrying.

The meaning of liberal

'Yes it's you, it's all you liberals, it's your fault, you have ruined this country ...'. One of the rudest things to do today is to call a South African, in particular a white South African, a liberal; the same applies to white Americans. This is because the word liberal has become associated with negative connotations such as racism, someone spineless, unprincipled, vague, a hypocrite, a person unable to take a strong stand or position except within the context of promoting their own agenda or interests, a weather cork, and someone loose. The meaning of liberal in South Africa has not only lost currency but also become confused.

In Europe, the word liberal is less used to describe people, politicians, or even political parties. Liberalism in Europe is so well entrenched that it is taken for granted that everybody espouses or practises some form of liberalism. The standard American sense of a liberal is the opposite of conservative. If you translate this sense into Europe, the definition of an American liberal is closer to what used to be called a socialist or a social democrat. The European sense of the word refers to the opposite of a socialist, and is rooted in the idea of favouring limited government and giving freedom priority over the supposed interest of society.

Even in political philosophy, the meaning of liberalism has become so broad and inclusive that it means almost nothing. Take for example Robert Nozick's view in *Anarchy, state and utopia* that a just society requires a minimal state because 'the demands of liberty are such that governments may legitimately carry out only the narrowest range of functions'. Contrast this liberal view with that of John Rawls, another liberal, who in *A theory of justice* allows for a large state that could decide the distribution of income among citizens (*The Economist* 1996). Clearly, Nozick would be a Eurosceptic in Britain or a Republican in America (he is also referred to as a 'libertarian' in the US), and Rawls could be seen as to the left of a social democrat.

Perhaps one of the fundamental sources of tension in liberalism lies in its definition, and the limitations imposed on individual freedoms that accompany this. These limitations are often best encapsulated in the 'harm principle' (*The Economist* 1996). John Stuart Mill's formulation of the principle was that 'the only purpose for which power can be rightly exercised over any member of a civilized community, against his will, is to prevent harm to others. His own good, either physical or moral, is not a sufficient warrant.' In other words, the individual does not have to prove that his actions harm nobody. The state that limits his freedom, if it is to act rightfully, has to prove the opposite. Equally, the issue of a civilized society – one that is mature and educated, as opposed to immature and uneducated – is open to different interpretations. Liberal freedoms were not given to people simply by virtue of their being people, but were selective, sexist, and, one could argue, elitist. Some of the liberal freedoms are in conflict with each other, and extensions of liberal freedoms, such as the relief of poverty, the provision of services such as education, and the transfer of income from rich to poor to attain a just society, pose severe contradictions that need continual justification. There is also conflict between what are described as positive and negative freedoms. A lack of clarity regarding the harm principle, its different interpretations, the inherent contradictions within liberal freedoms, and the circumstances under which people justify liberal freedoms are major sources of tension and difficulty.

So it seems that the meaning of liberal changes over time and place to mean different things: the meaning has become contextual, it depends where one is. This change has resulted in one consistent impact: the corruption of the meaning of 'liberal'. This has occurred even in societies that at some stage shared an identical civilization, such as Europe and America. It is no wonder that in the new South Africa, after the fall of apartheid, liberals are facing new challenges. The liberals during the apartheid era faced enormous hurdles of a different type. Perhaps it is true that liberals exist only under draconian, dictatorial, or authoritarian regimes, that it is only when denied that the value of liberalism is realized. It thus appears that liberalism as a concept in both academic and popular discourse has become so corrupt as to mean everything to everybody, or, alternatively, to mean nothing (*The Economist* 1996).

In South Africa a different meaning of liberal is fast emerging, that of a conservative racist, and this meaning is also closer to the meaning imparted to the world by African-Americans and Afro-Caribbeans in the USA and the UK. Liberalism has acquired a racial connotation in those societies in which diverse populations exist. The word racism keeps cropping up in particular in the South African and American contexts, for we come from a racist past and are committed to a non-racial society with equal opportunity in our respective constitutions. There is also an increasing recognition and acceptance, especially in the American and South African literatures, that conventional liberal dogma has failed the racial question, and a new phenomenon that may be appropriately termed 'liberal racism' is emerging (Hooks 1995; Makgoba 1997; Steinberg 1995; West 1995).

Perhaps the crucial thing about all these differing interpretations, nuances, or meanings of liberalism is that they underscore the critical importance of liberalism as a dominant cohesive force. Its inclusivity, its breadth, and the almost corrupt meaning of liberalism are ironically its strength. Liberalism, like swallowing or breathing, is so universal and integral to us that we take it for granted. A human swallows about 1.5 litres of fluid a day. It is only when one has a total occlusion of the gullet and cannot swallow one's saliva that one appreciates the importance of this process. Sometimes the most important things in life or society are recognized only when they are not there or are denied. Liberalism as a political theory falls into this category; its absolute necessity becomes obvious only in its absence under oppressive and totalitarian regimes such as the apartheid system.

Although there are several ways in which liberalism can be defined or described, I shall confine myself to two definitions: (1) the freedom of the individual to act without constraint from society or government (freedom of speech and religion, freedom from coercion, freedom from illegitimate government, and freedom to buy and sell property, including one's labour); and (2) the humanistic (social-democratic) type, which deals with the attitudes and/or responses of the individual to society, such as human rights, tolerance, accommodation, and respect for others. While the two broad definitions both revolve around the individual and self-reliance, they differ in the sense that in the first the individual is dominant or exalted, while in the second the individual is closely linked to society, is responsive, and hence less dominant. It is important to reflect on these two ways of looking at liberalism in South Africa, for therein may lie the clues to our confusion, difficulties, tensions, or solutions.

Who are the liberals or champions of liberalism?

South African liberals and the self-declared champions of liberal values are in general English-speaking white South Africans. According to this logic, it seems there are no Afrikaners, Africans, or Indians who are recognized as liberals. Some even argue that Africanism or Africanist thought is contradictory to and incompatible with liberalism. The denial or exclusion of this recognition of others, combined with the perceived association of a particular race group, is not only alienating but is also associated with arrogance, lack of racial sensitivity, and feelings of superiority (the holier-than-thou approach) that have become the features of some of our liberals – all, I might say, recognized features of racism.

A significant percentage of English-speaking South Africans are Jewish and this has important implications for the South African liberal/African debate. The present tension between Jews and African-Americans, both minorities and both with long histories of oppression and persecution, is rather interesting and may be a warning as to what the future holds in this debate.

The present champion of the liberal cause is the Democratic Party (DP). So the liberal label and liberalism's present champions in South Africa are perceived to be defined by race of a certain type. In short, the fundamental and dominant basis of defining liberalism in South Africa is race. This perceived description/definition is problematic for obvious reasons: it is based on wrong assumptions about Africanism and about liberalism itself, and also shows very little knowledge of African people. The association of race with liberalism is contradictory, at least in the classical definition of liberalism. It is also problematic for a nation coming out of such long institutionalized racism.

It therefore appears that the first major source of tension and difficulty with liberalism lies in its definition or description, its interpretation within our historical and cultural contexts. If liberals themselves – academic, practising, and otherwise – cannot define or do not seem to agree on or deliver a simple message, and are vague and confused about their identity, is it surprising that others are interpreting them in their own way, thus corrupting liberals and liberalism? In South Africa, the poor definition of liberalism, the glaring lack of identity, is further compounded by the issues of race, privilege, and transformation. These can only lead to further distortions and tensions.

The concept of society

Margaret Thatcher's famous quote 'There is no such thing as society. There are individual men and women, and there are families' is perhaps an extreme illustration of the exaltation of the individual above society in some form of liberalism. Rightly or wrongly, this was perceived to emphasize selfishness, naked competition, and individual greed. In contrast to this view of society is the almost universal saying 'Motho ke motho ka batho' or 'Umuntu umuntu ngabantu' in Sotho and Zulu respectively, meaning 'You are only human through the humanity of other people' which is characteristic of African society and its humanism, a recognition of the exaltation of the individual *within* society. This saying is generally perceived to emphasize altruism and the common good. The place of the individual in and in relation to society are inextricably linked in Africanist thought. There is obvious tension in the two statements in that they represent polarities.

South African society today is still largely divided along two major cultures with distinct interpretations of the world: the African and the European. Looking at our society today, one can deduce that the dominant view of liberalism is towards the humanistic, responsive type or the societal or social-democratic form, and that present tensions and difficulties arise as a result of over-emphasis of the first rather than the second, without a middle ground. The differences are more cultural than logical and relate to the way we conceive and construct society. White society in the form of the DP, for historical and cultural reasons, still emphasizes the first version of liberalism and hence the tensions, the apparent contradictions, and strong opposition from the majority. It is worth recalling that even in the West, particularly in Britain and the USA, this form of liberalism is fast disappearing, if not under pressure or contested all the time, to be replaced by the second form.

So, African thought is not incompatible with liberalism but incompatible with one version of it, the individualistic-dominant type, which is perceived to over-emphasize divisions within society: between elites and non-elites, superiors and inferiors. It is not that African society has no class or hierarchical structure, but it is the manner and tone of emphasis. The strong self-reliance principle within Africanist thought is a good example of a liberal principle.

One of the major reasons the African majority has not warmed up to the present DP is the conflict between individualistic and humanistic liberalism. Despite three centuries of western influence and domination, Africans have retained certain patterns of governance, hierarchies, operations, and socializations that are distinctly theirs. Most Africanists find the conflict between the individualistic and humanistic type of liberalism too much to handle coming from their particular social and cultural experiences. Individualistic liberalism flies totally against most things that Africans have stood for and cherish – Ubuntu, humanism, tolerance, the elimination of racial and class divisions, and the emphasis on society. Secondly, the majority of Africanists subscribe to the humanistic type of liberalism. A third reason for the failure to attract Africanist liberals to DP-style liberalism is the almost universal perception that the present champions of liberalism in South Africa still harbour racist tendencies because of their socialization, upbringing, privileges, and their incessant protection of privileges in their daily arguments. This notion is further supported by studies of race in other liberal societies such as the USA and the UK. One has just to glance at some of the personalities and compare them with their recent predecessors. A further difficulty and tension clearly relates to the way in which Africanists and conservative English-speaking whites place the individual in society or the different ways we construct social hierarchies. This naturally leads to the type of liberalism we choose to adopt and entrench in society. Perhaps the tension is not whether liberalism per se but which type.

Let us not forget the distortions of Africanism and English-speaking liberalism that have occurred as a result of prolonged institutionalized racism. The identities and underlying principles of both were strongly subjected to and shaped by apartheid South Africa. It is only now, with all this baggage, that each is trying to reconstruct itself in the new democracy. The recent distortions of 'one bullet and one settler' statements as representing the Africanist perspective are not only inflammatory and racist but also a serious distortion of Africanism, for they do not reflect the humanism and tolerance that are so characteristic of Africans wherever they are. This distortion is a consequence of apartheid and the liberation struggle rather than an integral component of Africanism or African thought. With the sensation and the obvious fear such statements induced or created in white South Africa, it is no wonder they remain fixated in the memory of most people. But to use these slogans as representing African thought is preposterous. The classic and certainly correct Africanist thought is underlined in the statement by the late Robert M. Sobukwe: 'The Africanist takes the view that there is only one race to which we all belong, the human race' (Sobukwe 1959 and 1960). Thus non-racism is established and entrenched in Africanism and the principle of ubuntu. If this statement alone does not represent classical liberal thinking, then one has problems with the whole concept of liberalism from whatever definition.

South Africa has entered a phase of multi-party democracy: the African National Congress, the Azanian People's Organization, the Democratic Party, the Inkatha Freedom Party (IFP), the National Party, and the Pan-Africanist Congress (PAC), to list just a few. In all these parties there is a liberal pattern of thinking and behaviour and liberal practices of varying degrees. Liberalism is rooted in each party's culture, tradition, history, and social experiences, and has acquired either an African or a European emphasis. So there are many African, Indian, and Afrikaans-speaking liberals.

Using the second description of liberalism as humanistic rather than individualistic, the ANC is the most liberal party in South Africa, for it is a broad church with an amazing degree of diversity and tolerance in terms of membership, race, gender, class, and ideas. The ANC is humanistic, tolerant, and inclusive in terms of race and class. However, it is rooted in African thought and traditions. It is largely a party of African social democrats. The ANC has long recognized freedom of thought, speech, and association, freedom from authoritarian government, and the rule of law. Everybody finds a home within the ANC, from the right to the left. In fact, most recognized white liberal-minded South Africans such as former members of the Liberal Party are today either members of the ANC or aligned to the ANC in thinking, Justice Goldstone and Sir Raymond Hoffenberg, for example. Nelson Mandela is the classic example of a liberal with an African perspective.

The present leader of the PAC, Dr Mmutlanyane Mogoba, has been described as a liberal. The leader of the IFP, Dr Mangosuthu Buthelezi, is another example of a liberal rooted in African nationalism. These are Africans leading large parties with entrenched liberal values, but from an African perspective. Prof. Kader Asmal, Dr Pallo Jordan, and Dr Mamphela Ramphele are other examples of hybrid liberals with African perspectives.

However, the DP has hijacked the liberal mantle for itself. As a minority party of largely white people, the DP has operated on the false premise that Africanism is incompatible with liberalism. The above examples not only question or disprove this false theory but also reveal that South Africa has its own brands of liberalism rooted in the diverse cultures of its people and political nuances. Liberalism is alive and kicking in South African society without one group claiming its exclusive ownership or success. Therefore, part of the tension between African and English-speaking liberalism is a lack of middle ground, as they are polar and pursued as such in a society where polarity is intrinsic and takes place amid a major societal transformation where the larger battle is defining the agenda and direction of the 'new society'.

The larger and more fundamental issues of this agenda for the majority are: who determines knowledge production and intellectual direction, culture and value systems, the meaning and value of life, and the identity of the nation in the global context in the new dispensation. These are what create the tensions between the two types of liberalism. Any rise in polarity within our society easily brings the ugly issue of race to the surface. Perhaps the fallacy has been the propagated notion that African societies are inherently anti-liberal.

The Liberal Party was the only party of the past that championed liberal values and fought for a non-racist South Africa. When liberal-minded South Africa aligned itself with the ANC, not-so-liberal-minded South Africans formed the Progressive Party. There thus emerged over time two types of white liberals in South Africa: the genuine liberal whose central theme was liberalism, and the masquerading type whose central theme was progressiveness. While progressiveness was essential to the anti-apartheid struggle, it does not equate with liberalism.

The present Democratic Party emerged from the joining of the Independent Party (led by Dennis Worrall), the Progressive Federal Party (led by Zach de Beer), and the National Democratic Movement (led by Wynand Malan), which were not intrinsically liberal in a classical sense. All these groups represented slight variations of conservative English-speaking ideology with elements of democracy, progressiveness, arrogance, and superiority. A mere glance at the names reveals much in terms of the central theme of each one of these groups. These various conversions represented some of the identity crises that have shaped the politics of English-speaking South Africa during apartheid.

So historically, the DP, which has today assumed the 'liberal' mantle, has done so from a wrong assumption and basis. It does not represent the genuine or the only liberal voice, but that of conservative English-speaking South Africans, the masquerading type of liberal. So for the DP to champion genuine liberal values without this qualification is like a heathen appearing in church to preach or to transform Christianity. It is hypocritical, for the aims of the party and its strategies have been to preserve and propagate a conservative English-speaking ethos and values very similar to Margaret Thatcher's or the Republican Party under Ronald Reagan.

The xenophobia and racism associated with these Eurocentric types of conservatism in the British Conservative Party and the American Republican Party are well documented. A recent illustration of this comes from statements by David Evans, a right-wing conservative, who when asked about the promotion of women politicians said of Virginia Bottomley (the British Minister for National Heritage) that she was 'dead from the neck upwards'. In relation to a rapist he said 'some black bastard' had raped a schoolgirl (*Star* 7 March 1997). It is as a result of these that the European Union declared 1997 Europe's Year against Racism and Xenophobia.

It is this close association and identification with, or shall I say the drawing of inspiration by our champions from, these elements that continue to stifle the evolution of a coherent and independent South African liberal cause. The DP has become, or is perceived to be, an imitation of European and American conservative parties within South Africa. This perception can only conjure up the past and its legacy of neo-colonialism, racism, superiority, and lack of commitment to Africa. In support of this, I quote Kaizer Nyatsumba who writes that 'the DP as presently constituted has no future. And for as long as it is seen as a party representing a small band of liberals promoting Thatcherite economic policies, nobody in government will take it seriously, no matter how much noise it makes in Parliament'. Which genuine liberals in the world would align themselves with Thatcherism or Reaganomics, let alone promote such ideas publicly today in a society striving for non-racism and emerging from a prolonged racial past?

Perhaps it is easily forgotten that long before the Nationalists came to power 'that most English of Englishmen' Cecil John Rhodes laid the foundations for apartheid when he decreed in a packed House of Assembly that 'the native be treated as a child and denied the franchise. We must adopt a system of despotism, such as works so well in India, in our relations with the barbarians of South Africa' (Thomas 1997). So, for historical and cultural reasons, a distorted version of liberalism has emerged in South Africa. By analysing these and making international comparisons, one can only conclude that conservative English-speaking liberals have a strong and long history of racist personae.

Liberals and racism in South Africa

In the struggle for the liberation of South Africa, the oppressed fought alongside the so-called liberals to remove Afrikaans-inspired racism, an authoritarian regime. It must be equally stated that the Afrikaner has never been associated with subtle racism: he has always tended to be open, frank, and hence crude in his practice of racial discrimination. The meaning of liberal then was simple, and different from today's: it stood for someone opposed to apartheid. It is unwise to equate anti-authoritarianism with non-racism or liberalism. Also, if one is anti-apartheid, that does not necessarily mean, or imply, that one is non-racist. The dynamics of 'anti' and of 'non' are quite distinct and different.

It is also quite foolish to equate the situation then and now. What people did then matters not an iota; it is what they do now, and how they behave in the new dispensation, that counts. However, there was a subtle but major distinction in objectives between the fight of the oppressed and that of the liberals, and it was this: the oppressed fought to remove all forms of racism, both the crude and the molecular types (sometimes referred to as subliminal, subtle, or unintentional racism), while the liberals fought to protect privilege and remove only the crude form of racism. They could not fight to remove the subtle version, which is part of their life, their socialization, their culture, and history. This form is generally linked to privilege. Privilege, the sense of identity and culture offered by 340 years of colonialism and apartheid, could not simply be erased by the ushering in of genuine democracy. The fight against this subtle form of racism would also be totally inconsistent with other conservative liberals in the western world.

Now that crude racism has been removed, the majority as part of their long-term agenda are focusing their energies on racism's subtle forms. It happens quite often in nature that by resolving one problem, another emerges as part of the solution. In attempting to create a non-racial democracy, in getting to understand each other better and learn more about each other, a different degree of discrimination or racism has been unveiled. The formerly disadvantaged experience and recognize this easily. Instead of defensiveness about this, I would counsel careful reflection on it. This is where so-called liberals are perplexed, for they do

not understand why they are under attack to redefine and articulate their agenda, and this time not only from the previously
oppressed but also from the previous oppressors. They seem to
work on the assumption that once the majority has tasted the
opium of power and the removal of naked apartheid, they will
either not recognize subtle racism or else they will leave it alone
to flourish in the new dispensation. Liberals are under attack
not to destroy liberalism but to strengthen it. They are under
attack so that the principles of equality and social justice can be
accomplished and strengthened between all members of South
African society.

The present South African champions of liberal values are
driven in their cause by the protection of apartheid-gained privileges and the acceptance of the consequences of inequality;
these are but disguised forms of racism. As a result of these, they
do not take into account the context, the history, and the social
experiences of the African majority. They operate as if things
have been and are now equal. While on the one hand they speak
non-racism, their everyday practices reveal just the opposite.
Their daily actions reveal that they are insensitive to the long
history of racial oppression. They have not yet succeeded in
exorcizing the scourge of racism that has been part and parcel of
their socialization throughout history. The greatest challenge to
democracy is no longer the naked crude Afrikaans-driven apartheid racism represented by the Afrikaner Weerstandsbeweging
(AWB), the Ku-Klux-Klan, and the British National Front, but
conservative English-speaking-driven racism, which is subtle,
molecular in nature, and very sophisticated in approach. It is
this latter form that is rampant among the champions of liberalism in South Africa and worse in other western democracies.
Because it is so subtle and deceptive in type, because it is not
crude or obvious, even the liberals in their everyday actions do
not realize that they harbour racism inherently – it has become a
subconscious phenomenon to them.

The new form of racial ideology in South Africa is characterized by the following features: (1) sanitized, coded language about
race that adheres to rather than departs from generally accepted
liberal principles and values, mobilized for illiberal ends; (2) an
avid disavowal of racist intent and the circumvention of classical
anti-racist discourse for potentially exclusionary ends (for
example, new racists would argue that their views do not represent racism but realism, or that affirmative action is 'reverse
racism'); (3) a shift from focus on race and biological relations
of inequality to concern for cultural differentiation and national
identity; (4) white racial attitudes that remain by and large contradictory and constant – with much progress on the commitment to the abstract principle of racial equality coexisting with
opposition to the implementation of these very same principles.

In this new terrain there is a broad conservative reinterpreta-
tion of the liberal legacy. The conservative liberals ironically
define racism as irrational and prejudiced attitudes certain individuals hold against others. In this new definition the question
of power and its role in the organization of social relations is
totally removed. As a result, a false assumption of symmetry in
social relations is created and with the neglect of the role of
power, justifies the notion that blacks, for example, are practising
or indulging in reverse racism. Because racism in this new
definition is defined in individual terms, the state can play very
little or no role in addressing and reversing the phenomenon.
Instead, the role of a liberal state is criticized as harming the
natural functioning of society by trying to intervene. A classic
example of this is affirmative action. In South Africa it has been
labelled 'reverse racism' and has been thought to harm rather
than improve society (Ansell 1997).

Subtle, conservative English-speaking racism manifests itself
in such patterns of behaviour as arrogance, we-know-what's-
good-for-you attitudes, paternalism, condescension, and an
assumption of superiority. It shows a lack of respect for other's

traditions, value systems, language, and identity; it seeks to enforce imitation through the manipulation of knowledge and inform-ation. These people have a burning desire to reproduce themselves and their system of values in others without compromising or in turn modifying their own behaviour. Such behavioural patterns are rampant in our society. Perhaps the best way to deal with the issue of liberals versus racism is to cite some recent experiences of eminent South Africans:

- Hlengiwe Mkhize, commissioner of the Truth and Reconcil-iation Commission (TRC) has said that 'Liberals think they can deal with the poor by doing things for them, but they cannot deal with you as an equal. They can't reason with you' (*Star* 1997), and Professor Smangele Magwaza complained of a 'Eurocentric and unrepresentative' delegation (*Star* 1997). Both of these men are respected clinical psychologists.

- Helen Suzman has in the *Sunday Times* (1997) cited two examples in her career of conflict between so-called liberals and society. One was in 1966 after the assassination of Dr Hendrik Verwoerd, when P. W. Botha said, 'Yes. It's all you liberals, it's your fault. Now we will get you.' P. W. Botha accused her and the liberal fraternity of planning the assassi-nation. The second was an angry lady who accosted her and said, 'Yes, it's you, it's all you liberals, it's your fault, you have ruined this country. Look what is happening with all the crime and violence, and people leaving in droves. It's your fault, it's you liberals.' One can only assume that similar utterances accusing the liberals of everything that is going wrong within the country have been made.

- In 1995, Barney Pityana, chairperson of the Human Rights Commission, accused Prof. Dennis Davis, a renowned liberal legal academic in public of being racist, again bringing the issue of liberal racism to the fore (Gevisser 1996; Husemeyer 1997).

- The debates and resistance around the transformation of the health system of the country were perceived to be a racial agenda by the liberal fraternity against Dr Nkosazana Zuma and Dr Olive Shisana (Gevisser 1996). The protection of privilege and multinationals was central to the issue.

- The debates between the Freedom of Expression Institute and Thami Mazwai have revealed further racial division between the black media and the English-speaking press. These debates have been corroborated by Rafiq Rohan in the Sowetan (1997) and recent submissions to the TRC by several black journalists in which they provide clear and unambiguous evidence of discrimination and racism within the English-speaking liberal press. There are many other alleged instances of racial discrimination that are ascribed to the liberal press during the apartheid era.

- In October 1995 a group of thirteen largely liberal academics at the University of the Witwatersrand set out to unseat me (I was then deputy vice-chancellor). This conflict was seen nationally and internationally as racially motivated and quintessential of South African liberal racism. This perception of 'racial motives' by liberals was widely reported by Nature (Cherry 1995, 1996), The Economist (1995), Marby (1996) in Newsweek, Mamdani (1997) in Social Dynamics and the Mail & Guardian, Statman and Ansell (1996) at the second annual congress of the Psychological Society of South Africa, the Washington Post (1995), and many other leading scholars and publications nationally and internationally. Of course, these issues were also compounded by the poor journalism and the poor research and analytical skills of the South African press, largely the English-speaking press. The racial divisions within the press, the differing perspectives, and the legacy of racial agendas are what produces sensational journalism rather than responsible and informative reporting (Makgoba 1997).[1]

What happened to me at Wits was not unique for a black South

African. Many of my brothers and sisters have suffered under the so-called liberal attack. Their identities, their self-worth, their credentials, and their confidence have been questioned, battered, and destroyed by these people. Ask any black academic anywhere in South Africa about academic harassment. Ask any prominent black person. Most of us have wounds or deep scars as a result of this vicious psychological destruction by whites. How do conservative English-speaking liberals hope to recruit Africans by alienating the very African role models, the filters and opinion-makers of African society, that they most need to develop and build their type of liberalism?

South African English-speaking liberals are riddled with guilt; they are superficial in their analyses and understanding of racial and sociopolitical problems. They have failed to engage with the systems of identity, values, and culture that are central to and hold together the oppressed majority. They have failed to engage with African culture as part of their socialization. How many English-speaking liberals today speak or understand an African language? Yet they live within a sea of Africans. Instead, they have from a superior position tended to expect the African simply to imbibe their culture and language. They have failed to reciprocate culturally, linguistically, and socially.

Like all liberals throughout the world, they have constructed a profile or persona of the African people that does not exist, but that fits their preconceived notions; they tend to concentrate on evasive structural approaches to real problems. They are more interested in the statistics of crime, the falling rand, more education, and more good bureaucracy and so forth. The little liberal thought that does exist, or that is left, lacks guts and courage. Hence they are perceived to be like a snake, twisting and turning, a chameleon, or a mirage, never to be caught. They have failed to adapt or integrate fully into their present environment. Instead, they have decided to sit on the fence or margin, so to speak.

All the examples cited earlier, from diverse sources, represent a major battle that is looming large between the majority and the so-called conservative English-speaking liberal. It is not simply that many Africans perceive and believe that South African liberals are racist, but this belief extends across class and the political divide; it also extends across the racial divide. Worse still, it extends across the African diaspora and the international arena. Many non-South African blacks and whites from the UK, the USA, Australia, and Germany also share this belief. These comments not only surprise many of us but also confirm our fears vis-à-vis our English-speaking compatriots. How could so many different people of different backgrounds, nationally and internationally, be so united in this perception of racism and still get it wrong? Could the majority be wrong in their perceptions, experiences, and understandings of these issues after 340 years of experiencing relentless racism? Surely they cannot be totally wrong, for the following reasons: the majority have experienced racism and through experience have formulated ideas, theories, and coping mechanisms to deal with different levels of it, and what it means to them; most of the examples cited earlier are from members of the majority (the likes of Dr Zuma, Dr Shisana, Dr Pityana, and myself) who have lived, experienced, and participated in mature democracies, so they clearly understand racism and liberalism from a broad perspective through their exile and life experiences; many Afrikaans-speaking people agree with the oppressed that the present champions of liberalism harbour racist tendencies; and finally, blacks across the African diaspora and non-South African whites of British and American origin agree with and confirm this perception.

So-called South African liberals remain unpopular, because in the eyes of the majority and the international community they are subtle racists. This perception is universal irrespective of the class and political persuasion of the oppressed. One thing all the oppressed share today, unfortunately even with the former oppressor (Afrikaans-speaking South Africans), is that the South

African liberal is a sophisticated racist and not a genuine liberal at all. As the agenda of the new South Africa is to eliminate all forms of racism in order to bring about transformation, liberals have no choice but to face this analysis within themselves. Liberals have to analyse their individual socialization, their politicization, their intellectual inspirations, their paradigms, and their privileged position within many generations of racist forefathers, and ask the simple question: have they finally exorcized racism over generations, or has racism been evolving so well with adaptation over time that they have become unconscious of it? Alternatively, can white English-speaking South Africans, with such a strong inheritance and long history of racism, have outgrown racism in a country that legitimized and internalized racism and practised it for so long? If they opposed crude racism, did they ever look at how to rid themselves of the subtle molecular forms of it?

It is because Africans detest, are allergic to, and have suffered racism so much as part of their history and socialization that any sniff of this induces a reflex dislike. This racial tag of the liberals is a major source of tension and opposition.

Liberalism and the racial question

'Racism and liberalism are incompatible ... Though liberals might sometimes lapse into racist ways of thinking, no true liberal can be a racist'. So said John Kane-Berman in 1996. This statement is not only profound in interpretation and meaning but clearly admits the sometimes racial tendencies of liberals. It also challenges whether our liberals are true or not by implication, suggesting that there may be liberals who are not true to liberal values. The major question is this: in a racist society such as ours, what are the chances that a liberal would lapse into racist ways of thinking and thus betray the true values of liberalism?

Liberalism is a dominant theme of most classical western democracies. It has contributed to great advancements in these democracies. In other words, liberalism is a universal principle that encompasses tolerance, freedom, objectivity, and independence, and recognizes the uniqueness of the individual and his rights. It does not matter whether the governing party is Democratic, Christian, Socialist, or Labour: these values are deeply entrenched and always respected.

Liberal philosophy, be it associated with conservative or true liberalism, has in general failed to deal with matters of race, be it in South Africa, in the UK, in France, in Germany, or in the USA. The repeated racial crises in each of these countries over the last thirty years bear testimony to this failure. The USA and the UK are generally accepted as the countries with the most entrenched and successful liberal values today. In a survey by the *Washington Post*, Harvard University, and the Kaiser Family Foundation in 1995, 47 per cent of American citizens felt racism had increased over the last ten years. In particular, 68 per cent of blacks and 38 per cent of whites thought that 'racism was a big problem in our society'. Perhaps even more startling were the differences in the way blacks and whites view the world. As Professor Robert Blendon put it, 'it really seems that blacks and whites may as well be on different planets'. While 70 per cent of blacks saw discrimination as their biggest obstacle, 58 per cent of whites saw the break-up of the black family and 'lack of discipline' as the major obstacles to black advancement. A similar pattern was found in a national survey in the UK, where 85 per cent of British whites in 1995 admitted to racism, or to still harbouring racist tendencies, compared to 95 per cent ten years ago. In South Africa today there can be no doubt that whites and blacks exist in two different spheres in the way they look at and interpret life and their social experiences.

These two studies are revealing, for both countries over the last thirty years have instituted aggressive national policies on discrimination, racism, and affirmative action. In both countries liberalism is so entrenched that it is not questioned or debated.

How can South African liberals believe and hope to convince anyone that they are immune from racism with these findings? 'Race relations are deteriorating as a result of persistent features in our political economy and the consequences of ambitious policies', reported Prof. Lawrence Schlemmer (1996) about the South African situation since the 1994 elections.

While this philosophy has provided liberty and success within the classical western democracies, largely to people of European descent, it has failed to accommodate the issue of race in these societies. The question is, Why? Is it because this philosophy is inadequate or inherently racist, or is it because there has been a deliberate fear to develop the liberal philosophy to its near-ultimate potential? In short, has there been a lack of courage on the part of liberals to expound and propagate the liberal ethos to its logical conclusion?

An honest analysis is that the liberal philosophy of the West is adequate, or at least could have been developed to accommodate the issue of race a long time ago. The development of liberalism in the West took place in the midst of entrenched white male supremacy and racism. Hence liberals evolved historically in the context of racial and gender inequality. As a basic philosophy liberalism is not inherently racist, but it is often championed with an arrogant, superior attitude that reveals racist tendencies. The champions of liberal values (for example, the English-speaking media, the English-speaking universities, and other English-dominated institutions such as the TRC) are not practising what they preach.

English-speaking universities in particular are neither democratic nor liberal. They are cloisters of some of the most illiberal and racist activities. Who benefited most from the protestations of the so-called liberals in South Africa on issues such as sanctions and university autonomy? White South Africans themselves.

These protestations increased alienation and discrimination and provided added advantage to an already advantaged community. Wherever the English-speaking South African is, there is covert racism.

Throughout the history of liberal thought and debate, liberalism has never taken the race issue and made it central to its dogma in the same way in which it has tackled education, poverty, and free enterprise. In fact, liberal philosophy and liberal writings are silent on the issue of race. Many liberal-minded whites who lapse into racist or illiberal actions hide behind the notion that the liberal philosophy is non-racist. As a result, liberal racism is rationalized instead of being confessed within the South African liberal community. What went wrong was fundamentally the lack of courage within all liberal communities to get out of this racial scourge completely.

The trouble with liberals is that they are arms-length people. They want to be good to everybody and in the end they are good to nobody. They do not get their hands dirty, for they are forever sitting on the fence. They are good at sending food posters to famine-stricken places and are quite happy to construct their own heroes of the natives without actual or hands-on experience. Instead of being courageous, they have allowed themselves to wallow in guilt all the time. They cannot face reality head-on but enjoy skirting it. For these reasons, the liberal philosophy has ignored the values and cultural systems of other groups and has tended to concentrate on statistics about crime and affirmative-action programmes. What liberals have failed to absorb or grasp is the masked psychological depression, the total loss of hope, and the reduction in the value and meaning of life that is so pervasive within the communities that are disadvantaged.[2] These are the root causes of racial tensions and would naturally be part of finding the solution. It is no fault of theirs that these developed through long periods of colonialism or slavery. It is their fault that these still persist. What they need to do is to confront these issues head-on rather than keep avoiding and passing them on to the next generation.

Liberalism in the West has failed in general to solve the racial question for a number of reasons. Western democracies are in general democracies of white people, pursuing and propagating the values of western civilization. Their main concern has been the role of the European ethos and values in shaping the world. Racism originated from Western civilization largely as part of intellectual inquiry (D'Souza 1995). It has been part and parcel of white people's socialization; whites have for generations lived with the assurances and certainties that they are 'the people' and define the norm. Liberals have in general adopted strategies that are essentially soft and do not go to the root of the racial question, which is *equality*. Their acceptance of, and acquiescence in, the consequences of inequality, their protection of privilege, and ordering of values, such as their preference for freedom above dignity in constitutional matters, are but a few examples to illustrate their subtle racism. They do not grasp the central tenet of humanistic liberalism, 'Motho ke motho ka batho', 'You are only human through the humanity of other people'.

Years ago we heard the anti-sanctions campaign; we heard the protection of university autonomy above academic freedom; they removed academic apartheid but supported social apartheid – all these in the name of liberalism. We hear today how we should be tough on immigrants and tough on crime, for example; just in the recent past when immigrants to South Africa were Europeans and crime was rampant in the townships, no one challenged the past regime to deal with these issues. At universities such as the University of the Witwatersrand, the University of Natal, the University of Cape Town, and Rhodes University, university autonomy was defended disproportionately at the expense of individual freedom. These universities in effect sanctioned discriminatory and racist practices that became the order of the day (Murray 1996). In short, university autonomy became a means of protecting Anglo-Saxon racism. The liberals never took a strong public stance on sanctions-busting and the deep and wide-ranging National Party government corruption that we now see emerging through the Truth and Reconciliation Commission. All these experiences tend to lend themselves to a racial interpretation of liberals in South Africa. These very features are sadly consistent with so-called liberals throughout the Western world. The universal failure of liberals to solve the racial question within Western-type democracies has left a worrying question about liberals and liberalism. If the liberal philosophy is inherently non-racial and enjoys such success, why has it failed to solve the race question? This is a major source of difficulty.

Conclusion

The apparent major tensions, difficulties, and opposition to liberalism lie in the definition, the concept of society, and the place of the individual in it. The history and evolution of English-speaking liberalism in a racist context has in South Africa led to a unique form of liberalism. This is characterized by the internalization of racist behaviour and language. This 'racist liberalism' is so subconscious that it has become the norm and hence unintentional. Racist and illiberal practices are rampant within the South African liberal community. These practices, despite their subtlety, show that South Africa's English-speaking liberals are unique in their racism. The repeated denials and rationalization of racism by South African liberals can only lead to a delay in advancing genuine liberalism and curing racism. Africanist thought is compatible with humanistic liberalism. The failure of liberalism to deal with race worldwide remains a worrying issue about the strength and level to which it can go as a social theory.

Finally, I wrote this article from the perspective of an African, from an African idiom. There has not been any rigorous academic research of liberalism in South Africa. The deconstruction of white identity, power, racism, and the construction of social relations and how these fed into the whole socialization and development of the so-called liberals and liberalism have not been studied, either by black or white intellectuals and academics. This article is to my mind one of the first commentaries or critiques on liberals and liberalism in South Africa from this perspective. It deals with liberalism as a phenomenon that requires serious and rigorous academic research from an African perspective in order to deconstruct its myth. It is in this light that it must be read and interpreted.

13

THEMBA SONO

Why are there so few black liberals?

BY 'BLACK' I PRESUME is meant, and I shall take it to mean, the erstwhile Bantus. Africans, that is. The term has been corrupted since the halcyon days of the Black Consciousness Movement to mean Africans, coloureds, and Indians. Despite this quilt-patch definition, the term is definitionally and representationally confined, and appropriately so, to Africans. Similarly, the concept 'black liberals' would refer to liberals in this group. This is an important hurdle to clear from the outset because one is frequently embroiled in nomenclatural incongruities and generalizations when one engages in conventional and analytical discourse on society, politics, and economics in South Africa. Precision in applying the term 'black' is of considerable importance.

This notwithstanding, the title of my paper is itself problematic in four respects. For one, liberalism, as a belief system, is an ethic that eschews group-consciousness, but fastens instead on individual-consciousness. The values of liberalism itself, as I show later in this work, are clear and specific, however, regardless of the ambiguity of the concept itself. Objectively, therefore, it is a simple matter to describe who a liberal is. By this objective device, rather than by a conventional ideological device, Africans, in contrast to the misleading question of my title, would most likely turn out to be overwhelmingly liberal. In the interim, however, I shall employ 'liberal' in the conventional ideological sense rather than in the objective sense. In South Africa, true liberals sought to achieve aims that included universal adult suffrage, reform rather than revolution, constitutional change rather than violent eruptions, a bill of rights, rule of law, a market economy, liberty, and equality.

Liberalism is to this extent non-racial and universal, regardless of the fact that it was inaugurated in South Africa by people of European descent, some of whom, wittingly or unwittingly, gave the concept an unwarranted stench because of their frequent lapses into illiberal attitudes and practices even while claiming to be liberals. Genuine liberals opposed arbitrary rule, repression, and violent means to achieve political ends. But more important-ly, they aroused suspicions of pretense and insincerity in their interpersonal relations with their black interlocutors. It is liberals nevertheless who first introduced the notion of individual liberty as a fundamental right, the right to own private property, and the rights of individuals qua individuals. It is they who first insisted on a constitutional state for all citizens. White liberals were in the forefront of this pursuit, for obvious reasons.

To put it differently, as Kierin O'Malley does, 'The history of organized liberalism in this country has been a predominantly white affair' (1994). But this in itself is not a serious observation since other political concepts as we know them today are European in origin: democracy, communism/Marxism, and even the name and state 'South Africa', let alone the term 'Africa'. Some may argue that even racism was European in origin. British liberals and Boer conservatives joined hands to sideline the Bantus. Such was the progressive conservatism of British liberalism in 1910. The point here, however, is that the notion of *racial* categorization in a *non-racial* context is anomalous, albeit very real in South Africa. In any event, there have been black liberals in South Africa, though they have not been as numerous as their white counterparts for obvious historical reasons. But because 'race' has had a sustained and traumatic role in the political life and history of South Africa, its legacy has remained powerful even in discourse among liberal circles. (I shall in due course visit the reason there is less emphasis on race in the discourse on communism *à la* 'white communists' and 'black communists'.)

The second problem with my title is this: why does a liberal foundation such as the Helen Suzman Foundation still define Africans by the colour of their skin? Talking of 'black liberals' is as unfortunate as it is unnecessary. It is as futile as agitating for 'black nationalism' in 1997. Incidentally, of the sixteen topics for this workshop, only this one identifies itself by the skin colour of the target population. Not a single topic carries the moniker 'white liberal'. Please look at the programme of this workshop for yourselves. Only the peculiar label 'black liberal' is a worthy racial topic for examination, implicitly suggesting that it is less the norm – that the concept 'liberal' should be understood to mean primarily white. This is the mind-set that hence rushes to conclude that 'there are few black liberals in South Africa', a conclusion not so much ill-conceived as lacking in empirical validity. Liberalism should appropriately not define itself in racial terms.

The third problem with this title is one of empirical validity: is it true that there are few black liberals in South Africa? In comparison with which group? With whites of course, but how do we know that this is the case? I am aware of no major studies that have surveyed African political attitudes in terms of categories that include liberal/liberalism. Certainly, numerous studies have been undertaken by such groups as the Human Sciences Research Council (HSRC), the Institute for Democracy in South Africa (IDASA; previously the Institute for a Democratic Alternative for South Africa), the Institute for Multi-Party Democracy (IMPD), Market Research Africa (MRA), Markinor, the UNISA Market Research Bureau, and the Helen Suzman Foundation. But none of these studies offer empirical evidence in support of our title question, since they confine themselves largely to attitudes towards *political parties* and not to the ideology of the respondents. Thus, while these surveys are helpful, they do not inform us about African identification in terms of ideology qua ideology.

The other side of this black/white coin of liberalism is: do we really know how many white liberals there are in South Africa? How do we know it? Have these studies given us an inkling of the magnitude of white liberalism? Do we really know whether there are more white liberals than black liberals? These questions automatically insinuate themselves the moment the type of question contained in this paper's title is raised. The title question is therefore as unscientific as, for example: Why are there so few (or many) African tribalists? Such questions are simply speculative, and thus of little value.

The fourth problem with this title is that it takes it as a given that blacks understand what is meant by liberalism or liberal. There are African liberals in the African National Congress (ANC), for instance, just as there are in the Inkatha Freedom Party (IFP), the National Party (NP), and the Democratic Party (DP). Even though the latter is probably the staunchest advocate of liberal principles, its message is obfuscated by the racially skewed composition of its leadership. It is seen, even by some African liberals, as oriented towards white leadership more than as a repository of liberal values, regardless of the fact that it *is* such a repository. In the crafting of the new constitution, liberals, especially in the DP, fought strenuously for liberal principles, most of which are now enshrined in the Bill of Rights. Illiberal forces strongly opposed the idea of property rights, for example. They succeeded only in blunting the property rights clause, however, not in expunging it altogether.

The character of our society and representative system is itself illiberal to some extent. Even the constitution (in section 1) defines South Africa as a *multi-party democracy*. Please note that a multi-party democratic state is *not* the same as a democratic state. The emphasis in our constitution is on *parties* as representative vehicles rather than on *individuals* as constituency representatives.

While it is theoretically possible to establish a political party that is specifically and definitionally a liberal party in a society that has known nothing but racial politics, it is not likely that a truly non-racial party can be formed, regardless of the non-racial tag of the ANC. This is not a deficiency in the ANC, however. It is not so much the non-racial nature of a given party that is significant, it is the degree of 'racialness' perceived in its non-racialism. Perceptions of racial degrees are more important than the weight of liberal values in any party. This is why the ANC, the Pan-Africanist Congress (PAC), and the IFP are predominantly black and the NP and the DP are predominantly white, regardless of the fact that all these parties welcome members and supporters of other races. All of them are defined by their racial heritage and appearance. It is blackness versus whiteness, not liberalism versus conservatism, or socialism versus liberalism, that is the primary factor. In any event, these parties are still defined by and operating according to the values of apartheid South Africa. They were all established in the era of apartheid.

These difficulties are clearly compounded by the fact that there is no organizational political vehicle that is specifically identified as liberal and which is seriously committed to the recruitment of Africans into its ranks. The defunct Liberal Party was one such vehicle, but it was systematically ground to extinction by the apartheid government and was not allowed to implement its strategy of recruiting Africans. The 1968 Prohibition of Political Interference Act was designed to prevent Africans from identifying themselves as members of the Liberal Party. But even this party failed to defy the system and elect Africans to prominent leadership roles. Could it be that there were no Africans worthy of top leadership positions? How about Jordan Ngubane, for instance? African critics of liberals first detected the 'hypocrisy' – or what they called the 'great pretence' – of white liberals on this very issue of leadership exclusivity. They saw the Liberal Party talking tall principles, but walking short roads of insincerity. Despite its efficiency and professionalism, the same fate awaits the DP if it fails to correct similar errors.

As already noted, the Democratic Party is a political organization dedicated to liberal democracy, so it could be argued with some measure of plausibility that if there are any African liberals in South Africa, here then is a political vehicle to which most of them could attach themselves. Membership of and/or electoral support for the DP in national and local elections since 1994 would constitute a veritable barometer of African support for liberalism. If statistics indicate that there are few African members of the DP, then new issues are raised. In that case, the question should rather be: why are there few blacks in the Democratic Party? But this question leads to many problems, as I shall detail momentarily.

Perhaps a slight digression might help to illustrate this issue of numerical notation of black liberals. A corollary question to the title of this paper might be: Why are there so many African communists in South Africa? Of course, this question presents problems similar to those raised by our title question. For instance, we do not really know how many African communists there are, simply because communists, unlike some of our liberals, hardly ever focus on the racial numbers of their membership. South African communists have perhaps learned the lesson of the 'Black Republic' racial saga of their party during the 1920s.

Their concern is simply to increase the number of communists, not for the purpose of winning electoral power, because they are not likely to, but to influence power-holders; that is, to act as a pressure group. Even if we may know that some 75 000 persons are members of the South African Communist Party (SACP), it would not follow that membership in the SACP is an accurate barometer of African communists in South Africa. Had it been so, the argument would be problematic because embedded in it are at least two fallacies: (a) that party membership is identical with ideology; and (b) that likeness is identity.

On the first fallacy: we have recently seen the spectacle of communists who, though still espousing the rhetoric of their ideology, are nonetheless involved in cobbling capitalist corporations and becoming captains of commerce and industry (Gevisser 1997; Koch 1997; Day 1997). The point here is: to be a 'communist' does not necessarily mean one wants to practise communism. The concept is meaningless in today's South Africa. The ideology of communism thus degrades into instrumentality. It becomes a simple tool, like a hammer or a sickle. The theory, in any event, is impracticable. In practice, communism, as history shows, inevitably leads to capitalism. The communist members of the labour unions, by and large, now have one major thrust: to support the growth of the black business class. They have established union corporate companies which are frenetically engaged in capitalist endeavours (Reuters 1997). The SACP is currently examining capitalist options, such as floating an investment company, to fund its activities.

The second fallacy is similar to the first. In reality, likeness is not identity. To look like a communist is not necessarily to be one. This is why communists in practice are non-existent except as political authoritarians. At the economic level, communists are nowhere to be found except as critics of neo-liberalism, even as they surely drift towards the benefits of neo-liberal economics. Communists don't exist. Only capitalists, proto-capitalists, or wannabe-capitalists are found at the level of practical reality. One is Being, the other Non-Being. So much for the digression. But what does this mean in relation to black liberals?

The simple answer is that there has never been, in South Africa, an accurate barometer for measuring liberalism either. My view is that were such a measure to be devised, it would most likely confound our title question and convert it to: Why are there so many African liberals in South Africa? Survey studies in South Africa may provide startling results, however: for instance, a recent Market Research Africa survey showed that 37 per cent of urban blacks polled favoured a one-party state![1]

Using the values classed as liberal as an empirical measuring rod, one may construct a more valid profile of African liberals. I shall show momentarily how such a survey could look.

Although South Africans are less ideologists than 'partyists', an ideological survey rather than a party-support survey may give us a somewhat better picture of the state or degree of liberalism among Africans. But even this is fraught with problems, because many liberals in the ANC, for example, focus more on *democracy and equality*, while their counterparts in the DP focus more on *democracy and liberty*. Despite some disagreements among the liberal camps in either party about what democracy means, not so much as an idea but as practice, the ideology of democracy is a source of both unity and divisiveness. In the ANC, democracy is *party-representation*, whereas for the DP the concept is closer to *individual-representation*. Proportional representation, rather than single-constituency representation, stresses the *party* as a democratic vehicle. Ours is thus closer to a party-state than a democratic state, albeit a constitutional one. That aside, the ANC liberal stresses *equality* while the DP liberal stresses *liberty*. The two concepts can of course become mutually exclusive at a certain point. For instance, to enforce equality may suppress liberty. To seek equalitarianism may extinguish libertarianism. To compel group identity may deny individual difference. On the other hand, to extend liberty invariably sprouts or enhances inequalities. The historical tensions between equality and liberty have been amply documented by others, and need no further elaboration here.

Be that as it may, an improved survey method on African liberalism might conceivably study a six-way relationship among *status*, *ideology*, *party*, 'race', *region*, and *religion*, as illustrated below. Other critical factors could of course be added, such as income and education. But the six-categories analysis could be sufficient to provide a fairly comprehensive profile, not only of who is liberal, conservative, or revolutionary/socialist, but also the race, party, class, or religion of these respondents:

Categories	Camp 1	Camp 2	Camp 3
Class or status	Upper	Middle	Lower
Ideology	Conservative	Liberal	Revolutionary/Socialist
Party			
Race			
Region:			
(a) Urban			
(b) Rural			
Religion			

Of course, such a survey will be useful only if there is a priori agreement on what the three ideological classifications mean. Even then, tendencies in these directions are restrained by numerous cross-cutting cleavages. Each of the tendencies is certainly important, but none is strong enough to exert a dominant pull on South African political life. It may, for example, be asked: are liberalism and conservatism not more powerful in stimulating a clear-cut split? The answer to this is that outside the apartheid environment, the ideologies are vague at best; coherent and lucid ideological thinking outside party affiliation is very uncommon in South Africa. This society has been heavily riven by the apartheid/anti-apartheid dichotomy, and beyond that, nebulosity reigns supreme: epithets such as 'progressive' and 'reactionary' for socialist/revolutionary/nationalist and conservative/liberal respectively begin to substitute for analysis and discourse. There is of course no absolutely certain method of correlating ideology with class/status. How do we classify, say, the boss of a taxi fleet, who despite being a multi-millionaire, enforces most of his business operations with the barrel of a gun? Is he upper, middle or lower class? Is he a liberal or a conservative? A democrat, socialist, or capitalist? How do we classify him ideologically?

So do black liberals exist in South Africa? The answer depends on our measuring rods. If we define liberalism in terms of political party affiliation, a superficial response would be that very few exist. But even this is a problem, because how are we to see these liberal trees when the racial forest is the character of South African political life? For instance, instead of seeing Tony Leon or Helen Suzman simply as liberals, we see race first, hence the silly tag 'he or she's a white liberal'. South African politics are overwhelmingly racial, though not necessarily racist. Black South Africans emotionally and traditionally identify with something that has the name 'African' or 'Black' in it. This is the reason many Africans today find it uncomfortable to belong to a party that is led by a non-African. White leadership mutes black followership, regardless of the authenticity or integrity of such leadership. Still, the DP's leadership remains largely white, not because whites seek to monopolize leadership roles (though a few may secretly hanker after that), but rather because its African support base is thin. And the black support base is thin because – oh, vicious circles – the white leadership base is thick!

Many whites have accepted the realities of our times, that they shall be ruled for the foreseeable future by a black person. Many others begrudgingly accept this point. For still many others, this is a bitter pill to swallow. On the other hand, I am not certain whether most Africans are emotionally willing to be ruled or led by a white person in today's South Africa. This is the reason more black liberals are in the ANC than in the DP. There is nothing fundamentally different between the ANC and the DP except degrees of emphasis, of efficiency, of certainty. The ANC emphasizes *distributive equality* while the DP emphasizes *funda-*

mental liberty. Both espouse democratic principles. Their emphasis differs.

After the ANC changed its name from 'Native' to 'African' some seven years after the founding of the Union of South Africa – in an era during which blacks called themselves 'Africans' and whites called themselves 'Europeans' – one's racial group became the dominant criterion of political identification. The small band of liberals who emphasized individual rather than group rights were hampered by the exclusivity of white leadership of their political or cultural organs. The implied 'therefore' of this situation was black followership. In a racially polarized society, long before the advent of formal apartheid, this became a non sequitur. The pull of the group-rights doctrine became more alluring than that of the individual-rights doctrine.

African political activists, like most of their Afrikaner counterparts, followed the group-rights doctrine. These two were the only major groups in a contest for political hegemony. A pertinent question may be: why did the overwhelming number of Africans, unlike the small band of largely English-speaking whites, follow the group-rights doctrine? Two answers appear pertinent:

(a) group-mindedness was a combat doctrine;
(b) Africans have been socialized to value traditional/
ethnic/tribal/clan cohesion or solidarity.

If these answers are true and valid, a group-oriented approach, as opposed to an individual-oriented approach, would invariably take precedence in an African world-view and personal evaluative preference. If Africans are seen to depart from the group-orientation norm to the individual-orientation one, they are likely to feel uncomfortable because they would allegedly be betraying their cultural background. But this hypothesis in reality is making a larger claim for the cultural thesis than is warranted. (In another paper, 'Is African culture incompatible with liberalism?' (Sono

1997), I have sought to show that the cultural thesis lacks sufficient empirical validity. For those who need to engage in this discourse, I refer them to the above-mentioned study.)

The point here is that an ideological-survey method of discovering the degree of liberalism among Africans in South Africa is itself not much better than the party-identification survey method. Most Africans know how to *live the liberal way*, even if they do not know what liberalism means. The majority would probably deny that they are liberals or that they espouse liberalism, especially since liberalism has been so demonized and denounced by black nationalists since the 1960s (Sono 1993). They would probably conclude that 'liberal' means 'white liberal' without knowing what a liberal is, and they would most likely be unable to define liberalism or describe its values. Most, in any event, would take refuge in epithets because of their lack of understanding of liberalism, or their fear of its political pull.[2]

Yet were an opinion survey to be conducted that did not use the term 'liberal' but was confined only to agreeing or disagreeing with the *values* and *interests* that are characteristically and classically liberal (such as those I enumerate below), a more valid and accurate picture of liberalism amongst Africans in South Africa would emerge.

An interests, beliefs, and values survey

		A	B
1	Ideal human relationships are those based on free individual choice.	Agree	Disagree
2	The right of free association, free assembly, is important and necessary in a democratic society.	Yes	No
3	Every person is entitled to freedom of speech, thought, and conscience.	Yes	No
4	The right to own private property should be extended to every citizen or legal resident of South Africa.	Yes	No

5	Group rights are more important than individual rights.	No	Yes
6	Government/public ownership or control is more important for society and the economy than individual/private ownership.	No	Yes
7	Should the government increase income tax for the employed in order to support the unemployed and poor?	Slightly disagree	Strongly agree
8	Governments should have as much right as private individuals to own and run businesses.	No	Yes
9	Competition in the market-place is a good thing.	Yes	No
10	It is the function of government to protect the rights of each citizen even against state abuse.	Strongly agree	Slightly agree
11	Common ownership is better than individual ownership.	No	Yes
12	I prefer equality to liberty.	No	Yes
13	Freedom is better if it is for the group than if it is for the individual.	No	Yes
14	Liberty is more important than equality.	Yes	No
15	Liberal tradition emphasizes the pursuit of freedom and individual dignity.	Yes	No
16	Every individual should subordinate his or her interests to the group.	No	Yes
17	It is vital for consumers to have choice in economic activities.	Yes	No
18	Everybody should be allowed to stand for elections and run for office even if he or she belongs to no political party.	Yes	No

Conclusion

All those whose answers fall mainly in the 'A' column are clearly liberals, regardless of their protestations to the contrary. Liberalism is *not* what one professes to subscribe to, but rather what one adheres to and upholds in one's day-to-day life. It is an attitude to life, an attitude that one would like to see in practice. Any respondent whose answers fall in column 'A' but who nonetheless professes to be either a non-liberal, a socialist, or a conservative is, at best, surely confused.

The interests, values, and beliefs survey as outlined above provides an accurate yardstick of who is or is not a liberal. I want to hazard a prediction: if Africans were asked to fill in this questionnaire, the majority of them would tick the column 'A' responses. African culture is neither illiberal nor organically incompatible with liberalism.

14

R W JOHNSON

The best of enemies? Black intellectuals and white liberals

SINCE THE ADVENT OF DEMOCRACY in South Africa in
1994, liberals – especially white liberals – have found themselves
the target of endless vituperation from black intellectuals. This
onslaught has surprised and bemused many liberals who, having
fought against apartheid for nearly fifty years, now watch as any
number of erstwhile Broederbonders and conservative businesspeople are easily preferred to them by the new black elite. Some
liberals have attempted to defend themselves by citing their record
of resistance to apartheid, but this appears to enrage their critics
even more. The phenomenon has already attracted a useful
compendium (Husemeyer 1997). Among white liberals, the
overwhelming reaction is one of angry puzzlement: 'have our
accusers gone mad?' they ask.

The question is not wholly rhetorical, for much of the criticism
seems unreasoned, and overheated. Certainly, most of it does
not stand up to even the most rudimentary analysis. Firstly, not
all liberals are white, and not all whites are liberal. There have

This chapter was added after the seminar at which Themba Sono's and William
Makgoba's papers were presented. Both complained – correctly – that no paper
dealt with the 'white liberal' category. So David Welsh and I both felt that this
point should be taken up. I am grateful to Prof. Makgoba for his extremely useful comments on this paper, providing me with points which I have tried to
accommodate wherever possible – R. W. Johnson.

307

always been African, coloured, and Asian liberals (though there is no way of estimating their number), but their existence is almost wholly ignored by many black intellectuals.

The fact that two of the most famous sons of the Asian and African communities, Mahatma Gandhi and Albert Luthuli, clearly belong within the liberal tradition is simply brushed aside as irrelevant – for in effect, what is being attacked is not liberalism but white liberals. As the black nationalist Bennie Bunsee put it, 'The worst political insult to a black radical is to refer to him as a liberal. It immediately brackets him with the enemy – liberals are supposed to be white, and all whites are generally liberals, according to the black tradition'(Husemeyer 1997, 226).

In fact, this equation of whites with liberals is a bizarre distortion of history. Among whites, liberals have always been a small group – at its very peak in 1989 the Democratic Party could muster no more than twenty per cent of the white vote, and during the 1960s and 1970s the proportion supporting its liberal predecessor, the Progressive Party, was no more than five to ten per cent. By definition, the other eighty to ninety per cent of whites were either supporters of apartheid or, at best, complaisant in the face of apartheid. The first point to notice is that by condemning white liberals one is effectively saying that there were no good whites at all, save perhaps the tiny handful of white communists – a judgment, of course, in which the latter would concur.

If one examines the tirades against 'conservative English-speaking white liberals', it is quickly apparent that the key word is white. The frequent attachment of the word 'conservative' is partly just a ploy. Most liberals would define themselves by their opposition to racism and their attachment to individual rights, a market economy, and the rule of law. In their eyes it merely confuses the issue to qualify such principles with the term 'conservative': liberals are in the first place liberal.

In practice, the real distinction is between the fringe of former liberals who have attached themselves to the ANC, either out of conviction or for reasons of preferment, and those who have used the same critique of hegemonic nationalism against the ANC that they used against its National Party predecessor. Typically, members of the former group (described by some as 'social-democratic liberals') have made themselves apologists for the ruling party and are strongly supportive of such highly contested notions as affirmative action, 'transformation', and the 'national democratic revolution'.

The liberals who are truly despised are thus those who embarrass black nationalists by exposing burgeoning corruption in the new regime, who point out the weaknesses and failings of affirmative action policies elsewhere in the world, and who deplore the ANC's party-mindedness, which frequently places the party above the law and the constitution and often equates the party with the state. Affirmative action is a particularly significant benchmark. Opinion polls have repeatedly shown that a majority of black voters are unsympathetic to such a policy (Johnson and Schlemmer 1996; Johnson 1997), but it is a matter of almost religious belief among the black intellectuals who are its main beneficiaries. The 'tough liberal' insistence on meritocracy finds particular disfavour in such circles.

There is a fierce parochialism to such definitions and divisions. If one questions black anti-liberals about their opinions on liberal theorists like John Stuart Mill, or on British, European, or American liberal politicians, they are happy to accept that their quarrel is not with liberalism as an ideology or even with its foreign practitioners: their strictures apply only to white South African liberals. So what is so bad about this group in particular? They are arrogant, hypocritical, and covertly racist, one is told. But these are merely alleged descriptions of individuals. Let us imagine for the sake of argument that such strictures were true of some individual white South African liberals; surely that would not be enough to condemn the species as a whole? To discover one or several bad Catholics or bad Jews does not, after all, invalidate either Catholicism or Judaism. So either one has to abandon the use of these individual descriptions as irrelevant, or (as is more normally the case) one must insist that they apply to each and every individual liberal – which is ludicrous, for it means that no South African liberal is capable of anything good if he or she is white.

Certain other twists in the argument are worth noting. One is often told that white liberals are 'perceived' as racist, a sort of crab-like approach to the issue in which the accuser takes no responsibility for the charge he or she makes, insisting that the accusation merely reports what is in the minds of others. Sometimes there are attempts to broaden the issue – as, for example, in William Makgoba's assertion that 'Liberalism has acquired a racial connotation in those societies in which diverse populations exist'. Apart from being factually questionable, this statement seems to imply that other policies have been more successful in combating problems of racial injustice than the liberal means used in countries such as the US and Britain. But surely one cannot argue, in the light of the fate of the Soviet Union and Yugoslavia, that these countries' ways of dealing with ethnic problems were superior?

Frequently, the accusation is made that liberals are Eurocentric. But one cannot help noticing that the 'Afrocentric' values of 'Africanist thought' with which this is contrasted are usually extremely imprecisely captured – typically just a few phrases about community and ubuntu. The fact is that the old pre-colonial African world of tribes, chiefs, and subsistence agriculture has extremely limited appeal to most black intellectuals. However, much that contributes to Africanist politics originated in its present form in Europe: nationalism, liberalism, social democracy, communism, constitutionalism, human-rights doctrine, elections, political parties, trade unions, capitalism, nationalized industries, and the republican state, not to mention such cultural manifestations as team sport. In other words, African intellectuals are in many ways as Eurocentric as those they criticize. Perhaps the key fact here is that it was only in pockets of Islamized Africa that the Arabic script penetrated. Apart from that, Africans south of the Sahara, unlike Asian or Arab intellectuals, have no ancient literate pre-colonial culture on which to draw in their critique of western liberalism – or, in the last analysis, on which to fall back.

This leaves one at an impasse. On the one hand, the criticisms that African intellectuals make of liberals and liberalism do not make much logical sense. The only real uniting thread often appears to be a racist dislike of whites – which they would certainly wish to disclaim. On the other hand, there is no doubting the vehemence of their critique. They are angry about something. But if their stated reasons do not make much sense, perhaps one must look instead at some unstated reasons.

One possible way forward lies in Themba Sono's exploration of 'the constrictive nature of African culture' (1994). Sono emphasizes the profound and continuing effect of the non-literate nature of African culture. Literacy permits a degree of abstraction, conceptualization, and systematization that is simply unknown under conditions of orality alone. One result, he argues, is that 'a non-literate culture merely reflected and stimulated the prejudices and parochialism of communal sectarianism'. The development of conceptual thinking is necessary to making the distinctions which in the end make the individual the focus; without it, the group remains primary. 'The role of the group in African consciousness', Sono writes,

> is overwhelming, totalistic, even totalitarian. Group psychology, though parochially and narrowly based (village thinking is necessarily so), nonetheless pretends to universality. This mentality, this psychology, is stronger on belief than on reason; on sameness than on difference. Discursive

rationality is overwhelmed by emotional identity, by the
obsession to identify with and by the longing to conform
to. To agree is more important than to disagree; conformity
is cherished more than innovation. Tradition is venerated,
continuity revered, change feared and difference shunned.
Heresies are not tolerated in such communities. Such a
culture belongs to a civilisation of consent rather than that
of the Occident, which belongs to a civilisation of dissent.
(Sono 1994, 7)

If one accepts Sono's argument, there is an almost intrinsic
opposition between traditional African culture and Western
liberalism, with its emphasis on individual rights and its history
of 'here I stand' dissent. But one is tempted to go further. A key
point about a literate culture is that documents exist, accuracy
can be checked, truth is not a moving target. This is not so in an
orally-based culture, where the immediate emotional truth of
the moment has a natural primacy over whatever happened
yesterday and the day before.

Certainly, South African liberals have frequently found themselves open-mouthed at the twists and turns of African nationalist politics, which seem to follow entirely different rules from
those they know. Thus, for example, throughout the 1980s the
claim by the apartheid government that the United Democratic
Front (UDF) was little more than the ANC in disguise was treated
as a foul slur. Yet upon legalization of the ANC in 1990 the UDF
was announced to have indeed been merely the internal wing of
the ANC and was accordingly dissolved. There were, of course,
strong political and even security reasons for both stances: the
UDF would have been banned by the apartheid regime had its
ANC provenance been admitted. But the point is simply that in
the course of the many twists and turns of the struggle the liberation movement became accustomed to treating truth as an
instrumental quantity. Or again, the ANC has alternately

denounced Winnie Madikizela-Mandela for all manner of gross crimes, then supported her to the hilt and elected her to high office, then reverted to previous practice, through at least three such cycles of truth/non-truth. At each stage, the political convenience of the movement is clearly the paramount factor, and liberals, determined only to know what the truth is, find themselves swept aside by the circumstantial tide. At the least, one should note the similarity between the old Communist Party style of making sudden radical changes to the party line to which all members must adhere (and, given the SACP's centrality within the ANC, the party was, of course, crucial to both the above instances) and the practices of an orally based political culture.

There are, however, several other reasons why liberals – especially white liberals – have become lightning conductors in a new South Africa charged with the wounded yet triumphant emotions of African nationalism at its apogee.

The first issue is that of hegemony. In a society in which many of the commanding economic heights are still held by whites, there is an overweening Africanist demand for political, intellectual, and cultural hegemony. The ANC trumpets the 'national democratic revolution' and attempts to define a 'new patriotism' to which all must subscribe save the active 'agents of the counter-revolution'. This hegemony means that all must genuflect to a series of new shibboleths – 'the African renaissance', 'transformation', affirmative action, 'black empowerment', and so on. The problem is that there is no elaborate theory underpinning 'the African renaissance', nor any real cultural depth to any of its associated notions: in effect they are little more than slogans and maxims. Thus these ideas do not and cannot achieve the sort of cultural dominance that Gramsci had in mind when he spoke of hegemony. For that to happen the new ruling culture has to be imbibed and internalized by the dominant intelligentsia who then re-propagate it throughout society where it secures the status of a confidently shared set of values. There is really no prospect that African nationalist slogans, let alone the old-style Marxism of COSATU and the SACP, can achieve that sort of acceptance among South Africa's educated classes, dominated as they are by white business people and professionals. This creates a major dissonance within the new South Africa which is only partially lessened by the fact that business circles are often silent as they continue to make money from a position of internal exile, while the professional classes equally tend to keep their heads down while they quietly fill in the emigration forms to New Zealand or Canada.

In practice, the culture of the new South Africa is the same old mix of Christianity, western consumerism, and pop culture, with continuous infusions from the business world. This is only thinly leavened by the new dash of Third Worldism and African-ism. To be sure, the electronic media are just as deferential to the new government as they were to the old, and much of the press seems bullied to the point of self-censorship — just as it was under apartheid — but the new ruling elite is uncomfortably aware that beneath this somewhat coerced deference the once dominant white group continues to harbour strongly critical views about the sky-high crime rate, governmental corruption or incompetence, and so on. Not surprisingly, the elite reacts with extreme sensitivity to such criticism and tries to insist that those who truly share 'the new patriotism' should not talk like this.

In this context, Afrikaner nationalists are tolerated as just another lesser – and superannuated – species of nationalist: old bulls put out to grass on the mountain slopes now that the young bulls are in the main pasture with the cows of the herd. The plaintive protests that emanate from these old bulls about the fate of Afrikaans or the plight of old-regime civil servants are simply what one would expect and are discounted in advance. But liberals who speak out, who expose the corruption, who articulate a vision of a different society in which race is finally removed as a basis for promotion or demotion, who want to see market-recognized merit – above all, who feel no guilt in speaking out because they opposed apartheid on similar grounds – these are the true irritants, the real intolerables.

The issue of guilt is primary. The Truth and Reconciliation Commission (TRC), set up to expose the crimes of apartheid, progressively widened its sphere of inquiry until one could actually hear black journalists claiming in the TRC hearings that the white-controlled press of yore was guilty of mass murder. The real atrocities of apartheid – the torture, the bannings, the detentions, the forced removals, the denials of educational opportunity and individual rights in every sphere – seemed no longer enough as the net was cast ever wider. Desmond Tutu, the TRC's chairperson, made an impassioned plea to *all* whites to acknowledge their collective guilt for the wrongs committed under apartheid: 'Please, I beg you to take this last opportunity to rid yourselves of the burden of the past' (SABC SAFM broadcast, 31 March 1998).

The problem is that liberals cannot accept the doctrine of collective guilt – the doctrine under which the Jews were so long hounded for the crucifixion of Jesus, the doctrine on which every racial war from the Holocaust to Serbia has relied. To liberals, guilt is individual, and blanket appeals to all whites to atone for the sins of apartheid not only leave out of account the minority of whites who fought hard against that evil but also the far larger number who had little say in the matter either way. It was all very well at the end of the American Civil War to hold the plantocracy guilty of having owned slaves, but what to say of abolitionists or poor white sharecroppers? One can debate such cases, but in the short term what one faces is the electric tension between white liberals who feel they have a clean conscience and African nationalists who feel furiously that all whites are guilty.

This liberal refusal to accept collective guilt is critical. Nothing seems to madden African nationalists more than a white person

who says, 'I opposed apartheid root and branch. I did all I could.
So I feel no guilt. And I feel just as free to point out what's wrong
with African nationalism as I did with Afrikaner nationalism.'
What is offensive, in the end, is the unbowed knee. This refusal
has often produced emotional tirades from black intellectuals in
which the term 'liberal' becomes wholly detached from historical
reality: one may hear nineteenth-century imperialists such as
Cecil Rhodes misdescribed as liberals, or hear the Democratic
Party condemned for having been part of the apartheid regime,
which in fact it always bitterly opposed. As Ken Owen has pointed
out, 'The word liberal was no longer a political definition for those
who believed in a non-violent path to a humane, non-racial
society: it was a racial code-word for English-speaking whites
who might claim the moral authority to speak out, to criticize,
to set norms, to shape the new nation' (1997).

Other dynamics are at work too. One of the most revealing
causes célèbres of the new South Africa was that of Professor
William Makgoba, a deputy vice-chancellor of the University of
the Witwatersrand, who was accused by a group of thirteen
academics in 1996 of professional misconduct including the
falsification of his curriculum vitae. In the resulting fracas – until
the rift was patched up in a compromise deal – the solidarity of
the black elite with Makgoba was total and paid no attention to
the detailed allegations made by the other side. Typically, the
thirteen were quickly typecast as 'white liberals', although one
was black and another avowedly Marxist.

In one sense this was a case of complete racial polarization, but
in a subtler sense it was also a case of class solidarity. Makgoba
was a totem for members of the rising black middle class because
the Makgoba affair occurred at the precise moment when they
had at last been told that the future belonged to them, that the
sky was the limit. This class is torn by conflicting emotions –
determination to take its rightful place in the sun, eagerness for
the fruits of middle-class status, but also anxiety over its ability

to fill these new roles and a fear that it might fail and thus incur the withering contempt of whites. The sight of a black professor – a leading medical scientist at that – being brought low by 'white liberals' thus conjured up a nightmare that threatened the upward social mobility of the entire group. Hence both the solidarity which cut across party lines, and the fury this group felt with Makgoba when he climbed down in the end, thus apparently validating some of the objections made about him.

The Makgoba case also drew attention to the power of internalized stereotypes. Africans are acutely aware of old white stereotypes of blacks and often react with extreme sensitivity to those stereotypes rather than to actual behaviour. Thus, for example, most blacks know full well that whites frequently predicted that black rule would lead to misgovernment, incompetents in jobs they were unable to do, and increased corruption. If white liberals now point to actual instances of such things, they are seen as lending support to the old negative stereotype of blacks, and the knee-jerk response is to accuse them of racism, even at the cost of maintaining in office those known to be egregiously incompetent or corrupt. No doubt this was in Deputy President Thabo Mbeki's mind when he announced pre-emptively that if the ANC government failed, it would be the fault of whites (Kane-Berman 1997). The even greater fear in the minds of many Africans is that events might unfold in such a way that those stereotypes are fulfilled and thus, horror of horrors, appear to have been 'justified' after all.

Many of the difficulties between black social commentators and white liberals derive from this problem of internalized stereotypes. In many cases whites who have been better educated than Africans are quickly accused of being condescending and patronizing, and of having superiority complexes. No doubt in some cases these accusations have been deserved, but their universality leaves no room for the examination of individual cases. If liberals argue for free competition based on merit, it is immediately assumed that this will amount to no more than the protection of white privilege, an accusation which jars with many white liberals because they feel the pursuit of meritocracy is intrinsically opposed to privilege. And always there is an overwhelming consciousness of what whites might say or think about any African failure. This hypersensitivity may appear absurd, but there is a real pain beneath. It was easy, for example, to find Africans who were greatly concerned that South Africa's soccer team might fare badly in the World Cup 'because whites would then say we won the rugby world cup because rugby is essentially a white man's game, but we failed in soccer because the soccer team is mainly black'.

Thus whites are often conceived of as a homogeneous, even monolithic group critical of all blacks. But one of the commonest jibes made against white English-speaking liberals is that many blacks prefer Afrikaners to them. Although there may often be a degree of deliberate provocation in such taunts, there is also perhaps a kernel of truth here too: many blacks feel comfortable with Afrikaners because they share group-think attitudes, but uncomfortable with the more instinctive individualism of English-speaking whites. To quote Sono again:

> Apartheid did such damage. Many Africans still identify with it. They find 'security' in group think, group rights, communal solidarity. The characteristics of group think are a tendency to moralise, an illusion of invulnerability – because the group is powerful – and a willingness to surrender all moral and intellectual judgement to the dictates of group solidarity. One reason why Africans often find it easier to get on with traditional Afrikaners than with liberals is that deep down they were convinced by apartheid, the separate 'groupness' of ethnic consciousness. (1996, 11–12)

One is driven back ineluctably, in the search for understanding, to Frantz Fanon's analysis of the tortured world of the colonial personality (1967a; 1967b; McCulloch 1983). Fanon believes that every black child has suffered trauma as a result of colonialism, and that this trauma manifests itself in self-hatred and 'exceptional sensitivity', in a dreadful anxiety that he will reveal his supposedly 'innate inferiority', and in a pathetic attempt to erect a mythology of Africanism or negritude as an escape route from colonial despair. There is no doubt that contemporary South Africa presents all too rich a field for Fanonist analysis, for if colonialism inflicted damage on the black child throughout Africa, then nowhere was the damage likely to be greater than in South Africa, where the impact of colonialism was exceptionally harsh and heavy. Moreover, to the damage inflicted on black consciousness by apartheid one must add in many cases the damage inflicted by imprisonment or exile, or by the liberation movement itself, or by the extraordinary and confusing euphoria of the triumph of 1994 which has seen many former stalwarts self-destruct, as if unable to cope with 'normal' life after a lifetime's abnormality.

A white liberal might respond: all very sad and all very regrettable, but why pick on us? One cannot quarrel with that. But to ponder the magnitude of the damage inflicted in Fanonist terms is also a humbling experience. South Africa has escaped a possible future in which a racial war might have left millions dead. Instead, it is living through a cultural revolution in which a frenzied cacophony of voices and actors attempts to settle old scores, to salve wounded pride, to achieve impossible targets of 'transformation', to achieve hegemony, to strive towards symbolic liberation – and to get rich. Living through such a period is not easy, and there is much unfairness in the targets that are singled out for blame or retribution. But it too will pass. It is, moreover, a mild experience compared to what has been avoided. Liberals who have to walk through this period suffering the slings and arrows of outrageous fortune need not feel guilt about their past, but neither they nor anyone else can avoid that past.

15

RACHEL C C JAFTA

Affirmative action: is the light worth the candle?[1]

A dismal state of affairs

The statistics telling the story of South Africa's inequalities are well documented and quoted often. With respect to the affirmative-action debate, unemployment and income distribution figures are particularly relevant:

- Unemployment as a percentage of the labour force is estimated in 1994 at 32.6 per cent by the team of economists who wrote the government's *Macro-economic strategy* (Department of Finance 1996, 29).
- The Labour Market Commission (Department of Labour 1996a, 141) has submitted that this unemployment rate broken down by race gives an even more alarming result: the African unemployment rate for 1994 reached 41 per cent compared to rates of 6.4 per cent, 23 per cent, and 17 per cent for whites, coloureds, and Asians respectively. Furthermore, while women fare worse in all racial groups, African women are worst off with an unemployment rate of 50 per cent.
- The *Green paper: Policy proposals for a new employment and occupational equity statute* (Department of Labour 1996b, 15) quotes figures from the 1995 issue of the World Bank's *World development report*, showing that the poorest 20 per cent of

South Africans received only 3 per cent of national income while 63 per cent went to the richest 20 per cent.

- Dividing the population into deciles, McGrath and Whiteford (1994, 17–19) calculated income shares for each decile (each 10 per cent) for each racial group for 1975 and 1991. The results for 1991 were then expressed as a percentage of those for 1975 to obtain the change in income distribution. They found that in all racial groups, the bottom 40 per cent had become worse off, while the top 10 per cent had improved their income shares. They show further that from 1975 to 1991, inequality in income distribution *between* racial groups became a relatively smaller contributor to overall inequality (only 22.7 per cent), while inequality *within* racial groups grew steadily more significant (from 57 per cent in 1975 to 77 per cent in 1991).

The Labour Market Commission report, the green paper on employment equity, and no doubt other proponents of affirmative action use these statistics to substantiate demands for affirmative action based on race and gender. While it is painfully obvious that these conditions are quite unacceptable, it is less obvious that affirmative action is the best means to eradicate them. This chapter therefore sets out to assess whether affirmative action really is the only answer or whether there are other options that may be better suited to achieve the same goals while promoting social harmony and enhanced standards of welfare for *all* South Africans. To this end, this chapter firstly weighs the expounded benefits (and real-life results) of affirmative action against the social and economic costs of such measures to society as a whole. Secondly, it asserts that an argument against forced, race-based affirmative-action programmes is not an argument for the status quo. On the contrary, several less costly and less divisive alternatives are explored. References to the experiences of countries that have implemented affirmative-action programmes are used throughout.

Affirmative action: Benefits and costs

Proclaimed benefits

According to the proponents of affirmative action, benefits from affirmative-action programmes derive from both equity and economic efficiency considerations. The equity argument is basically that 'discrimination on the basis of non-productivity-related characteristics such as race and gender is unjust on purely humanitarian grounds' (Department of Labour 1996a, 144). While the argument for equity is perfectly valid, it remains questionable whether an affirmative-action programme based on race and gender attributes will be successful in eradicating discrimination of this nature.

Affirmative action is also credited with being able to eliminate past economic inefficiencies such as inefficient resource allocation, labour market distortions, depressed domestic aggregate demand deriving from inequitable distribution of income (resulting in lower economic growth), higher cost structures, and poor international competitiveness (Department of Labour 1996a, 1996b).

At the firm level, it is claimed (Eskom 1994) that affirmative action will result in:

- a better understanding of and respect for different cultures and values;
- increased loyalty and commitment towards company goals;
- enhanced racial sensitivity, mutual respect, and trust, leading to better teamwork;
- less stress on all employees by nurturing their full potential;
- the eradication of discrimination;
- improved industrial relations to boost/increase productivity;
- improved company image;
- improved and harmonious interpersonal relations; and
- focus on performance.

Similar outcomes were aimed for in other countries where affirmative action has been implemented. Since the experiences of these countries present us with valuable information on the real-life outcomes of these policies, these results will now be examined more closely.

Real-world outcomes

Affirmative-action programmes have been implemented in various countries around the world, including Canada, the United States of America, India, Malaysia, Sri Lanka, Zimbabwe, and Namibia. Since space considerations do not allow a review of the results from all these countries, America and Malaysia are selected because they represent more than thirty and twenty years' experience respectively. Indicators of success (or lack thereof) include performance of preferred groups in the areas of employment, education, income, and wealth distribution, as well as improvement in general social conditions.

Outcomes in America

After more than thirty years of affirmative-action measures in America, outcomes have been, at best, mixed:

- Since the enactment of the first affirmative-action measures in 1964, black Americans have become worse off in the unemployment arena. In 1964 the ratio of black to white unemployment was 2 : 1, while in 1990 this ratio stood at 2.76 : 1 (Bolick 1996, 61).
- The economic status of minorities and women has not improved significantly. It is true that women's share of professional degrees grew from 2.7 per cent in 1960 to 36 per cent in 1990, and their average earnings as a percentage of men's increased from 61 per cent to 72 per cent over the same period. However, a study of 138 firms by Alison Konrad and Frank Linnehan (quoted in Bolick 1996, 61-62) found that

although companies with race-conscious policies had at least one woman at a higher rank and more minorities in management positions than companies with race-neutral employment policies, in four other categories[2] the results were the same for both types of company. Why did aggressively pursued, government-coerced affirmative-action policies produce such meagre gains? Bolick (1996, 62) explains that this is because they had a mainly redistributionist impact – in other words, these measures have largely shifted employees from some employers to others instead of facilitating new entries into employment opportunities.

- In education, black and white college participation rates now show a wider gap than in the 1970s. In 1976 about 22.6 per cent of blacks aged 18 to 24 were at colleges compared to 27.1 per cent of whites in the same age group; by 1990 black participation rates had grown to 25.4 per cent, while the rate for whites stood at 32.5 per cent (Brimelow and Spencer 1993, 101–102).

- General social conditions for blacks have become worse. In 1950 only 9 per cent of black families were headed by a single parent; in 1965 that figure had increased to 28 per cent, and by 1993 to almost 50 per cent. In 1959 only 15 per cent of black births were illegitimate, in 1992 66 per cent were. One in four black men in their twenties is either in jail, on probation, or on parole (Brimelow and Spencer 1993, 99).

- In terms of earnings distribution, the black middle class did well during the period 1970–1990: the percentage of black families earning more than $50 000 p.a. increased from 10 per cent to nearly 15 per cent (but this might have happened without affirmative action, since the percentage of white families in high-income categories also grew during this period). Meanwhile, the percentage of black families earning below $15 000 was nearly 40 per cent in 1993 (Brimelow and Spencer 1993, 102).

In summary, there have been gains and losses in the American experience and it is difficult to say whether the gains are entirely attributable to affirmative-action measures. It remains important, however, to establish at what cost these gains were garnered.

Affirmative action in Malaysia

The Malaysian experience claims reasonable success in that poverty has decreased from 49 per cent of the population in 1969 to 19 per cent in 1987, and access to education and employment for Malays has improved so that the distribution of employment in different sectors of the economy as well as in better-paying occupations is approaching target figures (Emsley 1992, 113).

In an economy dominated mostly by the Chinese, progress has been made in establishing a Malay business community (Puthucheary 1993, 23). However, after twenty years of affirmative action, Malays are not proportionally represented in management positions and the professions, and they still find themselves over-represented in the less productive parts of the economy. Ownership of equity has not reached the 1970 targets and although great strides have been made towards equalization of income per capita *between* ethnic groups, income inequality *within* ethnic groups has worsened. This is explained by the fact that richer Malays found it easier to use the opportunities in tertiary education, better-paid managerial positions, cheap shares, loans, and government contracts provided by ethnic preferment. Once again, the beneficiaries of affirmative action have been predominantly those who already had a comparative advantage over their poorer compatriots (Emsley 1992, 114).

It is important to note that affirmative-action measures in Malaysia were supported by remarkable economic growth of between 6 per cent and 7 per cent over twenty years. New employment opportunities were created and non-Malays did not lose their jobs to make room for Malays (Loxton 1993, 29).

As was the case everywhere else, the affirmative-action gains in Malaysia involved some costs. The nature and extent (where relevant information is available) of these costs will now be considered.

Costs

Calculating the costs of affirmative-action programmes is notoriously difficult, and reliable estimates of inclusive costs are hard to come by. Nevertheless, like everyone else, governments have limited resources, and they have an obligation to use these scarce resources optimally. In order to do so, regular assessments weighing the costs of government programmes against their realized results are necessary. Should the costs significantly outweigh the realized benefits, a logical next step would be to look for alternative means of achieving the desired objectives.

Economists divide costs into direct, indirect, and opportunity costs, where the opportunity cost of a particular choice refers to the value of the best alternative foregone. In the context of affirmative-action issues, it is necessary to add another category of costs, which are difficult to quantify but have a significant bearing on the desirability of race-based affirmative-action policies. For lack of a better term, these costs are described as social costs. Each of these cost categories will now be discussed in turn.

Direct costs

Direct costs derive from the expansion in the bureaucracy in order to create the institutional machinery to implement affirmative-action measures. In America this machinery comprises the Equal Employment Opportunity Commission, the Office of Federal Contract Compliance, the Department of Education, and several other federal, state, and local agencies. In an estimation for 1991, Brimelow and Spencer (1993, 82) found that the cost of regulation by these agencies amounted to approximately

$545 million. When the costs of complying with affirmative-action regulations (including private-sector costs) are added, direct costs are estimated at $17 billion to $20 billion.

In South Africa, the proposed affirmative-action institutional framework comprises the Department of Labour, the Directorate for Equal Opportunities, the Labour Inspectorate, industry-wide collective-bargaining forums, the Commission for Conciliation, Mediation, and Arbitration, the Labour Court and the Labour Appeal Court, and the Employment Equity Advisory Council. Neither the Labour Market Commission report nor the green paper on employment equity (Department of Labour 1996a, 1996b) contain any cost estimates for running this operation. Mention is made of compliance costs for private-sector firms, but these are considered negligible and justified in the interest of racial equity.

Indirect costs

Indirect costs involve no direct cash outlay but constitute real costs in the sense that delays in hiring and recruiting are caused by time-consuming affirmative-action regulations in, for example, the private sector and educational institutions. Similar problems are experienced in the construction sector in South Africa in that uncertainty about government's affirmative-action requirements has resulted in long delays in allocating housing projects and a slowdown in growth in the building industry (Robertson 1996).

Brimelow and Spencer (1993, 82) put indirect costs of US affirmative action at an estimated $96 billion for 1991.

Opportunity costs

With reference to Malaysia, Emsley argues that the allocation of human and financial resources 'away from areas of highest return reduced possible productivity gains'. He further observes that while inefficiencies arising from giving preference to and subsidizing Malay firms may have been reduced by the phenomenon of having non-Malay business partners (in the form of a sleeping partner) and sub-contracting to Chinese firms, such behaviour did not encourage the development of entrepreneurship amongst Malays. In the field of education, race-based preferential policies, particularly in awarding educational certificates, led to the devaluation of certain degrees and the further complication that more prosperous Chinese had their children educated at international educational institutions. The result was a double standard of education for Malays and others (Emsley 1992, 115).

In America the opportunity costs of affirmative action arise from bad hiring decisions under government coercion, negative effects on morale, and the misallocation of financial resources (Brimelow and Spencer 1993; Bolick 1996). Brimelow and Spencer believe that the opportunity cost of affirmative action is by far the highest ($236 billion for 1991). This figure includes an estimate of $150 billion, representing the opportunities lost if employers under pressure to get the numbers right hire people who cannot do the job efficiently, perhaps because of a lack of skills or aptitude. Sufficient data to quantify the effect on morale was not available, but the cost of not allowing financial resources to seek optimum returns is estimated to be a further $86 billion. The authors argue that investing this money in research and development or plant modernization could have added this much to the country's overall output.

Put simply, it needs to be asked what results might have been achieved if such resources had been invested in efficient education, essential infrastructure, or other efforts to empower the truly disadvantaged outside of the economic mainstream.

Social costs

The social costs of enforced race- and gender-based affirmative action are varied, and once incurred cannot easily be eliminated. Virtually all affirmative-action policies have set out to remedy some form of past discrimination and have been meant to be temporary measures. Despite their noble intentions, such policies have generally undesirable side-effects:

- Affirmative-action policies based on race must use racial attributes to be implemented. This emphasis on race leads to the reinforcement of negative stereotypes, racial tension, and a stigmatization which thwarts the efforts of members of the preferred groups to pursue their goals on merit and hard work rather than preferential treatment. The American affirmative-action landscape is littered with stories of abuse of the affirmative-action provisions, simply because race had become a proxy for disadvantage. Don Caldwell cites the example of Harvard University's financial aid to all minority students irrespective of need. When asked whether he had to maintain a certain standard of performance to receive the financial aid, one of the beneficiaries of the programme responded: 'No, I have to prove I am still black!' (1992, 71)

- Race-based affirmative-action programmes encourage a culture of entitlement which undermines initiative, self-confidence, and self-reliance. The beneficiaries of racial preferences may always have to prove their worth more than others because of lingering suspicions of undue advantage; even the beneficiaries themselves often wonder whether they are in demand because of their abilities or because they happen to be the 'right' colour. This is a far cry from the days of Black Consciousness when the mood was one of pride, confidence, and a sense of capability. Shelby Steele, a professor of English at San Jose State University in California, abhors the message that current affirmative-action policies in America send to young blacks:

> ... that extra entitlements are their due and that the greatest power of all is the power that comes to them as victims. If they want to get anywhere in American

life, they had better wear their victimization on their sleeve and tap into white guilt, making whites want to escape by offering money, status, racial preferences, anything – in return. Is this the way for a race that has been oppressed to come into their own? Is this the way to achieve independence? (quoted in Bolick 1996, 64)

- The worst factor of all, for a nation attempting to restore the fragile fabric of a society torn apart by years of racial discrimination, is the racial polarization resulting from policies that insist on using race as a means of achieving racial harmony.

In considering the proposals aimed at employment and occupational equity, South Africans will have to decide whether the costs deriving from race-based affirmative-action policies are worth enduring for the meagre results that they have shown to date.

An argument for the status quo?

Should an argument against race-based affirmative action therefore be construed as an argument for the status quo? Certainly not. Efforts should be made to find ways in which all South Africans would become better off, but especially the truly disadvantaged, those with the least access to employment, food, security, and productive assets. The following suggestions are offered as ways which would treat all South Africans as equal in the eyes of the law, but would still reach those who need it most.

Sustainable rural development

Since the poorest of the poor are found predominantly in rural areas[3] and are more often than not women and youths, a sustained effort to help the rural poor to help themselves could go a long way towards solving problems of marginalization and inequality.

Such an attempt could conceivably include measures to 'increase the quantity and productivity of assets owned by the poor; increase the price of services yielded by assets sold by the poor (including their labour time), and increase the volume of market sales by the poor' (Ingham 1995, 242).

Obstacles to rural development are generally poor infrastructure and provision of services, which hamper rural productivity and access to markets, and limited access to financing facilities, agricultural support services, and skills acquisition. In this regard, South Africa has experienced serious problems in that funds which had been budgeted for development of infrastructure and provision of services had to be rolled over from one financial year to another.[4] The biggest obstacle to efficient implementation of programmes budgeted for seems to have been a lack of capacity in the delivery systems. One way of addressing this problem may be to cultivate better cooperation amongst all levels of government as well as the intended beneficiaries of such programmes. This will expand participation in delivery and hopefully spawn improved capacities through experience. In development literature, the latest approach in the battle against poverty is to focus on the poor as a source of development potential and opportunities for investment. Sustainable rural development is greatly enhanced by learning from the 'coping strategies' of the poor, as is currently the trend in trying to provide credit to small-scale operators along the lines of the strategies followed in the informal sector (Ingham 1995; Elkan 1995; Schoombee and Smith 1995).

To a large extent, the success of the New Economic Policy in Malaysia can be credited to its commitment to rural development and particularly to efforts to raise the incomes of rural Malays through gains in agricultural productivity (Emsley 1992, 113).

Increased efficiency in education and training

It is clear that major improvements in the South African education and training delivery system are required to meet the demands of a growing economy. It is of very little use to watch statistics to assess the racial representativeness of the South African workforce while the workforce of the future has to contend with situations where there are not enough textbooks to go round or chairs to sit on or, even worse, where no teaching or learning takes place because teachers are disgruntled over government's education policies. To ensure that all South Africans will have access to rewarding employment, sufficient education and skills acquisition are non-negotiable requirements. Nor could we have different standards based on race; building capacity through hard work and endurance will take longer, but it will certainly be a better use of resources than attempted short cuts via affirmative action. South Africans will do well to learn that many mistakes are bred by impatience.

Enlightened self-interest: private-sector involvement

By now, it should be evident to business leaders that the environment in which they do business has a bearing on the future success of their business endeavours. This environment also includes the opinions and the well-being of the communities in which they operate. Recognition (sometimes grudging) of this fact has led to the development of various new approaches to the organization of work, recruitment and promotion criteria, training, and community involvement:

- Efforts to reduce the demands on the time and attention of women (and to minimize the perceived reasons for discrimination against women) include paternity leave, opportunities for men to take time off to take children to the doctor or dentist, child-care facilities in the workplace, and better use of flexitime and opportunities for working at home provided by information technology.

- In some business organizations a new perspective on recruitment and promotion involves a move away from the 'paper mentality' of requiring certificates for every job to a greater reliance on competence so that skills acquired informally or through work experience can be recognized and rewarded.
- A new approach to training means that training is no longer pursued simply for the sake of training: the new brand of trainers believe that the benefits from training should be quantifiable – in fact, they guarantee a measurable improvement in a company's bottom line after training. This approach promises better returns on investment in human capital by the private sector.
- Many firms see for themselves a social responsibility role which ranges from providing educational scholarships to sports development sponsorships to training for the unemployed.

By reviewing these contributions by the private sector, it is of course not implied that these efforts are entirely sufficient to redress the imbalances created in the past. One thing is certain, though, and that is that coercion is not the best means to encourage the private sector to do its bit to eliminate racial inequalities.

A growing economy

It is imperative to understand that a rapidly growing economy is a necessary (but not necessarily sufficient) condition to enable the eradication of past inequalities. As was seen in the case of Malaysia, a steadily growing economy created new job opportunities to absorb the Bumiputra ('sons of the soil') into the labour force. A growing economy will also enable government to provide much-needed infrastructure without putting too much pressure on an already stressed budget deficit.

Conclusion

This chapter set out to compare the costs and benefits of a race-based programme of affirmative action. Despite the good intentions of such programmes, the negative side-effects and direct costs seem to outweigh the benefits. That being the case, attempts should be made to find ways that will benefit all South Africans in the long term, and particularly those who are least in a position to exploit the opportunities in employment and education offered by race-based affirmative-action policies. To this end, programmes and policies including rural development, better education and training, private-sector involvement, and economic growth should be considered. These are not the only feasible solutions, but they would certainly go further towards avoiding the divisive effect on society of race-based policy measures.

16

DENIS BECKETT

The holy cause that ends in tears

I CAN THINK of better formulas for popularity than trying to argue that affirmative action is a mistake. Some people will ascribe a multitude of foul motives to me: I'm insecure, I'm nostalgic for supremacy, I want blacks to feel inferior so that they will not threaten my career, and so on. Some people will resort to that drearily overworked term 'racist!'.

Whilst I do not think there is much value in replying with that equally dreary protest 'I am not a racist', I do think it is worthwhile establishing a few basics that apply to the affirmative-action debate.

Firstly, I concede that yes, quite frequently when you hear white voices saying that affirmative action is wrong, there is a kind of racial trade unionism lurking in the background. Quite often there is a *schadenfreude*, a happiness in beholding black glitches and black failings. Perhaps that is a response to threat, perhaps it is a response to a concealed sense of inadequacy, perhaps it is a response to affirmative action itself and the distortions it creates; perhaps all three.

Many liberals have their doubts about affirmative action, but given the prevailing climate, such doubts are most often expressed in private and only between consenting adults. Denis Beckett's chapter, however, is based on a talk he gave to the Black Management Forum – on this topic, the equivalent of the lion's den.

Whichever, I do admit that such a thing exists, and I do understand that when blacks hear white intellectuals denouncing affirmative action, their hackles tend to rise and they tend to respond as if to a declaration of racial war or racial insult.

Secondly, I submit that there is also a certain amount of racial righteousness in this matter, a righteousness that is all the more strident for being misplaced. The current and very vocal fashion among black columnists who deal in these issues is to project a society of perfect and faultless (may one say 'lily white'?) black people whose sole problem in life is the wicked whiteys who keep thinking up obstacles to put in their way. The idea is that whites are racists and blacks are pure, and I have to say that is serious twaddle. You can listen in shebeens and you can even listen to the conversation in the corridors of the Black Management Forum at teatime, and you will easily hear observations not a whit less stupid than anything you might hear from the Michaelhouse old boys in the change room at the squash club. You'll hear *schaden-freude* this side too, a kind of dumb delight at white unemployment and white discomfiture, perhaps partly motivated by the assumption that white pain means black gain, perhaps just a result of envy or jealousy.

Either way, it rings a touch hollow to constantly hear the high priests of affirmative action thumping their little tub for everybody to please notice their halo. If there is stupidity and irrational rank-closing on the one side, it's on the other side too. Half the reason the whiteys are giving blacks good reason to perceive racial insults is that they perceive racial insults coming their way too. Both 'sides' of this debate behave fairly abysmally fairly frequently, and there is no point trying to elevate one above the other or trying to ascribe blame, because it ends up as a useless rerun of that useless old argument about whether the police pulled the triggers before the klipgooiers gooied the klips or vice versa.

The third and last basic that I wish to establish in respect of this debate is this: that while the above mentioned pathetic racial debate rages forth, occupying inordinate amounts of column centimetres and contributing to the famous decline of news circulations, there is another and better debate coming up. This is the debate that is predicated on the simple recognition that for the success of anybody, you need reasonable contentment of the whole. It does me no good in my white middle-class cocoon if all around there are angry blacks sharpening pangas. It does neither Eugene Terre'Blanche nor Clarence Makwetu nor John Smith any good to cultivate the cheer of any single segment of society while leaving any other segment angry and embittered.

Now, I do not guarantee that every Terre'Blanche, or every Makwetu, necessarily recognizes the depth of his need to cultivate the confidence of people unlike him, but I do say that this is the arena of the emerging debate, the new debate. It is not about 'we whites doing better than you blacks' and it is not about the reverse either. It is a better debate and it is way beyond these silly blinkers. It is way beyond racial categories and well into the basic liberal perception that the only way we can make sense of this country is by respecting the individual as individual, equal and unique.

I set all this out because I want it to be understood that when I say affirmative action is a mistake, I am not wishing to make black people feel bad, I am not into racial status stakes, I am not wishing black people to carry hods or hew wood. I am saying: this distortion now on the go is at least as bad for blacks as it is for whites, and probably very much worse. I am saying that I take living in South Africa seriously enough to want black advancement to be real and sound and lasting, and not the flimsy charade that affirmative action makes it.

We are all aiming for the same end target, it's just that the routes diverge. It's a pity that so much of what ought to be the South African debate is stifled at birth because of the overuse of 'racist!' It's too boring for words.

Now, everybody knows affirmative action is not working to order. It is legitimate, even approved, to say that. Invariably, though, one promptly adds that the reason it is not working is that it is applied wrongly. The principle, it is said, is great, superb; just a pity that silly people, like employers, mess it up.

Funny, we've heard that line before. We heard it of apartheid. For years, in many quarters, it was absolutely insisted that the fault was not the principle; the fault was how it was implemented. We heard it even more, and longer, of communism. That the theory was right, the implementation flawed by human error. Now we hear it of affirmative action. I believe we'll see the same end. We will look back and say: no, the principle was wrong.

Let us be quite clear what the principle is. Some people use 'affirmative action' as a synonym for good management – training, opportunity, the quest to raise people's ceilings as far as they can reach. In that sense, of course, affirmative action is right. But in that sense, why use the term at all? Why not just call it common sense?

The significant meaning of affirmative action is the one that wants to engineer a change in the colour-coding of individual jobs. This is the sense in which affirmative action is contentious, and this is the sense in which it needs to be discussed. Unfortunately, discussion is not easy, because when matters get sensitive, which is early on, the focus goes floppy and people start relying on the other, apple-pie, definition. I am talking about the contentious meaning: racial or gender engineering to make institutions of control less white or less male. I ignore the easy meaning as there is no argument there.

As I see it, affirmative action in the hard sense necessarily and inherently has four anti-social effects. First, it installs tokenism as a way of life. Second, it is criminally wicked to its alleged beneficiaries. Third, it entrenches the idea of second-class black professionalism. Fourth and greatest, it sabotages the economy. Let us go through these four effects one by one. Everybody who argues for more and faster affirmative action says, 'We don't want tokenism. Tokenism is out.' In the next breath they turn to Company A or Council B and say, 'Where are your black executives? Where are your black members?' The company replies: 'We can't find a suitable person', whereupon the critics say, 'There are forty million black people. You must be able to find one.'

Under pressure, the company thereupon identifies a person whom it would not have identified by the normal criterion of an expected ability to master the job, but who is black, to become a general manager. Invariably, this process begins with high hopes and a certain trepidation. Commonly, it ends in tears. Bit by bit the new exec's functions are de facto taken over by someone else – perhaps a deputy, perhaps the predecessor (who is now a 'consultant' making more than he used to).

The new exec blames the company, and puts it about that they wilfully block him from real power. The company blames him, saying he didn't measure up. Regardless of who is right and who is not, the reality is that this excessively familiar process has led to the creation of a token, a person who has the rank and the income, but not the task.

Of course, there are times that our new general manager, selected for reasons other than being the most likely person to carry out the job, rises extremely well, even majestically, to the task. In which case, hooray, affirmative action has worked.

Unfortunately, it has only worked temporarily, because another sadly well-worn syndrome then swings into play. Within a very short period that person is head-hunted into a higher position by another company under the same pressure to demonstrate its affirmative-action credentials. And if there is again a success story, there is another head-hunt, until eventually another token is added to this society so opposed to tokenism, another person with more rank than function.

Of course, this does not apply to every affirmative-action case. Let those whom the cap fits, wear it. Of course there are people who hop off the roller-coaster; and of course there are people who keep matching up to all the new demands. But the process I describe is a fair generalization as generalizations go, and the point is that it builds in a pressure that virtually ensures the tears at the end.

We know of the Peter Principle, which states that managers are promoted until one step beyond their level of competence. What we have here is a Beyond-Peter Principle, a structural imperative to promote managers multiple steps beyond their levels of competence. The tears are not accidents or by-products, they are created by the process. The effects are tragic not only for the individuals caught in the machinery but also for the overall quest to bring a real, lasting black presence into the executive echelons, because it leaves a smell of failure attached to the very notion of black management.

One of the central hallmarks of the thrust for affirmative action is the cry that goes: 'Produce top blacks, and don't dare have tokenism.' I submit that this approach is no less impossibly illogical than saying: 'Produce children, but don't dare make love.' As long as companies feel they are judged by their complexions, tokenism will be entrenched and perpetuated.

Let us turn now to the matter of personal destruction. The scene is a conference, on 'Black empowerment' or 'Furthering the RDP', or any similarly proper subject. Speakers are saying all the right things, such as how vital affirmative action is, and how the employers should do a lot more of it.

Tea-time comes around and people are milling in corridors, and one group is talking about who's who, and up comes the name of some person currently prominent, climbing the corporate ladder, and his black brothers and sisters promptly respond with one voice: 'Him, oh no, he's just an affirmative-action appointment.'

Maybe I can mention another scene. The one where a leading (black) personality, in impeccable suit with BMW outside, is addressing a suburban discussion group on the extreme holiness of affirmative action, and afterwards an innocent wide-eyed lady comes forth all gushing and well-meaning and says: 'Eow Mr So-and-so' (she mispronounces his name; if he is an Mphahlele he comes out as a spluttered amalgam of mff's and shh's), 'I see quite how important affirmative action is. Look how much it has done for you'. Whereupon our speaker chokes on his cucumber sandwich and turns strange colours and in very firm terms informs her that: no, affirmative action is for other people, his career owes absolutely nothing to affirmative action, whatsoever.

Now I ask myself: if this cause is so noble in the abstract, why is it such an insult in the personal? And I think the answer goes to the flaw in the core. No matter how much you set out to sugar-coat affirmative action as a development programme, deep down inside everybody knows it is charity, and there's nothing people hate like receiving charity.

And what's even worse than receiving charity is receiving charity that goes sour. Take a fellow who gets fast-tracked by affirmative action and suddenly finds himself with carpet and secretary and three-window office and all, and it's great. A year later friends are asking what he actually does and it's less great. Five years later the carpet's worn out and he's tired of the view and he's really seriously gnarled up inside. He's telling friends: 'These whites won't let me have authority, because they're scared I'll show them up'. His boss is telling his own friends: 'Nice chap, but no manager, can't take responsibility'.

I've seen people messed up this way. I myself once messed a guy up. It was long ago, before affirmative action was the in thing. This guy was in a humble job, and he was good, and I manoeuvred him into the fast lane, because he was black. Had he been white I would have let time take its course; because he was black I wanted him to be a visible success. The lane was faster than his speed. He left the rails. And crashed. I see his widow from time to time. She blames me. So do I.

Turn to part three: second-class professionalism. I was talking a while ago to an eminent black businessman, about a legal problem he was facing. He said it was in good hands, with his lawyers. I asked who they were. He told me: one of those old established names with pompous pictures of bygone partners all down the corridors, that had been in Main Street since Oom Paul's day (until a year ago when they defected to Sandton because, you know, 'the blacks are taking over town'). I said: 'It's strange for a guy who talks affirmative action from breakfast time to close-down to go to this firm. Why not black lawyers?' And he replies: 'Don't try to be funny. This is a *serious* case.'

In one sentence, the unsanitized truth of what one advocate of affirmative action really thinks of it: that it's a nice thing to have around and a nice line to punt at seminars, but when you're on the table for a triple bypass, well, call for Dr Cohen.

Fifty years ago or so, stockbroking was a one hundred per cent English activity. Afrikaners featured nowhere. Now, there are plenty of Afrikaners. There are Afrikaans firms, and so many Afrikaans people in other firms that nobody notices, and no client is about to get agitated about being referred to a Van der Merwe or a Van Schalkwyk or whoever.

This, as I see it, is a satisfactory outcome, and it was arrived at because there was no affirmative action for Afrikaners. There was a natural ingress. No stockbroker firm employed Van der Merwe because they thought they'd better have his name on the letterhead; they employed him because they needed the services he was offering. No firm pushed Van Schalkwyk into a rank above what they believed he could handle; they put him into the slots where they needed what he could deliver. Between English and Afrikaans we ended up with a single professional standard and professional reputation, and the same applies in the professional realm as a whole: accountancy, medicine, law, whatever.

Will our children face the equivalent? Will they be equally freely consulting a Khumalo or a Montgomery? Or will they see an A-team professional world, consisting of whites or anyway non-Africans, and a B-team they'll call affirmative action?

As I see it, there is a core choice here. The affirmative-action route will produce higher numbers of black professionals, but at the cost of investing black professionalism with a third-world stature whereby it is employed only by those who have no choice. The avenue which you might call 'ruthless merit', or somewhat more far-sightedly 'ruthless *potential* merit', would mean a slower rate of blackening the boardrooms and the chambers, but with sounder long-term consequences.

On count four of the case for the prosecution, I talked of treason against the economy. Is this melodramatic? I might have thought so, I might have admitted to a little hyperbole, except that last week I was in Zambia, and I return shocked. After thirty years of Zambianizing – their version of affirmative action – nothing worked. The main local industry is crushing stone at the roadside.

There is now a stirring, some things are beginning to work, because they have been taken over by outsiders – by Lebanese, by Greeks, or especially South Africans. I found this a painful sight – far more painful than the average Zambian I spoke to, I might say, whose basic view is that it's great to be able to drink beer again, or buy insurance. It was painful to me nonetheless, and I wish never to see any echo of it here.

Thus, I stick to the talk of treason. The wheel of history turns. Where we are now, our views and attitudes, our children will not be. They will be somewhere else. I submit that insofar as we do anything to soften the cutting edge of the economy, making policies or appointments for any reason other than to maximize growth, our children will curse us.

As I speak in this vein, some people imagine me to be saying 'blacks can't do it'. What I am in fact saying is that once you appoint people for reasons other than their perceived ability to do it, you are not only damaging them, and not only stigmatizing all other people in the same bracket; you are also playing fast and loose with the one thing you are not allowed to play with – the economy. Insofar as you may, to rainbowize ten or a hundred executive offices, jeopardize the future of thousands or millions of artisans or labourers, you do no service.

I do not think many people will seriously deny that this jeopardy is real. We see the strident columnists telling us of the fantastic merits of black managers as a class, but most people, of whatever colour, know that the stridency is a cover for lack of conviction. As a class, black managers have not covered themselves with glory. I will never say 'blacks can't do it' because I will never think in terms of 'blacks'. It is affirmative action that thinks in terms of 'blacks', and that mangles or wrecks the prospects of each new black individual coming into the management echelon by having created an image that colours the performance of blacks as a category.

I would rather say: 'Can Khumalo do it? Can Moloi do it? Can Mudau do it?' I am not oblivious to the fact that these people are black. I therefore am all the more keen to see them do it. But I do not measure them as blacks, I do not slot them into this rank or that post by virtue of blackness.

My way would mean a much slower rate of ingress of black managers and directors and professionals into the top echelons of the economy than the affirmative-action route would mean. However, my route would also mean fewer heart attacks, much less skindering among friends and acquaintances, the eradication of the standing idea that black success stories are there because it suits some white institution to have put them there, and so on. It would also mean a great diminution in the number of (black) patients who, arriving at Lesedi and being told they need a major operation, gulp and find an excuse to relocate to Rosebank Clinic.

To me it is a matter of a simple choice: a choice between having large numbers of derided and discontented black bigshots in the short term, with a stonecrusher economy in the longer term, and having an irritatingly slow black incursion into the executive offices that in the end means both a surer incursion and a good deal better life expectancy for the jobs of those famous 'masses' to whom affirmative action is nothing but two strange words.

17

LAWRENCE SCHLEMMER

Liberalism, democracy, race relations, and the rising black middle class in South Africa

The middle classes and the amelioration of political conflict

In the very anxious years between the 1976/77 Soweto uprising and the start of the transition to democracy in the early nineties, corporate business in South Africa involved itself in various reform and development initiatives. These initiatives were driven by a variety of motives, one of which was to attempt to create conditions of greater stability in the operating environment of business. The Urban Foundation was one of the more prominent and generally successful development organizations established.

As a member of the Council of the Urban Foundation, I can recall repeated assertions by prominent business leaders that the key to future stability would be a growing black middle class. The assumption was made, and often openly stated, that a black middle class would develop the same values and interests as the white middle class, and would identify with goals for society which would be compatible with the interests of business. My cautionary comments on this issue had little effect. The conviction was firm, and the image of a sympathetic black BMW class was captivating.

Quite understandably, the radical and activist communities

understood these motives of business as a desire to 'co-opt' a class of black social, economic, and political 'bodyguards' in anticipation of the conflict of interests that would inevitably ensue after South Africa's political transition. To some extent, obviously, they were right.

The concerns of the radicals were misplaced on two counts, however. The first is debated here. I will argue that the black 'middle class', to the extent that it is a category of interests, has a mixed political and ideological profile, and is likely to include categories of people who take the lead in attacking white business and middle-class interests.

Second, the radicals at the time underestimated the philanthropy, good intentions, and benevolence of the leadership of business organizations, however superficial these sentiments may have been, and completely overestimated the strategic coherence of their planning. In the end, the Urban Foundation achieved its greatest successes in the fields of low-cost housing, mass educational reform, and opposition to laws like influx control and discriminatory tenure regulations – fields that probably had a greater impact on the black proletariat than they did in promoting the growth of the much-vaunted black middle class. An initiative of the Urban Foundation to promote and monitor black occupational advancement in industry was dropped soon after a rather incomplete pilot investigation.

Various small business development initiatives were pursued but the business initiatives of the time fell far short of the intensive training and career sponsorship that would have been required to stimulate a surge in the growth of a business-friendly black middle class. In fact, the greatest single source of stimulation of the black middle class in the apartheid era was the rapid growth of a black bureaucrat and professional class in the former homelands, significantly assisted, deliberately or otherwise, by the mass-production of second-rate Bachelors of Arts in new black universities, or apartheid 'bush colleges' as they were once called.

The beguiling notion among white opinion leaders that a black middle class will cushion whites' business interests in the interplay of interests in the open political economy is probably still alive and well as an abstract concept, however. Even the fact that Cyril Ramaphosa, the 'flagship' protégé of business in the field of black empowerment, has made fairly recent speeches keeping up the pressure on business by lamenting how little it has done to 'transform' itself has probably hardly dented the notion.

Businessmen were not alone in their (ineffectual) belief in the benefits of a black middle class. A great deal of early political science literature on democracy broadly supports the notion that social mobility and a large and growing new middle class will strengthen trends supporting democratic pluralism. Tom Bottomore (1966, ch. 2), for example, argues that the emergence in industrial societies of the new middle classes created status groups which bridged the formerly stark division between labour and ownership of capital, and introduced more complex concepts of interest conflict into societies which might otherwise have been dominated by conflict over the ownership and control of production. Seymour Martin Lipset (1959) has also talked of the 'emollient effect' of a growing middle class on political conflict. William Kornhauser (1960) saw the middle classes as essential to the 'mediating structures' which would allow a greater variety of interests to be effectively articulated in a competitive political system. Gabriel Almond and Sidney Verba in their famous work *The civic culture* (1965) implied in various arguments that the middle classes, through their enhanced education and citizen competence, were an essential part of the resources for a network of lobbies and social pressures which would constrain the structures of power to respect a greater variety of interests than their own agendas would otherwise accommodate.

Because of the logical correlation between levels of development and the relative size of the middle classes in any society, middle-class influence is virtually a given factor in all the propositions to the effect that stable democracy and liberal tolerance depend in most instances on at least certain thresholds of economic development having been achieved (see, for example, Robert Dahl 1971, chs. 5 and 6).

In a very broad sense, I would not challenge these established views. It is perfectly logical to assume that a growing black middle class in South Africa's new democracy will strengthen or deepen the articulation of a diversity of interests in the political system and add to the weight of influence of the numerically small but established and largely white middle classes. Ordinary logic would suggest that a growing black middle class must to some extent take the edge off the potential conflict between the mass of black 'have-nots' and the minority of largely white 'haves'.

The problem, however, lies in the generality and over-simplicity of the broad proposition. Even the most cursory glance at current conflicts in the world today will suggest that the most extreme, irrational, and even murderous intentions are not mouthed by peasants or workers but by *middle-class* activists and the relatively privileged militant intelligentsia, and there is an abundance of literature to support that simple observation. It is obviously not sufficient to talk of the 'middle class' as if it were a uniform and consistent phenomenon. Notions of the political significance of a 'middle class' are quite as absurd as the notion of some inevitable solidarity and class action among all industrial workers. The question to be asked is, What middle class, and when will its influence become salient in the ways suggested above?

Empirical indications in South Africa

Before continuing with this argument it is appropriate to consider some available empirical evidence. No special study has been undertaken for this purpose, but recent surveys in which I have been involved contain items and correlations with class-related background variables which are instructive. Difficulties in defining the 'middle class' will become apparent as this argument proceeds, but I will hold discussion on this to the end.

A study which I conducted in 1991/92 (fieldwork by Market and Opinion Surveys (Pty) Ltd, black sample size 1 642 nation-wide, rural and urban) contained findings which tended to offer slight support for the thesis that middle-class blacks had attitudes to whites which were more accommodating and gentler than those of blacks polled generally across class. For example, fourteen statements on race relations were included in the survey, to which respondents could agree or disagree. (The items are listed in the appendix.) The mean proportions of replies across the fourteen items in a positive direction (lack of hostility/acceptance of whites/rejection of racial solidarity) were as follows:

Table 1: Rejection of negative and/or endorsement of positive statements on race relations by black respondents; 1991/2 mean proportions across 14 statements

All black adults (n 1 642)	51.6%
Top 7.5% of household incomes (n 60)	55.4%
Top 10% of educational qualifications grade 12 (std 10) or higher (n 85)	54.9%

The contrasts are not very large, and quite clearly some 45 per cent of respondents in the 'middle-class' categories identified had not 'softened' their attitudes in regard to racial issues. The balance of responses in the two middle-class categories hardly allows one to generalize for the 'class' as a whole. If the more hostile 45 per cent of the 'middle class' happened to contain the most articulate and confident sentiments, it would quite easily overshadow the more benign 55 per cent in its effects on a popular consciousness.

The study was conducted before the major political transition of 1993/94, a change in political context which might qualify the results of a similar, more recent study. Some people might assume that race relations have improved since 1991/92, or others might consider that hostile and competitive attitudes at the time were still constrained by white power and authority and that more recent research would produce more 'valid' hostile responses.

Two more recent surveys, conducted after the transition to majority rule and the assumption of power by a party dominantly supported by blacks, provide more detailed assessment. One was conducted by myself in collaboration with Hermann Giliomee in December 1994, and the other was conducted by R. W. Johnson with input by myself in October 1996. The fieldwork in both instances was undertaken by MarkData (Pty) Ltd among representative nationwide samples of over 2 200 adults of eighteen years and older (1 500 African), and was based on personal interviews in the home languages of respondents.

The so-called middle class is a complex amalgam of characteristics, and no single indicator can be used to identify its constituents. The following indexes of 'middle-class' status were used, on the assumption that each represents an aspect of being 'middle-class' or of what is termed the 'emerging middle class' in South Africa. (The sub-sample sizes given are those of the 1996 survey, but they are almost identical to those of the 1994 study. The sample sizes show that the sample-design incorporated deliberate over-representation of these categories, allowing for subsequent 'rectification' by means of computer-weighting.)

Indexes of 'middle-class' status

- Educational: post-matric (tertiary, or after grade 12) qualifications: ± 1.5 per cent of black adults (sample size: n 63);
- Material: household and personal income of R2 500 or more per month: ± 7.5 per cent and 2 per cent of black adults (n 176, 59 respectively);
- Occupational: professional, semi-professional (teachers and

nurses etc.) and white-collar occupations: <1 per cent, 1.5 per cent, and ± 18 per cent of black adults (n 23, 43, 294 respectively);

- Consumer patterns: the so-called *Living Standards Measure*, categories 6, 7, and 8, at which patterns of purchasing and possession of consumer durables reflect what are typically regarded as part of an emerging or established middle-class lifestyle: 9 per cent, 4 per cent, and 1.5 per cent of black adults (n 199, 118, 30 respectively).

I have not provided data in tabulated form for reasons of brevity; instead, I will describe relevant trends from the results under various headings. The small sizes of the relevant sub-samples do mean that the conclusions are often suggestive rather than conclusive.

Material aspirations

In the 1994 survey an open question was asked about desirable objectives that government should attempt to achieve in the new South Africa. Among the wide range of answers, some referred to levels of remuneration. Compared to the 14 per cent among the general population wanting the government to ensure *higher salaries*, we have the following proportions in 'middle-class' categories:

- those with post-matric (tertiary) qualification: 40 per cent;
- with personal income above R2 500: 26 per cent;
- independent professionals and semi-professionals: 33 per cent. (1994)

A wide range of policy objectives was presented to respondents, who were asked to indicate how important they considered each to be. Some 11 per cent of all respondents considered salaries, incomes, and *working conditions* to be 'most important of all'.

This 11 per cent compares with the following proportions among the middle-class respondents:

- those with post-matric (tertiary) qualification: 24 per cent;
- independent professionals: 25 per cent;
- semi-professionals: 24 per cent. (1994)

Virtually all the respondents expected the government to 'create' *work for the unemployed*. When asked what these make-work jobs should pay, some 24 per cent of all respondents considered that pay should be R1 250 per month or more. Among the middle-class categories the proportions were generally very much higher:

- those with post-matric (tertiary) qualification: 51 per cent;
- Living Standards Measure (LSM) 7/8: 49 per cent;
- household income above R2 500 per month: 40 per cent;
- independent professionals: 61 per cent;
- semi-professionals: 37 per cent. (1994)

Hence, although not consistent across all categories, there seems to be a tendency among the middle-class respondents to be more concerned with incomes and material rewards than the black respondents in general. There were no instances in which any of the middle-class categories were less concerned with money than the population at large. This manifest materialism is perhaps rather typical of a new middle class – more established or old middle classes can perhaps afford to place less emphasis on salaries and incomes because they have accumulated assets, have paid for their more expensive durable possessions, have no housing bonds or have lower housing bonds, and hence have relatively less debt.

Expectations

After the respondents' attention was drawn to the Reconstruction and Development Programme (RDP) of the new government, they were asked when they expected to derive benefits from it.

Some 47 per cent of all respondents expected *benefits immediately*, compared with the following proportions in 'middle-class' categories:

- LSM 7/8: 54 per cent;
- independent professionals: 53 per cent. (1994)

Some 45 per cent of all adults felt that the government had *not performed 'as well as they expected'* by the end of 1994, and this broad level applied to the middle-class categories as well, with the exception of LSM 7/8, among which only some one-third were disappointed (1994).

By 1996, roughly 24 per cent of all adults felt that the government had *met 'almost none' of its promises*, compared with far fewer people in the middle-class categories who were critically disappointed. For example:

- those with post-matric (tertiary) qualification: 19 per cent;
- LSM 6/7/8: 13 per cent;
- personal income above R2 500 per month: 8 per cent;
- in middle-class occupations: ±20 per cent.

Similarly, the proportions of middle-class respondents who felt that the government had matched its promises partly or completely were higher than among the population at large (1996).

Among the black population at large, only some 23 per cent were satisfied with their *incomes and standards of living*. Among the LSM 7/8 group this figure stood at roughly 37 per cent, among the higher-income categories 38 per cent, and among clerical and sales occupations 33 per cent. None of the middle-class groups were less satisfied than the general population.

The trend here seems to be that despite evidence of a high level of material concerns, and the tendency to want to see benefits very quickly, the middle-class categories tend to be more satisfied with the performance of government than poorer people. Possibly it is because the areas in which the new government has produced results most quickly are those in which the middle classes and aspirant middle classes are able to benefit.

Policy concerns

Acceptance of the private sector

The middle classes seem to be more concerned with the economy than people polled irrespective of class. While some 39 per cent of all respondents considered *investment for economic growth* to be very or most important among policy concerns, the figures for other categories were:
- those with post-matric (tertiary) qualification: 57 per cent;
- LSM 6/7/8: 49 per cent;
- semi-professionals: 50 per cent;
- independent professionals: 33 per cent. (1994)

Only some 18 per cent of all respondents identified the *encouragement of private-sector growth* as a solution to unemployment, while the proportions among the middle classes included the following:
- those with post-matric (tertiary) qualification: 33 per cent;
- LSM 7/8: 39 per cent;
- with a household income above R2 500 per month: 29 per cent;
- white collar-clerical occupations: 31 per cent;
- independent professionals: 57 per cent.

On the issue of the *privatization of state assets*, roughly 26 per cent of the general population were in favour of the policy. No category in the middle class was less positive than this, and the support for privatization rose to well above 30 per cent among LSM 6, lower professionals, and clerical workers (1996).

The issue of *the freedom of business to make profits versus regulation* was raised in 1996. Overall, some 32 per cent of the black population favoured the freedom of the market, while this figure fell slightly in the following categories:

- those with post-matric (tertiary) qualification: 28 per cent;
- LSM 8: 11 per cent
- higher-income categories and independent professionals: 23 per cent.

No category of the middle class favoured business freedom more than the population average.

The middle-class categories we have identified, therefore, seem to be marginally more supportive of economic concerns and in favour of private-sector-based development than the population at large, but with important qualifications. The trend is not very marked, and the high-status category of independent professionals appears to be ambivalent. The middle class in any event appears to want more government regulation of business than the population at large. The trend in these middle classes is to want the market to be so guided by government as to favour their interests.

Redistribution

The *redistribution of wealth to help the underprivileged* was strongly supported by some 25 per cent of the population at large. Support among the specific categories varied, however. It was similarly low among all categories except independent professionals:

- those with post-matric (tertiary) qualification: 20 per cent;
- higher-income categories: 20 per cent;
- clerical and sales occupations: 7 per cent;
- independent professionals: 37 per cent. (1994)

The principle of securing the *socio-economic* equality of all groups in society was endorsed as very or most important as a policy issue among 34 per cent of the population as a whole, and among the middle-class categories the support tended to be the same or very slightly higher (among the independent professionals it was much higher at 52 per cent). Among the semi-professionals, however, support dropped to 15 per cent (1994).

Special measures for the *promotion of the interests of people who suffered under apartheid* are endorsed as very important or most important by 30 per cent of all respondents, and the level of support is much the same among the middle-class categories, except:

- LSM 7/8: 45 per cent;
- higher-income categories: 37 per cent;
- independent professionals: 36 per cent.

On the broad issues of equality and redistribution, then, the responses of the middle-class categories are very mixed, with some categories significantly less in favour of the principle than black voters in general. Generally, however, the independent professionals are more in favour of equalization and redistribution of wealth than the population at large.

Law, order, and social discipline

This is an issue of considerable salience in a society with a high crime rate and many other indications of a breakdown in respect even for legitimate authority. In the 1994 survey, 48 per cent of the population at large considered *law, order, and respect for authority* to be very or most important among policy issues, and it emerged as the fifth-highest issue of general concern after employment creation, housing, incomes, and welfare and social services. No category in the middle-class groupings gave a lower priority to the issue, but LSM 6/7/8 categories were higher at 62 per cent and independent professionals marginally higher at 55 per cent.

Some 30 per cent of the general public considered strong action to restore respect for authority to be very or most important, and the level was marginally higher among the specific middle-class categories, except semi-professionals:

- those with post-matric (tertiary) qualification: 37 per cent;
- LSM 6: 36 per cent;
- higher-income categories: 35 per cent;
- independent professionals: 57 per cent;
- semi-professionals: 13 per cent.

The *restoration of discipline and standards in schools* was regarded as very or most important by 34 per cent in the general population and the level of endorsement was moderately higher in most middle-class categories but with LSM 7/8 and the white-collar groups at 50 per cent or more. Here again, lower professionals were less concerned, at some 31 per cent (1994).

Generally, then, the middle-class categories are somewhat more concerned than average about social order and authority, but the semi-professionals are clearly an exception. These are mainly teachers and nurses, and it is possible that the high levels of unionization in these categories have produced a protest approach which is not consonant with other middle-class concerns on this and similar issues.

Racial balance in public and private affairs

In the 1996 survey, respondents were probed on their views on racial representation in government. Only 15 per cent of the general black population thought that there were too many minorities in government and that there should be more Africans. Compared with this, no fewer than 45 per cent of independent professionals wanted a greater dominance of blacks in public representation. The other middle-class categories were much the same as the general population in their views.

Some 7 per cent of the population at large wanted to see more whites in government, a proportion which doubled in the LSM categories and rose to 20 per cent among clerical and sales workers.

In the same survey, 30 per cent of the general population felt that affirmative action should be applied, involving *no white appointments* for a long period of time or until representativeness has been achieved. Among the middle-class categories we found the following proportions:

- those with post-matric (tertiary) qualification: 24 per cent;
- LSM 7/8: 22 per cent;
- higher-income categories: 26 per cent;
- independent professionals: 18 per cent;
- semi-professionals: 12 per cent;
- those in clerical and sales occupations: 44 per cent.

The position on racial balance is therefore complex. Independent professionals want more blacks in power, but they are less concerned with affirmative action than the general population. White-collar categories want black affirmative action but more whites in power. Generally speaking, the middle-class groupings are somewhat less in favour of special black advancement than the general population and are not markedly more insistent on a greater black dominance in government, with the exception of the independent professionals.

In similar vein, in the 1996 survey, and in other earlier surveys, we asked whether the respondents supported the notion that *'South Africa is mainly a country for blacks and others should take second place'* (that is, as opposed to equal and non-racial opportunity). The proportion in the general population supporting the 'black country' position was 24 per cent, and the responses in the middle-class groups included the following:

- those with post-matric (tertiary) qualification: 18 per cent;
- LSM 6: 30 per cent;
- LSM 7/8: 12 per cent;
- higher-income categories: 20 per cent;
- independent professionals: 15 per cent;
- semi-professionals: 14 per cent
- those in clerical and sales occupations: 34 per cent.

What appears to be the pattern here is that the lower-middle class supports the notion more strongly than the general population and the middle class somewhat less strongly than voters in general.

It would seem, then, that the lower middle class tends to favour black entitlement and that middle-class professionals are less concerned about it than the general population. The professionals, however, are certainly more concerned than other groups about the issue of increasing the political dominance of blacks relative to whites.

Democratic opposition

This critical issue is one on which the middle class is normally assumed to be rather distinctive. On the issue of support for a strongly *critical opposition* (1996), the overall support was 43 per cent, and the middle-class categories included the following:

- those with post-matric (tertiary) qualification: 48 per cent;
- LSM 8: 57 per cent;
- clerical and sales: 66 per cent;
- all other categories were no more supportive of critical opposition than the general population.

When asked whether they favoured *many political parties or fewer to promote unity*, the 'democratic' position was supported by 42 per cent in the general population, while figures for the specific middle-class categories were as follows:

- LSM 6/7: 48 per cent;
- higher-income categories: 55 per cent;
- high professionals: 66 per cent;
- LSM 8 (a particularly wealthy category): 27 per cent.

On the issue of a *vigilant and critical press*, the population support was at no more than 16 per cent. The figure for the LSM 8 category stood at 29 per cent, and independent professionals at 22 per cent.

The other categories were not meaningfully different from the general population.

In the 1994 survey we asked whether or not the respondents felt that there should be more opposition in the Government of National Unity (GNU), and only 6 per cent in the general black population wanted it, compared with 16 per cent among LSM 7 respondents. The independent professionals were completely united in not wanting any greater opposition to the African National Congress (ANC) in the GNU.

These indicators of support for the principle of democratic opposition produce very mixed signals from the 'middle classes'. At best, one may say that there is a slight increase in support for the principle among some of the middle classes, mainly the high-consumption categories, but with the professionals rather inconsistent in their views.

When one draws together these various indications it seems that any assumption that the black middle classes are closer to the interests and values of the established (white) middle class would be hugely oversimplified. The black middle class, to the extent that there is any coherence of positions within it, is marginally closer to the views of the established middle classes in regard to business, provided it is regulated, slightly less concerned with redistribution policy, and slightly closer in support of the principle of critical political opposition and law, order, and social discipline. In many areas, however, the high-status professionals are inconsistent and ambivalent. There is also a strong sense of 'entitlement' in the lower middle class, which weakens in the higher-status groups, but the professionals in a sense 'compensate' with their concern with black political dominance.

The relatively marked materialism of the middle classes is a reminder that it is very much a new middle class with a great deal of catching up to do in terms of establishing a sense of material security. Like most middle classes, it might also be very concerned with the acquisition of visible status goods.

In general, one is left with the impression that there is a degree of mild convergence between the new and the established middle classes on some issues, but that a fairly large gulf remains. Furthermore, on some very sensitive issues, there are categories in the black middle class which diverge from what might be typical white middle-class patterns very sharply.

The issue of the gulf between the two racially-based classes is most easily grasped if one considers the issue of party political support patterns. Overwhelmingly, the white middle class supports opposition parties, and broadly it is a stance taken in defence of interests and public standards that protect the everyday culture and lifestyle of an established middle class. The attitudes are very similar to those of middle classes in all industrialized countries. Underlying much of the speculation about the role of a black middle class in South African politics is the expectation or hope that the black middle class will gravitate towards support for the same norms and standards, and hence towards support for the two political parties that are most closely associated with middle-class interests, the National Party (NP) and the Democratic Party (DP).

In 1991/92 there were indeed signs in survey data that the reputation of President F. W. de Klerk was achieving considerable support for the NP among blacks – over 20 per cent of blacks indicated that they would support either the NP or De Klerk as an individual. This trend has been very sharply reversed since then, however.

In the 1996 survey shown in Table 2 , the following are the percentages supporting the ANC, the Pan-Africanist Congress, the NP, and the DP, among the categories of the middle class identified. The results indicate that there is a slight increase in support for the NP, but also for the PAC, among the middle-class voters. The DP, which is frequently seen to be the party of the private-sector middle classes par excellence, gains virtually no additional support among the middle classes, except among the higher-income category. The NP also gains more as a second-choice party than does the DP.

Table 2: Partisan choice among categories of black voters

	First choice				Second choice		
	ANC	PAC	NP	DP	PAC	NP	DP
All black voters	72	3	2	<1	23	11	3
Post-matric (tertiary)	80	2	5	0	30	16	3
LSM 6	77	5	3	<1	28	14	1
LSM 7	67	5	7	0	22	15	7
LSM 8	77	3	3	0	26	19	6
R2 500 p.m. or more	72	3	4	2	13	14	5
Indep. Professionals	59	4	3	0	16	18	0
Semi-professionals	67	0	6	0	17	5	5
White-collar occupations	76	4	4	<1	22	13	4
Clerical/sales	80	4	4	0	34	18	4
White voters	4	–	32	9	–	15	9

The strong position of the PAC as a second choice emphasizes the weakness of the parties of the established (white) middle class even further. The pattern suggests that if there is a drift away from the ANC among middle-class blacks, it will be towards the PAC much more than towards the NP or the DP.

The most dramatic evidence of the difference in the political agendas of blacks and whites with roughly middle-class status is in regard to the specific priorities for state action in the socio-economic field. These differences are presented in Table 3; the index of middle-class status chosen is that of levels of qualification above matric.

Table 3: Responses of post-matriculants to the item: 'What should government do for people like you?' (First, second, and third responses; three answers coded, hence totals exceed 100 per cent)

	Blacks	Whites
EDUCATION	44	37
EMPLOYMENT	18	25
SERVICES/AMENITIES	89	0
INCOME	41	8
HOUSING	29	10
TAX RELIEF	1	50
COMBAT CRIME	8	28
EQUAL RIGHTS	9	29
BOOST ECONOMY	0	11
HEALTH SERVICE	6	11
NO AFFIRMATIVE ACTION	0	9
FACILITIES FOR AGED	2	9
PRESERVE RIGHTS	0	6
PRICES/INFLATION	0	4
OTHER	<3	<3

In Table 3 the responses between black and white post-matriculants converge in respect of education and employment, but thereafter diverge sharply on virtually all other expectations of government. The expectations of the black group are far closer to those of the black poor, even though their circumstances are very different from those of poor people. To some extent this is explained by the fact that the black post-matriculants have not yet accumulated the comforts and capital of the white middle classes, but these differences persist even when incomes are compensated for in statistical calculations. There is, thus, a very different political culture among the black emerging middle class than that which typifies the white middle class.

All these results, with the exceptions identified, tend to underscore the fact that racial divisions remain a more pervasive cleavage in our politics than class – a division which the consolidation and further growth of a black middle class will begin to bridge only very slowly. The different goals, demands, and expectations of government action among blacks and whites in the middle classes, broadly defined, are understandable in view of the persisting differences in residential location and lifestyle. But these differences have also become lodged in political culture. This reinforces the argument that a 'middle class' which is socially equivalent to the white middle class cannot emerge quickly enough to create a cross-racial class solidarity which will make an impact on South Africa's current and short- to medium-term politics.

Discussion and some implications for the future of liberal values

The comments above on convergence and divergence cut both ways in a party-political context. The vulnerability of South Africa's pluralist democracy lies not only in the fact that there is a cross-class racial solidarity among black voters, but also in the fact that the same pattern applies in white politics. Very few whites support the ANC, the PAC, or the Inkatha Freedom Party at the moment, and the trend of support away from these parties has strengthened slightly in very recent months. This pattern has been a source of concern in the ANC, and in recent provincial congresses of that party resolutions have been passed aimed at increasing white support. This is not likely to be any more successful than attempts by the NP and the DP to attract black support. In a sense, the only effective demonstrations of democratic choice and of the valuable principle of a floating vote are found to some extent among coloured and Indian voters.

The same broad conclusions can apply to the other indications of convergence and divergence of the white and black middle classes in the empirical results quoted. While great care was taken to identify the instances or issues on which the black middle class does shift towards the pattern of the established middle class, a broader view of the patterns would suggest that the overall trends are so mild that they make very little difference to the pattern of racial division. One can quite safely say that the majority of the populations in the middle-class categories identified conceive of their interests in ways which deny politically significant middle-class commonality.

One must accept the obvious fact that it is problematic to approach any 'class' as a cohesive and internally consistent social phenomenon. One must remain very cautious and not be pushed into the assumption of class cohesion by Marxist analyses, which have seldom been empirically verified. A 'middle class' is a complex collection of potentially divergent interests. The assumptions made in much of the literature referred to earlier are notably oversimplified.

This very intra-class divergence and inconsistency, however, is perhaps the basis for more modest claims that a middle class can strengthen democratic pluralism in a society. This will occur not by creating a pattern of common values and goals among all middle classes but simply by making political allegiances less 'bloc-like' and therefore more varied and diverse. This effect, however, would be unpredictable as regards the extent to which it might protect the interests of the established middle classes in South African society. It could, for example, lead to fierce competition between populist factions, all drawing on black middle-class leadership.

The more predictable pattern, however, is that of a division between the black and white middle classes. South African society is still faced, as it has been since the beginnings of contact between its component communities, with the fact that classes and interest categories can and often do compete within 'class' boundaries more fiercely than classes will compete with each other. The competing intra-class divisions need only find some identity or status concern with sufficient emotional resonance to cause class solidarity or even a mild commonality to fly out of the figurative window.

The most important question is how quickly this racial division of classes in South Africa might soften. The impressions and the evidence from elsewhere in the world do not suggest that progress will be at all rapid, particularly as far as the middle classes are concerned. In Zimbabwe, more than a decade after liberation, black middle-class opinion leaders are if anything intensifying demands for special black entitlement.

As far as I can discern, the black middle class in the USA has achieved more rapid upward mobility than most other minorities with the exception perhaps of Asian and Jewish minorities, but racial consciousness within the class still appears to be intense. Although less publicized, the same seems to apply to colour minorities in Europe, although various accounts suggest that race divisions are softening in the UK; casual observations do suggest that this applies to the lower-middle and working classes more than to the professional and managerial classes.

We are faced with the very real possibility that race conflict will re-emerge as the hallmark of South African society. It is quite clear that the condition of the black poor will take a very long time to improve in relative terms. The most basic condition for the alleviation of poverty is a marked reduction of unemployment, and even the optimistic assumption of 6 per cent growth by 1999 as embodied in the government's macro-economic policy (in conjunction with technological change and continued low skill in-migration into South Africa) means no more than a stabilization of an already high rate of unemployment. We already know that there are serious fiscal and administrative constraints on an effective expansion of welfare at the lower levels of subsistence and survival, and these will endure as well.

Any interest group, not only the black 'middle class', will utilize whatever competitive advantages it can in promoting itself. As some authors have pointed out in the United States, the presence of social discrimination and a black underclass provides an enduring rationale for special treatment of all blacks. It would be naive to expect black interest groups in South Africa not to adopt this rationale to the hilt.

The established middle classes, furthermore, find it very difficult not to appear to discriminate against outsiders in the social field, no matter how hard they may try to remove objective forms of discrimination in the occupational and economic fields. The established (white, western) middle classes tend to place a premium on privacy (even within the family circle), on fairly exclusive lifestyle pursuits, and on distinguishing social mannerisms. They do not necessarily mean to maintain social distance between themselves and others, but it is almost impossible for them to avoid the image of some snobbishness and exclusivity (the social burden of the WASPs, perhaps).

If one combines this pattern with the very visible presence of black poverty and deprivation as a basis for racial claims, then it is difficult to imagine the racial distance, and even racial hostility, among the middle classes ameliorating very significantly.

Furthermore, it now seems fairly inevitable that there will be an ethnic revival and re-mobilization in the Afrikaans middle classes. A small but substantial proportion of English-speakers will, I predict, begin to align themselves with that revival, particularly in towns and cities in which the Afrikaans middle class is numerically powerful among whites (some 40 per cent of English-speakers polled in Pretoria evinced sympathy for the Volkstaat idea in the poll conducted by the Volkstaat Council). Here again we will have a phenomenon dividing the 'middle class'.

Perhaps this scenario is too gloomy (liberals are today quite frequently accused of unpatriotic pessimism). The fact that it is a possible scenario can hardly be rejected out of hand, however. If so, the most depressing thing about it is that the basis for division will continue to be defensible and understandable, and is likely to remain so, on all sides.

Affirmative action and special measures aimed at black empowerment are very deeply divisive and aggravating to those whose world-views are based on hallowed principles of individualism and merit. These measures are stoking the fires of Afrikaans ethnic counter-reaction all the time to boot, but it is indefensible and futile to suggest that the black middle class should not attempt to defend the rationale underlying them.

Liberals should continue to take their own established values very seriously and try to demonstrate the superiority of merit and individually-based approaches for national development. This means promoting and supporting training, training, and more training, in contexts free of the negative externalities and impediments of bureaucracy. Perhaps the first challenge for liberals is to mobilize resources to demonstrate that effective training for occupational self-reliance is the only enduring answer to South Africa's most racially divisive problem of unemployment. It is also a way to demonstrate that 'black advancement' can be vigorously pursued without the unease which racially-based empowerment generates among both victims and beneficiaries.

Appendix: abridged attitude statements

- Would it be good or bad if many whites were to leave South Africa because of new laws or higher taxes paid to assist blacks? Yes/No
- South Africa is a country for Africans – whites should take second place. Agree/Disagree
- A new government should protect *all* people: white people as well as black people, rich people as well as poor people. Agree/Disagree
- The behaviour of most white people makes me angry. Agree/Disagree
- Blacks have a great deal to learn from whites (the reverse was also presented). Agree/Disagree
- South Africa needs people with skills, no matter if they are immigrants from the West, eastern Europe, or Asia. Agree/Disagree
- African people cannot be blamed for stealing because white people have been selfish and kept their wealth to themselves. Agree/Disagree
- Black people would be wealthier and happier if whites had never come to South Africa. Agree/Disagree
- No matter what they say, Asians and coloureds will join with whites rather than with Africans. Agree/Disagree
- I do not want to be given opportunities just because I am black. Agree/Disagree
- We should value the things which whites have brought to Africa. Agree/Disagree
- Blacks should preferably all support one particular political party. Agree/Disagree
- All people in South Africa should try to be members of a great new nation and forget about their different traditions and language groups. Agree/Disagree
- It makes me angry when I see that most whites are wealthy and most blacks are poor. Agree/Disagree

18

Liberalism and the future of South Africa's new democracy

THE FATE OF LIBERALS and liberalism in South Africa's new democracy may appear a matter of parochial concern to a few small and weak organizations and scattered individuals. Yet it is a question with a significance far beyond itself. When South Africa held its first universal-suffrage election in 1994, many realized that the fate of Africa as a whole was riding on the success or failure of this transition: for if a recognizably liberal polity could be consolidated in Africa's most advanced state, it would exercise a strong gravitational pull towards democratization in the rest of the continent – but if South Africa slips towards the chaotic authoritarianism that characterizes much of Africa, it is difficult to see how the continent could avoid entering a new dark age.

The question, moreover, has to be situated in an even wider context – the fate of liberalism and liberal democracy around the world in the new millennium. This has been the subject of much debate in the wake of Francis Fukuyama's famous 'end of history' hypothesis, which argues that all of humanity is moving towards the same liberal-democratic and capitalist form of society.

Among those contesting Fukuyama's view is Samuel Huntington, who argues in *Clash of Civilizations* that the cultural differences between western liberal-democratic systems and those of Asia (especially China) will inevitably produce conflict, even if these systems converge on a common capitalist economy. One does not have to take sides in this debate to agree with Huntington that liberal democracy cannot be discussed in a disembodied way, without reference to the societies in which it has become entrenched. Historically, it emerged in Western Europe, whence it was transplanted to North America and Australasia, its successful expansion deriving from the colonial dominance of west European societies in the nineteenth century and the economic dominance of North America in the twentieth.

If the twentieth century was 'the American century', however, it is tolerably certain that that sort of dominance will not be seen again in the new millennium. Economic and military power is becoming increasingly dispersed. If liberal democracy is to continue to expand, it will have to depend less and less on Western dominance and increasingly on its ability to develop its own deep and authentic roots in societies beyond the Western core. South Africa is very much a case in point. The liberal democracy that was born in 1994 owed a good deal to the concerted pressures of West European and American states, but if it is to survive, it will have to build a liberal society and liberal culture to underlie the present, formal apparatus of its liberal constitution.

This will not be easy. Liberalism arose in relatively homogeneous societies where the atomistic notion of individual rights was not countered by the group solidarities of race or ethnicity. As it spread to societies that were divided on those lines, such as Ireland, Belgium, and Spain, it encountered serious difficulties. In some cases, as in the USSR and Yugoslavia, the advent of liberal democracy had the effect of imploding the state altogether.

The fact is that less than ten per cent of all contemporary states are 'nations' in the traditional sense of possessing a single, overarching identity based on a common history and language. South Africa, for example, has eleven official languages, and its various groups nurse memories of very different and often bitter histories.

The liberal tradition in South Africa has a long and distinguished history, but it was not until the 1950s that it acquired an organized political voice in the Liberal and Progressive Parties. By the late eighties, the Progressive Party's successor, the Democratic Party (DP), had grown to become the official opposition within the whites-only parliament. Throughout its long period of opposition, South African liberalism reflected the diversity that liberalism has shown internationally – one could find everything from Thatcherites to social democrats within its ranks – but liberals were united by a common rejection of racial discrimination, a preference for reform over revolution and for federalism over centralization, a belief in the superiority of market-driven economies over command economies, and a rejection of Marxism-Leninism.

The relative weakness of liberals within white politics was matched for much of the century by their strong influence within black politics. The furious insistence of the National Party (NP) that liberalism was tantamount to communism was based on the clear realization that the doctrines of non-racialism and individual rights were deeply subversive of the ethnic and racial solidarities on which the NP depended. Moreover, until the late 1950s the African National Congress (ANC) was led by such classic liberals as Albert Luthuli. At this point, however, liberalism suffered a series of calamities. In 1968 the NP government passed the Prohibition of Political Interference Act, which made it impossible for whites and blacks to combine within the same political organization. This Act led to the dissolution of the Liberal Party in 1968. A number of younger liberals opted for violent action by establishing the African Resistance Movement, a short-lived and futile initiative that gave credence to government claims and left liberals discredited and split. And above all, young ANC radicals, impatient of their elders' reformism, turned towards more Marxist solutions.

The ANC's radical turn to the left saw the South African

Communist Party (SACP) gain a dominant organizational grip of the movement for several decades, but ANC ideology during this period was only incidentally communist: in essence it was Third-Worldist. Except that ideology is really the wrong word: Third-Worldism denoted an outlook and a state of mind rather than an ordered system. It embodied a radical critique of imperialism, exploitation, and racism, a Fanonist view of violence as a purifying instrument of liberation, and solidarity with Gaddafi, Saddam Hussein, Louis Farrakhan, and almost every other anti-imperialist leader on the block. It was a heady mix, and liberals could not compete with it. Their insistence on constitutional and procedural forms, their belief that limitations should be placed on popular sovereignty by restraining the power of government, and above all their apparently symbiotic link with capitalism meant that they were all too easily portrayed as privileged middle-class whites concerned essentially with the protection of property rights and the staving-off of revolution.

Nevertheless, liberalism enjoyed an ironic triumph as the apartheid era drew to a close. This development was accompanied by – and, indeed, was to some extent the consequence of – the collapse of Marxism-Leninism throughout the Soviet empire. This, together with a growing challenge to one-party states in Africa and the demonstrable superiority of market-driven economies, all combined to give liberalism a powerful new impetus. Moreover, President F. W. de Klerk's abandonment of apartheid in 1990 made it clear that liberals had won the domestic political debate completely. A portrait of Helen Suzman, for so long the DP's lone parliamentary voice, was unveiled in parliament by De Klerk, who frankly admitted that he had at last come round to her views. At the same time, the ANC began to disengage itself from its commitment to nationalize industry and to move towards an acceptance of the market economy. Most striking of all, the NP and the ANC found common ground in liberal constitutionalism. True, the constitution that was finally adopted contained elements that some liberals cavilled at, but it was in many ways a liberal document with a bill of rights occupying a central role within it.

At the end of all this, however, the DP won only 1.8 per cent of the vote in the 1994 election and saw large numbers of Indian and coloured voters flock to the NP, which had persecuted them, rather than to the liberals who had fought for them. The NP, which had been outpolling the DP by only 5 : 2 within the old white electorate, increased that margin to nearly 12 : 1 within the new non-racial electorate. Moreover, liberals found themselves under headlong attack from the black intelligentsia and the ANC. Indeed, it was soon clear that far from feeling kinship with a group that had always fought against apartheid, the new regime viewed liberals with greater hostility than it did the old NP. Thus, the ironic result was that liberalism had persisted and won, only to be rewarded with defeat and hostility. The DP played no part in the government of national unity that presided over the new liberal-democratic order. The organizations that did – the ANC, the Congress of South African Trade Unions (COSATU), the SACP, the NP, and the Inkatha Freedom Party (IFP) – were a motley collection, but they had one thing in common: throughout much of their history they had in practice (and often in principle too) displayed scant regard for, or even outright hostility to liberal democracy.

The reason for this is not difficult to discern. The continuity between South Africa's old and new political systems lies in the way political mobilization still occurs largely along ethnic and racial lines. This was dramatically apparent in the 1994 election, which as far as whites and blacks were concerned had more the character of a racial census than of a fluid contest in which debate or issues counted for much. For most of its history the NP had mobilized on an essentially ethnic (Afrikaners only) basis, but by the 1970s had broadened this into a more explicitly racial appeal as the party sought – with considerable success – to mobilize whites as a whole. At the same time, the NP attempted to extend the principle of ethnic mobilization to others; this was, of course, the rationale behind the foundation of the ten black 'homelands' and the establishment of separate parliaments for coloureds and Indians.

The homeland system was anathema to the ANC, which contrasted it with its own commitment to non-racism. In practice, however, the ANC is opposed to ethnic mobilization but not to racial mobilization. Indeed, the party has itself opted for two overlapping forms of racial mobilization: on the one hand, it has attempted to corral all coloured, Indian, and African voters, and it was both pained and indignant when majorities of the two former groups supported the NP in 1994. The ANC regards such voter options as morally and politically repugnant, because it is unwilling to accept that they may result from a rational expression of interests: it believes they can be explained only by the manipulation of anti-African racism. On the other hand, the ANC has increasingly relied on the racial mobilization of Africans as such, not only by the use of Africanist language and symbols, but by a similar insistence that there is something indecent about the idea of an African voting for what the ANC has persistently referred to as 'one of the white parties', meaning any party that was represented in the old whites-only parliament, or white-led parties, such as the Freedom Front, that have sprung up since then. In addition, it has branded the United Democratic Movement, led by Bantu Holomisa and Roelf Meyer, as 'counter-revolutionary' and thus not worthy of black support. It has also suggested repeatedly that the IFP and the Pan-Africanist Congress (PAC) join or merge with the ANC – not because the ANC needs their votes, but because this would complete the political unity of the African racial bloc. In effect, therefore, the ANC believes that racial voting lines should be maintained as tightly as possible and that an ANC-led bloc of parties is the only fit object of black support.

The ANC's recourse to the language and tactics of racial mobilization has set up powerful emulatory waves throughout the political system. These have been particularly noticeable among coloureds and Asians, who have felt increased African pressure in the housing, labour, and other markets. In the Asian community Amichand Rajbansi's Minority Front, a Hindu communalist party, has risen to heights never achieved under NP rule, while amongst the coloureds of the Western Cape there have been increased demands for a separate coloured party. The only new white-led party, the Freedom Front, has taken the same communalist attitude towards the defence of Afrikanerdom, announcing that it is willing to include coloured Afrikaans-speakers within that definition but not English-speakers of any kind.

Liberals have found themselves fundamentally at odds with this recurrent pattern of ethnic and racial mobilization. Whereas the ANC pretends to a non-racialism in principle which, at the hustings at least, it by no means always practises, and the NP, a latter-day convert to non-racism, still looks to an ethnic and linguistic core of Afrikaans-speakers, liberals have never posses-sed an ethnic base on which to fall back: even at its height the DP could muster the votes of fewer than half of English-speaking whites. Thus, even if ethnic and racial mobilization did not clash with liberal principles, there has been little temptation or opportunity for liberals to renege on those principles. This has put liberals in a position where their intent is subversive of the racial and communal appeals of other parties, a position which makes their critique particularly offensive to many.

This dynamic has another aspect: both Afrikaner nationalism (in its heyday) and African nationalism now are hegemonic movements. That is, they are not merely political parties glad to have achieved a spell in office and eager to carry out their policies before the inevitable swing of the democratic pendulum puts their opponents in power. Rather, both movements tend to believe that they are or were in power more or less in perpetuity, that their mission is nothing less than to transform society in their own image, and that opponents who criticize or hinder that process are unpatriotic and dangerous (they are 'subversives' or 'counter-revolutionaries', for instance). This conception not only elevates a nationalist movement above all other parties but also tends to make it coterminous with the state.

Movements with such a strong sense of self-righteousness and mission are quasi-religious in nature; they require absolute loyalty from their followers and, like religious movements, evangelize endlessly beyond their ranks. That is, there is no question of such a movement resting on its laurels when it wins fifty or even sixty per cent of the vote: it always wants more, and the ideal would be for everyone to join it. President Nelson Mandela has frequently made this explicit, claiming that 'there is a home for everyone in the ANC' and arguing, for example, that the solution to violence in KwaZulu-Natal is for everyone to join the ANC. The ANC makes no bones about its ambition to win all nine provinces in the 1999 election and also to win a two-thirds majority nationally, a result which would allow it to change the constitution at will. It is in no way abashed by the fact that such a result would create a virtual one-party state.

Liberals, on the other hand, are intrinsically opposed to such hegemonic claims and are horrified by the whiff of a single-party regime that such conceptions conjure up. In their view the state belongs to no one and everyone, the boundaries between party and state have to be rigorously observed, and democracy relies on a regular alternation in power and ready acceptance of whatever the electorate decides.

All of this has left liberals in a difficult and embattled position since 1994, the more so as many of them were weary after decades of resisting apartheid. In any case, they have found that the world wants to celebrate the 'miracle' of democratic change in South Africa and does not much wish to be told that South Africa's new majoritarian nationalism has the potential to threaten democracy in much the same way as the preceding wave of nationalism had done. Together with the pressure exerted by the rising juggernaut of the ANC, this had already led in the 1980s to the phenomenon of 'slideaway liberals', those who had stood up bravely for liberal principles against apartheid but showed a marked disinclination to stand up for the same liberal principles when these were abused by the ANC.

After 1994 the 'slideaway' phenomenon was greatly strengthened by a host of material and social incentives to be on the right side of the new government; these inducements led to the rapid emergence of a new wave of former Broederbonders (ardent Afrikaner nationalists), opportunistic businesspeople, and ambitious socialites undergoing instant conversion to the ANC. The slideaway developed into a full-blown and suffocating form of political correctness in which the ANC was allowed to define what was correct, and the overall effect divided and demoralized liberals.

Political correctness was particularly prevalent in the universities, the press, and the churches, three institutions that had been bastions of liberal thought in the past. A bruising political battle had been fought between Marxists and liberals in the universities in the 1970s and 1980s, at the end of which the former were everywhere triumphant. Their control continued easily into the 1990s, untroubled by the collapse of so much that the Marxists had campaigned for. For example, Marxists had intellectually 'established' as orthodoxy the idea that capitalism and apartheid were inseparable; but in 1990, apartheid disappeared while capitalism continued.

Similarly, with the lonely (and brief) exception of Desmond Tutu, few leading clerics could be found to comment upon rampant corruption within the new elite, just as few university leaders could be found to criticize the government's policies for higher education – even though they were at least as interven-

tionist and careless of academic freedom and university autonomy as anything the apartheid government had attempted. The
English-speaking press was at best sporadic and inconsistent, at
worst downright cowardly in its reaction to the excesses of the
new elite – though, to be fair, even the coverage it gave was sufficient to arouse the government's ire. Many of the journalists
who had campaigned bravely against apartheid took shelter in a
curious form of 'sunshine journalism' once the ANC took office,
writing only about anodyne subjects or ethereal 'think' pieces.
The generally fellow-travelling *Mail & Guardian* (formerly the
Weekly Mail) slowly recovered a little of its old critical spirit but
only within well-defined limits. Ironically, the boldest and often
the most consistent liberals in the press emerged in the Afrikaans
newspapers, *Die Burger*, *Rapport*, *Beeld*, and the *Citizen*, despite
its disgraceful origins as a secretly funded apartheid propaganda
sheet.

Similarly, when an attempt was mounted to legislate government control over all voluntary associations – including the
right of the government to confiscate their funds, rename them,
and appoint a new set of trustees – some of the most prominent
anti-apartheid non-governmental organizations (NGOs) failed
to register a public protest of any kind. The initiative was killed
thanks to the determined efforts of only two NGOs, the Helen
Suzman Foundation and the South African Institute of Race
Relations, which managed to rally enough support to force the
withdrawal of the measure. But the thinking behind such initiatives had not disappeared. In December 1997 President Mandela
launched a major attack on NGOs that had fallen out of the ANC
orbit: clearly, in his view the duty of such organizations was to
support his party and the government. Dr Blade Nzimande, the
number-three man in the Communist Party, wrote an article in
which he named the two liberal organizations mentioned above
and one individual, the eminent historian Hermann Giliomee,
as 'counter-revolutionaries', making it clear that they, rather

than racists or true reactionaries, were the targets of the ANC's ire (1997).

The attitude of the white business community was schizophrenic. Many businesspeople greeted the advent of the ANC with a shower of money as they desperately sought to re-position themselves, buy favours, and buy clients. When the ANC demanded R1 million from each of twenty leading companies in 1994 they got what they asked for in all but one case. The DP, regularly attacked by the ANC as the party of business, had never enjoyed largesse such as that. In the early days after 1994, businesspeople also happily accepted the government's promises of a new partnership, even a new corporatism, and were strongly disinclined to oppose government policy in any way. Within a few years, however, a more sober mood had dawned. Business participation in the National Economic Development and Labour Council had led precisely nowhere: all it meant was that business representatives had to sit and listen to vulgar Marxist tirades from second-echelon trade unionists. Moreover, when business tried to show reasonableness by agreeing to labour legislation they did not like, they found it bought them no favours at all. When government brought forward even more draconian labour legislation – the Basic Conditions of Employment Act – business was promised that the act could not become law without their agreement, but this promise was then snatched back in order to allow the ANC leadership to buy COSATU votes at the 1997 ANC conference.

After a few years many businesspeople began to retreat into a state of internal exile, fed up with government but unwilling to criticize it or take a public position on anything. Although logic dictated support for a strong liberal presence in South African society to act as a barrier to the sort of evolution that had seen hegemonic African nationalist governments wreak enormous social and economic damage in neighbouring states, only a minority of businesspeople actually did so.

The situation in which South African liberals thus found themselves after 1994 was certainly embattled, but it was far from hopeless. South Africa had got through its founding democratic election, and even though the election may have been flawed by serious voting irregularities and a final result which seemed to be 'negotiated' rather than achieved by counting, the outcome was accepted as crudely correct by everyone, a remarkably positive sign. The long night of apartheid had created a real hunger for democracy, and although the process of building a democratic culture to consolidate the democratic institutions thus launched would be long and arduous, the work had at last begun. Of course, this enormous change could not take place without a virtual cultural revolution in society, particularly since the ANC and the SACP had to adapt to a world very different from the one they had expected to inherit. In such a situation a good number of adjustment pains, wild flights of rhetoric, and political 'noise' of every kind was to be expected. Jarring and alarming though some of this was, it was a mild experience compared to the racial war that had been clearly in prospect until the turn towards peaceful democratic transition after 1990.

Great hopes were placed on the rapid growth of a black middle class after 1994: these, surely, would be the liberals of the future? The radical scholar Barrington Moore put it simply: 'No bourgeois, no democracy'. However, Lawrence Schlemmer cautions that such hopes may, at the least, prove premature (see his chapter in this volume). The new black middle class depends heavily on the political patronage of the ANC elite, and any hopes that it will rally quickly to the liberal cause are likely to be in vain, as were similar hopes of the Afrikaner middle class that emerged in the wake of the NP victory in 1948. But that example also makes the point: in the end – after some thirty or forty years – the Afrikaner middle class did become the bearer of liberal values, a flowering which had full issue in the post-1994 era. Thus, while only very small percentages of new middle classes may support liberal parties at the polls, their support for the core liberal values that undergird the democratic state seems likely to grow over time.

Liberals have also been able to draw strength from several other sources. First, there was a dawning realization among many white Afrikaners that South Africa's evolution had made liberals of them: indeed, one NP leader privately estimated that as much as eighty per cent of the NP parliamentary caucus had now, slightly to their own bemusement, discovered that they were liberals at heart. With apartheid dead and unmourned, they looked towards a future in which their best hope lay in their being allowed to compete on fair terms in an open society and economy in which the power of government was restrained by a free press and a vigorous opposition. By 1997 it was clear that many such voters were, for the very first time, willing to consider transferring their support from the NP to the DP. More promising still was the possibility that the other non-African groups, the coloureds and Asians, would in time also see the futility of minority communalism and rally to the liberal cause for similar reasons. The National Party, for which most of these groups had voted in 1994, has already evolved in a liberal direction, and is now separated only by its own history from the DP.

None of this addresses the exiguousness of black support, in any guise, for liberal politics. Here, liberal-democratic hopes have to rest on other factors. First and foremost there is the constitution, which, whatever criticisms some liberals may have (see, for example, Anthea Jeffery's chapter in this volume), is clearly liberal in spirit. Provided the constitution is respected, there is hope that democratic constitutionalism will acquire legitimacy and seep down into the pores of society, gradually influencing even those parties and groups that have historically rejected liberalism. If such a process is accompanied by political stability and economic growth, there is a real chance that liberal values will grow by a process of political osmosis rather than by a sharp ideological break. It should not be forgotten that the values underlying western consumer culture – imbibed from an early age by South Africans of all races – also work in that direction. It is worth noting, too, that the experience of opposition in the post-1994 period saw the radical Pan Africanist Congress evolve in a noticeably liberal direction, a development paralleled by the clearly liberal bent of the new United Democratic Movement led by Holomisa and Meyer. And, of course, the Inkatha Freedom Party, though too wedded to African traditionalism to be regarded as a liberal party, has adopted a thoroughly liberal set of economic policies. A number of its leading figures would, indeed, not be out of place in an avowedly liberal movement.

Some of the same tendencies were noticeable even within the ANC, but these have been counterbalanced by a strong communist influence, a general penchant for quasi-Marxist populism, and an insistence on a military loyalty to the movement: cadres did not move but were 'redeployed', resignation from the party was often regarded as tantmount to treachery, and corruption and even more serious crimes were often overlooked in the case of loyal party members. Such a style is not compatible with liberal democracy, and the sheer enormous weight of the ANC within the polity also means that it faces a far greater anti-democratic temptation than any other party. Judges who reached verdicts of which the ANC disapproved were roundly attacked and the party made it clear that it wanted more control over judicial selection and over all independent power centres such as the attorney general, auditor general, and Reserve Bank. The government assumed greater powers over higher education than the apartheid government had ever dared, and Ministers happily spoke of their ambition to 'transform' everything from university curricula to sport. Nothing was off-limits to the new ANC elite.

But even the ANC elite is constrained: it cannot make the economy work without having full regard for the interests of the business community and for South Africa's integration into the

international political economy. That integration is not uncon-
ditional. The modern world is increasingly intolerant of governments that renege on democratic commitments, and powerful
sanctions can be imposed on those who do renege. In this sense
the internationalization of the South African issue which began
in the 1960s has become a double-edged sword. The dismantling
of apartheid and the creation of a new democratic system were a
famous victory for liberty. No political leader in his or her right
mind will wish to incur the international odium that any derogation from that liberty would cause. As a result, many of the
devices used by African nationalist regimes to the north are
simply not available to the ANC: even if it wanted to, the ANC
cannot afford to institute a one-party state, to detain people
without trial, to censor the press, or to otherwise suppress political opponents. This internationalist constraint alone will create
a series of spaces and openings within society which will allow a
natural pluralism to develop. This is a sea in which liberal values
can swim.

The liberal tradition in South Africa is older than any other,
yet no liberal party has ever stood a chance of gaining power.
This remains the case, but liberal values have progressed all the
same. There were times when liberalism looked as if it might be
crushed by a wave of Afrikaner nationalism, but that wave has
spent its force and liberalism has scored a belated and ironic
triumph. Now it must show the same resilience in the face of a
new wave of nationalism – until this wave too spends its force.
The years ahead promise to be a testing time for liberals, but
provided they can keep their nerve, there is no end of their tradition
in sight.

Notes

Introduction: The liberal inheritance

1 The Liberal Party existed as a small non-racial grouping from 1953 to 1968 but never achieved parliamentary representation. The Progressive Party was founded in 1959 as a breakaway from the United Party. Thereafter, it was successively joined by other breakaway elements, changing its name on each occasion to the Progressive Reform Party (1975), the Progressive Federal Party (1978), and the Democratic Party (1989).

2 The new constitution: a triumph for liberalism? Some doubts

1 Dr Anthea Jeffery is special research consultant to the South African Institute of Race Relations. This contribution has been written in her personal capacity and does not reflect the views of the Institute itself.

2 See Chemerinsky, E. 1985. 'Rethinking state action'. 80 *North Western University Law Review*, p. 503, and the criticism of his views in Marshall, W.P. 'Diluting constitutional rights: Rethinking "Rethinking state action"'. 80 *Northwestern University Law Review*, p. 558.

3 The Constitutional Court found against the government on two occasions, invalidating proclamations made by President Nelson Mandela under the Local Government Transition Act of 1993 (*Executive Council, Western Cape Legislature* v *President of the Republic of South Africa*, 1995 (4) SA, 877 (CC)) and upholding the validity of KwaZulu-Natal legislation on the payment of chiefs (In re KwaZulu-Natal Amakhosi and Iziphakanyiswa Amendment Bill 1995, In re Payment of Salaries, Allowances and Other

Privileges to the Ingonyama Amendment Bill 1995, 1996 (7) BCLR 903
(CC)). In both instances the Court found that the central government had
overstepped its powers.

4   Must contemporary South African liberals be Thatcherites?

1   Rawls's two principles read as follows:

> *First Principle*
> Each person is to have an equal right to the most extensive total
> system of equal basic liberties compatible with a similar system
> of liberty for all.
> *Second Principle*
> Social and economic inequalities are to be arranged so that they
> are both:
> (a) to the greatest benefit of the least advantaged, consistent with
>   the just savings principle, and
> (b) attached to offices and positions open to all under conditions
>   of fair equality of opportunity. (Rawls 1972, 302)

5   The rule of law since 1994

1   Dr Anthea Jeffery is special research consultant to the South African
    Institute of Race Relations. This contribution has been written in her
    personal capacity and does not reflect the views of the Institute itself.
2   It is not possible in this analysis, which focuses on events in the post-
    apartheid period, to provide an adequate description of the numerous
    violations of the rule of law that occurred under apartheid law. Further
    details may be obtained from the *South Africa survey*, published annually
    by the South African Institute of Race Relations since 1936. See also Dugard,
    J. 1978. *Human rights and the South African legal order*. New Jersey: Princeton
    University Press.
3   The Cradock Four were four prominent UDF activists from Cradock in the
    Eastern Cape. Matthew Goniwe was a key UDF leader in the area. He was
    accompanied by Sparrow Mkonto, Fort Calata, and Sicele Mhlauli in
    driving from Port Elizabeth to Cradock in June 1985. All four died during
    the journey in mysterious circumstances, and their bodies were found
    later in their burnt-out car. Security police were widely believed responsi-
    ble for their deaths, but this could not be proved in legal proceedings

(*Citizen* 3 March 1998).

4   The Pebco Three were UDF activists from Port Elizabeth who were
members of the Port Elizabeth Black Civic Organization (Pebco). Sipho
Hashe, Champion Galela, and Qaqawuli Godolozi were abducted from
Port Elizabeth airport in May 1985 and killed in a bid to cripple Pebco,
which police believed responsible for unrest in the region (*Business Day* 7
November 1997).

6   Liberal institutions under pressure: the universities

1   See the remarkable case of Durban-Westville (UDW) in 'La luta continua'.
October 1996. *KwaZulu-Natal Briefing*. No. 4. (Available from the Helen
Suzman Foundation.)

10 What role for the churches in the new South Africa?

1   These figures are derived from annual press releases from the WCC's
Programme to Combat Racism.

2   *The road to Damascus* was an international initiative which grew out of a
meeting between Frank Chikane, then general secretary of the ICT, and
members of the theologically radical Ecumenical Association of Third-
World Theologians in 1986. It was simultaneously published in America
and Britain.

3   During 1987–1990 the 'Church and Mission' Department accounted for
only 1.5 per cent of SACC expenditure, but even this is an overestimation of
expenditure on evangelism or traditional missionary activity (Tingle,
1992, 172–4).

4   Financial report to the SACC National Executive Committee Meeting, 27
November 1996. (However, the SACC was expecting to carry over R9
million in cash reserves to 1997).

5   The Truth and Reconciliation Commission has provided jobs for several
radical church leaders, including Prof. Charles Villa-Vicencio as Director
of Operations; the Rev. Khoza Mgojo, formerly SACC President; and the
Rev. Bongani Finca. (At the time of the WCC's 1985 emergency consultation
on South Africa held in Harare, Finca issued a widely-distributed statement
declaring that 'what we need at this hour ... in South Africa is action
calculated to intensify and escalate conflict'.)

6   This was confirmed by IFCC general secretary Chris Lodewyk (personal
interview (unpublished), January 1997).

7   *Signposts* magazine devoted the whole of edition No. 1, Vol. 12, 1993 to a critical discussion of the issue.

8   In 1997 Lodewyk stated his aim (see note 6) to set up a Christian Political Movement, which he believed could attract over a million members within a year, and which would hope to influence all political parties in a 'Christian direction'. It is difficult to discern exactly what this might mean.

9   Noel Wright, general secretary of the Church of England in South Africa and a member of the former EFSA executive, has stated that in order to prepare a TEASA budget he repeatedly asked for information about CE membership and budget, but at the date of our interview this request had been ignored (personal interview (unpublished), January 1997).

10   Interview with the Rev. Peter Hammond, Director of United Christian Action, and one of the leaders of Christian Voice, January 1997.

11   Radio Khwezi, which started broadcasting in September 1995, has four studios with state-of-the art technology. It broadcasts seventeen hours a day, seventy per cent of the time in Zulu, with wide-ranging programmes teaching life-skills, as well as news, entertainment, and basic Christianity.

12   Interviews with two black Christian leaders, Dr Elias Mashao, principal of the Timoth Training Institute, which trains many of the leaders of the black independent churches, and Dr Kenneth Meshoe, an African Christian Democratic Party MP and senior pastor of a large black church (personal interviews (unpublished), January 1997).

12 Oppositions, difficulties, and tensions between liberalism and African thought

1   See Husemeyer (1997) for further discussion of these issues.

2   See West (1995) and Makgoba (1997). The discussions offered in these works capture the experiences of black intellectuals in their communities in contrast to those of white intellectuals.

13 Why are there so few black liberals?

1   The Power Sharing study referred to was conducted for *Business Day* in October 1996. The total coverage represents approximately 92 per cent of the urban adult population and approximately 53 per cent of the total adult population (correspondence, Market Research Africa, Johannesburg, 7 July 1998).

2   The most vicious attack on liberalism and 'black liberals' I know has been

made by the former president of the Azanian People's Organization
(AZAPO), Prof. Itumeleng Mosala:

> [Liberalism] is a powerful tool by means of which black people
> can be paralysed into perpetual slavery and dependence. It is a
> useful and highly valued weapon in the hands of white people.
> They love it, it works for them, and they will kill anybody who
> threatens to disarm them of this weapon ...
>
> On the whole our struggle against white liberalism has been
> successful ... Of more danger to the freedom of black people is
> black liberalism. Like all diseases which emanate from white
> people, black liberalism is fatal ... There is a new breed of black
> liberals. This class of liberals is more than a cultural photocopy of
> Europe or the West. It is made up of political types who have their
> eyes on certain stakes in the future which white people are designing
> but for which there must be black signatures and endorsement.
> (Mosala 1993)

Mosala was of course denouncing the ANC as a liberal organization. But
when those same ANC liberals offered him a 'gravy-train' position (the sort
of job he was denouncing as a liberal trap), the professor jumped at it and
promptly fell quiet about his anti-liberal rhetorics. Until the end of 1997 he
was the chief director of higher education in the Department of Education.
In 1998 he took up the position of rector at the Technikon of the North-West
in Ga-Rankuwa.

15 Affirmative action: is the light worth the candle?

1 This chapter is the revised version of a paper delivered at the South African
   Institute of Race Relations Seminar on Affirmative Action, Johannesburg,
   23 August 1996.
2 The rank of the highest-ranking minority, the percentage of women in
   management, and the percentage of women and of minorities in the
   company as a whole.
3 In South Africa, the Northern Province is the least urbanized (8.8 per cent
   of population) and also one of the poorest, followed by the North West
   (30.4 per cent), Mpumalanga (31.0 per cent), Eastern Cape (36.0 per cent),
   KwaZulu-Natal (37.8 per cent), and the Free State (55.7 per cent),while the
   Western Cape, Northern Cape, and Gauteng have urbanization rates of

86.2 per cent 75.7 per cent and 95.6 per cent respectively. All figures are for 1993 (FRD 1995, 20–37).

4 It was estimated that an amount of R9 billion will remain unspent at the end of the 1996/1997 financial year (Department of Finance 1997, 3.7).

Bibliography

Introduction: The liberal inheritance

BIKO, STEVE. Edited by Millard W. Arnold. 1987. *No fears expressed*. Johannesburg: Skotaville Publishers.

DAVENPORT, RODNEY. 1987. 'The Cape liberal tradition to 1910'. Chapter 1 in *Democratic liberalism in South Africa*, edited by Jeffrey Butler, Richard Elphick, and David Welsh. Middletown: Wesleyan University Press.

DRIVER, C. J. 1980. *Patrick Duncan: South African and Pan-African*. London: Heinemann.

HELLMANN, ELLEN. 1979. 'Fifty years of the South African Institute of Race Relations'. Chapter 1 in *Conflict and progress*, edited by Ellen Hellmann and Henry Lever. Johannesburg: Macmillan South Africa.

LUTHULI, ALBERT. 1962. *Let my people go*. London: Collins.

MCCRACKEN, J. L. 1967. *The Cape Parliament* 1854–1910. Oxford: Clarendon Press.

PATON, ALAN. 1964. *Hofmeyr*. London: Oxford University Press.

PATON, ALAN. 1988. *Journey continued: An autobiography*. Cape Town: David Philip.

SCHREINER, OLIVE. 1960. *Closer Union*. Cape Town: Constitutional Reform Association. (Reprinted articles originally published in the *Transvaal Leader*, 1908).

SLABBERT, F. VAN ZYL and David Welsh. 1979. *South Africa's options: Strategies for sharing power*. Cape Town: David Philip.

SMUTS, J. C. 1942. *The Basis of Trusteeship*. Johannesburg: South African Institute of Race Relations.

SUZMAN, HELEN. 1993. *In no uncertain terms: Memoirs*. Johannesburg:

Jonathan Ball.

SWART, RAY. 1991. *Progressive odyssey: Towards a democratic South Africa.*
Cape Town: Human and Rousseau.

VIGNE, RANDOLPH. 1997. *Liberals against apartheid: A history of the Liberal
Party of South Africa, 1953–68.* Basingstoke: Macmillan.

WALSHE, PETER. 1970. *The rise of African nationalism in South Africa: The
African National Congress 1912–1952.* London: C. Hurst.

1   The new constitution: a triumph for liberalism?
A positive view

GILIOMEE, HERMANN. 1997. 'The offensive against even-handedness'.
Frontiers of Freedom 11:8.

3   Liberalism and politics

ASMAL, KADER and Ronald Roberts. 1995. 'Liberalism's hollow core'. *Sunday
Times*. 1 October.

BIKO, STEVE. 1978. 'White racism and Black Consciousness'. Speech delivered
to a student conference in January 1971. Reprinted in Biko, *I write what I
like*. London: Bowerdean Press.

MAZWAI, THAMI. 1996. 'Liberal conspiracy surfaces again'. *Business Day*.
19 April.

SLABBERT, F. VAN ZYL. 1993. 'Fashioning a new role for fashionable liberalism'.
Sunday Times. 6 June. Edited version of his Alan Paton Memorial Lecture
delivered on 4 June 1993.

SOBUKWE, R. M. 1959. Pan Africanist Manifesto adopted at the inaugural
conference of the Pan Africanist Congress, 5 April 1959.

SOBUKWE, R. M. 1977. 'The future of the Africanist movement'. Originally
published in *The Africanist*, January 1969. Reprinted in Thomas Karis,
Gwyndolen Carter, and Gail Gerhardt (eds.). 1977. *From Protest to
Challenge* Vol. 3. Stanford, California: Hoover Institute.

WELSH, DAVID. 1994. 'Liberals and the future of the new democracy in South
Africa'. *Optima*. Vol. 40, No. 2. November.

4   Must contemporary South African liberals be Thatcherites?

ADAM, HERIBERT. 1971. *Modernising racial domination.* Berkeley: California
University Press.

BARBER, BENJAMIN. 1996. *Jihad vs MacWorld: how the planet is both falling apart and coming together*. New York: Ballantine.

DE SWAAN, A. 1988. *In care of the state: health care, education and welfare in Euope and the USA in the modern era*. Cambridge: Polity Press.

MANN, MICHAEL. 1988. *States, war and capitalism: studies in political sociology*. Oxford: Basil Blackwell.

MCGRATH, MICHAEL D. 1979. 'The racial distribution of taxes and state expenditure'. Black/White Income Gap Project Final Research Report 2. University of Natal, Durban.

MCGRATH, MICHAEL D., C. Janisch, and C. Horner. 1997. 'Redistribution through the fiscal system in the South African economy'. Paper presented at the Economic Society of South Africa, Pietermaritzburg, September 1997.

MIGDAL, JOEL S. 1988. *Strong societies and weak states: state-society relations and state capacities in the third world*. Princeton, New Jersey: Princeton University Press.

PEI, MINXIN. 1994. 'The puzzle of East Asian exceptionalism'. *Journal of Democracy* 5 (4). October.

RAWLS, JOHN. 1972. *A Theory of Justice*. Oxford: Oxford University Press.

SKOCPOL, THEDA. 1992. *Protecting soldiers and mothers: the political origin of social policy in the United States*. Cambridge, Massachusetts: Harvard University Press.

5   The rule of law since 1994

Frontiers of Freedom. 1995. 'The attorneys'-general's general'. January. South African Institute of Race Relations.

GILIOMEE, H. 1995. 'A struggle for the high moral ground'. *Frontiers of Freedom*. Second Quarter. South African Institute of Race Relations.

JEFFERY, A. J. 1991. *Riot policing in perspective*. Johannesburg: South African Institute of Race Relations.

JEFFERY, A. J. 1997a. *1996/97 Bill of rights report*. Johannesburg: South African Institute of Race Relations.

JEFFERY, A. J. 1997b. 'Presuming guilt and rewriting the law'. *Fast Facts*. No. 7. South African Institute of Race Relations.

JEFFERY, A. J. 1997c. *The Natal story: 16 years of conflict*. Johannesburg: South African Institute of Race Relations.

JOHNSON, R.W. 1996. 'The unresolved mess over spying'. *Focus Letter*. No. 2 February. The Helen Suzman Foundation.

JOHNSON, R. W. and A. Johnston. 1998. 'Pressure builds for an election deal'. *KwaZulu-Natal Briefing*. February. Helen Suzman Foundation.

KANE-BERMAN, J. 1979. *Soweto: Black revolt, white reaction*. Johannesburg: Ravan Press.

LAURENCE, P. 1998. 'The full Nugent'. *Frontiers of Freedom*. Second Quarter. South African Institute of Race Relations.

MOTALA, S. 1987. *Behind closed doors*. Johannesburg: South African Institute of Race Relations.

MYBURGH, J. 1996. 'Wiser than ours?' *Frontiers of Freedom*. Third Quarter. South African Institute of Race Relations.

MYBURGH, J. 1997. 'The TRC and the rule of law'. *Finance Week*. 26 June.

NZIMANDE, BLADE. 1997. 'The real agenda behind Meyer and Holomisa's new political party'. *Mayibuye*. November/December.

PEREIRA, P. 1996. 'Malan: A disgraceful episode'. *Fast Facts*. No. 11. South African Institute of Race Relations.

PEREIRA, P. 1997a. 'Few limits on people's spies'. *Finance Week*. 18 September.

PEREIRA, P. 1997b. 'Sniffing the wind'. *Frontiers of Freedom*. Second Quarter. South African Institute of Race Relations.

POTTER, E. 1998. 'National crime trends'. *Fast Facts*. No 1. South African Institute of Race Relations.

SAFRO, W. 1995. 'Shell House probe nearing end?' *Frontiers of Freedom*. January. South African Institute of Race Relations.

SCHOENTEICH, M. 1997a. 'Justice delayed ...' *Fast Facts*. No. 8. South African Institute of Race Relations.

SCHOENTEICH, M. 1997b. 'National boss for attorneys general'. *Fast Facts*. No. 3. South African Institute of Race Relations.

SCHOENTEICH, M. 1997c. 'Open to abuse'. *Frontiers of Freedom*. Third Quarter. South African Institute of Race Relations.

SCHOENTEICH, M. 1997d. 'The odds against conviction: 20 to 1'. *Fast Facts*. No. 6. South African Institute of Race Relations.

SCHOENTEICH, M. 1998a. 'Privatise faster to prevent collapse'. *Frontiers of Freedom*. First Quarter. South African Institute of Race Relations.

SCHOENTEICH, M. 1998b. 'The return of people's courts?' *Finance Week*. 22 January.

South Africa survey. Published annually since 1936. Johannesburg: South African Institute of Race Relations.

WENTZEL, J. 1998. 'A callous public relations stunt'. *Frontiers of Freedom*. First Quarter. South African Institute of Race Relations.

7 Closer to home: student unrest and the welfare function

JAFF, R., J. Hofmeyer, and G. Hall. 1995. *National Education Teacher's Audit.*

RAMPHELE, MAMPHELA. 1996. 'South Africa and the Culture of Philanthropy: What is the Missing Ingredient?' Ernest Oppenheimer Memorial Trust Address. 19 March.

9 The press since 1994

BRAND, R. 1997. 'Independent group redressing wrongs of past'. *Star* 18 September.

BRIDGLAND, F. 1997. 'Only those who look can see the truth'. *Sunday Times* 26 October.

GINWALA, F. 1997. Unpublished speech given at Sowetan Media Freedom Day, Johannesburg 20 October.

HUNTER, C. 1997. 'No crisis between press and govt'. *Star* 10 July.

MASIPA, M. 1997. 'Mainstream press "colluded with apartheid"'. *Star* 18 Sept.

SAPA (South African Press Association). 1997. 'Times Media will "transform itself"', says Cyril Ramaphosa'. *Star* 18 Sept.

TYSON, H., ed. 1987. *Conflict and the press.* Johannesburg: Argus Publishing.

WILLIAMS, M. 1997. 'She gets away with it'. *Citizen* 18 Oct.

10 What role for the churches in the new South Africa?

BERGER, PETER and Richard Neuhaus. 1977. *To empower people: The role of mediating structures in public policy.* Washington: American Enterprise Institute.

CHALLENGE. 1996a. 'Is the new economic plan bad news for the poor?' Johannesburg: Contextual Publications. October/November.

CHALLENGE. 1996b. 'Justice for the poor'. Johannesburg: Contextual Publications. August/September.

DE GRUCHY, JOHN. 1986. *The church struggle in South Africa.* London: Collins.

DE GRUCHY, JOHN. 1995. 'Becoming the ecumenical church', in *Being the church in South Africa today*, edited by Barney Pityana and Charles Villa-Vicencio. Johannesburg: South African Council of Churches.

Ecunews. 1996. 'SACC finances in good shape'. Johannesburg: South African Council of Churches. No. 1.

EvangeLENS. 1995. 'Reflections and projections'. Pietermaritzburg: Evangelical Fellowship of South Africa. No. 4.

Evangelical witness in South Africa: South African Evangelicals critique their own theology and practice. 1986. London/Oxford: The Evangelical Alliance and Regnum Books. (Also published in South Africa by Concerned Evangelicals, Dobsonville.)

FROISE, MARJORIE (ed.). 1997. *South African Christian Handbook*. Welkom: Christian Info.

ICT Review. 1995. Johannesburg: Institute for Contextual Theology.

Kairos '95: At the threshold of jubilee. 1996. A conference report. Johannesburg: The Institute of Contextual Theology.

KANE-BERMAN, JOHN. 1993. *Political violence in South Africa*. Johannesburg: South African Institute of Race Relations.

KANE-BERMAN, JOHN. 1997. 'Let the priests confess'. *Frontiers of Freedom*. SAIRR Fourth Quarter.

MAYSON, CEDRIC. 1983. 'The liberation of Christians'. *Sechaba*. November.

NOLAN, ALBERT. 1994–95. '... and Chikane moves on'. *Challenge*. Johannesburg: Contextual Publications. December/January.

PITYANA, BARNEY and Charles Villa-Vicencio. 1995. *Being the church in South Africa today*. Johannesburg: South African Council of Churches.

Signposts. 1994. 'Nicaragua – A blueprint for South Africa?' Pretoria: Signposts Publications and Research Centre. Vol. 13 No. 3.

Signposts. 1996. 'Has TEASA joined the ecumenicals?' Pretoria: Signposts Publications and Research Centre. Vol. 15 No. 2.

SOUTH AFRICAN COUNCIL OF CHURCHES. 1995. *Expenditure budget for 1996 – 1998*.

TINGLE, RACHEL. 1992. *Revolution or reconciliation? The struggle in the Church in South Africa*. London: Christian Studies Centre.

The Kairos document – Challenge to the church: A theological comment on the political crisis in South Africa. 1985. Braamfontein: The Kairos Theologians. Also published by the Catholic Institute for International Relations/British Council of Churches, London, 1985. References here are to the British edition.

VILLA-VICENCIO, CHARLES. 1992a. *A theology of reconstruction: Nation-building and human rights*. Cape Town: David Philip. (Also published in England by Cambridge University Press, Cambridge.)

VILLA-VICENCIO, CHARLES. 1992b. 'Religious identity and voluntary commitment'. *African Communist*. First Quarter.

VILLA-VICENCIO, CHARLES. 1993. 'Beyond liberation theology: A new theology for South Africa'. *Challenge*. February.

11 Freedom of education: a privilege or a right?

ADEA Newsletter. 1996. 'Languages of instruction and language policies –
A synthesis of research'. Vol. 8 No. 4.

BOT, M. 1991. *The blackboard debate: Hurdles, options, and opportunities in
school integration.* Johannesburg: South African Institute of Race
Relations.

BOT, M. 1993. 'Language use in schools: A survey of teachers' opinions'.
EduSource Data News No. 3, Johannesburg.

CARRON, G. and T. N. Châu. 1996. 'The quality of primary schools in different
development contexts'. IIEP/UNESCO.

CLARK, S. B. 1993. 'The schooling of cultural and ethnic subordinate groups:
Essay review'. *Comparative Education Review (CER)* Vol. 37 No. 1.

COHN, E. and R. A. Rossmiller. 1987. 'Research on effective schools:
Implications for less developed countries'. *CER* Vol. 31 No. 3.

COOMBE, C. 1996. 'Local/district governance of education in South Africa:
Learning from experience', in Coombe, C. and J. Godden eds.

COOMBE, C. and J. Godden eds. 1996. *Local/district governance in education;
Lessons for South Africa.* Centre for Education Policy Development.

CROUCH, L. A. 1996. 'A public-private partnership for self-replicating quality
in people's schools'. Unpublished preliminary draft.

DIJKSTRA, A. and J. L. Peschar. 1996. 'Religious determinants of academic
attainments in the Netherlands'. *CER* Vol. 40 No. 1.

DONALDSON, A. 1996. 'Opportunity to improve financial planning at all levels'.
Budget Watch Vol. 2 Issue 3.

DURHAM, K. 1996. 'Learning the home way'. *Indicator SA* Vol. 13 No. 3.

FOON, A. E. 1988. 'Non-government school systems: Funding policies and
their implications'. *CER* Vol. 32 No. 2.

GILIOMEE, H. 1996. 'Liberal and populist democracy in South Africa:
Challenges, new threats to liberalism'. Presidential address, South African
Institute of Race Relations.

GORDON, A. 1996. 'New schooling policies – Widening rural inequalities?'
Matlhasedi, July/August.

HANF, T. et al. 1975. 'Education: An obstacle to development? *CER* Special
Issue Vol. 19 No. 1.

HANF, T. 1980. 'Education and consociational conflict regulation in plural
societies' in Van Zyl Slabbert, F. and J. Opland. *South Africa: Dilemmas of
evolutionary change.* Grahamstown: Institute of Social and Economic
Research, Rhodes University.

Hansard, 10. Interpellations, questions and replies of the National Assembly. 4 September 1996 col. 1944.

HENNING, M. 1996. *Towards a funding policy framework for independent schools*. Independent Schools Council, 19 November 1996.

HILL, A. C. 1987. 'Democratic education in West Germany: The effects of the new minorities'. *CER* Vol. 31 No. 2.

JITA, L. 1996. 'The South African experience of local government involvement in schooling and some stakeholder positions'. *Education Monitor* Vol. 7 No. 3, Education Policy Unit (EPU), University of Natal, Durban.

KARSTEN, S., I. Groot and M. A. Ruiz. 1995. 'Value orientations of the Dutch educational elite'. *CER* Vol. 39 No. 4.

LAUGLO, J. 1996. 'Forms of decentralization and their implications for education', in Coombe, C. and J. Godden eds.

MONDSTUK. April 1996. 'Twee kante van die munt'. Vol. 22 No. 283.

NAIDOO, J. P. 1996a. 'The racial integration of schools: A review of literature on the experience in South Africa'. *EPU working paper* No. 8, University of Natal, Durban.

NAIDOO, J. P. 1996b. 'Racial integration of public schools in South Africa: A study of practices, attitudes and trends'. *EPU research paper*, University of Natal, Durban.

POTTERTON, M. and P. Christie, with A. French, K. Cress, L. Lanzerotti, and D. Butter. 1997. *School development in South Africa: A research project to investigate strategic interventions for quality improvement in South African schools*. Education Department, Univ. of the Witwatersrand.

'Report of the task team on education management development'. 1996. In *Changing management to manage change in education*. Department of Education, December.

SAMOFF, J. 1987. 'School expansion in Tanzania: Private initiatives and public policy'. *CER* Vol. 31 No. 3.

SCHREINER, D. 1997. 'Signposts from Sweden'. *Frontiers of Freedom* Issue No. 11, First Quarter, South African Institute of Race Relations.

STONIER, J. L. 1996. 'Implications of "Africanness" for educational planning in the Republic of South Africa: A qualitative study of educational needs'. Unpublished Ph.D. thesis, University of Stellenbosch.

TALBANI, A. 1996. 'Pedagogy, power and discourse: Transformation of Islamic education'. *CER* Vol. 40 No. 1.

VAN DER ROSS, R. E. 1996. *The concept of equity in the provision of education in South Africa: An Essay*. Belhar, Western Cape.

VAN RENSBURG, C. 1996. 'Onderwys kan SA kelder'. *Insig*, June.

WELTON, J. and N. Rashid. 1996. 'Local governance of schools in England and Wales', in Coombe, C. and J. Godden eds.

12 Oppositions, difficulties, and tensions between liberalism and African thought

ANSELL, A. E. 1997. *New Right; New Racism: Race Reaction in the United States and Britain.* New York: New York University Press.

CHERRY, M. 1995. 'Black scientist faces inquiry at South African university'. *Nature* 378: 324.

CHERRY, M. 1996. 'Witwatersrand seeks to diffuse "race row"'. *Nature* 379: 199.

D'SOUZA, DINESH. 1995. *The end of racism.* New York: The Free Press.

GEVISSER, MARK. 1996. *Portraits of power.* Cape Town: David Philip.

HOOKS, B. 1995. *Killing rage.* New York: Henry Holt.

HUSEMEYER, LIBBY (ed.). 1997. *Watchdogs or Hypocrites?: The Amazing Debate on South African Liberals and Liberalism.* Johannesburg: Friedrich-Naumann-Stigting.

KANE-BERMAN, JOHN. 1996. 'Copy Helen Suzman and keep going'. *Frontiers of Freedom* 9: 11–12.

MAKGOBA, M. W. 1996. 'In search of the ideal democratic model for SA'. *Sunday Times* 27 October.

MAKGOBA, M. W. 1997. *Mokoko – The Makgoba Affair: A reflection on transformation.* Johannesburg: Vivlia Publishers.

MAMDANI, M. 1997. 'Makgoba: Victim of the "racial power" entrenched at Wits'. *Mail & Guardian* 5 September.

MAMDANI, M. 1997. 'Makgoba: Victim of "racial power" entrenched at Wits'. *Social Dynamics* 23: 1–5.

MARBY, M. 1996. 'Joined at the hip'. *Newsweek* 1 April.

MURRAY, BRUCE. 1996. 'Defending the "open university"'. *Perspectives in Education.* 17:27–50.

NYATSUMBA, KAIZER. 1997. 'First salvos in election '99 race: We need effective opposition'. *Star* 22 January.

ROHAN, RAFIQ. 1997. 'We were victims of apartheid too – The English press say so'. *Sowetan* 10 March.

SCHLEMMER, LAWRENCE. 1996. 'The nemesis of race: A case for redoubled concern'. *Frontiers of Freedom.* 9: 21–24.

Star. 21 January 1997. 'The TRC is run by a "clique of liberals"'.

Star. 7 March 1997. 'Report'.

SOBUKWE, R. M. 1959. Pan Africanist Manifesto adopted at the inaugural conference of the Pan Africanist Congress, 5 April 1959.

SOBUKWE, R. M. 1960. Trial 23 Case No. L 173/60. Magistrate Court for the Regional Division of South Transvaal Johannesburg before Mr J. De. K. du Plessis.

STATMAN, J. M., and A. Ansell. 1996. 'The war at Wits: Symbolic conflict and the William Makgoba affair'. Annual congress of the South African Sociological Association. 11 July.

STATMAN, J. M., and A. Ansell. 1996. 'A boyfriend with balls: Symbolic conflict and the Makgoba affair'. *Second annual congress of the Psychological Society of South Africa*. September.

STEINBERG, STEPHEN. 1995. *Turning back*. Boston: Beacon.

SUZMAN, HELEN. 1997. 'Feeling happy after all these years'. *Sunday Times*. 19 January.

The Economist. 1996. 'Liberalism defined'. 17–20. 21 December.

The Economist. 1995. 'Black in academe'. 23 December – 5 January 1996.

THOMAS, A. 1977. *Rhodes*. Johannesburg: Jonathan Ball.

Washington Post. 1995. 'The Washington Post, Harvard University, and the Kaiser Family Foundation study into race in America'. 8–10 October.

WEST, CORNELL. 1995. *Race matters*. New York. Vintage.

13   Why are there so few black liberals?

DAY, JIM. 1997. 'Unionists make "hot-shot" investments'. *Mail & Guardian*. 24–30 January. p. B4.

GEVISSER, MARK. 1997. 'The Mark Gevisser page'. *Sunday Independent*. 2 February. p. 4.

KOCH, EDDIE. 1997. 'The new unionist: Suit, silk tie, and chequebook'. *Mail & Guardian*. 24–30 January. pp. B4–B5.

MOSALA, ITUMELENG. 1993. Speech to AZAPO's National Council. Edited version published as 'Focus on Azapo'. *Sowetan*. 18 August.

O'MALLEY, KIERIN. 1994. 'The fundamentals of liberalism in South Africa today'. *The New Liberals*. Johannesburg: South African Institute of Race Relations. p. 29.

REUTERS. 1997. 'Marxist unionists try capitalism'. *Citizen*. 20 February. p. 24.

SONO, THEMBA. 1997. Unpublished paper presented at a conference in Tripoli, Libya.

SONO, THEMBA. 1993. *Reflections on the origins of black consciousness in South Africa*. Pretoria: Human Sciences Research Council (HSRC). Especially pp. 5–31.

14 The best of enemies? Black intellectuals and white liberals

FANON, FRANTZ. 1967a. *The wretched of the earth*. London: Penguin.

FANON, FRANTZ. 1967b. *Black skin, white masks*. London: Penguin.

HUSEMEYER, LIBBY, ed. 1997. *Watchdogs or hypocrites? The amazing debate on South African liberals and liberalism*. Johannesburg: Friedrich-Naumann-Stiftung.

JOHNSON, R. W. 1997. 'The South African electorate at mid-term'. *Focus 6*, Helen Suzman Foundation.

JOHNSON, R. W. and Lawrence Schlemmer. 1996. *Launching democracy in South Africa. The first open election, April 1994*. London: Yale University Press.

KANE-BERMAN, JOHN. 1997. 'White scapegoats for government failures'. *Fast Facts*. South African Institute of Race Relations. December.

MCCULLOCH, J. 1983. *Black soul, white artifact. Fanon's clinical psychology and social theory*. London: Cambridge University Press.

OWEN, KEN. 1997. 'A coat of many colours'. *Leadership 16*: 4.

SONO, THEMBA. 1994. *Dilemmas of African intellectuals in South Africa: Political and cultural constraints*. Pretoria: University of South Africa.

SONO, THEMBA. 1996. 'Interview: Themba Sono'. *Focus 2*: Helen Suzman Foundation.

15 Affirmative action: is the light worth the candle?

BOLICK, C. 1996. *The affirmative action fraud: Can we restore the American civil rights vision?* Washington DC: Cato Institute.

BRIMELOW, P. and L. Spencer. 1993. 'When quotas replace merit, everybody suffers'. *Forbes*, 15 February: 80–102.

CALDWELL, D. 1992. *No more martyrs now: Capitalism, democracy, and ordinary people*. Johannesburg: Conrad Business Books.

DEPARTMENT OF FINANCE. 1996. *Growth, employment, and redistribution: A macro-economic strategy*. Pretoria: Government Printer.

DEPARTMENT OF FINANCE. 1997. *Budget Review*. Pretoria: Government Printer.

DEPARTMENT OF LABOUR. 1996a. *Restructuring the South African labour market: Report of the presidential commission to investigate labour market policy*. Pretoria: Government Printer.

DEPARTMENT OF LABOUR. 1996b. *Green paper: Policy proposals for a new employment and occupational equity statute*. Pretoria: Government Printer.

ELKAN, W. 1995. *An introduction to development economics*. Revised second edition. London: Prentice Hall.

EMSLEY, I. 1992. 'Affirmative action: The Malaysian experience'. *Optima*, Vol. 38(3): 111–117.

ESKOM. 1994. *Generation group social harmonization strategy*. Johannesburg: Internal publication.

FOUNDATION FOR RESEARCH DEVELOPMENT (FRD). 1995. *Research, science and technology in South Africa: Comparative strengths of the nine provinces*. Pretoria: FRD.

INGHAM, B. 1995. *Economics and development*. London: McGraw-Hill.

LOXTON, L. 1993. 'Learning from others'. *De Suid-Afrikaan*, May–June: 29.

MCGRATH, M. and A. Whiteford. 1994. *Inequality in the size distribution of income in South Africa*. Stellenbosch Economic Project, Occasional Paper No. 10. Stellenbosch: Centre for Contextual Hermeneutics.

PUTHUCHEARY, M. 1993. 'Malaysia: Safeguarding the Malays and the interests of other communities'. *Development and democracy*. Johannesburg: Urban Foundation (now the Centre for Development and Enterprise (CDE)).

ROBERTSON, D. 1996. 'Do-good housing policies do badly'. *Sunday Times*: 'Business Times', 2 June.

SCHOOMBEE, G. A. and A. Smith. 1995. 'Getting commercial banking services to the informal sector: A comparative study of Asian countries and South Africa'. Paper delivered at the Conference on Business Dynamics and Management Challenges in East Asia, Brunei, November.

17 Liberalism, democracy, race relations, and the rising black middle class in South Africa

ALMOND, GABRIEL, and Sidney Verba. 1965. *The civic culture*. Boston: Little, Brown.

BOTTOMORE, TOM. 1966. *Classes in modern society*. New York: Vintage Books.

DAHL, ROBERT. 1971. *Polyarchy: Participation and opposition*. New Haven: Yale University Press.

KORNHAUSER, WILLIAM. 1960. *The politics of mass society*. Glencoe, Illinois: The Free Press.

LIPSET, SEYMOUR MARTIN. 1959. 'Some social requisites of democracy'. *American Political Science Review*, Vol. 53, March.

18 Liberalism and the future of South Africa's new democracy

FUKUYAMA, FRANCIS. 1992. *The end of history and the last man*. London: Hamish Hamilton.

HUNTINGTON, SAMUEL P. 1997. *The Clash of Civilizations and the Remaking of World Order*. New York: Simon and Schuster.

NZIMANDE, BLADE. 1997. 'The real agenda behind Meyer and Holomisa's new political party'. *Mayibuye*. November/December.

Index